City Fights

City Fights

Selected Histories of Urban Combat
from World War II to Vietnam

EDITED BY

Col. John Antal

AND

Maj. Bradley Gericke

PRESIDIO
PRESS

BALLANTINE BOOKS • NEW YORK

The views expressed in this book do not reflect those of the Department of Defense or any government agency but are solely those of the authors.

A Presidio Press Book
Published by The Random House Publishing Group
Copyright © 2003 by Col. John Antal and Maj. Bradley Gericke

www.presidiopress.com

Library of Congress Cataloging-in-Publication Data is available upon request from the publisher.

ISBN 0-89141-781-8

Book design by Joseph Rutt

Manufactured in the United States of America

First Edition: September 2003

10 9 8 7 6 5 4 3 2 1

Contents

Contents

Preface

by John Antal and Bradley T. Gericke

> *Thus the highest form of generalship is to balk the enemy's plans; the next best is to prevent the junction of the enemy's forces; the next in order is to attack the enemy's army in the field; and the worst policy of all is to besiege walled cities.*
>
> —Sun Tzu

This book is about urban combat. *City Fights* presents a series of essays that provide insights into the evolution of modern urban combat. The essays describe urban battles that occurred from 1938 to 1968 as told by fourteen writers who arc among the best and brightest military thinkers in the United States today. These men are officers currently serving in the armed forces of the United States or working as Department of Defense civilian analysts. All are military veterans, and each is a student of the art and science of war.

The intent of *City Fights* is to describe the details of specific urban battles and extract the lessons learned. Urban combat is not new. Wars have been fought in open terrain, mountains, and deserts, on the seas, in the sky, and frequently in cities. In fact, cities tend to draw troops during war. Often these fights have been grinding, bloody slugfests that consume armies.

If urban combat is so horrible, why do military forces fight in cities?

In ancient times, city fights were avoided at all costs. As Sun Tzu, the ancient sage of war, emphasized, a wise commander assaults a city only as a last resort. Assaults on fortified cities are dangerous, bloody, and difficult. Sun Tzu preferred to dislocate his enemy and take away his strength rather than fight him on equal terms.

Dislocation, the art of rendering the enemy's strength irrelevant, has often been the goal of the superior commander and was considered the highest order of strategy by Sun Tzu. Rather than pit force against force, the most skilled commanders have rendered their enemy's strength useless and won seemingly fantastic victories. Alexander at Arbela, Napoleon at Ulm, and the 1991 Gulf War are three examples of the power of dislocation; these successful actions avoided the slow and deadly travail of urban combat.

Dislocation, however, has been the exception in military history rather than the rule. Cities are frequently of critical tactical, operational, strategic, political, cultural, and economic value. They contain critical infrastructure centers such as ports, airfields, food distribution centers, industry, and, most important, people. Cities and urban areas play a crucial role in military operations because all these things underpin the strength of nations. If a state loses its cities, it has lost the war. Armies, therefore, continue to fight for cities in spite of Sun Tzu's admonitions.

Battles have been fought in cities since the transition from tribal warfare to organized city-state conflict. Many of the earliest wars that were recorded in stone reliefs depict conflict against walled cities. These city fights were largely settled by long sieges where starvation was the weapon of choice. Jericho is the earliest known fortified city whose walls were breached by Joshua's invading Hebrews in the mid–thirteenth century B.C. Battering rams, catapults, siege towers, and eventually cannon soon replaced the horns used by Joshua's divinely inspired trumpeters, and made the smashing and breaching of walls a central feature of the art and science of war.

In the past sixty years, some of history's most horrific conflicts have been played out in the steel and concrete forests of the urban battlefield. The dynamic of city fighting is often straightforward. Throughout history, cities have become battlegrounds when weaker forces assumed the defensive to attempt to negate the advantages that an otherwise superior attacker possessed in more open terrain. For a defending force, a city is a natural stronghold, because maneuver and command inside of cities is extraordinarily difficult. A defending army that seeks to sustain combat power or retain a political advantage may therefore choose the urban battlefield as the best available opportunity to prolong a war. Military commanders confronting an urban fight must overcome a tremendous number of complex variables. Unlike "natural" or rural landscapes little touched by human activity, urban terrain is designed by its occupants to perform numerous functions. Hence modern cities are constructed densely in a particularly multidimensional manner. People live, work, and move below the ground, at the surface, and overhead, in buildings. Combatants must learn to navigate this "jungle" if they are to win the city fight.

After World War II, the U.S. Army was so concerned with operations against the Soviet Union in Germany that it organized a team to study urban combat operations during the war. The team discovered that 40 percent of all Allied combat resources were consumed in the villages, towns, and cities of Europe. It predicted that a modern conventional war would involve 70 percent of all combat resources. And since that time, urban areas across the world have expanded. Not only will today's soldiers have to deal with combat in villages, towns, and cities, they will have to contend with large areas of urban sprawl. There is little doubt that as urban areas expand, conflict will occur for tactical, operational, strategic, and political reasons in these areas. As far back as 1979, the U.S. Army believed that "the worldwide increase in sprawling urban areas has made it almost impossible for forces conducting operations to avoid cities and towns."[1]

Despite the probability of urban combat, current military doctrine, reinforced by the memory of the tough urban battles from World War II to the Vietnam War, rightfully advocates the avoidance of urban combat. Our military prefers to fight instead in open terrain, where the tremendous effect of its sophisticated military systems can overmatch any other force on the planet. It has demonstrated a remarkable ability to apply precision firepower from a distance to achieve its policies. Some experts even believe that we can dominate the land through the application of standoff precision weapons alone. These proponents argue that troops are no longer needed to close with the enemy and fight him in close combat.

It is clear, however, that only foolish enemies will come into the open to be destroyed. Intelligent opponents have studied the American way of war and will be reluctant to play our game. They realize that they cannot match us in the open, force on force. They are learning that they must engage our forces with different methods. The attack on the United States on September 11, 2001, is proof of this asymmetric approach.

Urban terrain is anathema to the doctrine of standoff warfare where many high-tech weapons are negated by the close-in, three-dimensional urban battle space. In addition, this dangerous battle space is extremely complicated, because traditional maneuver advantages are neutralized and firepower must often be tempered by considerations to reduce collateral damage. The presence of noncombatants and friendly governmental and nongovernmental agencies, and the powerful cable news effect of having to fight under the ever-watchful eye of the world's media, all

combine to make a city fight perhaps the most dangerous battle-
ground facing us today and in the future.

In war the enemy always gets a vote, and he doesn't have to
play by our rules. We must expect that intelligent adversaries will
attempt to negate the current advantage held by the United
States in technological, standoff warfare by forcing us to fight in
areas where our brilliant weapons aren't so smart. Our dramatic
battlefield defeat in Somalia is a case in point.

Today our military has begun work to find answers to the
complexities of urban warfare, but what if urban combat cannot
be avoided? What if we must place our soldiers once again into
the concrete and steel confines of an alien city and fight house to
house against a determined enemy?

The chapters that you are about to read relate how combat
in cities is deadly, slow work. History is a sound tool to examine
fighting in cities. Its study offers a window into past battles to
learn the lessons that were once paid in blood. Since the dawn of
warfare, military forces have sought to dislocate the enemy and
avoid urban combat, but they were often forced into deadly city
fights. The history of war in the modern era points to the fact
that no silver bullet solutions exist to avoid close combat in the
restricted terrain of the urban battlefield. These fights always
took time, blood, and treasure and significantly influenced the
outcome of campaigns and wars.

The battles that were fought in cities during the period from
Tai-erh-chuang in 1938 to Hue in 1968 span thirty years of urban combat. The purpose of this book is to present tactical
lessons from the past and provide a select series of campaigns for
those who wish to study the tough, bloody close combat that oc-
curs in a city. These studies offer the modern-day reader important lessons relevant to urban combat today and important
insights into the nature of the battles that will be fought in cities
in the future.

If urban warfare is a topic of increasing relevance, it is essential for those who plan, prepare, and execute such missions to determine how to dominate enemies in this environment. In these chapters you will learn that war has no boundaries. What remains certain, however, is that the professional military, policy makers, and concerned citizens need to know the difficulty, horror, and cost, both human and material, of urban combat operations. Military forces will have to deal with close-combat issues, which will not go away, or surrender the initiative to the enemy in such situations. The future of war, therefore, may be less like the movie *Star Wars* and more like *Saving Private Ryan*.

ENDNOTES
  1.   U.S. Army, Field Manual 90–10–1: *An Infantryman's Guide to Urban Combat* (Washington, DC: Department of Defense, 1979), 240.

City Fights

ONE

Tai-erh-chuang, 1938:

The Japanese Juggernaut Smashed

by 2d Lt. William M. Waddell

The tactic of attacking fortified cities is adopted only when unavoidable. . . . If the general cannot overcome his impatience but instead launches an assault wherein his men swarm over the walls like ants, he will kill one-third of his officers and troops, and the city will not be taken. This is the disaster that results from attacking fortified cities.

—Sun Tzu

In early April 1938 a lone Chinese soldier stood on a wall in the town of Tai-erh-chuang to survey his surroundings.[1] Tanks, armored cars, and trucks were strewn about the countryside, abandoned once they had run out of fuel. Dead horses, broken machine guns, and deserted field guns lay across the landscape. The soldier could detect the faint smell of burning flesh. Interspersed among the quiet chaos lay 16,000 dead Japanese soldiers. For the first time in 340 years, China had defeated Japan in battle.[2]

The Imperial Japanese Army faltered in Tai-erh-chuang because it was lured into a vicious city fight for which it was dangerously unprepared. The semimodern Japanese army had not achieved the necessary combined-arms integration to prosecute such a battle. Japanese infantry hid behind the strength of their firepower, tanks advanced without adequate protection, and neither of them effectively used maneuver to gain a tactical advantage over the opponents. Furthermore, the Japanese commanders themselves committed operational blunders as their minds become dangerously fixated on the consuming fight within the city's bounds.

Chinese acumen stood in contrast to Japanese deficiencies. Perhaps owing to their material inferiority, the Chinese in and around Tai-erh-chuang displayed remarkable imagination. Their situation forced them into creative tactical and operational solutions, which served to frustrate the disjointed and uncoordinated efforts of the Japanese invaders. The disasters that beset the Japanese and the forethought that benefited the Chinese provide insightful lessons for the modern military.

The story of the Sino-Japanese War is one of immense struggle punctuated by catastrophe. Taken as a single event, the victory at Tai-erh-chuang illustrates that the Chinese could be capable planners and organizers. It also highlights the sophistication of their military thought. The Chinese not only understood their adversaries' mind-set but manipulated it to advantage. In effect, the Chinese laid a trap at Tai-erh-chuang. The Japanese were lured into and systematically destroyed in a brutal street fight, punctuated by sweeping maneuver.

Early Days of the Sino-Japanese War

The opening of the Sino-Japanese War had not gone well for the Chinese. The defense of Shanghai had been a valiant but an ultimately futile effort. Chiang Kai-shek's German-trained Central Army held on to Shanghai through a series of gruesome offensives and equally foolish dare-to-die defensive stands. The height of China's military modernization perished in Shanghai. Casualties for the battle may have been as high as 300,000. By December 13, 1937, the Japanese had pushed their way to Nanking. Chiang shifted his headquarters to the relative safety of Wuhan in December. Things were equally worrisome in the north. Paoting and Tsangchow fell to the Japanese First and Second Armies, respectively, on September 24. Chinese resistance was crumbling before the Japanese advance, while Chiang carefully hoarded his remaining units in order to preserve his delicate hold on Chinese leadership.[3]

The Japanese intended to force a Chinese capitulation by endangering the ad hoc capital at Wuhan. Rail and river provided the primary means for the Japanese advance. The Tientsin-P'ukow railroad line provided one such high-speed avenue of approach. Japanese efforts in this area should have been stalled by the presence of Han Fu-Chu's 80,000–strong 3d Army Group. Such was not to be as Han fled Tsinan, thereby leaving this front wide open for Japanese exploitation. Chiang Kai-shek paid Han the traitor's wage by executing him in Hankow on January 25.[4]

The opportunity was not lost on the Japanese. If the Japanese could strike south quickly, they could seize the junction of the Lunghai and Tientsin-P'ukow railway lines at Hsuchow. From there, the way to Wuhan lay before them. The object of the Japanese southern drive was the hodgepodge 5th War Area under the command of Li Tsung-jen, who had been given the task of defending Hsuchow.

Troops and Terrain

Li's command structure was certainly convoluted. Owing more to political expedience than military necessity, many of Li's subordinates commanded units noticeably larger on paper than what the unit could actually put into the field. Many army group commanders were concurrently corps commanders, and in two cases officers were serving simultaneously as army group, corps, and division commanders. For instance, P'ang Ping-hsun nominally commanded the Third Army, but it consisted of only one corps, in which there was only one division.[5] The layering of command, primarily for political reasons, served to confound the modern perspective and undoubtedly complicated command and control of Chinese armies.

Chinese troop dispositions reflected the confusing nature of the Chinese command structure. A standard division, on paper, consisted of at least two infantry brigades, one artillery battalion, and a variety of support units. In sum, the Chinese division was nominally 10,000 men strong. Two divisions or more made up a corps, and at least two corps formed an army.[6] Unfortunately, few Chinese armies were actually organized in such a manner. The rapid integration of the various warlord armies into the Kuomintang (KMT) force structure invalidated any organizational uniformity. Even a cursory glance at the command structure of the 5th War Area reveals how few units adhered to this rigid prescription. It is probably safe to assume that only the Central Army units under Li's command even approached this strength.

Despite the awkward arrangement of his command, Li chose his battlefield well. He was able to do this because Japanese attention shifted to his area only as their drive to seize the Nationalist major political organs had been frustrated by their timely withdrawal to Wuhan. Furthermore, Li had been in the area as early as November 1937 and hence understood the terrain.[7] The defensive line of the 5th War Area extended below the relatively impassable mountains in southern Shantung. The position of the mountains channeled an attacking force around the heights through two widely separated routes. One avenue passed on the western side of the range through the cities of Tsouhsien and T'enghsien in succession. This course also coincided with the vital Tienstin-P'ukow main rail artery. The second approach brought an adversary around the mountains to the east through the strategically significant city of Linyi. Once a force had cleared this obstacle, it still would find itself separated from its supporting column by roughly eighty kilometers. The quality of this defensive sack is further heightened by Wei-shan Lake and the Grand Canal, which effectively shore up a defending force's left flank. Below the Wei-shan the Grand Canal turns abruptly east, creating a significant barrier to attacks as well as a convenient rallying point for defenders. Below the mountains and to the east of Tai-erh-chuang, the terrain becomes broken by a series of rivers, canals, and marsh. Any attacker moving into this region would find his area of operations increasingly limited. Furthermore, the nature of this region necessarily caused defensive pockets to form around the various cities, which, in turn, were hedged by the already mentioned natural fortifications.

In essence, any invading host's push into this region on a broad front had to be widely dispersed and incapable of mutual support. Once the mountains were cleared, the area where a juncture of forces could be made was significantly limited. Forces entering the cul-de-sac would find themselves advancing obliquely into the bowl with their lines of communication trailing behind them at widely divergent angles. This arrangement forced the attacker to seize the cities in order to effectively control the rail lines.

The Preparation for Battle

It is quite likely that some Chinese officers were mentally prepared for this battle. Henri Johan Diederick de Fremery, a retired Dutch artillery colonel and military advisor to China, reported that the Chinese had indeed foreseen such a circumstance. Recognizing this area as a potential threat to Nanking, staff officers conducted several staff exercises and the matter was

discussed in earnest at the Central Military Academy. This information was partially corroborated by the work conducted at the
Chinese Staff College at Lu-ta. The students at Lu-ta engaged in
several wargames focused on "mobile defense." The scenarios
postulated a deep penetration by enemy columns into Chinese
territory. Once the enemy formations reached the height of their
advance, they were to be subjected to violent attacks from the
rear and on the flanks.

The general concept of the Japanese effort, as it developed,
was that Japanese troops would speed south to effect a juncture
at Tai-erh-chuang. From there they would consolidate for the
siege of Hsuchow.[8] The task to press the attack to Hsuchow
fell to Lt. Gen. Juzo Nishio's Second Army. Nishio's 10th and
5th Divisions would take the Japanese to the vital Lunghai
railway. The Lunghai offered a high-speed route for the Japanese to reach Wuhan and the interior of China. David Barrett,
the assistant American military attaché to China, aptly described
the Lunghai as "China's jugular vein."[9] Han Fu-Chu's ignomin-
ious withdrawal had placed Taian, Yenchow, and Tsining into
Japanese hands in quick succession and further placed the Lunghai at Japan's mercy. Nevertheless, Nishio threw his 10th Division (Lt. Gen. Rensuke Isogai) against Wenshang/Tsining. The
5th Division, under Lt. Gen. Seishiro Itagaki, was dispatched
from Taian with the object of ultimately seizing Tai-erh-chuang
via Linyi.

The early Japanese successes in the north had come without
much of a price. The relative ease of these initial conquests inspired a certain degree of military adventurism in the Second
Army. It is interesting to note that the Second Army believed
that it faced no less than eleven Chinese divisions to its front.[10]
With this fully in mind, it plunged ahead. The commanders in
the 5th War Area quickly surmised their danger, but, more importantly, they perceived their opportunity.

The Japanese Attack

The 10th Division opened the attack by throwing its Nagase detachment, consisting of four and a half infantry battalions and two field artillery battalions, against Tsining. The Chinese resistance around Tsining broke on February 20. Chiahsiang came soon after, falling on the twenty-fifth. Simultaneously the 5th Division, spearheaded by the Katano detachment, motored out of Weihsien. In short order Chuhsien and Ishui fell to the 5th Division. Itagaki stood poised to throw the weight of his motor column against the Chinese at Linyi. To ensure success, the command of the Katano detachment was placed under Maj. Gen. Jun Sakamoto.

Li Tsung-jen was not idle as the Japanese daggers thrust ever closer to the heart of his defense. Recognizing Linyi's importance, Li transferred P'ang Ping-hsun's Third Army to defend it. The term *army* is deceiving, because P'ang commanded, in fact, only five infantry regiments. His force had been discriminated against by the Central Government and labeled an "unattached" unit.[11] Li was certainly risking much by entrusting this defense to such a questionable organization.

Li knew better. P'ang's troops formed a highly cohesive unit. They had fought for years together under the same banner. Even captured soldiers would try to return to their regiment if they were offered an opportunity for escape. All of P'ang's regiments were at full strength, although they were short of ammunition. Li requisitioned additional equipment for P'ang, notably mortars, and sent him off to stop Itagaki. There would be no retreat from Linyi.

Li recognized his situation for what it was. He understood that his forces could not hope to stop both advancing divisions at the same time. Defending a line south of the mountain range would have surrendered the operational initiative and condemned the 5th War Area to a slow retreat at best. Instead the main effort of the Japanese attack was to be drawn in and destroyed. Li identified the main effort as the 10th Division. It traveled down the railroad and posed the greatest potential threat to Hsuchow. Although Li could not hold the 10th for long in any one place, he could draw it in and predict its movements given its dependency on the rail line. Furthermore, the cities along the rail could be used as a series of nominal stopgaps to slow and entice Isogai's advance. To accomplish this, Li would have to hold Linyi at all costs. The fulcrum of his defense, Tai-erh-chuang, would not be able to withstand the combined attack of both Itagaki and Isogai. What Li needed most was time. He required time to bring in reinforcements capable of closing his planned salient and time to get them where they needed to be.

Itagaki wasted little time. By the end of February he had engaged P'ang Ping-hsun around Linyi. The earlier string of relatively bloodless victories stood in stark contrast to what now developed in and around Linyi. Much to Itagaki's consternation, the Chinese in Linyi stood fast. The Japanese quickly escalated the scale of their attack. Despite their vigor, however, the Japanese attacks against Linyi were largely frontal. The nature of the city fight canalized Japanese endeavors into bloody assaults on staunchly held pockets of resistance. These mobile forces would have been better used to surround the Chinese rather than batter aimlessly at P'ang's men. No concerted effort was made to encircle and isolate the vital road junction. This allowed the Chinese to repeatedly reinforce the beleaguered defenders.

P'ang had done well, but in the face of nearly the entire 5th Division, his situation became desperate. The subsequent calls for help did not go unnoticed by Li Tsung-jen in Hsuchow. Chang Tse-chung's LVIX Corps stood ready for deployment to Linyi. Chang, however, had been lambasted by Chiang Kai-shek and China at large for his failure to defend Peiping the previous autumn. Li petitioned Chiang in Chang's defense, then offered Chang a chance to repudiate his former infamy and stand boldly against the Japanese. Chang would do that and more.

The Chinese Counterattack

The LVIX Corps reached Linyi on March 12. By the thirteenth, Chang was preparing for a counterattack against the besieging Japanese. This growing resolve triggered a similar response from the Japanese. Reinforcements continued until the seventeenth, when Sakamoto achieved a strength of six full infantry battalions supported by two field artillery battalions and a mountain artillery battery. The growing Japanese frustration is best evidenced by the Second Army directive of March 13 ordering the 5th Division to take Linyi immediately, then proceed toward Ihsien to facilitate the 10th Division's parallel assault. The stalemate at Linyi had placed the onus of the attack squarely on Isogai. This situation would substantially militate against the 10th's ability to carry out its primary mission.

The pressure on Isogai became intense. On the thirteenth he received an order to press his attack along the Tientsin-P'ukow rail line. Major General Hajime Seya set out from Tsouhsien as the lead element of the 10th the next day. He rumbled through Chieho that same day and placed his detachment within ten kilometers of T'enghsien.[12]

Li Tsung-jen had achieved transitory success in Linyi, but the situation along the Tientsin-P'ukow was rapidly deteriorating. Li could not allow Isogai to continue at this pace. More time was needed to garrison Tai-erh-chuang and prevent Isogai from rushing over to break the siege of Linyi. The evacuation of women, children, and the elderly from Tai-erh-chuang had almost been completed, but Li needed a few more days to replace these people with fighting men. The trap was nearly set.

Teng Hsi-hou's 22d Army Group (Sun Chen acting commander) became the bait for this trap. Li dispatched the 122d Division under Wang Ming-chang and the 124th under Wang Shih-chun to Tsouhsien to stem the Japanese assault.[13] As with many of Li's units, the 22d Army Group was considered of poor quality due to its Szechwan origin. Li equipped the 22d with five hundred new rifles, ammunition, and a quantity of trench mortars.[14] The troops marched north in early March to face Isogai in Tsouhsien.

The 22d arrived south of Tsouhsien in time to hear of its fall. Li immediately reallocated his troops to the defense of T'enghsien, the next major hurdle along the rail artery. The 122d was ordered to defend within T'enghsien; the 124th remained outside the city, most likely to prevent its encirclement. Seya's detachment, reinforced for its coming fight, plunged forward on March 15. Seya battered T'enghsien with heavy artillery and his substantial tank arm. For three days and three nights Seya pounded T'enghsien. It is uncertain exactly when it fell, but by March 18 the Japanese had occupied the city. The entire 122d Division, including the commander, Wang Ming-chang, fell in its defense.

The division's sacrifice purchased the necessary time. The intense fighting north of Hsuchow convinced Chiang to transfer the 2d Army Group under Sun Lien-chung and the Twentieth Army under T'ang En-po to the 5th War Area from the 1st War Area. T'ang's army represented the best of what was left of the Chinese Central Army.[15] Of his five divisions, both the 4th and the 25th had been formed from the 2d Capital Guard Division, which had been highly trained by the German military mission.[16] As the lead elements of T'ang's army reached Hsuchow, they were sent forward to T'enghsien to cover the retreat of the 22d Army Group.

As the Twentieth Army pushed north, the 2d Army Group

of Sun Lien-chung arrived in Hsuchow. Sun's three full-strength divisions were sent to Tai-erh-chuang to secure the village. Sun himself arrived in Tai-erh-chuang on March 20 to assume responsibility for its defense.[17] It was a fitting choice. Sun's height was six feet—tall enough to rise above the political infighting so fashionable at the time. He graduated with the first class for general officers from the staff school at Lu-ta. Sun would develop somewhat of a reputation for his defensive skill throughout the war. His aptitude was certainly demonstrated in Tai-erh-chuang as well.

The 10th Division, spurred by its success, drove on. Isogai's position, despite his success, had grown dangerous. His division was ill prepared to have advanced so far without support. Isogai left only weak garrisons in vital locations west of Yenchow. His lines of communication would have probably required a full division to defend them adequately. No such force was available. He wagered instead on the power of the offensive and once more struck south.

Lincheng (Xuecheng) fell to the 10th Division just after the capture of T'enghsien. Seya then divided a portion of his force into right and left pursuit units. Each consisted of one infantry battalion and a field artillery battery. On March 19 the right pursuit unit captured Hanchuang on the shore of Wei-shan Lake. The troops defending Hanchuang withdrew below the Grand Canal. The Japanese made no effort to pursue them further. Simultaneously the left unit pushed on to Ihsien (I-cheng). Also labeled the Fukuei column, it was opposed every step of the way by the withering efforts of T'ang En-po. The 23d Regiment of T'ang En-po's 4th Division defended Ihsien to the last man, suffering 100 percent casualties in the twenty-four-hour battle.[18] Nevertheless, the Fukuei column pushed into Ihsien between March 19 and 21.

The second battle for Linyi began in earnest on March 20.

Chang Tse-chung began his planned counterattack. March 24 saw a major action raging fifteen kilometers to the northeast of Linyi in Tangtouchen when the Japanese struck back. P'ang Ping-hsun, in front, managed to hold on until Chang Tse-chung arrived the following day. In front of Linyi the Chinese army held a line with the 180th Division on the left, the 38th in the middle, and the 39th on the right. The Japanese pressed the attack around the left flank, forcing the Chinese to fall back to the southern portions of the city. On March 28 the Chinese held only the southern tip of Linyi, but by then Japanese efforts had eased dramatically. Sakamoto was preparing to turn south, causing the lull in the fighting. The American military attachés noticed the severity of the fighting in Linyi. The impressive Chinese counterattacks had made things difficult for the Japanese in Shantung.[19] According to Colonel de Fremery's Chinese sources, the intense fighting in and around Linyi resulted in the deaths of three thousand Japanese, including two colonels. Although this figure was probably inflated, it does reveal the level of conflict that engulfed Linyi in late March.

The Chinese counterattack continued apace. On March 19 several Chinese divisions struck along the Tientsin-P'ukow route between Hanchuang and Tsinan. On the twenty-first they re-crossed the Grand Canal and wrested Hanchuang from Japanese control. The seeds of Isogai's poor defensive measures were beginning to bear bitter fruit as Lincheng, T'enghsien, and Yen-chow were all struck at once. The rail line was battered and severed at "hundreds of points." The Chinese attackers destroyed bridges, tore up the rails, and sometimes actually plowed the rail bed under. These attacks effectively stymied many Japanese chances for reinforcement. Tsingtao, in the east, had not yet been converted into a major logistical port, so the western railway represented their only significant logistical tail. Tied to the rail lines, the Japanese found themselves isolated.

Isogai, at his headquarters in Tzuyang, ordered Seya to press the attack. The luxury of carrying the assault to Hsuchow would have to wait. The 10th Division, once the Second Army's main effort, would have to bail out the 5th Division, previously its support. Isogai ordered Seya to secure the Grand Canal line in the vicinity of Hanchuang and Tai-erh-chuang, to garrison Lincheng and Ihsien, and then to support the 5th Division operations.

Seya was faced with a difficult situation. He had neither the troops nor the time to pursue the wide array of objectives laid out for him by Isogai. In Seya's haste to attack, he had not noticed or did not care to notice that a large portion of T'ang Enpo's 80,000 men had furtively slipped into the hills to his left flank. T'ang gave way before the Japanese assault in order to draw them in, just as Li planned. For the moment, T'ang waited for the Japanese.

Now Seya had to rescue Sakamoto in Linyi, secure Tai-erh-chuang, and hold his present position. On March 23, he dispatched a force of one infantry battalion, one light armored car company, one field artillery battery, and one mountain artillery battery to Linyi. Fatefully labeled the Linyi detachment, this force would do no better than the Japanese already engaged at that spot.

The Anvil at Tai-erh-chuang

Sun Lien-chung arrived in Tai-erh-chuang on March 20. Three days later a portion of his 31st Division met the Japanese 10th Division at Nikou, nine kilometers north of Tai-erh-chuang. The Chinese troops were sent there to entice the Japanese southward. The 31st Division commander, Chih Feng-cheng, having left only one brigade in Tai-erh-chuang, advanced north. When the initial Japanese attack did not disperse the Chinese troops, the Japanese reinforced their effort with an additional battalion.

Chih moved his force to an adjacent hill and allowed the Japanese to circumvent his position. He had, in fact, moved one of his battalions to a concealed position to the south. As the Japanese struck the rear of the Chinese position on the hill, the hidden battalion attacked them, in turn, from behind. Shaken badly, the Japanese withdrew for a time, only to strike back in earnest on March 24. Allowing the Japanese to pass by him, Chih conducted a series of flank attacks that ended as the Japanese brought on even more forces. In light of this, the Chinese succeeded in their endeavor to attack Ihsien and draw the Japanese south. It would seem that the feint worked, because the Japanese were forced to dispatch their left pursuit column to Tai-erh-chuang even as Seya attempted to mass his strength in Ihsien and Lincheng.

The left pursuit column struck Tai-erh-chuang on March 23. The desperate situation for the Japanese 10th Division was compounded by the grim defense it confronted in the walled village. The heavy rock used to construct Tai-erh-chuang made her walls and houses veritable castles. Sun's 31st Division, which held Tai-erh-chuang, endeavored to make its capture as difficult as possible. In the city, defensive positions were constructed in the corner of each house. Roofs of houses were then removed to prevent them from catching fire. Due to this configuration the Japanese would have to expel each defender one at a time, because each position was largely self-sufficient. Adding to the rigidity of the town's interior defense, Sun kept the majority of his force outside the town to conduct attacks against the Japanese rear and flanks.

The Japanese pounded Tai-erh-chuang on March 24. As many as 6,000 shells fell on the 31st Division.[20] The Chinese responded by taking to the earth. Marine captain Evans Carlson noted in a discreet letter to President Roosevelt that "[d]ugouts were so thick that one could hardly take a step without walking on part of an excavation."[21]

As the 10th hammered fruitlessly at Tai-erh-chuang, the men of the Linyi detachment motored east to relieve their beleaguered 5th Division comrades. The detachment, operating essentially alone, was surrounded in Kuolichi on March 25. The seemingly ubiquitous forces of T'ang En-po, which had also secured control of the rail junction in Lincheng the very same day, carried out this encirclement. It would take the Japanese four days to recapture it.

Seya's ability to set the pace of events was completely lost. He didn't have the strength to save Sakamoto in Linyi or to break the Chinese hold on Tai-erh-chuang, yet he attempted both. Spurred by his horrendous casualties and the dire condition of the Linyi column, Seya was forced to redirect his attention toward relieving his relief force. On March 26 he withdrew the majority of his forces from Tai-erh-chuang to break the death ring around Kuolichi.

The seesaw battle in Tai-erh-chuang continued as Seya drove north. The Japanese managed to occupy only a small corner of the village by March 27. The fighting strength of the Chinese defenders had been dramatically heightened by their fortified positions. But the accomplishment did not come without significant loss. Owing to their lack of tanks and adequate antitank guns, the defenders were forced to dislodge successive Japanese thrusts by hand. Thus despite the success, the Chinese in Tai-erh-chuang had lost nearly half their strength.[22]

Even as the Chinese drew in the majority of Isogai's division, they took horrendous casualties. Their hold north of the Grand Canal became increasingly tenuous. Tai-erh-chuang could not fall, or the well-laid trap would come undone. T'ang En-po was ordered to close the salient as early as March 27 but did not make substantial progress. This probably was due to Seya's northerly shift in attention. As an interesting aside, the Japanese minister of war, General Sugiyama, flew to Peiping in this period; most likely to take stock of what he saw to be the disintegration of his Second Army. The deterioration would soon become annihilation.

Seya extricated his lone detachment from Kuolichi on March 28 after repulsing the attacking Chinese forces. In Tai-erh-chuang the remaining Japanese succeeded in punching a hole through the wall. The Japanese ability to advance with limited numbers was in part because of additional air support granted the Second Army in late March. Four heavy bombers, a light bomber squadron, and a portion of a fighter squadron were all assigned to support the Second Army, but it was to no avail; the Japanese were promptly expelled from their hard-won gains.

Seya had, in a belated way, learned his lesson. Shunning his disparate efforts, he took his entire detachment to smash Tai-erh-chuang. The Japanese, fully intent on breaking the Chinese, brought up their heavy guns and tanks. Indicative of their overweening pride, Japanese radio mistakenly began reporting a victory. The April 5 issue of the *New York Herald Tribune* even ran a story covering the continued southern drive of Japanese forces after capturing the "smoldering ruins" of Tai-erh-chuang.[23]

Sakamoto knew better. He received reports in Linyi that Seya's effort was meeting with failure, so he canceled the attack on Linyi on March 29. The Second Army was in its death throes. Leaving one element southwest of Linyi and another at Hsiancheng to guard his rear, Sakamoto struck out blindly to the south. He passed around Linyi, leaving Chang Tse-chung and P'ang Ping-hsun unmolested in his rear. The decision is explicable only in terms of the intelligence and communications blackout that seized the Second Army. T'ang En-po sat astride any potential lines of connection between the two divisions. The depth of this isolation and confusion would grow progressively worse.

Annihilation of the Japanese

In Tai-erh-chuang the Japanese faced a decidedly resolute and dynamic defense. The nature of the city's layout favored a Chinese stand. Its heavy stone walls served to reduce the Japanese preponderance in firepower. To this end, the Chinese also limited their major operations to the night. The men of the 2d Army Group were well prepared for such operations. Sun Lien-chung made a habit of sounding an alarm at night so his men would become familiar with dressing and reporting in complete darkness and silence. As Captain Carlson would learn immediately following the battle for Tai-erh-chuang, the emphasis on night attacks negated Japanese superiority in the air and rendered their artillery ineffectual as the Chinese resorted to close combat.

The Chinese artillerymen in and around Tai-erh-chuang also may have outshot their Japanese counterparts. Captain Carlson observed young battery and battalion commanders, trained at the Central Military Academy under German tutelage, computing firing data based on the latest methods. With their medium batteries of 155mm howitzers, the Chinese engaged their Japanese adversaries at ranges of 10,000 to 15,000 meters and accurately controlled and observed the distribution of their fire.

In one instance Carlson, an artillery officer himself, stood at a Chinese artillery observation post as the Japanese guns attempted to range the position. From the upper reaches of the hill, he watched as Japanese high-explosive shells pummeled the bottom of the hill. Expecting a good battery to bracket any target in three salvos, Carlson watched in awe as the Japanese lamely poured fifty salvos into the now unoccupied hill. All burst short of the desired target.

Showing special interest in artillery, Carlson moved the following day to observe a battery of camouflaged 75mm guns shelling Japanese positions from the east flank of the Chinese position.

There, windlasses from local wells were set up to resemble guns. A single actual gun was then fired from various locations among the dummies. The Japanese expended large quantities of ammunition to silence the phantom gun, only to fail to destroy even one of its wooden brothers.

This is not entirely surprising, because Japanese artillery units did not generally engage targets farther than 5,000 meters distant. Similarly, Japanese artillery doctrine called for batteries to deploy within 450 to 750 meters of the front line when attacking organized positions.[24] Although Japanese artillery was useful for close-in assaults, its inflexibility proved its undoing against the creative Chinese gunners. It is evident, therefore, that Chinese artillerymen in and around Tai-erh-chuang engaged their opponents at ranges nearly triple that of the Japanese.

Much of the Chinese defense in Tai-erh-chuang relied on a heavy use of machine guns to impede the doctrinaire Japanese movements. In ways reminiscent of World War I, Chinese soldiers retreated to their earthen shelters during heavy bombardments and emerged with their machine guns as the Japanese infantry advanced. This worked well due to the large number of machine guns in Tai-erh-chuang. The Japanese were probably surprised not so much by the equipment present as by the Chinese ability to use it so well.

This ability did not stop the Japanese from trying. By March 30, they had little room and little resupply. As Seya once again turned south to Tai-erh-chuang, T'ang En-po began to close the salient. Meanwhile Sakamoto rushed from Linyi to support the Seya detachment in Tai-erh-chuang. He arrived in Puway, a small village several miles east of Tai-erh-chuang, on April 2. He had a force of no more than four infantry battalions and two artillery battalions. The rest of the detachment, as has been noted, had been left to guard against any movement in Linyi. Furthermore, given the heavy fighting in Linyi, it is doubtful that Sakamoto commanded even this large a force.

Sakamoto attempted to advance west to meet Seya in Tai-erh-chuang. A large Chinese force promptly surrounded him near Puway. Savage fighting continued around the Japanese pocket for the next three days. T'ang En-po sent a powerful force to stop Sakamoto from reaching Tai-erh-chuang. In doing so he ensured that Sakamoto did not threaten Tai erh-chuang or his own Twentieth Army. This move also placed T'ang's LII Corps north and east of Tai-erh-chuang to prevent any escape. From this point forward the separated Japanese units showed almost no coordination. In the final days of the battle, the actions of the Japanese army more closely resembled the spasms of a dying beast than the calculated steps of a modern military host.

Pressed from all sides, the Japanese redoubled their efforts to seize Tai-erh-chuang. To divert strength from the Japanese frontal assaults, Sun Lien-chung launched the majority of his forces against the Japanese flanks and rear. The 30th Division of Chang Chin-chao struck on the left while the 27th Division of Huang Chiao-sung pushed from the right. On April 2 the Japanese increased their hold on Tai-erh-chuang with the help of massed firepower. April 3 saw the Japanese in possession of a full four-fifths of the town. The Chinese just managed to hold the western gate, because it represented the only remaining means for communication between this force within Tai-erh-chuang and those outside. The Japanese proceeded to engage the Chinese outside of the city with thirty tanks and sixty armored cars. They succeeded in pushing Huang Chiao-sung's 27th Division back across the Grand Canal. The battered 31st Division was reduced to one-fourth its strength by April 3. The next day marked the high point of Japanese confusion as this command group struggled to react to the many divergent threats.

Early April witnessed separate Japanese units stabbing blindly in the dark. Cut off from accurate intelligence in his head-quarters in Tsingtao, Itagaki ordered the Sakamoto detachment to "destroy the enemy to its front and capture Linyi." This order not only reveals Itagaki's lack of appreciation for the situation but also implies that he was generally unaware of his detach-ment's whereabouts.

Believing that Seya had already taken Tai-erh-chuang and that no more concerted action would be required, Sakamoto in-formed Seya that he was going to wheel about and return to fin-ish off Linyi. Sakamoto learned on April 6 that Tai-erh-chuang was not occupied. Inadequate communication prevented the timely passing of information. Unaware of Sakamoto's contin-ued presence, Seya crumbled in the face of a vigorous Chinese assault on the same day.

Out of gasoline, ammunition, food, and water, the Japanese clung to Tai-erh-chuang because they had nowhere else to go. Air-dropped supplies failed to find their intended starving recipi-ents.[25] Soldiers in the 31st Division reported to General Chih that the Japanese had used tear gas the previous night. Under-standing this to be a move of desperation, Sun Lien-chung or-dered an assault for the night of April 6. At 4 A.M. on April 7, the Chinese crushed the remaining Japanese defenders in six to seven hours of furious combat.[26] As the main force carved up the Japanese, two other columns moved to encircle the forces within Tai-erh-chuang itself. These divisions belonged to T'ang En-po. T'ang had his columns cross the Grand Canal at 8 P.M. on April 6. The western division raced eight kilometers north of the city to occupy the village of Changlu. The eastern force struck out for the village of Nanlo, situated five kilometers southeast of Tai-erh-chuang. It then moved north and west to meet up with its western counterpart, drawing the noose tighter. Some Japanese soldiers, realizing the extent of their entrapment, committed ritual suicide.

As the Japanese fled the town, many attempted to incinerate their dead to hide the depth of their failure.[27] At least four hundred men managed to break out of the northeastern gate and flee toward Ihsien. Three hundred more, unable to escape, barricaded themselves in a building at the southeast corner of town. Because they were unwilling to surrender, the Chinese burned them out.[28]

A "brilliant sunlight" cascaded through the streets of Tai-erh-chuang on April 7. Captain Carlson surveyed a scene of "utter destruction." The city was riddled with barbed wire and sandbag barricades. Of the twenty tanks that assaulted Tai-erh-chuang, thirteen had been disabled, but four remained on the field outside the city wall. The rest managed to withdraw. The lifeless crews of these four tanks were sprawled about the vehicles in silent testimony to their futility. Unguarded by infantry, the tanks proved easy targets. Chinese soldiers, hiding in the folds of the earth, destroyed the tanks by throwing bundles of four grenades into the tracks.

During the final days of Tai-erh-chuang, the Japanese massed nearly 20,000 soldiers in and around the city.[29] Sixteen thousand of these never left. Chinese losses were also high. When the valiant 31st Division fell in to assess its damage, only 2,000 of the original 9,000 were able to answer the roll call.[30] The exhausted Chinese pursued the fleeing Japanese as far as Nikou on April 7. Ihsien was as far as the Chinese pursuit would go.

The failure to pursue grated on the mind of the head of the German military advisor, Alexander von Falkenhausen, in Hankow. He wished that the Chinese had followed up their victory and destroyed even more Japanese as they ran. This criticism was not realistic. The Chinese army, after Tai-erh-chuang, was in no position to chase down the Japanese. The elite Central Army units had been largely worn down and the remaining units were probably not operationally capable of large-scale pursuit. The decision not to advance probably saved a good portion of the Chinese 5th War Area. Had Li gone forward, the ten Japanese divisions that poured into Shantung to crush the Chinese would have likely caught him. Li's successful defense and measured retreat actually saved the Chinese from this fate as well as allowing the Chinese to extricate their precious heavy equipment.

Indeed the Japanese belief in the attack was indoctrinated often at the expense of good sense. When faced with ambiguous situations the Japanese would invariably go forward. Directives given to Japanese commanders before the war urged them to continue the assault at all costs. Retreat in the face of the Chinese was unconscionable. Bold, swift, and merciless assault was the only recipe for victory. The Chinese understood this and used it to their advantage. By holding firm in Linyi while falling back before the 10th Division, the Chinese effectively induced the Japanese to greatly overextend themselves. Each new setback caused the Japanese to gamble more heavily on the offensive. Consternation, confusion, and ultimately panic seized the Japanese as they contemplated what, in essence, had never happened before—defeat.

Conclusion

The Chinese at Tai-erh-chuang took into account a sophisticated understanding of ends and means. Poorer quality units were assigned simpler tasks. The defense of Linyi required resolve and a do-or-die attitude. Li found this in Chang Tse-chung, who desperately wanted to redeem himself after his earlier failures. The finesse of better-trained units such as T'ang En-po's army would have been wasted in such a grinding battle of attrition. The heterogeneous nature of the Chinese army at the time made matching the unit's ability to the task important. Li must receive high marks in this category. The well-trained and equipped 2d Army Group and Twentieth Army were used to draw in the Japanese as well as hunt down their lone columns as they moved across the countryside.

The battle at Tai-erh-chuang fully exposed the Japanese weakness in combined-arms warfare. Japanese attacks were habitually one sided. When Japanese artillery and airpower pounded an objective, the infantry remained stationary. As with many modern armies, the Japanese developed an overdependence on firepower. Although seemingly cheaper in lives, a reliance on firepower alone is less dynamic in its application. A determined foe, such as the Chinese in Tai-erh-chuang, can take to the ground in earnest and survive even heavy barrages. Any dislodgment of the Chinese from their fortress-town required a more tightly knit integration of fire and maneuver.

Likewise, the imperial army's mechanized forces advanced without the effective support of available infantry. Without this protection, Nishio's substantial tank arm was isolated and eliminated by industrious Chinese antiarmor teams. In urban terrain more so than anywhere else, armored forces must be accompanied closely by supporting infantry. Similarly, Japanese infantry, lacking in firepower, needed the addition of the tanks. Success, however, required close integration.

These problems were exacerbated for the Japanese by the ineptitude of their commanders. Nishio, Itagaki, and Isogai frequently dictated unrealistic orders to their subordinate commanders without the slightest understanding of their positions. Japanese directives were untimely, uninformed, and often contradictory. The staunchness of Chinese resistance called for unified action. In response, the Japanese offered only uncoordinated, divergent thrusts. Japanese belief in the supremacy of the offense

was misguided. The attack should unbalance a foe psychologically and physically. Japanese linear drives served only to confuse
the Japanese commanders. Their confusion allowed them to become fixated on the fighting within Tai-erh-chuang. The smaller,
mobile Japanese army quickly found itself trapped in a battle of
attrition while the larger, unwieldy Chinese moved with speed to
surround it. Chinese commanders exercised a clear knowledge of
their superior's intent without any hint of rigidity. Chinese command was diffuse yet coherent.

Perhaps the most interesting aspect in this study of pre-
World War II urban warfare is the use of maneuver. Japanese advances, as has been noted, adhered rigidly to the railroad lines,
because they provided the sole means for logistical support. This
fact forced Japanese units into easily identifiable pockets of resistance in the form of cities. The retention or loss of these nodes
of conflict rested not so much on those units inside the town but
actually on those that operated around them. The Chinese defense of T'enghsien, Linyi, and Tai-erh-chuang depended upon
the skill of forces fighting outside the city limits. Especially at
Tai-erh-chuang, Li Tsung-jen's forces used the city as a pivot for
their maneuver rather than the locus of their efforts. Though
violence engulfed the city itself, the decisive actions took place
on the flanks and in the rear areas. The linearity of the Japanese
assaults within Tai-erh-chuang was countered by Chinese moves
to the exposed wings. Only after the Japanese in Tai-erh-chuang
were isolated did the Chinese hack their way through the remaining imperial troops.

Throughout history, cities have been the scenes of military
operations for two primary reasons: military importance or political value, and sometimes both. The various street fights leading
up to and including the battle for Tai-erh-chuang were fought
because the Japanese supply system and their requirements for
speed necessitated the capture of these way points. Controlling

the outlying regions, however, best effected controlling these points. This is the didactic key. Thus the strongpoints were viable only until obviated by maneuver. The Chinese at Tai-erh-chuang knew this far better than their Japanese adversaries.

ENDNOTES

1.   Joris Ivens, *The Spanish Earth/The 400 Million,* 108 min., Slingshot Entertainment, 2000, dvd.

2.   Frank Dorn, *The Sino-Japanese War, 1937–1941* (New York: Macmillan Publishing Company, 1974), 157.

3.   Edward L. Dreyer, *China at War 1901–1949* (London: Longman Group Limited, 1995), 216–222.

4.   Henri Diederick de Fremery, *A Dutch Spy in China,* ed. Ger Teitler and Kurt W. Radtke (Leiden: Brill, 1999), 164. Chiang had Han court-martialed, then sent before the firing squad.

5.   Hsu Long-hsuen and Chang Ming-kai, *History,* 223.

6   Evans Carlson, *The Chinese Army: Its Organization and Military Efficiency* (New York: Institute of Pacific Relations, 1940), 27.

7.   Paul Kesaris, ed., U.S. military intelligence reports. *China, 1911–1941* (Frederick: University Publications of America, 1983), Nov 1937, No. 9607, 7, 8.

8.   Te-Kong Tong and Li Tsung-jen, *The Memoirs of Li Tsung-jen* (Boulder: Westview Press, 1979), 343.

9.   U.S. military intelligence reports, 13 Jan–1 Feb 1938, No. 9627, 7.

10.   Taksuma Shimoyama, *North China Area Operations,* 141. The Second Army believed it faced three KMT divisions, three divisions of the Shantung army, four Szechwan divisions, and a single division of irregulars.

11.   Te-Kong Tong and Li Tsung-jen, *Memoirs,* 343.

12.   U.S. military intelligence reports, 17–23 March 1938, 3.

13.   Te-Kong Tong and Li Tsung-jen, *Memoirs,* 349.

14.   Ibid., 350–51.

15.   Ibid., 352. T'ang's army consisted of the 2d, 4th, 25th, 89th, and 110th Divisions.

16.   Leng Hsin, interview by Col. William Whitson, 16 September 1965, interview 48, Military History of Modern China, Taipei, 7.

17.   Evans Carlson, *Twin Stars of China* (New York: Dodd, Mead & Co., 1940), 141.

18.   Dorn, *Sino-Japanese War,* 152.

19.   U.S. military intelligence reports, 17–23 March 1938, No. 9649, 3.

20.   Te-Kong Tong and Li Tsung-jen, *Memoirs,* 353.

21.   Evans Carlson, *Evans F. Carlson on China at War, 1937,* ed. Hugh Deane. Letter dated 15 April 1938 (New York: China and US Publications, 1993), 32.

22.   Te-Kong Tong and Li Tsung-jen, *Memoirs,* 353.

23.   *New York Herald Tribune,* 5 April 1938.

24.   U.S. War Department, *Handbook on Japanese Military Forces* (Washington, DC: U.S. Government Printing Office, 1944), 69–73.

25.   Dorn, *Sino-Japanese War,* 157.

26.   Joris Ivens, *The Camera and I* (New York: International Publishers, 1969), 161.

27.   Carlson, *Twin Stars,* 146.

28.   Ibid., 144.

29.   de Fremery, *Dutch Spy,* 176.

30.   Dorn, *Sino-Japanese War,* 157–58.

Stalingrad, 1942:

With Will, Weapon, and a Watch

by Col. Eric M. Walters

In war and work, every minute counts! [1]
—Soviet World War II propaganda poster

I wanted to get to the Volga and to do so at a particular point where stands a certain town. By chance it bears the name of Stalin himself. I wanted to take the place, and do you know, we've pulled it off, we've got it really, except for a few enemy positions still holding out. Now people say: "Why don't you finish the job more quickly?" Well, the reason is that I don't want another Verdun. I prefer to do the job with quite small assault groups. Time is of no consequence at all. [2]
—Adolf Hitler, November 8, 1942

Beginning on August 23, 1942, the German Sixth Army under Col. Gen. Friedrich Paulus attempted to capture the Soviet metropolis of Stalingrad, on the west bank of the Volga River. By mid-November, it succeeded in wresting approximately 90 percent of the city from Maj. Gen. Vasili Chuikov's Sixty-second Army. At 6:30 on the morning of November 19, large Red Army forces attacked the weak Romanian Third and Fourth Armies on the left and right flanks of the Sixth Army. By November 22, spearhead units of the Soviet pincers met at Kalach, severing

Paulus's line of communications. Hitler would hear nothing of allowing the trapped army to escape. Despite a December effort to relieve the encircled force, the Sixth Army was unable to break the Soviet stranglehold and perished on February 2, 1943.

In spite of the battle of Stalingrad's significance as the largest and longest-running urban fight of the twentieth century, its tactical lessons and the relevance of those lessons to warfare in the twenty-first century are not clear to many soldiers, students, and historians in the West. Part of the problem lies with English-language source materials; although nearly all of them discuss the city fighting, it takes a back seat to the drama of the November 19 counteroffensive and abortive German relief effort.[3]

But the real issue is primarily one of perspective. How are we to judge the success of urban warfare tactics in Stalingrad? At first glance, this would seem simple enough. The Germans, despite great difficulty and heavy casualties, took 90 percent of the city in approximately two months of hard fighting. Although the Sixty-second Army defenders were provided succor and reinforcements from the east bank of the Volga, they failed to stem the Nazi tide. Only the November 19 Soviet counteroffensive appears to have prevented the Sixth Army from taking the remaining fraction of the city still left in communist hands. From this perspective, one might think that the best tactical lessons concerning military operations in urban terrain (MOUT) would be found on the German side.

Certainly a tactical-level examination of the correlation of forces and combat ratios—the influences and impediments of terrain; the number and sizes of units committed, spent, and destroyed; the quantity and size of city blocks gained and lost—seems to confirm this view. To many, the Soviet defenders closely resembled an armed mob.[4]

Looking at the battle of Stalingrad from an operational-level perspective, however, another conclusion may be drawn. The

Sixty-second Army could not resist German advances in the urban landscape at all points without siphoning off reinforcements destined for the counteroffensive.[5] Once the Soviet leadership decided to trap the Nazi enemy, Chuikov's role evolved from defending the city to delaying inevitable German success. The concept was to encourage the Germans to keep attacking, enjoying victory after tactical victory but consistently falling short of conquering all of Stalingrad.[6] For the Germans to continue their effort to vanquish the Red Army, they would have to draw on additional troops from the Sixth Army's flanks and elsewhere in the theater, making themselves vulnerable to the Red Army counteroffensive.

Although there is evidence that the Germans were always aware of the risks in committing more forces of the Sixth Army into the maelstrom that was Stalingrad, this did not change their basic tactical approach. The German leadership consistently believed that its troops would conquer the remainder of the city in just enough time to redeploy units to the threatened flanks and defeat any Soviet counteroffensive.[7] Possessing this faith, the Germans saw little reason to alter their offensive technique inside the city. Paulus nearly won the battle for the city by mid-November 1942, only to definitively lose it in late January to early February the following year.[8] Like the hare versus the tortoise in the children's story, the Sixth Army lost the race for Stalingrad despite its potential superiority. The Germans underestimated their opponent's will and failed to realize that the crucial dimension of conflict in the city was temporal, not physical. Although space and forces were important, time mattered most.

The very possibility that the Soviets were using their defensive tactics in Stalingrad to shape the operational situation suggests that the Germans are not the only source for lessons learned on urban warfare. Indeed, although German MOUT tactics, techniques, and procedures provide insights into how to destroy an urban enemy, the Soviet experience suggests how to make a superior enemy pay for such gains—and pay for them in terms of time. Seen in this light, German urban warfare tactics lose much of their luster. It is more worthwhile to examine Soviet tactical patterns, especially because they challenge conventional military thought. Thus, we are given a glimpse into how the Soviet defenders succeeded in luring German forces into the city, and took heavy casualties to absorb the blow to gain the time necessary to achieve an operational-level victory.

The Operational Context

We can conclude, then, that generally the stronger side in war seeks to shorten the duration of the conflict, while the weaker side generally tries to lengthen it in order to increase opportunities for a favorable outcome. As Clausewitz noted: "Time, then, is less likely to bring favor to the victor than to the vanquished."[9]

To place any tactical analysis of Stalingrad city fighting in proper context, an understanding of the operational-level situation is essential. Taking the city wasn't always considered a bad idea. Originally, operations near Stalingrad were designed to interrupt rail and Volga River traffic from central Russia to the outlying Caucasus region and destroy armament factories in the city. The oil fields in the Caucasus were the primary objective of the German 1942 summer offensive, code-named Operation Blue.[10] Stalingrad happened to be a convenient anchor point for the left flank of the Axis drive. But when the advance to seize Soviet oil sources in the Caucasus foundered in late summer, Hitler focused on conquering Stalingrad as the primary prize for the year's campaigning. Historians fault Hitler for putting too much emphasis on the perceived psychological importance of seizing "Stalin's City" as a war trophy.[11]

The problem for the German campaign was that Stalingrad and the upper Don River area were natural places to attract Soviet reinforcements. Stalin and Stavka (general headquarters of the Soviet high command) worried that the German 1942 summer offensive was intended to drive east, then swing north to Moscow. It was only well after the German focus of effort was revealed to be aimed against the Caucasus region that Stavka contemplated an offensive use for the forces making up the newly established Don and Volga River defenses.

The Sixth Army's major military challenge in its advance to Stalingrad was to maintain enough combat power to its front and flanks—particularly its left—simultaneously. The dilemma was that if too many forces massed to the front, Soviet attacks on the flanks would interrupt the army's lengthening line of communications. This would degrade the continuous flow of precious supply to the Sixth Army, especially fuel and artillery ammunition needed to take the city. If the Germans focused too much combat power on securing the flanks, the forces spearheading the drive would be robbed of sufficient strength to perform their task.[12] Paulus faced the typical problem of balancing the need for mass against Stalingrad with the requirement for effective economy of forces on his flanks. This problem would increase as the assault on Stalingrad proper continued.

Once he reached Stalingrad in strength, Paulus did not have enough force to spare for an attack against the whole city at all points simultaneously. He initially hoped to take Stalingrad on August 23 by coup de main from the north using the relatively small and strung-out XIV Panzer Corps. When this failed, he ordered aerial terror bombing in preparation for larger German assaults that could not materialize in time to take advantage of the shock effect of the bombing. From the first, the Germans believed they could preempt the Soviet defensive efforts in the area by moving quickly, even if that increased their vulnerability. After their preliminary efforts failed, the Germans lunged into south and central Stalingrad on September 13. Despite impressive gains, the German Sixth Army foundered on the rocks of Soviet defenses in key areas by September 24. Thus ended the first phase of what would become a three-phase offensive by the Sixth Army to conquer the urban ruins of Stalingrad.[13]

By this time, the Germans had already achieved the original operational objective set for taking Stalingrad—interrupting river and rail traffic to the Caucasus. Additionally, Stalingrad's industrial contributions to the war were seriously degraded.[14] Hitler's insistence on obtaining a symbolic victory, however, meant that the deadly contest would continue.

When the Germans failed to take Stalingrad in a rapid operation during the first phase of the battle, they mounted more deliberate efforts. The second phase witnessed the reallocation of German combat power, beginning on approximately September 27, to reduce the triangle of Soviet defenses in the north and northwest suburbs and surrounding area. Through these dislocating attacks the Germans hoped to open a path to the industrial northern end of the metropolis, gaining room to maneuver and sufficient attack frontages for future assaults there to complete the conquest of the city. This phase continued until October 8.

The third phase consisted of an intermittent series of German offensives that began with preparations for a massive assault that commenced on October 13 and ended just prior to the Soviet November counteroffensive. This phase was characterized by a series of huge and sequential deliberate assaults on Stalingrad's three major industrial complexes, located in the northern part of the city: the Dzherzhinsky Tractor Works, the Red Barricades Ordnance Factory, and the Red October Metallurgical Works. The German offensive ended before the last Soviet defenses were eliminated. Subsequent Sixth Army operations no longer aimed at conquering the city but attempted to maintain the integrity of German gains after the Soviet encirclement until the army's surrender on January 31, 1943.

Influences of the Urban Terrain

The geography of Stalingrad itself contributed to the Soviet ability to confound German designs of conquest. The city ran thirty miles in length along the west bank of the Volga River and was only four thousand yards at its widest point. In many places, the width of the city was less than fifteen hundred yards.[15] Although such urban terrain seemed shallow and vulnerable to seizure along a wide front, the Sixth Army could not muster enough combat strength to mount such a general offensive effort along the city's entire length. The Germans had to focus overwhelming combat power against one part of the city at a time.[16]

The southern portion of Stalingrad consisted of mostly wooden structures, which were gutted and laid to rubble by German aerial attacks beginning on August 23. Later on, this would create problems for German tactical mobility within the city.[17] The center of Stalingrad was split by the heights of the Mamayev Kurgan, known to the Germans as Hill 102, affording observation over nearly all of the city and adjacent Volga River. North of the Mamayev Kurgan lay the large industrial complexes of the Red October Metallurgical Works, the Red Barricades Ordnance Factory, and the Dzherzhinsky Tractor Works with adjacent workers' housing. The work halls and surrounding machinery/foundry buildings and work bays formed natural fortresses within the industrialized northern section of the city. Deep gullies and ravines cut through Stalingrad from the surrounding terrain, forming natural covered avenues of approach and defensive positions.

The most important terrain features in Stalingrad were the landing stages on the west bank. These stages facilitated the movement of Soviet reinforcements, replacements, and supplies ferried across the river from assembly areas on the lower east bank for movement into the city.[19] The only way to defeat the Soviets in the city was to prevent their reinforcement and resupply; therefore, as Gen. Hans Doerr explains, the means to achieve a decision "lay in the last hundred meters before the Volga."[20] Interdiction of Soviet movements on the lower-lying east bank of the Volga was problematic, owing to the dense forests there.

The east bank of the Volga River has a slightly concave bend along the length of the city and is topped with bluffs overlooking the water. River islands interrupt the line of sight from these points along the length of the waterway, inhibiting the Germans' ability to interfere with river-borne traffic. Most Soviet reinforcements and supply crossed the Volga during darkness, further complicating German attempts to interdict Red Army trans-Volga resupply and reinforcement.[21] Until the Germans seized the bluffs in any locality, the Soviets could use the "dead space" created by the cliffs above the riverbank to unload and concentrate ammunition, reinforcements, and replacements. Soviet defenders dug tunnels into the cliffs to store ammunition and artillery as well as house Katyusha truck-mounted multiple rocket launchers.[22] Ravines and industrial drainage pipes provided covered access from the Volga's west bank to the city's interior.

Stalingrad the battle turned out to be as big as Stalingrad the city. A few case studies drawn from each phase suffice to illustrate the development of Soviet tactical patterns throughout the battle.

Demonstrating the Will in the First Phase: The Battles for the Grain Elevator and Central Railroad Station

This problem is, broadly, how to maintain a continuous and sustained effort throughout an attack, so as to take instant advantage of initial success and to achieve complete victory before the enemy reserves can intervene. It really resolves itself into a time problem between the onrush of the attacker and the enemy reserves. [23]

At 6:45 A.M. on Sunday, September 13, the Germans opened the battle of Stalingrad with an artillery and air bombardment into the central and southern sections of the city. That same day, Maj. Gen. Vasili Ivanovich Chuikov replaced the disheartened Anton Lopatin as commander of the Sixty-second Army and set about reviving its fighting spirit. This was not easy, because local crises mounted under the relentless German offensive and communications with the front line were often lost. Also complicating matters was the fact that the decision to defend the city was made at the last minute, as J. Bowyer Bell relates:

No one had foreseen a stand at Stalingrad. The city was totally unprepared for a siege. An abortive last-minute start had been made on fortifications, but nothing had been done about the evacuation of civilians or machinery. No supplies had been accumulated. More revealing, not only did the Soviet Sixty-second [Army] . . . have no idea of how to defend a modern city under siege, but the Red Army itself had no formal doctrine concerning the techniques of city fighting.[24]

Yet, from the outset, the sheer force of Chuikov's personality did much to raise the flagging morale of the Sixty-second Army.

Given that his superiors at the Stalingrad Front, Marshal Andrei Yeremenko and Nikita Khrushchev, expected him to defend Stalingrad or die in the attempt, Chuikov's personal purposefulness is perhaps not so surprising.[25] Still, his fatalistic, no-nonsense attitude struck a responsive chord in Soviet soldiers.[26] Chuikov kept his headquarters close to the front lines when his subordinates moved their headquarters farther to the rear. He also had no tolerance for cowardice, no matter how horrible the fighting conditions became. Some claim that roughly 13,500 men were executed for failing to rise to the challenge.[27]

Chuikov had grown tired of the poor leadership he witnessed during July and August once he was assigned to the Stalingrad Front. To him, poor troops were the natural by-product of poor leaders; good troops naturally resulted from good leaders.[28] He saw his job as providing determined leadership to the army. This he did in short order, instilling a sense of urgency in whomever he came into contact. Over time, his grim ruthlessness infected small units and soon larger ones, until—like a seed crystal dropped into a supersaturated solution—the Sixty-second Army suddenly solidified into a single extension of his will.

The German aerial bombardments of August 23–25 and September 3 had turned most of southern Stalingrad into a burnt-out pile of rubble. The few structures that survived dominated the surrounding terrain. One of these buildings was a grain elevator in the southern part of the city, located at the end of a rail spur. The large concrete silos and adjacent corrugated metal–covered elevator structure on the northern side made for an ideal protected position from which to observe the surrounding area.

Approximately fifty survivors of the 35th Guards Division holed up there, defending the site against German attacks of XLVIII Panzer Corps surging in from the south and west on Monday, September 14. But the ground west of the grain elevator

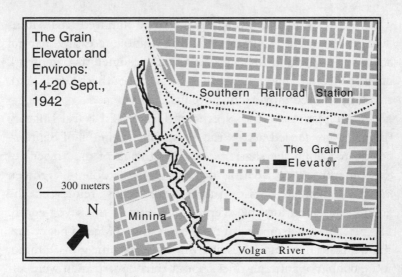

The Grain Elevator and Environs: 14-20 Sept., 1942

Southern Railroad Station

The Grain Elevator

0   300 meters

N

Minina

Volga River

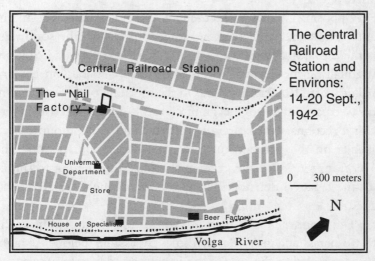

The Central Railroad Station and Environs: 14-20 Sept., 1942

Central Railroad Station

The "Nail Factory"→

Univermag Department Store

House of Specialists

Beer Factory

0   300 meters

N

Volga River

First phase case[29]

was not nearly as built up along the three hundred to six hundred yards to the Southern Railway Station, creating natural fields of fire. Behind the silo, the terrain resumed its patchwork of broken buildings and debris typical of southern Stalingrad, enabling covered movement of vehicles and men.

Arctic marines of the North Sea Fleet's 92d Naval Infantry Brigade were ferried across the Volga on the night of September 16 to stiffen the shattered southern flank of the Soviet defense in the city. A marine machine-gun platoon of eighteen men, commanded by Lt. Andrei Khozyaynov, reinforced the grain elevator during the evening darkness of the seventeenth. The platoon was armed with two water-cooled Maxim heavy machine guns, a light machine gun, three submachine guns, a radio, and a couple of antitank rifles. About thirty guardsmen were left in good order inside the grain elevator; some wounded remained with the able-bodied men because they could not yet be safely evacuated.[30]

Opposing them was Lieutenant General Pfeiffer's 94th Infantry Division, a unit that had fought its way to the southwest of the elevator and onward to the Southern Railroad Station. Augmenting the infantry was the armor of General von Hauenschildt's 24th Panzer Division. On the morning of the eighteenth, the Germans attacked the grain elevator, adjusting artillery fire with a reconnaissance aircraft. Infantry and tanks mounted ten assaults on the structure in one twenty-four-hour period. The explosions set fire to the grain in the silos, threatening to smoke out the fanatical defenders. Despite this, all the German attacks failed.[31]

The marines crept up to the top of the elevator during the day to harass and stop German infantry assaults below. At night they descended to the base of the structure and formed a defensive perimeter to prevent night infiltration. From November 18 to 20, the Germans continued ad hoc attacks against the composite platoon so that the division could resume its advance to the Volga bank. Once, German soldiers finally reached the corrugated elevator tower itself but were tossed out when the marines caught them creeping up the metal stairs.[32] Again, all these assaults failed. When water ran out, the marines urinated into the cooling jackets of the Maxims to keep the barrels operational. After reallocating the remaining ammunition on November 20, Khozyaynov's men found they had no more grenades or antitank rifle rounds left.[33]

Twelve German tanks rumbled into view at high noon, splitting up to pump rounds into both sides of the pockmarked and blackened structure. This took time, because their small-caliber tank cannon and armor-piercing shells could do no more than punch holes in the walls. With no more antitank weapons left to combat them, the Germans grew bolder and were able to put both Soviet Maxim machine guns out of action. Lieutenant Khozyaynov's marines had only the remaining light machine gun to stop a ground assault on one side of the building at a time. Without automatic fire to break up German infantry attacks from all quarters simultaneously, several companies of infantry from the 94th Division were able to depart from behind their tank cover, tossing grenades in front of them. They soon infiltrated into the bottom of the elevator. The marines and guardsmen could not see them and fired at sounds, which seemed to drive the Germans to ground.[34]

That night during a lull, Lieutenant Khozyaynov redistributed his marines' remaining ammunition. All they had left was a drum and a half of ammunition for the light machine gun, about two dozen rounds per man for the submachine guns, and fewer than a dozen rounds left for each rifle. Water and food had long since been consumed. The marine platoon commander decided to sneak out of the elevator under cover of darkness. Surviving marines escaped, driven more by their maddening thirst than by fear of the enemy.[35] Thus ended the battle for the grain elevator. The actions of these few Soviet defenders held up the German offensive in southern Stalingrad from November 14 through the evening of the twentieth—a total of six days.

This was not an isolated example of what could be accomplished with a small group of determined soldiers. Although the Soviet defense eventually succumbed, it cost the Germans time. Chuikov and his German opponents realized this during the battle for the Central Railway Station in central Stalingrad.

Lieutenant General Hartmann's 71st Infantry Division enjoyed easy progress on Sunday, September 13, commencing its attack west of Stalingrad near Hills 144.9 and 153.7. Even on the morning of September 14, resistance seemed light all the way into the city. A subordinate unit of the 71st Infantry Division— the 194th Infantry Regiment, commanded by Lieutenant Colonel Roske—approached the Central Railroad Station just northwest of the governmental and commercial downtown district of Stalingrad. Assault columns of the 3d Battalion, commanded by Capt. Gerhard Meunch, were losing men to Soviet snipers shooting from third- and fourth-floor windows as well as from concealed infantry guns at ground level. For Meunch to eliminate the threat, he would have to get his battalion off the streets and root out the defenders in the neighboring buildings. That was going to take more time than he had. By 2:00 P.M. he was a few hundred meters from the Central Railroad Station main building next to Red Square when Roske ordered him to seize the Central Ferry Landing on the Volga.[36]

Back at the Sixty-second Army command post, the 71st Infantry Division's success was causing Chuikov a great deal of consternation. He had only one reserve left to deal with the crisis: the depleted 6th Tank Brigade. Chuikov sent for one battalion from the brigade; it arrived with nine tanks. The Sixty-second Army chief of staff collected a scratch force of foot soldiers from the headquarters guard company combined with the tanks and officered by the army staff. One group was assigned to block the streets running from the Central Railroad Station to the Central Ferry Landing stage. Chuikov ordered the other group to take the House of Specialists (an apartment building for engineers), where the Germans had set up heavy machine guns to fire on ferries bringing reinforcements to the landing stage.[37]

The sudden commitment of this small reserve caught the German advance elements off guard as they were closing in on the Central Railroad Station. Lieutenant Colonel Roske commented:

> I walked up the street to the advance party—the left column was still within a sea of houses. My estimation of the enemy seemed to be right, so I was in good spirits, for there was no significant resistance and only occasional artillery fire from the other side of the Volga. Finally, we reached the railroad station. It was on the upper edge of a steep slope, from which one could see the wide body of tracks north of the main railroad station, with numerous criss-crossing tracks, and, beyond that, the magnificent 1800 meter wide band of the Volga. This is where the stone quarter began, and so did the fire from the tanks and mortars from beyond the railroad barrier and from individual guns on the east bank of the Volga. It was noon and I thanked God: one could see the camouflaged enemy for a great distance, and then I exhaled, for this line had been designated as the second sector. Then all of a sudden everyone stopped and took cover. Something unexpected happened. There was confusion. Then the sight of T-34s crossing to and fro, the mortars, the machine guns, and enemy artillery observers disembarked and marked the beginning of the end.[38]

The 194th Regiment's 1st Battalion was trying to reach the ferry on Meunch's left flank. By dusk, its troops had taken the beer factory and could see the ferry pier just 750 yards ahead. Other German soldiers of the 194th Regiment had taken the House of Specialists and the five-story State Bank. Defending the area were sixty NKVD troops (People's Commissariat of Internal Affairs, also called the Soviet Secret Police) reinforced by the 1st Battalion, 42d Guards Regiment, 13th Guards Division. On September 14, General Chuikov had ordered the 13th Guards Division to shore up the collapsing center defenses of Stalingrad. Colonel Yelin, the 42d Guards Regiment commander, and his 1st Battalion arrived to bolster the defense of the Central Railroad Station area.[39]

The suddenly tenacious Soviet defenses had taken the wind out of the sails of the 194th Infantry Regiment, at least for the rest of Monday evening. Captain Meunch lost nearly two hundred men in the fighting near Red Square and the Central Railroad Station. Attacking through the rail yard made him nervous. Surrounded by the devastated urban area, the Central Railroad Station complex was a linear feature running northeast to southwest and consisting of relatively open ground. Wrecked and serviceable rolling stock dotted the network of track, lending some cover for Meunch's troops not already occupied by Soviet snipers. After the day's heavy losses to sniper fire, Meunch decided not to risk an advance through this kind of terrain. He called in an air strike and attempted to bypass the station. Unfortunately the Ju-88 pilots had difficulty discriminating between friendly and enemy troops; they missed their target and rained bombs on Meunch's infantry. With fifty men left, there was no way the 3d Battalion could take and hold the Central Ferry Landing without support.[40]

The Soviet guardsmen of the 1st Battalion, 42d Guards Regiment, had difficulty sorting out the situation and forming a coherent defense during the night, despite Yelin's prodding. The Germans seemed to revive on the morning of September 15; the Luftwaffe pounced on anything that moved and the 71st Infantry Division renewed its assault on the Central Railroad Station. The Germans seized the station but lost it to a Guards counterattack that morning. The relative lack of cover in the station complex, compared to the rubbled stone and concrete around it, meant that the Central Railroad Station was relatively easy to take from a defender but harder to hold against a counterattack. The afternoon brought another successful German attack. Could the Soviets take the station back?[41]

Chuikov stepped outside his bunker and stopped the first combat officer he saw, Lt. Anton Kuzmich Dragan, who was commanding the 1st Company, 1st Battalion, 42d Guards Regiment. The general ordered the lieutenant to collect his surviving men and retake the station. Dragan massed his men near the main station building near one firing but immobile tank and started the attack with celerity: "A sudden attack, the throw of a grenade, a soldier after it." The Germans broke and ran away. By the time they realized that only a company had attacked, Dragan had set in his defense. The Soviets owned the Central Railroad Station by the end of the night.[42]

From September 16 to 18, the 1st Battalion, 42d Guards Regiment, and elements of the 71st Infantry Division sparred over the Central Railroad Station, which changed hands eleven more times. Dragan was pried loose from the station by a German enveloping move in the vicinity of the nail factory.[43] The guardsmen shifted their combat power to blunt it but were pushed out of the station and into the adjacent nail factory. Close-quarter fighting broke out between Dragan's troops and the Germans in the nail factory, supported by the Soviet 1st Battalion mortar company. The rest of the 1st Battalion was disintegrating. The 3d Company attempted to reinforce the beleaguered

Dragan, running the gauntlet of German fire to arrive at the nail factory with only twenty men left. September 18 ended with the Germans in control of the coveted rail yard.

Fighting in the nail factory continued throughout September 19. Local citizens informed Dragan that the Germans were regrouping, pairing up the infantry with tanks of the 24th Panzer Division and arranging for artillery support. No longer could the Germans hope to take the ground on the fly. September 20 was a relatively quiet day for Dragan's men as their German opponents prepared to renew the attack. The guardsmen prepared, too, setting in antitank rifles and making Molotov cocktails (gasoline firebombs).[44]

The morning of the twenty-first witnessed a ferocious, coordinated German attack. By the afternoon, the German 71st Division had cut the Soviet 1st Battalion in half, surrounded the remnants, and digested them. Ammunition was low. Dragan collected the survivors around his company in the nail factory and began a retreat to the Volga, consolidating his positions against vicious enemy attacks as he went. Only six men, Dragan included, were able to eventually make their way back across the Volga River to safety.[45]

Why had the Germans done so well until they reached the built-up areas of the city? What had given the Soviets so much heart? Chuikov's energetic measures to instill the will to resist certainly had contributed.[46] So, too, had the arrival of fresh troops, such as the 92d Naval Infantry Brigade and the 1st Battalion, 42d Guards Regiment, in these two examples. But there is more to it than this.

It is commonly supposed that the close terrain of the ruined Stalingrad metropolis robbed the Germans of their ability to employ long-range weapons to good effect and achieve the measure of command and control of forces that they were long accustomed to enjoying. Accordingly, the Germans negated many of their tactical advantages by accepting battle in the urban environs of Stalingrad, where controlled long-range engagements were replaced by uncontrolled close combat.[47] Certainly this was true. But there was another major tactical effect that was primarily psychological, affecting the will to fight on both sides.

The German blitzkrieg technique was built on the concept of pitting offensive strength against enemy weaknesses, achieving local superiority and exploiting combat success by rapid movement. Advancing combat elements penetrated deeply and in many directions to disperse the defenses before follow-on exploitation forces drove in the direction of the greatest weakness. German forces unhinged and dislocated defenses before they even congealed, forcing the enemy to abandon them. Maneuver leveraged enemy forces out of position and set them up for encirclement and destruction before the enemy was able to counteract it. Preemption and dislocation was the dominant German tactical modus operandi.[48] The critical element here was that the defender's will crumbled because he perceived himself unprepared vis-à-vis his assailant. Flight often resulted.

John Keegan, in his excellent work *Face of Battle,* describes how men in the stress of combat are affected by the proximity of mortal danger in the same way as animals. That is, the farther away the threat, the more likely the intended victim is to flee. The nearer the threat, the more likely the intended victim will stand his ground and fight.[49] This perhaps seems to defy common sense until one realizes that turning one's back on an immediately adjacent enemy usually means certain death. Distance can provide a psychological buffer; the victim thinks he can escape through flight if he is fast enough. Close combat provides no such buffer. Turning away from the enemy actually increases risk and the level of fear. Combatants suddenly confronted with close combat are not given time to run; therefore, they are psychologically more predisposed to stand their ground.[50] In Stalingrad, closing forces could not sight or fire on one another until they were within a very short range; thus, perceived opportunities for safe flight were seldom available. Psychologically, it was easier to face the threat head-on and fight than to attempt escape.[51] The ruined cityscape naturally stiffened Soviet resolve to resist, diminishing German shock tactics.

Initial German attacks on the outskirts of the city had rapidly developed, and advance units tried to take the center and southern sectors of the city "off the cuff." But to gain speed, the German divisions sacrificed a measure of coordination of their combat power. This made them more vulnerable to Soviet defensive fires and counterattacking maneuvers. Certainly the ability to pick off Germans while quickly moving down the streets and squares from the relative safety of urban cover boosted Soviet morale. The German 94th Infantry Division repeatedly mounted locally improvised attacks against the grain elevator on September 18 to 20; these attacks failed. The German 71st Infantry Division did much the same thing against the Central Railway Station from September 14 to 18 and failed as well. Eventual German success in both cases was due to isolating the defenders and forcing them to run out of ammunition. Significantly, the Soviets had not lost heart as they had in earlier battles.[52]

By this time it was clear to the Soviets—from the lowest private in Stalingrad all the way to Stalin himself—that the Sixth Army intended to conquer the whole of the city. It was equally clear to the German leadership that although their attacks were successful, they were also wasteful. German infantry strength was seriously depleted and required replacement. Paulus reported even as early as September 20 that "the infantry strength of the army has been so weakened by our own and the Soviet attacks of recent days that a supplement is needed to activate it."[53] The only places from which reinforcements could come were the divisions left behind inside the Don River bend. The Soviets had maintained their bridgeheads across the Don at Kremenskaya Sirotinskaya and at Serafimovich on the Sixth Army's flanks, but the German leadership did not sense that these posed any immediate danger. The German divisions were pulled out and the eleven divisions of the Romanian Third Army were posted in their places. In response to Paulus's requests, the Army Group B commander released the 100th Jaeger (literally "hunter," but in modern parlance this means light) Infantry Division to the Sixth Army for employment in Stalingrad.[54]

Paulus originally hoped that his rapid, preemptive attacks would conquer the city. Robert Leonhard mentions the temporal relationship between preemptive tactics and concentration tactics. Briefly, preemptive tactics sacrifice synchronization of the discrete combat arms in order to achieve greater velocity, which equals the speed of the fastest unit. Concentration tactics aim at optimizing combined-arms effects through synchronization of the force, but at the price of reducing its speed to that of the slowest unit.[55] No longer would preemptive attacks against apparent Soviet weaknesses be possible or productive within the built-up areas. No longer could the Germans hope to take Stalingrad on the run. Attacking "on the fly" clearly did not work.

As the Germans reduced to rubble existing structures with bombing and artillery saturation strikes, it became more difficult to observe the enemy and move through the devastated urban battlefield. This situation favored the defender more than it did the attacker, because command and control of large units were soon lost once attacks began. Fighting often degenerated into small-unit versus small-unit duels, out of contact with senior headquarters. Without the ability to rapidly direct units toward weaknesses and through temporary gaps, German attacks lost momentum and stalled. The devastated terrain made large-unit maneuver impossible, and gains were measured by the room rather than by the city block. General Hans Doerr relates:

> The time for conducting "operations" was over for good. From the wide expanses of the steppes, fighting had moved into the jagged gullies of the Volga bank, with its copses and ravines, into the city and factory areas of Stalingrad, spread out over uneven, pitted, rugged land, covered with iron, concrete, and stone buildings. The kilometer was replaced as a measure of distance by the meter. GHQ's map was the map of the city. A bitter battle for every house, factory, water tower, railway embankment, wall, cellar, and every pile of rubble was waged without equal even in the First World War . . . The distance between the enemy's forces and ours was as small as it could be. Despite the concentrated activity of aircraft and artillery, it was impossible to break out of the area of close fighting.[56]

Within the ruined urban landscape of Stalingrad, small groups of Soviet soldiers found they could take on their enemy on somewhat even terms. Either the Sixth Army troops stayed out in the open, advancing as they had down the boulevards and plazas to maintain tempo—at a high price in blood—or they slowed down to scuttle into the buildings sheltering their assailants, eliminating the Soviet defenders in house-to-house combat. As the battles for the grain elevator and Central Railroad Station demonstrated, speed alone was not sufficient to seize the city. The actions of a few rugged and fanatical defenders could bring such preemptive attacks to a standstill.

For the Germans, they would have to deploy the full arsenal of weapons that the Sixth Army possessed, accepting a loss of tempo in order to conserve manpower and increase firepower. Especially given the debilitating effects that the shattered terrain had on tactical execution, the Sixth Army would have to use concentration tactics, pausing when necessary to prepare. Time would be required to orchestrate tactical evolutions optimizing German combined-arms combat power, saving lives. If the Soviets had the will to defend Stalingrad to the death, then Paulus would show that the Sixth Army had even more determination—and the tools—to take the city. If the battle for Stalingrad had been a trial of wills in its first phase, it would evolve into a contest of weapons by the second.

Perfecting the Weapon in the Second Phase: The Transition of Soviet Tactics into "The War of the Rats"

Things are going very slowly, but every day we make a little progress. The whole thing is a question of time and manpower. [57]

As the fight for the Central Railroad Station raged, the Sixty-second Army leadership realized the virtues of smaller, cohesive groups. Compared to larger formations, such teams had a greater proportional tactical impact on the situation. Chuikov observed:

The guardsmen fought to the death; the only ones who left were the seriously wounded, who crawled away one by one. The stories told by the wounded made it clear that the German forces which had seized the station were suffering heavy casualties. When they were cut off from the division, the guardsmen, singly or in groups of two or three, consolidated positions in pill-boxes, in the basements of station buildings, behind station platforms and under railway carriages, from where they would continue, alone, to carry out the job they had been given— to attack the enemy from the rear and flanks and destroy them night and day. In this way they forced the enemy into street fighting, which compelled the German officers to keep their companies and battalions on the alert round the clock, to throw in more and more troops in different places, in order to surround and overcome the "one-man fortresses" created by Soviet soldiers who had decided to fight to the last breath.[58]

Impressed by the measures that determined men such as Khozyaynov and Dragan devised under the pressure of combat, Chuikov and his immediate staff decided to revise their tactics. Because they could not reliably control their larger formations in coordinated action, they would not even try to, thus making a virtue out of necessity. No longer would units be tactically employed solely as regiments, brigades, and battalions. Instead, unit organization would include small storm groups, and these would be given mission orders. Decentralized command and control enabled these units to take the initiative, seizing local opportunities where and when they occurred. The staff began working out specific ideas on disposing these storm groups for both offensive and defensive missions.

Defensive employment was more easily figured out from what had happened in the first phase of the fighting. City buildings took a great deal of time to move through and clear; a rapidly moving enemy usually avoided these buildings if possible and went along the streets. The Soviets could slow a German attack by configuring particular buildings as miniature fortresses for a small storm group. These groups of buildings were selected for their ability to dominate local terrain by fire and by virtue of their stout stone or brick construction. Ideally, these buildings had already been gutted by fire, so the Germans could not set them ablaze and smoke out the defenders.

Soviet garrisons within these fortified locations were armed with machine guns, submachine guns, Molotov cocktails, antitank rifles, and grenades for all-around defense, at a minimum. Larger garrisons had antitank guns, flamethrowers, dug-in tanks, and artillery. Medics and medical supplies, water, rations, and especially ammunition were stockpiled in the garrisons to provide sustainment when isolated.[59] Chuikov and his staff quickly learned how powerful these small—but motivated and well supplied—groups of soldiers were in delaying the German advance and buying time for the defenders.

The tactical defensive scheme for multistoried buildings was to sweep the streets with fire using weapons sited from semibasement and ground-floor locations, ideally using concealed firing slits or loopholes. Infantry guns and all manner of machine guns were emplaced on the lower floors. On the topmost floors, Soviet defenders located heavy machine guns and Molotov cocktails to use on German forces taking cover in the streets from ground-level fire. Soviet soldiers and remaining local citizens constructed obstacles, maximizing the effects of the tactical dilemma that this disposition created.

The idea was to control a position that could bring fire on a larger area; the Germans would be forced to divert troops to encircle the garrison and take the time to eliminate it before moving on. To allow such a garrison to effectively exist in the rear increased the hostile "surface area" that German troops had to guard. Basically, the more Soviet garrisons allowed in their rear area, the more troops the Germans had to divert to watch or eliminate them. The existence of these fortified Soviet strongpoints in rear areas also slowed German reinforcements, replacements, and supplies headed for the front. A successful defense prevented the Germans from obtaining observation points, disorganized German attacks, separated the infantry from supporting tanks, kept advancing elements from spreading out when they had broken through, and created small, nonmutually supporting enemy pockets for local counterattacks to engulf and digest.[60]

The whole Soviet Sixty-second Army was disposed of in this way, from small groups up to larger formations—each unit able to endure isolation and continue fighting. As long as the will to fight remained and ammunition held out, Chuikov expected that his defensive system would absorb an attack and rob it of momentum quickly.

The army commander also gave up on launching coordinated offensives with large units. Storm groups were to fight automatically, without waiting for orders, and counterattack the enemy before the Germans consolidated newly won ground. These assaults were carried out by moving above and below the ground, burrowing through attics and basements and crawling through sewers, keeping out of the streets and squares, and infesting every structure and rubble heap. Storm groups were built around an existing platoon and given two or three machine guns, a couple squads of sappers armed with flamethrowers, demolition satchel charges, or portable pioneer equipment such as crowbars, picks, and shovels. Submachine guns and grenades were preferred over rifles, even though these weapons were expensive in terms of ammunition.[61] Chuikov refused to make his men be stingy with their bullets.

The attacking storm groups would be split into three teams, called assault groups, with six to eight men in each team. They were lightly armed, usually carrying submachine guns, grenades, and shovels (sharp-edged shovels were used as axes to break into buildings, or hack German soldiers to death). These units would initially enter a building and start a close-quarters fight. A reinforcement group, divided into teams, was then committed into the building from several points simultaneously while the enemy was still fending off the assault groups. Their job was to set up hasty defenses to prevent the Germans from coming to the aid of the attacked unit. They carried machine guns, mortars, antitank rifles, explosives, pioneer gear, and heavy guns.

These units would be supplemented by the reserve group if need be. The reserve group was intended to block enemy relief efforts outside the target building that the reinforcement group could not handle, or to augment the assault groups that had been depleted from the fighting.[62]

The Soviets encouraged night movement and attacks to prevent the Luftwaffe from interfering. Effective sniping, booby-trap construction, mining, camouflage, and other individual combat field-craft techniques became a point of pride among many Soviet soldiers. Tales of incredible innovation and weapons expertise spread throughout the Sixty-second Army, inspiring soldiers to become ace snipers, antiaircraft gunners, mortar men, or antitank riflemen. The slogan of the army became, "Look after your weapon as carefully as your eyes."[63]

No longer could the art of generalship be allowed to flourish; this was where the Germans excelled. The battle for the city would henceforth be transformed into the art of the individual soldier and his weapon. He alone knew best what the enemy in front of him was like, what he was thinking, what he was feeling. Chuikov's idea was to make every German feel as though he was "living under the muzzle of a Soviet gun."[64] This would make the Nazi enemy tired from lack of sleep and from nervousness. He was therefore more likely to go to ground at the slightest threat, to hesitate, to be more cautious. The Germans labeled this kind of fighting as *Rattenkreig,* or war of the rats. For the Soviets, these tactics bought valuable time.[65]

Through these new tactics the Germans were put into a

dilemma. Either they sacrificed time to economize their own blood—allowing bypassed strongpoints and infestations to be sealed up but not eliminated—or they sacrificed blood to gain time, eliminating defiant Soviet resistance nests at heavy cost. Either way meant that troops would be diverted from the assault forces at the tip of the advance.[66] Either way also meant that time would be lost eventually. Even if the Germans eliminated Soviet strongpoints threatening rapid transit through an area, the resulting exhaustion and gradual attrition of the unit forced a pause later in the operation. More time was needed to obtain and integrate replacements into the assault battalions. More time was necessary to plan, rehearse, and prepare for the next coordinated attack.

To defeat this defensive concept, the natural German tendency was to mass troops prior to an attack. Chuikov made this an expensive proposition as well; when the Germans gave the Soviets indications that they were marshaling infantry in assembly areas or moving en masse into attack positions, the Soviets would unleash artillery and rocket launcher defensive fires from both the east and west banks of the Volga. This greatly heartened the Soviet infantry.[67]

The only possible way out of these dilemmas was for the Germans to use profligate amounts of firepower instead of friendly troops to destroy the enemy. Artillery, mortar, and air attacks were their preferred means of eliminating Soviet resistance. The Soviets ensured that the Germans did not often get to use these options by staying as close as possible to their adversaries—"fighting by the belt."[68] For Soviet soldiers, keeping in the immediate proximity of their enemy meant that the Germans could not safely use artillery and air support without risking their own troops.

German infantry strength had been drained away in the fight for the urban areas during the first phase of the battle. It took time to gather replacements and integrate them into the depleted divisions. Fighting in the city died away on the evening of September 24 as the Germans shifted their main effort from central Stalingrad to the northern sectors. A day later, the 100th Jaeger Infantry Division arrived to augment the Sixth Army and was posted near the Mamayev Kurgan. The idea of reducing the triangle of the northern Stalingrad defenses—with the tip at Orlovka—had much to recommend it. Paulus had to open up needed frontage to attack industrial northern Stalingrad directly. All he had at the moment was a thin line in the vicinity of the Mamayev Kurgan in the south and a small front outside Rynok in the north. Chuikov had heavily reinforced and fortified both areas. Assembling remaining Sixth Army combat power against the Orlovka salient also pit German strength against Soviet weakness in terrain more suited to German tactical methods. If the assaults developed quickly enough, the Sixth Army might then penetrate into factory districts in northern Stalingrad before they could be seriously contested.

Chuikov detected the shift in focus through his extensive reconnaissance efforts and prepared his defenses. The goal was not to prevent the Germans from penetrating the outer defense perimeter of the Orlovka salient; that was not realistic. Chuikov simply aimed to keep the Sixth Army out of the workers' settlements just west of the three great industrial complexes there and retain the Mamayev Kurgan.[69] The Germans might eliminate the salient, but they were not to take northern Stalingrad.

Once the Soviets completed regrouping, Chuikov ordered a spoiling attack aiming southwest back into central Stalingrad as far as the Central Railroad Station. He hoped the Germans would be forced to divert units from their upcoming attack to parry his blow in the city. Although the last paragraph of his attack order exhorted his commanders to use the small assault group concept, it was very much a traditional-style attack. It commenced at 6:00 A.M. on September 27 and lasted all of two hours. By 8:00 A.M. the Luftwaffe had pinned down his assaulting elements. By 10:30, German artillery opened a bombardment on the Mamayev Kurgan, heralding the start of the Sixth Army's own offensive. When night came, the Germans had penetrated to the outer edges of the Red October Metallurgical Works and were threatening the Red Barricades Ordnance Factory as well. Reinforcement by the bulk of the 193d Rifle Division the night of September 27 brought German progress there to a halt. Fighting seesawed in the area all the next day, with the Germans sidestepping across the length of northern Stalingrad and reaching the silicate factory. The battle for the Kurgan raged continuously throughout, devouring men and materiel on both sides.

While Chuikov was occupied with the immediate defense of the industrial sector of Stalingrad, Paulus opened his offensive against the Orlovka salient on Tuesday, September 29, using the familiar pincer attack. Two battalions of the Soviet 115th Rifle Brigade were overrun, with the remnants retreating into the vicinity of Orlovka itself. These units held until their ammunition ran out; the survivors escaped to the Soviet lines on October 7. Like the smaller strongpoints in the city, they had diverted and tied up German troops, buying Chuikov some time.

The Sixth Army mounted attack after attack into the factory districts and the Kurgan in early October, but once again the fighting dissipated into a series of uncontrolled small-unit actions. Only prepared, coordinated German attacks appeared to work; unforeseen gaps opened by small units did not have reserves ready to exploit them. Local leaders often took the initiative and tried to push forward without adequate support. These often fell victim to small Soviet counterattacks.[70]

The losses incurred by this style of fighting were debilitating on both sides. The Sixth Army chief of staff communicated to Army Group B on October 2, warning that "in spite of the most intensive efforts by all forces, the low combat strengths of the infantry will prolong the taking of Stalingrad indefinitely if reinforcements cannot be supplied."[72] Paulus followed up this observation the next day to the Army Group B commander, explaining that "[a]t present even the breaking out of individual blocks of houses can only be accomplished after lengthy regroupings to bring together the few combat-worthy assault elements that can still be found."[73] The pace of combat was slackening, but despite great success the Germans were still short of their final objectives. Once again, the Sixth Army would have to halt, absorb replacements, and prepare for yet another exhausting offensive effort.

Because by this time it was clear that the Germans would stop at nothing to take Stalingrad, the Soviet objective was to protract the battle long enough to muster sufficient combat power opposite the Sixth Army's weak flanks. One of Stalin's senior military representatives at the Stalingrad battle, Marshal Georgi Zhukov, calculated that it would take approximately forty-five days from the beginning of October. The goal of the defense in the city was to gain time. Although historians debate when and whether Chuikov was ever explicitly told to do this, he probably would have guessed it anyway; adopting the defense to gain time is a concept as old as war itself. The defender normally desires a longer duration in order to gain opportunities to reverse the situation. The attacker nearly always wants a shorter conflict. If the Soviet operational-level objective for the Sixty-second Army was to prolong the conflict's duration in Stalingrad, how could this be achieved?

Clausewitz suggests that an unbroken continuation of combat theoretically should push the situation to a decision fairly rapidly.[74] Certainly the Germans aimed to ensure continuous attacks to achieve this. But Clausewitz also observed that several factors contribute to preventing this from happening. One is the problem of defense. Because defense is a stronger form of combat than offense, it contributes to prolonging the conflict, even against a robust attacker.[75] Chuikov appears to have realized this by eventually giving up on large-scale counterattacks, preferring instead to form defensive strongpoints for both large and small units. Soviet offensive action became purely localized and characterized by aggressive infiltration.

Clausewitz also says that uncertainty imposes a degree of caution or hesitation on the part of the combatants, further protracting combat action.[76] Chuikov's mandate to make every German in Stalingrad feel "under the gun" was successful in creating this degree of uncertainty. This caused combat to slow down as assault units proceeded more cautiously. Robert Leonhard adds his own observations on how duration may be affected. He says the most basic influence on duration is the objective: "As a general rule, the more distant or ambitious the objective of the aggressor, the longer the war will last."[77] Given Chuikov's will to defend Stalingrad, coupled with the weapon he quickly forged and wielded in the form of the Sixty-second Army, one could argue that rapidly conquering the city with the depleted Sixth Army was realistically ambitious. Additionally, Clausewitz states that the slower the combat action proceeds, the longer the periods of inaction between actions. This is because longer combat actions require longer periods of preparation in order to get sufficiently ready.[78] Certainly this was borne out by the Sixth Army's pause between September 24 and 27; more pauses were necessary as the battle dragged on slowly.

Friction, the nature of war to make the simple difficult, also is a drag on operations. This we may attribute to Clausewitz's province of chance.[79] Certainly the Sixty-second Army's tactical methods did everything possible to aggravate the play of friction on German operations, from the impact of bypassed strongpoints, to infiltration behind the lines, to massed artillery and rocket attacks on German assembly areas. If the Sixth Army intended to carefully prepare every attack, synchronizing its forces to optimize combat power, Soviet countermeasures ensured that delay was the price the Germans would pay to achieve this.

Last but not least, less frequent operations can prolong the conflict.[80] Any given event in war involves a loss of energy to the side conducting it and, if it is successful, to the side receiving it. The best events are those that cause a greater proportional loss to the side that receives it than the side that conducts it, all else being equal. Of course, this is rarely the case. A lesser effect is tolerable, provided the attacker causing the event has the capability to mount more events than the defender can successfully receive in aggregation. As Leonhard points out: "In any case, each event results in the loss of strength or capability on one or both sides of the conflict. Since strength is finite, each event brings the combatants closer to the termination of the conflict. As we might expect, then, low-frequency conflict . . . is typically longer in duration than higher frequency conflict."[81]

The Sixth Army's problem was that its opponent, the Sixty-second Army, learned to lower the frequency of combat on its own side, dragging out the battle. By decentralizing combat so that German attacks lost energy quickly, Chuikov rarely offered the Nazis an opportunity to speedily and decisively smash large formations.

This decentralization had another effect. By giving his small units a set of simple rules to operate by, Chuikov learned to give up explicit control of his army, contrary to Soviet doctrine and experience. Today's nonlinear theory scientists might claim that Chuikov was creating a Complex Adaptive System; such a system is made up of individual entities that act according to very simple regulations. The resultant emergent behavior is more than the sum of the parts; the aggregate interactions create their own patterns.[82] For Chuikov, each element of the Sixty-second Army could learn about its immediate environment and automatically act in consonance with his overall intent or purpose without waiting for orders. Local leaders could compare the results of their tactical actions and adjust them if they were found wanting. Previously successful techniques did not work as well the next time around for the Germans, because Soviet defenders quickly learned how to deal with them on a purely local level. This simultaneously simplified Chuikov's command and control problems and gave the Sixty-second Army the flexibility it needed to deal with German attacks. Trouble was, the Germans could not pinpoint a specific vulnerability in either the Red enemy or the terrain that would unlock the defense.[83]

The problem this posed for the Sixth Army was that the Soviet defense seemed formless, much like an armed mob, yet it acted and reacted with an overall and unifying purpose to thwart their offensives, a behavior not characteristic of mobs at all. Paulus was also chagrined that his assaults rapidly lost direction and coherence. To use complexity theory language, the Sixth Army tactical execution simply "went chaotic" in a short period of time. If Chuikov had foregone detailed control of his army, resulting Soviet tactical patterns absolutely confounded the Germans. Simply put, Paulus could not help but lose control of operations. Thomas Czerwinski suggests that certain military leaders of the caliber of a Napoleon, Rommel, or Patton can maintain a fragile level of coherence in their forces and operations where others would fall into chaos.[84] But Paulus was no Rommel.

What was worse, the German soldier did not develop a taste for urban warfare the way his Soviet counterpart did:

German infantrymen loathed house-to-house fighting. They found such close quarter combat, which broke conventional military boundaries and dimensions, psychologically disorienting. During the last phase of the September battles, both sides had struggled to take a large brick warehouse on the Volga bank . . . which had four floors on the river side and three on the landward. At one point, it was "like a layered cake," with Germans on the top floor, Soviets below them, and more Germans below them. Often an enemy was unrecognizable, with every uniform impregnated by the same dun-colored dust.[85]

If Chuikov had shown that the Soviets had the will to defend Stalingrad during the first phase of the battle, the second phase demonstrated his adaptive perfection of the weapon he had at hand—the Sixty-second Army. Although on the whole his Soviet units may not have been as good as their Sixth Army counterparts, they were good enough to get the job done. Certainly the Soviet soldier proved himself equal or even superior to the German in the ruined labyrinth of Stalingrad. The Sixth Army still managed to score tactical successes, but at tremendous costs in both lives and time. As the battle moved into its third phase, it remained to be seen whether the price paid would result in total victory.

Keeping One Eye on the Watch in the Third Phase: The Battle for the Barricades Ordnance Plant

". . . today we are just marking time."

"This marking time doesn't mean we haven't the chance of winning a great victory, my dear Schmidt."

Schmidt looked steadily at the Army Commander-In-Chief:

"No, but it decreases it, Sir." [86]

From October 9 until the morning of the fourteenth, the fighting in Stalingrad entered another pronounced lull. On October 11, elements of the 305th Infantry Division arrived to boost the Sixth Army's sagging infantry strength, augmented with the tanks of the 14th Panzer Division. Paulus was consolidating his gains and preparing his army for its next thrust.

The Sixth Army learned that it achieved its best successes when units had time to get ready (for example, the September 27 attack made the greatest progress in its first few days). Once the advance bogged down into small-unit fighting, little else could be expected despite a continued heavy expenditure of human life. The Germans made good use of the time they provided themselves, drawing infantry drafts from throughout the army rear, refilling the depleted ranks of the divisional assault battalions, and replenishing ammunition.

The shortage of infantry in the frontline forces drew even Hitler's attention. He realized that there were no reserves left to augment either the stalled drive in the Caucasus or the blunted main effort in Stalingrad. The German Führer noted with irritation the low combat strength of the divisions compared to that of the support units. On October 8, he requested that all his army commanders report on personnel muster statistics, justifying the "tooth-to-tail" ratios for frontline combat formations and rear-echelon elements.[88]

At 8:00 on Wednesday morning, October 14, Paulus launched a massive assault along a three-kilometer front using three infantry and two panzer divisions, aimed at taking the factory districts. Within two days, the Sixth Army divisions had wrestled the Dzherzhinsky Tractor Works from Soviet control, devouring the Soviet 37th Guards Division in the process. Once again, it seemed that time used to prepare a synchronized attack was well spent. Flush with their quick victory, the German 389th Infantry Division, supported by tanks from 14th Panzer Division, turned south along the Volga bank to the Red Barricades Ordnance Factory on the seventeenth to take advantage of temporary Soviet weakness in the area.

As was so often the case previously, German attempts at pre-emptive tactics in Stalingrad were short lived. The hasty assault was beaten back by remnants of the Soviet 208th Rifle Division and dug-in, camouflaged T-34 tanks of the 84th Tank Brigade. Here the Soviets used one of their favorite techniques. They allowed the attacking tanks to penetrate through the position with the infantry in trace; when the Germans were interested in moving quickly, they usually allowed the armor to run ahead of the infantry. If they were more cautious, the Soviets would drop mortar rounds right behind the tanks, forcing the accompanying German infantry to ground. The Soviets held their fire, opening up with antitank weapons only at close range, normally a hundred yards or less. At such short distances, the Soviet gunners usually could not miss their targets. With their tanks destroyed, German infantry became easy meat for hidden infantry guns. Avoiding these hidden Soviet firing positions often made the German infantry vulnerable to mortar and rocket barrages. Finding cover in the rubble from the overhead fire and snipers while maintaining the momentum of the attack was nearly impossible.

Still, German celerity paid some dividends. Undeterred by their setback, assaulting units of the 389th Infantry Division probed along the rail line and found a gap between the newly arrived 138th Rifle Division and its depleted neighbor, the 308th Rifle Division. Apparently, the two Russian divisions had not had time to coordinate and integrate their flank defenses when the 138th Rifle Division took up its position. Chuikov was so concerned about the Germans pouring through the hole that he held the local commanders personally accountable for repairing the tear in the lines and ejecting the Germans.[89]

Heavy fighting continued on the western edge of the Barricades complex, reaching the northwest corner of the factory. On October 18, the Soviets committed the local factory militia to the fight. During a pouring rain on the twenty-second, German troops broke through the Soviet lines and entered the larger work halls, making their way through the central and southwestern parts of the complex because they could not penetrate east to the river. For the Soviets, there was nowhere to retreat. Every night, Soviet soldiers would bind their boots in sackcloth to muffle their footfalls, crawling silently through the darkness to infiltrate back into previously lost strongpoints.[90] German aircraft roamed the skies during the day, preventing the Red Army from reinforcing threatened sectors. During the night, Red Army engineers constructed slit trenches and tunnels to connect separated strongpoints to counteract the immobilizing effect of German dive-bombers. Soviet defensive methods bled the German infantry white. So concerned were German commanders that they flattened whole buildings with artillery to defeat Soviet snipers. Soviet mortars, artillery, and rockets tried to disrupt the assembly of German troops in their attack positions.[91] Paulus introduced the 79th Infantry Division into the Stalingrad inferno a few units at a time, beginning on October 20. The last battalion did not close on the city until October 28, more than a week later.

Paulus forecasted that his massive attacks would lose steam and had already prepared a follow-up effort. During a torrential downpour on the twenty-fourth, he renewed "all-out" offensives against both the Barricades and Red October. This latest attack collapsed the Soviet defenses at the ordnance plant. German infantry scattered to the south and west of the complex, clambering over the wet, blackened debris. Because Paulus had no reserves to exploit this unforeseen opportunity, the German advance ground to a halt in the midst of pinprick Soviet counterattacks.[92]

On October 25, lead elements of the 14th Panzer Division reached Bread Factory Number 2, immediately south of the Barricades production complex. Fanatical attacks led by a noncommissioned officer of the 64th Motorcycle Battalion temporarily punctured the Soviet defenses there. But like so many other local opportunities, the Germans lacked on-hand reserves to make the most of the situation.[93] On October 26, the Sixty-second Army committed the 10th Rifle Regiment of the 95th Rifle Division to limit German success there, just in time to prevent further German breakthroughs.

That evening, following a massive artillery preparation, an aggressive patrol from the German 100th Jaeger Division infiltrated to the west bank behind the Barricades. The Soviets emerged from cover and quickly surrounded the patrol in position on the high ground. Throughout the night Soviet attacks failed to destroy the patrol, but the Soviets did stop a German relief effort mounted from the shattered factory work halls. The following morning only a dozen survivors of the patrol managed to exfiltrate back to German lines.[94] This was the only good news for the Soviets; their reinforcing unit, the 45th Rifle Division, could not get across the Volga the previous night because of heavy German fire on the landing stages.[95]

By October 27, the Soviet line was stretched taut. Any shifting of troops would open serious holes in the defensive line. Something had to be done to buy more time so that the 45th Rifle Division could be ferried over into the city. Soldiers of the Soviet 118th Rifle Regiment managed to recover three tanks from the front; one was a T-34 armed with a flamethrower. Chuikov used these tanks, along with thirty men recently released from the field hospital, and a few men from the Sixty-second Army staff, and formed them into a small force to counterattack the Germans. Despite artillery and rocket launcher barrages in support, only three enemy tanks were destroyed and a couple of German trenches captured in the predawn Soviet attack of October 28. The Germans, however, were exhausted. This latest instance of Soviet audacity gave them reason to stop once more to regroup. In the meantime, the 45th Rifle Division crossed the Volga in time to plug the holes in Chuikov's defenses.[96]

Fighting bogged down into company-level actions as each side continuously tried to get the upper hand on its adversary in every part of the rubbled cityscape. Even the Germans found they had to resort to decentralized small-group tactics just like the Soviets, reinventing "storm-wedges" used in early 1918. The newly formed ten-man squads armed with a single machine gun, a small mortar, machine pistols, and a flamethrower for clearing bunkers, cellars, and sewers looked much like their 1918 World War I predecessors, the *sturmtruppen*.[97] Perhaps when faced with World War I conditions, a World War I solution was a natural one to adopt.

But the spasms of small-unit combat achieved nothing of lasting operational, or even tactical, significance. Alan Clark relates:

A German tank would appear at a corner of the street; slowly it would swing around and grind cautiously toward the Soviet-held buildings; iron hatches closed tight, the crew trembling with anticipation of combat. The Soviet infantrymen would watch it pass, trembling too, while they waited for the rest of the German force to show its hand. Another tank appears at the street corner; it halts there, and follows its compatriot's progress with the gradual traverse of a still silent turret. Then suddenly an explosion. A Soviet 76mm anti-tank gun at the eastern end of the street opens fire; the range is less than fifty yards, but it seems to have missed and at once the whole scene becomes animated in a storm of noise and pain. The German tank accelerates desperately in reverse, the cover tank fires instantaneously at the Soviet's gun smoke; at the same time a section of German infantry-men, armed with sub machineguns and grenades, rise from the rat runs in the rubble where they have been crawling, and empty their magazines at the anti-tank gun. As they do so, Soviet snipers who have been lying mo-tionless for hours in the eaves of skeletal buildings, high on the ledges of tottering facades, pick them off one by one. If the action does not escalate, with each side call-ing in more and heavier weapon support, it will soon die away, leaving only the wounded exposed to view. . . .[98]

The last German offensive of October witnessed the 79th Infantry Division expending itself in fruitless assaults against the Red October Metallurgical Works. It was finally called off on November 1; Soviet artillery strikes and storm group counter-attacks had worn down the assault squads.[99] The troops were exhausted from two weeks of fighting and suffered from ammu-nition shortages. Soviet tactics made the German troops fearful. They shot at noises and shadows, consuming small-arms ammu-nition at an alarming rate.[100] As before, the Germans had run out of infantrymen, coordination, and energy to continue the attack.

The German high command had not been idle in dealing with its infantry shortage throughout southern Russia, even be-fore the third phase of the Stalingrad battle opened. On Octo-ber 8, Franz Halder's replacement as the German army chief of staff, Col. Gen. Kurt Zeitzler, issued a stern order to reduce headquarters and rear-area personnel counts by 10 percent, sending the excess manpower to bolster the thin ranks of the frontline infantry. Hitler even assigned Gen. Walther von Unruh to travel throughout the rear areas to identify excess personnel to send to the front.[101] On October 15, the German Führer authorized the formation of twenty Luftwaffe field divisions out of the manpower-swollen German air force.[102] But these measures did not significantly assist the Sixth Army inside the embattled city.

The problems the Germans faced were obvious to the local Soviet leadership. On November 6, they reported to Stalin in Moscow that "in the last two days, the enemy has been changing his tactics. Probably because of losses over the last three weeks, they have stopped using large formations."[103] Another pause descended upon Stalingrad as the Germans geared up for yet another push.

There was no infantry left to take the rest of the city. Army Group B combed the rear areas and gathered up combat engineer battalions to reinforce the Sixth Army and serve as the vanguard for the next offensive. The main effort would be the depleted 305th Infantry Division, reinforced with one additional pioneer (engineer) battalion to each assaulting regiment. A total of four pioneer battalions, armed with flamethrowers and explosives, would spearhead the attack. Further technological superiority would be applied in the form of a dozen experimental "citybusting" assault guns, the sIG33B (self-propelled infantry gun), mounting a 150mm short-barreled gun to blast apart buildings.[104] In their attack positions behind the hulking ruins of the Barricades, pioneer troops prepared for their attacks on two well-known Soviet strongpoints on the other side: the Chemist's Shop and the Commissar's House (also known as the Red House).[105]

In the predawn twilight of Wednesday, November 11, newly created assault formations built from the remnants of the remaining six German divisions, and reinforced with the pioneers, attacked the Soviet defenses from the Barricades to the Red October Metallurgical Works. In the Barricades area, the Chemist's Shop strongpoint fell easily to German assaults, involving ten battalions supported by tanks and pioneers, but the Commissar's House held fast. Advance units of the German 305th and 389th Infantry Divisions struggled to the Volga bank near the oil storage tanks, cutting off the survivors of the Russian 138th Rifle Division behind the gutted Barricades.[106] During the evening hours of November 11, Chuikov began an attack to disrupt German continuation of its offensive. The 95th Rifle Division attacked German lines in the southeast corner of the Barricades complex. The attack went nowhere; at 5:00 A.M. a "hurricane of fire" from German mortars and artillery was unleashed on the Soviet defenses.[107]

In the morning, the German assault troops resumed the attack and the pioneers set about reducing the Commissar's House strongpoint, which was still holding out. The Commissar's House was a formidable structure, with every opening sealed up save for weapon firing ports. After taking heavy losses, the pioneers of the 50th Engineer Battalion eventually took the building on November 13. The defending Soviets fled to the cellars to carry on the fight. The German troops ripped up the floorboards, threw in full gas cans, and ignited them with gunfire, then lowered satchel charges to kill Soviet defenders trying to escape from or fight the flames. That evening, all the German attacks dissolved into small, uncontrollable firefights.[108]

The labyrinth of Soviet defenses quickly frustrated the assaulting pioneers. Many had never before experienced anything like it. Even when they could reduce and take Soviet strongholds, the follow-on infantrymen were too weak to consolidate the ground they had won. Because further advances meant taking flanking shots from reinfiltrated strongpoints, often the pioneers had to give up ground. In two days of combat, pioneer casualties accounted for at least 20 percent of their original battalion rosters. The debris and rubble prevented use of flamethrowers and tanks within the Barricades complex. Unless there was infantry available to mop up behind the assaulting engineers, Soviet sharpshooters tried to ignite the fuel tanks of the flamethrower troops, and antitank teams attempted to engage slow-moving vehicles in close combat. Even the heavily armored assault guns—including the sIG33Bs—could not keep up with the vanguards. They could only lend supporting fire from behind, provided they had clear lines of sight to their targets.[109]

Chuikov's forces were unable to get much succor from the east bank of the Volga, because drifting ice prevented all but minimum reinforcement and resupply. The German 162d Engineer Battalion fought its way through to the Volga bank, suffering a total of 40 percent casualties in the process. On November 14, one of the pioneer battalions prepared to resume its attack to the east in conjunction with the 162d Engineer Battalion's advance northward along the Volga bank to erase the threat to its left flank.

The Soviet defenders had built a series of trenches halfway up the bluffs overlooking the Volga River. This strong defensive system was composed of fighting positions situated on the crest of the cliffs, its trenches connected by tunnels. The 162d Engineer Battalion found the advance north to be rough going.[110]

By November 15, the Russian 138th Rifle Division was isolated but still holding onto a 400– by 700–meter strip on the Volga bank. The division's regiments were weak; its 650th Rifle Regiment had 31 survivors, the 433d Rifle Regiment had 123. Sensing an opportunity, the Germans attacked into the division's lines with seventy submachine gunners and pierced the Soviet defenses. The Soviet division commander assembled a counterattack force of twelve survivors of the 179th Independent Engineer Company, six men from the headquarters guard company, and a few staff officers. They tore into the German attack—the combat turning into vicious hand-to-hand fighting—and eventually repulsed the enemy.

Immediately south of the Barricades complex, on that same day, elements of the Russian 95th and 138th Rifle Divisions were hanging onto a few blasted shells of the workers' housing project. The Germans had reinforced the area with the sIG33B self-propelled assault guns of the 244th Sturm Abteilung and pioneers. These forces hurled themselves against the Soviet defenders in the fortified ruins. Covered by the pioneers, the assault guns were able to pull up short of the buildings and pump 150mm high-explosive rounds into them at point-blank range. With such firepower, the pioneers were able to break into the Soviet defenses, initiating yet another round of close-quarters killing. Chuikov dispatched a few Soviet tanks to rectify the situation; that measure proved to be enough. While tanks shot at one another, the infantry on both sides died in the labyrinth of ruined buildings. Still, the Germans managed to reach the east end of the housing project, but Chuikov scraped together units from the 1053d Rifle Regiment to stop them. With no infantry to hold onto what they had already won, and without any more strength to press on, the Germans had to halt their attack. Bled white, the latest German offensive was spent.[111]

Paulus was desperate. The expenditure of the pioneers and assault battalions left him with no remaining infantry to win the city. He ordered tank crews from the panzer divisions to be formed as infantry teams. Appalled by the order, the panzer division staffs sent their signal troops, cooks, and medics into the fray rather than sacrifice the precious tank crews.[112] The Sixth Army had expended a great deal of its infantry and seized nearly all of the city, yet the Sixty-second Army managed to hold onto a few small slivers of land on the Volga bank. But Paulus had no more troops left within his army to attack; he had pulled in all the German forces he could from the flanks. Despite these measures, they had not been enough.

The Germans would never get another chance to eliminate the remaining Soviet defenders in the shattered rubble of Stalingrad. After the success of the Soviet counteroffensive that encircled it, the Sixth Army would focus all of its energies on sheer survival.

Previously, the Germans had been able to command the sequence of events, at least at first, until fighting fragmented into unfocused firefighting. The idea behind sequencing is to create a situation where today's events set up a favorable situation for tomorrow's. Ideally, one should sequence events so that the enemy is unable to interrupt a continuing, cascading flow of friendly actions.[113] Proper sequencing also ensures that one's own combat power is more ready to move and/or fight than that of the enemy's at any particular moment. A well-sequenced attacker seeks to use movement, engagement, and exploitation when the defender is resting or preparing and therefore not ready to effectively oppose the attacker. If one characterizes military action as a sequence involving elements of movement, strike, and force protection, much the same effect can be achieved by striking when the enemy is moving but not protecting—or moving when the enemy is protecting himself from strikes, or protecting when the enemy is striking.[114]

A pattern of competing rhythms is established, each side hoping to make maximum use of the time the opponent is resting in order to achieve objectives or catch him at a disadvantage.[115] Although some earlier German deliberate attacks at least tried to hit the Soviets when and where they were least prepared, Paulus's last assault on November 11 was purely a battering ram against a ready opponent. Chuikov's tiny perimeter left the Germans no other option because there was no flank to turn, no salient to pinch off, no way to preempt or dislocate the defense on a large scale. The Sixty-second Army commander generally restrained himself from ordering large-scale counterattacks; instead, he focused on placing Soviet reinforcements in the path of upcoming German advances, plugging holes in the line, and encouraging his commanders to keep fighting.

Yet the Germans were offered some opportunities when their assaults met with success. Leonhard describes opportunity as not merely a decision point but one that is time sensitive. But in order to take the advantages that fleeting opportunity offers, there must be resources available.[116] Taking opportunities, although increasing frequency for the moment, may end up sacrificing sequence. German small-unit commanders did take opportunities, but there were no resources at hand to follow them up. Without reserves to exploit success, the Germans did not generate proper sequence; they could not mount an uninterrupted flow of action. This had been a continuing problem for the Sixth Army since the beginning of the battle. Often they plunged ahead anyway for temporary gains, which could not be coordinated, reinforced, and therefore could not be held under the pressure of local Soviet counterattacks. The fate of the 100th Jaeger patrol, the eventual outcome of the suicidal assault of the 64th Motorcycle Battalion in the bread factory, and the attack of the seventy German tommy-gunners against the 138th Division headquarters are the outstanding examples during this phase of the fight.

The third phase of the battle for Stalingrad showcases the Sixth Army's focus on concentration tactics. But because the Germans were generally unable to balance proper sequence and opportunity when confronted with a decentralized Soviet defensive method, they inadvertently pushed the engagements across the threshold into uncontrolled, violent chaos once again. Because of the infantry shortage, the Sixth Army was not able to both hold onto territory and form enough strength to conquer the remaining sliver of ground that the Sixty-second Army still held.

The problem that Paulus faced was that of time. He needed time to reinforce and prepare his forces for the October 14 assault. Although the three-week-long attack gained ground, it lost synchronization and had to be halted. Only four days were needed to coordinate the November 11 offensive—an attack that had an equally brief life span. Soviet defense patterns ensured that each offensive that the Sixth Army launched would get dragged out over a long period of time. And in protracting combat, the Soviets also ensured that their enemy would need protracted periods of recovery, refit, and preparation between each exhausting engagement. If the Germans did not take the time to adequately prepare their attacks in order to take advantage of perceived fleeting opportunities, Chuikov's defensive methods would cause their offensives to bog down rapidly.

The Sixty-second Army had not been able to hang onto Stalingrad in its entirety. Despite this, Chuikov had accomplished the one other imperative of a successful defense: He had gained time. He kept an eye on the clock, all the while convincing the German high command that they should not do the same. The Sixth Army would eventually lose Stalingrad not because of their casualties or the ground they gave up once they were encircled. These problems were symptomatic of a larger cause, one that lay in the prosecution of the battle during the two months from mid-September to mid-November. The Germans lost Stalingrad because they ran out of time.

Conclusions

Time is blood. [117]

German leadership was obsessed with viewing the Stalingrad situation in terms of physical and moral forces. The operational-level disadvantage of pitting German strength against Soviet strength was seemingly turned into a strategic, psychological opportunity to make Stalingrad a gladiatorial arena, a symbolic microcosm of the entire Soviet-German conflict. The idea of pitting the best the Nazis could offer against the best of the communists was not something Hitler wanted to avoid. To the German Führer, whichever gladiator won at Stalingrad would foreshadow the eventual outcome of the war in the East. Historians since have criticized the German leadership for ensuring that insufficient German forces would be available to take Stalingrad, given the attempt to simultaneously seize divergent objectives in the 1942 summer campaign. Given Hitler's compulsion to prevent any appearance of German weakness by retreat or withdrawal anywhere, even to conserve forces, this is a legitimate observation. Yet such criticisms are also overly focused on force and space relationships. Hitler was certainly aware of these, but his focus was on the will of the combatants. He was gambling that Germany had more determination to conquer Stalingrad than the Soviets had the will to defend it. German hubris at the strategic level percolated down through the chain of command to the commander of the Sixth Army.

Hitler's problem was that Stavka made sure he was right. The Soviets would gradually fall back under the German assaults in the city. Here Stavka was putting more emphasis on mental forces, specifically on sacrificing a pawn—the Sixty-second Army—to gain time and eventually create a superior operational-level position. Time was more important to the Soviets than to the Germans. The operative Soviet problem was to make sure the Germans stayed fixated on Stalingrad long enough for the eventual trap to be constructed and then sprung before they could react. Although the role of Soviet operations security and deception contributed to the success of their counteroffensive, it was competing perceptions of time that mattered most.

From the start, Chuikov's first task was to instill a fighting spirit in his defeatist army. His fatalistic ruthlessness, coupled with the natural effect the close terrain had on the individual combatant, achieved this to a large degree by the end of the first phase of the fight. German attempts to take the city by storm in a series of hasty attacks broke down due to the will of a few determined Red Army soldiers to defend their positions to the death. The Sixth Army casualties were too high to continue such "off-the-cuff" attacks; speed would have to be sacrificed in order to optimize combat power. During the first phase of the battle, the Sixth Army leadership thought that preemptive tactics could win the city. The failure of such tactics at places such as the grain elevator and the Central Railway Station meant that concentration tactics would have to be adopted instead.

Yet merely having the will to win was not enough to ensure that the Soviets actually would win. And pouring masses of troops into Stalingrad would have been wasteful. Conservation of force dictated that reinforcement would be dribbled in piecemeal from Yeremenko's Stalingrad Front so that sufficient offensive power could be built for the upcoming Soviet counteroffensive. The Soviet weapon for the defense of Stalingrad—the Sixty-second Army—had to be sharpened. As Chuikov saw it, the fight for the city depended more on skill and less on sheer strength. The army commander and his staff observed the potential that small, cohesive groups possessed and built new tactics upon that foundation.[118] Certainly, the stinginess of Chuikov's superiors regarding reinforcement may have left him no other alternative; big-unit operations quickly broke down, and the units themselves were speedily consumed in the fighting.

Soviet tactical patterns evolved in the second phase to increase the uncertainty and friction that the German attackers faced, no matter whether they employed preemptive or concentration tactics. The Soviets accomplished this through decentralized tactical execution. The Sixty-second Army's success prolonged local combat action. German units were entangled in a web of mutually supporting fortified strongpoints that took time and casualties to eliminate, pushing the conduct of their tactical evolutions from over the edge of coherence into chaos, miring the attack. The combination of the requirement to optimize precious combat power using concentration tactics, the need to recover operations from uncontrolled chaos, and the necessity to fully prepare for time-consuming advances imposed a drag on the Sixth Army's operational tempo. With will and weapons in hand, the Stalingrad defenders made the Germans hesitate before committing themselves to combat.

The result was gradual but continuous German progress in gaining ground and destroying Soviet tactical formations, but at the cost of time. Because the Soviets were afforded more time by German preparations to prepare themselves, the rhythm of combat in Stalingrad became more favorable to protracting the conflict. This made it difficult for the Germans to mount effective preemptive or dislocating attacks. Thus, the Germans were unable to achieve rapid tactical decisions and settled for drawn-out attritional fighting, which sapped their strength, imposed frequent tactical pauses, and drew more forces into the city in order to maintain gradual, albeit halting, tactical momentum.

By the third phase, the Germans had resigned themselves to accepting "ordinary" as opposed to their preferred "extraordinary" victory.[119] Even when local circumstances afforded them purely tactical opportunities, Soviet defensive tactics ensured that these could be taken only at the price of heavy casualties that could not easily be replaced. Still the Germans hammered on, taking ground and killing Soviet formations until they ran out of time in mid-November, just short of final victory.

Chuikov succeeded not only in gaining the time Zhukov wanted for the November 19 counteroffensive, he also attracted

German forces away from the flanks and into the city. The September 13 attack opened with three infantry, one motorized, and two panzer divisions in the south and center, with elements of one other motorized division and panzer division performing economy of force operations in the north. By September 25, Army Group B committed the 100th Jaeger Division into the city. On October 11 the Germans brought in the 305th Infantry and 14th Panzer Division. From October 20 through 28, the 79th Infantry Division trickled into the fight.[120] For Paulus and his senior leaders, Stalingrad proved both a magnet and a tar baby, sucking in forces and never letting them go.

So the question remains: Given Soviet defensive tactics at Stalingrad, could the Germans have won? Perhaps they could not have done any better than they did at the tactical level.[121] If the Soviets intended to use tactical losses to gain time at the operational level of war, perhaps the German solution to this gambit lay at the operational level as well. Germany's problem was that the arrogance of her leaders prevented an accurate assessment regarding the nature of the Soviet threat to the Sixth Army's flanks. The German high command failed to comprehend that they did not have all the time in the world to take Stalingrad and more resources would be needed to speed up its conquest—resources that would have to be drawn from the Caucasus. As it was, both the Germans and the Soviets had the will and the weapons to do battle over the urban ruins of Stalingrad, but only the Soviets kept one eye on their watch. That made all the difference.

ENDNOTES
    1.   The poster shows a heavily cloaked Soviet soldier, submachine gun in hand, pulling up his left sleeve to expose his wristwatch. See the box art for Mark Simonitch's commercial board wargame, *Campaign to Stalingrad: Southern Russia, 1942* (Vallejo, CA: Rhino Game Co., 1992); the

rulebook credits the poster to the Hoover Institution, Stanford University, on p. 2.

2. Hitler delivered this speech to the Burger Brau Beer Cellar in Bavaria to celebrate the rise of the Nazi Party to power in Germany. See Heinz Schroter, *Stalingrad,* trans. Constantine Fitzgibbon (New York: E. P. Dutton Co., Inc., 1958; Ballantine Books, 1960), 34.

3. Of the English language sources this author consulted, Marshal Chuikov's monograph on the battle was overall the best work on the urban battle, despite some historical inaccuracies and sometimes excessive emotional rhetoric. Most secondary sources and commercially published board wargames rely on his work for detailed descriptions of the urban fighting. See Marshal Vasili Ivanovich Chuikov, *The Battle for Stalingrad,* trans. Harold Silver (New York: Ballantine Books, 1968), republished from *The Beginning of the Road* (London: MacGibbon and Kee, Ltd., 1963).

4. Veteran commercial wargame designer John Hill credits the Sixty-second Army as being the only "armed mob" that defeated the German army. See John Hill, *Battle for Stalingrad: The Struggle for the City, September–November 1942* (New York: Simulations Publications, Inc., 1980), p. 18 of the rulebook. Many take issue with this view, notably Fred Helferrich in his review of the game. See Friedrich Helferrich, "The Playing Man's Stalingrad: Close up Battle for Stalingrad" in *Fire and Movement,* No. 23 (September-October 1980) (La Puente, CA: Baron Publishing Co., 1980), 14.

5. Even if more reinforcements had been committed to Chuikov, it is doubtful whether they could have been sustained across the Volga River. Chuikov's memoirs are peppered with his descriptions of the difficulties he had in adequately supplying the forces committed in the city as it was. See Chuikov, 111, 126, 128, 165, 170, 199, and 227.

6. When Chuikov's role changed is open to conjecture. Sources and interpretations disagree. Chuikov suggests he was not aware of definite plans for the Soviet counteroffensive until he received word about them on November 18. See Chuikov, 234–35. John Erickson indicates that the intent of the Soviet high command to trap the Germans at Stalingrad was already well established when Marshals Georgi Zhukov and Alexander Vasilevsky briefed Stalin on the concept the evening of September 13, the day Chuikov assumed command; the intent was finalized late that same month. Erickson also maintains that in October, Chuikov accurately guessed his new role as live bait to trap the Germans. See John Erickson, *The Road to Stalingrad* (Boulder, CO: Westview Press, 1984), 390, 423–32. Dave

Parham argues that although the Soviets may eventually have intended to trap the Germans in Stalingrad, this was not the original concept when Chuikov took command. See Parham in Hill, 24.

7.   Numerous sources describe the indications and interpretations that German intelligence and Axis commanders had concerning the upcoming Soviet counteroffensive. See Gen. Walter Warlimont, *Inside Hitler's Headquarters: 1939–1945*, trans. R. H. Barry (Novato, CA: Presidio Press, undated reprint of Weidenfeld & Nicolson, Ltd., London, 1964), 255; David Glantz, *Soviet Military Deception in the Second World War* (London: Frank Cass and Co., Ltd., 1989), 108–17; William Craig, *Enemy at the Gates* (New York: Reader's Digest Press, 1973), 147–48; Joel S. A. Hayward, *Stopped at Stalingrad: The Luftwaffe and Hitler's Defeat in the East, 1942–1943* (Lawrence, KS: University Press of Kansas, 1998), 216–20; Edwin P. Hoyt, *199 Days: The Battle for Stalingrad* (New York: Tom Doherty Associates, Inc., 1993), 183; Albert Seaton, *The Russo-German War: 1941–45* (Novato, CA: Presidio Press, 1990, reprint of title from Praeger Publishers, 1971), 298.

Don Greenwood summarized Hitler's perspective: "German leaders grew increasingly alarmed at the dangers posed by their weak flanks, but Hitler was adamant. 'Take Stalingrad and you can winter there in relative comfort while withdrawing the necessary forces to back up the satellite armies." See Greenwood, "A New View of Stalingrad" in *The General Magazine,* Vol. 26, No. 2 (Baltimore, MD: The Avalon Hill Game Co., 1990), 13.

8.   Paulus surrendered to the Soviets on January 31, 1942. Remnants of the Sixth Army held out until February 2, when they were extinguished by Soviet forces. V. E. Tarrant, *Stalingrad* (New York: Hippocrene Books, 1992), 220, 228.

9.   Robert R. Leonhard, *Fighting by Minutes: Time and the Art of War* (Westport, CT: Praeger Publishers, 1994), 55.

10.   Anthony Beevor, *Stalingrad, the Fateful Siege: 1942–1943* (New York: Viking Penguin Press, 1998), 70.

11.   On October 2, Hitler admitted in a headquarters situation briefing that the capture of Stalingrad had little operational significance. His rationale for continuing the fight was to influence world opinion and boost the morale of the Axis allies. Joachim Wieder and Heinrich Graf von Einseidel, *Stalingrad: Memories and Reassessments,* trans. Helmut Bogler (London: Arms and Armor Press, 1997), 22. Hitler may have been thinking of the

old Russian proverb that says whoever crosses the Volga conquers Mother Russia; see Parham in Hill, 20.

   Hitler exhibited a tendency to view World War II through the lens of his experience from World War I. Russell H. S. Stolfi discussed this in the context of the German leader's conception for the Russian campaign. It is possible that Hitler easily became obsessed with the psychological and symbolic importance of places, paralleling many World War I operations such as Verdun. This could explain his contrasting of Stalingrad with Verdun in his speech of November 8. For details on Hitler's "siege mentality," see R. H. S. Stolfi, *Hitler's Panzers East: World War II Reinterpreted* (Norman, OK: University of Oklahoma Press, 1991), 201–22.

   12.   Paulus had been dealing with this dilemma ever since his army crossed the Don River; the Soviet First Guards Army was continuously harassing his left. Paulus chose to drive deeply for Stalingrad despite the threat this formation posed to his lines of communications, betting that the threat to Stalingrad would divert Soviet attention away from his Don River bridgehead. See Earl F. Ziemke and Magna E. Bauer, *Moscow to Stalingrad: Decision in the East* (Washington, DC: Center of Military History, U.S. Army, 1987), 385.

   The Sixth Army commander took another chance when he pushed XIV Panzer Corps out on a limb north of Stalingrad on August 23, in hopes of suddenly seizing the city. Strung-out divisions of the panzer corps were quickly contained by the Soviets and continually harassed by ill-coordinated but still dangerous Soviet incursions. By August 29, major elements of the corps were isolated and barely rescued by follow-on forces. See Walter Kerr, *The Secret of Stalingrad* (New York: Doubleday and Co., Inc., 1978), 149–61.

   13.   The author has drawn on Richard Woff's discussion on the phasing of Sixth Army offensives in Stalingrad. See Richard Woff, "Chuikov" in *Stalin's Generals*, ed. Harold Shukman (New York: Grove Press, 1993), 71.

   14.   By the end of September, the Sixth Army had effectively closed the Volga River to traffic headed for the Caucasus and possessed the rail terminals in the city. See Earl F. Ziemke, *Stalingrad to Berlin: The German Defeat in the East* (Washington, DC: Center of Military History, U.S. Army, 1968), 44. Originally, part of the strategic importance of Stalingrad lay in her industrial contribution to the war effort. In the northern part of the city, the Red October Metallurgical Works fed metals to the adjacent Barricades Ordnance Factory, which made artillery and tank cannons, and farther

north to the Dzherzhinsky Tractor Works, which fabricated tanks. German bombing attacks on August 23–25 and September 3 had put these facilities largely out of commission; occupation of southern and central Stalingrad by the Sixth Army would keep them that way. See Hayward, 189, 191–92, and observations by the Germans in Beevor, 149.

15.   Erickson, 387.

16.   Dave Parham relates that although the Soviets were weak, their dispositions were so dispersed in the city that they presented no single critical vulnerability that the Germans could strike for and achieve a rapid decision. He also relates that the Sixth Army had too few units to attack all along the wide front of Stalingrad. Because of the heavy commitment of forces and logistics to the Caucasus, which had been the German main effort, the Sixth Army was low on artillery ammunition and infantry replacements, particularly for the 71st, 295th, and 389th Infantry Divisions. Paulus's idea was to conduct a series of operations that would take sections of the city one at a time. See Parham in Hill, 21.

17.   The original intent of the bombing was to scare the Soviet defenders out of the city prior to an attempted German coup de main with elements of the XIV Panzer Corps from the north on August 23. It was tried again on September 3 when it appeared that the Fourth Panzer Army would seize the city in a similar lightning strike. Neither fait accompli materialized. In fact, the resulting rubble and debris made it much more difficult for the German attackers to rapidly mass combat power and exploit success. See Peter G. Tsouras, *The Great Patriotic War* (Novato, CA: Presidio Press, 1992), 82.

18.   Map compiled from "Stadtplan vor Stalingrad" (Map R-1), 1:20,000 scale, and legend, Armeeoberkommando (AOK) 6, Fuhrungsabteilung, Langenskarte No. 30a. zum Kriegstagebuch (KTB) No 13; Dana Lombardy and Dave Parham, *Streets of Stalingrad* (Rockville, MD: Phoenix Game Co., 1979), game map and map cards 1, 2, and 3. The author extends his personal gratitude to Dana Lombardy for providing the AOK 6 KTB 13 map.

19.   Paul Carell, *Stalingrad: The Defeat of the German 6th Army* (Atglen, PA: Schiffer Military History Publishers, 1993), 147–48.

20.   Ibid.

21.   Alan Clark, *Barbarossa: The Russian-German Conflict, 1941–45* (New York: William Morrow and Co., Inc., 1965), 221.

22.   Colonel Richard N. Armstrong, *Red Army Legacies: Essays on*

Forces, Capabilities, and Personalities (Atglen, PA: Schiffer Military History Publishers, 1995), 22.

23.   Paddy Griffith, *Forward Into Battle: Fighting Tactics From Waterloo to the Near Future* (Sussex, UK: Anthony Bird Publications, Ltd., 1981; Novato, CA: Presidio Press, 1990), 103.

24.   J. Bowyer Bell, *Beseiged: Seven Cities Under Siege* (Philadelphia, PA: Chilton Books, 1966), 132.

25.   This was by then a common Soviet practice used to stiffen commanders. The last time such threats had been issued was during the initial defense of Leningrad in 1941. See Harrison Salisbury, *The 900 Days: The Siege of Leningrad* (New York: Harper and Row, Publishers, 1969), 340, 343–46.

26.   John Hill, in *Battle For Stalingrad,* p. 18, comments: "Adding to Chuikov's problems was the fact that though he knew his men could hang tough and would contest bitterly each block of ground, he also was aware of another very Russian trait—the potential of a total morale collapse if his men sensed that total disaster was imminent. Von Mellenthin often commented on the unique Russian trait of fighting tenaciously with no regard to casualties and then suddenly falling apart, fleeing or surrendering in total despair, based on the occurrence of an 'unsettling event.' The Soviets feared that they would be abandoned on the west bank by their high command. . . ."

27.   Richard Overy, *Russia's War: A History of the Soviet War Effort, 1941–1945* (New York: Penguin Books, 1997), 176. Chuikov's ruthlessness in using the NKVD "Special Detachments" to summarily execute deserters and his personal threats against subordinate commanders are comparable to similar measures used by Georgi Zhukov in the defense of Leningrad in 1941. See Salisbury, 340–46.

28.   Alexander Werth, *Russia at War: 1941–1945* (New York: E. P. Dutton and Co., Inc., 1964), 443–50.

29.   Map compiled from "Stadtplan vor Stalingrad," AOK 6; Dana Lombardy, et al., game map, and Craig, 31.

30.   Chuikov, 110.

31.   Ibid., 110–12.

32.   Jack Decker, "The Grain Elevator, 14 September 1942," in *Critical Hit! Magazine,* 1997 Special Issue (Croton Falls, NY: Critical Hit! 1997), 29.

33.   Craig, 140.

34.   Chuikov, 112.

35.   Decker, 22.

36.   Craig, 89.

37.   Chuikov, 100.

38.   *The 71st Infantry Division in the Second World War, Hidlesheim, 1973,* quoted in Werner Haupt, *Army Group South: The Wehrmacht in Russia, 1941–1945,* trans. Joseph G. Welsh (Atglen, PA: Schiffer Military History Publishers, 1998), 171–72.

39.   Craig, 92.

40.   Ibid., 92–93.

41.   Chuikov, 105; Tom Morin, scenario notes for "Storming the Station," "The Valor of the Guards," and "Confidence Is High," in *On All Fronts Magazine* (Oct/Nov 1992) (Marshall, AR: On All Fronts, 1992), 5, 10.

42.   Chuikov, 134.

43.   Sources disagree as to the actual location of the nail factory and Dragan. The author has sided with those who argue that the nail factory is on the southwestern end of the Central Railroad Station complex, closer to Red Square and the Univermag Department Store. Others maintain that it is on the northwestern end, adjacent to 9th of January Square. The difference in opinion lies in what source one assumes to be more accurate: Chuikov's account of Dragan's fight, supporting the nail factory on the southwestern end, or the annotations that the Sixth Army put on their war diary map, locating it on the northeastern end. To arrive at his conclusion, the author conducted a competing hypothesis analysis, but the results were far from conclusive in disconfirming the opposing point of view based on sources consulted. For an exhaustive on-line discussion of this debate, see posts of Eric Walters, Art Lupinacci, Dana Lombardy, Tom Meier, and Thomas Morin from November 11 to December 11, 1999, on the Consimworld Discussion Board Web site at URL: http://talk.consimworld.com/WebX.cgi?230@^54809@.ee6d35b.

44.   Chuikov, 135–36.

45.   Ibid., 138–43.

46.   Indeed, the Sixty-second Army commander continued to be ruthless in ensuring that the army would fight. Chuikov himself threatened to shoot commanders who did not do their duty. Major Khopko, commander of the 6th Tank Brigade, had only one immobile but still firing T-34 and about a hundred submachine gunners left when he asked Chuikov what he

should do. The general ordered him to prevent the Germans from getting to the Central Ferry Landing or be shot for his failure to do so. Khopko and fifty of his men died carrying out the order. See Carell, 140. Although most of the Soviet soldiers would give good account of themselves, some elements did display cowardice during the opening stages of the battle. By October 6, the political organs of the Stalingrad Front confidently reported that the number of instances of cowardice and desertion within the Sixty-second Army had plummeted. Chuikov's methods may appear to have been brutal, but they were effective.

47.   Griffith, 177.

48.   Ibid., 107–8. Griffith summarizes the Blitzkrieg tactical technique well, which is worth repeating:

> When they were not crossing obstacles in extremely risky operations the Germans were often racing across relatively undefended territory to forestall the creation of fresh obstacles further to the rear. Much of the first four or five months of the Russian campaign had this aspect, with the armoured spearhead commanders constantly urging rapid advances to disrupt enemy building of new fortified lines. Far from exhibiting confidence in the assault strength of their tanks, therefore, they were actually doing everything they could to avoid a phase of positional warfare. The real strength of armor, in fact, lay not in battle but in the pre-emption of battle.
>
> Quite apart from fortified lines, the Germans were also anxious to avoid counterattacks by enemy reserve formations. The essence of "blitzkrieg" was to break the enemy's defences before he had time to gather his reserves together. It should disrupt his counter-attacks before they had been formed. Only then would the apparently decisive advantages of the defensive be totally broken.
>
> The secret of the "blitzkrieg" lay in moving a mechanised all-arms force through an enemy's front line before he had time to consolidate it, and then playing havoc in his rear areas before he could mount a counter-attack or build a fresh defensive line. The process did not rely particularly upon tanks—and in Norway it was effectively completed without their assistance. What it did require was rapid transport, surprise, and an overawed or demoralised enemy.

An alerted enemy, on the other hand, could do several things to make such an attack stop and fight, for without the benefit of surprise, a great deal of the power of the offensive melted away.

49.   John Keegan, *The Face of Battle* (New York: The Viking Press, 1976; The Dorset Press, 1986), 165–66.

50.   Lieutenant Colonel Dave Grossman, *On Killing: The Psychological Cost of Learning to Kill in War and Society* (Boston: Little, Brown, and Co., 1995), 127.

51.   Ibid., 127; Keegan, 166.

52.   It became clear to the Germans by the end of September that the Soviets could not be demoralized. Edwin Hoyt quotes one German diarist: "Sept 1: 'Are the Russians really going to fight on the very bank of the Volga? It is madness'; Sept 8: 'Insane stubbornness'; Sept 11: 'Fanatics'; Sept 18: 'Wild beasts'; Sept 16: 'Barbarism . . . not men but devils'; Sept 16: 'Barbarians . . . they use gangster methods.' " See Hoyt, 163.

53.   Extract from AOK 6 Ia KTB Nr 13, dated September 20, 1942, quoted in Earl F. Ziemke and Magna E. Bauer, 395.

54.   Ibid.

55.   Leonhard, 157.

56.   General Hans Doerr, *Der Feldzug nach Stalingrad: Versuch eines operativen Uberblickes* (Darmstadt: E. S. Mittler & Sohn, 1955), 52–53, quoted in Hayward, 200.

57.   Wilhelm Goerlitz, *Paulus and Stalingrad,* 170, quoted in Thomas N. Carmichael, *The Ninety Days* (New York: Bernard Geis Associates, 1971), 251.

58.   Chuikov, 118.

59.   Ibid., 306–7.

60.   Ibid., 308–9.

61.   Ibid., 314.

62.   Ibid., 317–18.

63.   Beevor, 154.

64.   Hoyt, 142.

65.   The Germans spent all day clearing a particular avenue; then, spent from the day's fighting, they tried to take cover and settle in for the night. The next morning they would discover that the Soviets had returned to their old positions, now behind German lines. The Soviets had cut holes

between attics, sometimes using planking to connect adjacent buildings, "running like rats in the rafters" to set up defensive positions with machine guns and Molotov cocktails. See Clark, 225–26.

66.   Ibid., 221–22. Alan Clark is critical of German methods in response to these Soviet tactics:

> The Germans adopted the most extravagant method of simply battering away at one block after another. Each of the three "major offensives" launched during the siege was aimed at cutting across the thin strip of ground the Russians held and reaching the Volga at as many points as possible. The result was that, even when they were successful in their aim, the attackers would find themselves stranded in a web of hostile emplacements, their access corridors too narrow to make the troops at their tip anything but a tactical liability.
>
> [T]he fact remains that while the Russians showed great skill and versatility in adapting their tactics as the battle wore on, Paulus mishandled it from the very start. The Germans were baffled by a situation hitherto outside their military experience, and they reacted to it characteristically—by the application of brute force in heavier and heavier doses.

67.   Edwin Hoyt quotes Soviet author Konstantin Simonov, expressing the infantry's love of the Soviet mortars, artillery, and rocket launchers. See Hoyt, 155.

68.   The image of "fighting by the belt" was meant to connote a way that a smaller, shorter-armed man could beat a taller, longer-armed man in a fistfight. The shorter man got belt buckle to belt buckle with his opponent when trading punches. No longer did the taller man enjoy the benefits of superior "reach." From this idea, the Soviet defenders learned to "hug" the positions of their enemy. See Seaton, 297.

69.   Chuikov, 150.

70.   One good example of this was when three hundred men of the German 295th Infantry Division, carrying mortars, crawled through the main drainage system adjacent to the Krutoy Gully and emptying out into the Volga. They emerged and turned south into the rear of the 13th Guards Division, coinciding with a raid against the division's right flank. Because

neither of these attacks was immediately reinforced and exploited, Major General Rodimstev's guardsmen were able to counterattack and restore the defensive lines. See Erickson, 416.

71.   Map compiled from "Stadtplan vor Stalingrad" (Map R-1), AOK 6, Dana Lombardy, et al., game map and map cards 4 and 5, and Chuikov, 379.

72.   Ziemke and Bauer, 397.

73.   Ibid.

74.   Carl von Clausewitz, *On War*, trans. Peter Paret and Michael Howard (Princeton, NJ: Princeton University Press, 1976), 79, 81–83.

75.   Ibid., 83–84.

76.   Ibid., 84–85.

77.   Leonhard, 56.

78.   Clausewitz, 85.

79.   Ibid.

80.   Leonard, 61–62.

81.   Ibid., 89.

82.   Thomas Czerwinski, "Non-Linearity: An Introduction," in Thomas Czerwinski, ed., *Coping With the Bounds: Speculation on Nonlinearity in Military Affairs* (Washington, DC: National Defense University, 1998), 14.

83.   This is a characteristic of Complex Adaptive Systems; past actions are absorbed as experience so that future, identical actions do not lead to the same results. As Robert Jervis explains in "Complex Systems: The Role of Interactions," in Czerwinski, 270, 272:

> Because actions change the environment in which they operate, identical but later behavior does not produce identical results: history is about the changes produced by previous thought and action as people and organizations confront each other over time.
>
>   Interaction can be so intense and transformative that we can no longer fruitfully distinguish between actions and their environments, let alone say much about any element in isolation.

84.   Czerwinski, "Towards a Non-Linear Reductionism," in Czerwinski, 45.

85.   Beevor, 148.

86.   Conversation between General Schmidt, Chief of Staff of the Sixth Army, and Colonel General Paulus, commander of the Sixth Army, in Schroter, 44.

87.   Map compiled from "Stadtplan vor Stalingrad" (Map R-1), AOK 6, KTB No. 13; Dana Lombardy, et al., game map, and Chuikov, 380–82.

88.   Major Timothy A. Wray, *Standing Fast: German Defensive Doctrine on the Russian Front During World War II—Prewar to March, 1943*, Research Survey No. 5 (Fort Leavenworth, KS: Combat Studies Institute, U.S. Army Command and General Staff College, September 1986), 126.

89.   Erickson, 439.

90.   Charlie Kibler, *Red Barricades: A Game of Tactical Warfare, Stalingrad, 1942* (Baltimore, MD: Avalon Hill Game Co., 1989), rulebook, O9, and scenario notes for "One Down, Two To Go."

91.   Kibler, O9.

92.   Kibler, scenario notes for "Blood and Guts," in *Red Barricades*.

93.   Kibler, scenario notes for "Bread Factory #2"; Charlie Kibler, Rex Martin, Don Greenwood, and David Pope, scenario notes for "Berserk!" in *Streets of Fire: A Game of Tactical Warfare, 1941–45* (Baltimore, MD: Avalon Hill Game Co., 1985).

94.   Kibler, *Red Barricades*, scenario notes for "To the Rescue."

95.   Erickson, 443.

96.   Brian Youse, scenario notes for "Oh Joy," in *Advanced Squad Leader Journal #2* (Gambrills, MD: Multi-Man Publishing, LLC, 2000), 32.

97.   Beevor, 148.

98.   Clark, 243.

99.   Sixth Army headquarters staff noted that "the effect of massed enemy artillery has decisively weakened the division's attacking strength." See Beevor, 211.

100.   One German general complained that the Soviet enemy appeared to be invisible, mounting ambuscades from cellars, wall fragments, hidden pillboxes, and factory ruins, creating heavy casualties among the assault troops. Ibid., 149.

101.   Wray, 126.

102.   Hayward, 207.

103.   Beevor, 212.

104.   This vehicle was a PanzerKampfwagen III chassis fitted out to mount the 150mm gun. Twelve were built for the Operation Hubertus offensive, commencing November 11; twelve more were constructed to take part in the relief effort in 9th Company, 201st Panzer Regiment in the 23d

Panzer Division. Don Greenwood, *Beyond Valor* (Baltimore, MD: Avalon Hill Game Co., 1985), H11.

105.   Schroter, 35–36; Kibler, *Red Barricades,* O9.

106.   Beevor, 216, and Kibler, *Red Barricades,* O10.

107.   Beevor, 217.

108.   Kibler, *Red Barricades,* O10.

109.   Schroter, 36.

110.   Ibid., 37–38.

111.   Peter Mudge and Joe Waldron, scenario notes for "No Farther," *Critical Hit!* Issue #2 (Croton Falls, NY: Critical Hit! 1995), 16; Kibler, *Red Barricades,* scenario notes to "Turned Away."

112.   Beevor, 218.

113.   Leonhard, 91–92.

114.   Ibid., 170–72.

115.   Ibid., 93–105.

116.   Ibid., 110.

117.   Chuikov, 89.

118.   Although the Soviets certainly economized on committing numbers of units into Stalingrad, they were not stingy with quality. Many of the units fed into the battle were Guards formations or earned the honorific title of Guards during the battle due to their tenacious conduct. For example, Major General Rodimstev's 13th Guards Division is considered by many to be the best infantry division the Soviets fielded during the war. The authors' thanks to Jack Radey for pointing this out.

119.   The famous Alfred von Schlieffen used to describe methods of combat in terms of seeking ordinary victory versus extraordinary victory. Ordinary victory was generally proportional; tossing in more forces meant more gains. The problem with this was its attritional focus and lack of economy in using forces; it usually did not achieve annihilation of the enemy force. Schlieffen preferred the extraordinary wins; these used small forces but in creative ways, gaining leverage to achieve significant results, ideally all out of proportion to the size of the force employed. Jehuda L. Wallach, *The Dogma of the Battle of Annihilation: The Theories of Clausewitz and Schlieffen and Their Impact on German Conduct of Two World Wars* (Westport, CT: Greenwood Press, 1986), 45–47.

120.   Some sources disagree regarding the September 13 order of battle. Many works include the 76th Infantry Division (ID) and 14th Panzer Division, relying on Chuikov's memoirs; the 76th ID never saw action in

Stalingrad. The 14th Panzer Division didn't arrive in strength until October 11. Units sent into Stalingrad in the south and center included the 29th Motorized Division, the 94th Infantry Division, the 24th Panzer Division, the 71st Infantry Division, the 295th Infantry Division, and the woefully understrength 389th Infantry Division. Units of XIV Panzer Corps in the north—the 60th Motorized Division and 16th Panzer Division—lacked sufficient sustaining power to drive deeply into northern Stalingrad. See Don Greenwood, *Turning Point: Stalingrad* (Baltimore, MD: Avalon Hill Game Co., 1989); and Dana Lombardy and Dave Parham, *Streets of Stalingrad*.

121. Some argue that the Germans could have won had they changed their concept of operations for the assault on the city. Alan Clark complained that the Germans did not see other possibilities: "[I]nstead of putting all of their energies into attacks at the extremities of the Russian position and working their way up and down the bank—a tactic which if successful would have ultimately left the garrison stranded on an island of rubble in the center—they switched their effort to different points of the city."

See Clark, 221. Could such an approach have worked? The problem was that Stalingrad was a long but narrow city; attack frontages on the extremities could have been only just under a kilometer. This would have eased the Soviet defensive problem, because small groups of soldiers could hold up such an advance. Additionally, German advances on the extremities would not be mutually supporting until the very end; each drive would operate in isolation of the other. Chuikov would have been spared the difficulty of predicting where the Germans would attack next. Given such foreknowledge, it would have been an easy matter for the Sixty-second Army commander to balance the allocation of reinforcements.

Such a concept also overlooks the need for the Germans to garrison a long eastern line on the western edge of the city, as well as slowly lengthening flanks for their north and south spearheads. The Soviet tactical scheme would have assailed these at the local level, siphoning away troops from the tip of the penetration to guard German lines of communication. The combination of reduced troops at the point of main effort due to a short attacking frontage and the need to guard against Soviet incursions on the thinly garrisoned and very long German lines looping around the city may very well have lengthened the duration of the battle. There would be no opportunity for preemptive or dislocating attacks—certainly none like the kind that

Paulus mounted in the first and second phases of the battle, achieving dramatic geographic results but at great human cost.

In fairness to Clark, a variation of his proposed strategy is sometimes used by hobby wargamers in at least one Stalingrad board game. The 1999 World Boardgaming Championships witnessed two top players compete in the *Turning Point: Stalingrad* tournament with the title champion "bidding" higher territorial victory conditions to play the German side. He formed a three-front attack: (1) the 94th Infantry Division led the attack on the south; (2) the 29th Motorized Division redeployed from the south to the north, circling around the city to attack Rynok; and (3) the 295th and 71st Infantry Divisions, heavily augmented by the 24th Panzer Division, attacked toward the Mamayev Kurgan. Faced with three narrowly focused and powerful concentric drives, the Soviet player faced one too many holes to plug with too few forces. The Soviet player capitulated on September 17, 1942, as he was faced with the prospect of much faster German progress in conquering Stalingrad. It is doubtful that Chuikov would have done the same even if such a German tactical concept had been successful. Despite this, the Germans might have won the city sooner using such a concept, possibly forcing the Soviet high command into launching their counter-offensive before it was fully prepared. See Bruce Monnin, "World Boardgaming Championships: Brief Summaries," in *The Boardgamer*, Vol. 5, Issue 2 (April 2000) (Minister, OH: Bruce A. Monnin, 2000), 40.

THREE

Warsaw, 1944:

Uprising in Eastern Europe

by Maj. David M. Toczek

We know how to die.
> —young insurgent in the 1944 Warsaw Uprising

I attributed our superiority over the enemy tanks to one element: the spirit of the soldiers and the general co-operation of the entire population. I was fully aware that the army under my command was a revolutionary one. Its successes were due to the drive which enabled its soldiers to charge and take a strongly fortified enemy position, often without the help of even a machine-gun.[1]
> —Tadeusz Komorowski, Polish Home Army

Early on the morning of August 1, 1944, the inhabitants of Warsaw met another day of German occupation with uncharacteristic anticipation. After five long years of suffering at the hands of their oppressors, the Varsovians knew that at five that afternoon, the Polish Home Army (Armia Krajowa, or AK) would attack the Nazis and liberate their city within a few days. Unfortunately, they were only partially correct in their estimate. The Home Army did begin its attack on the afternoon of August 1, but instead of liberating Warsaw after a short time, the Poles entered a protracted urban battle with the Germans, resulting in hundreds of thousands of casualties and the near complete destruction of

Poland's capital. Despite the presence of the Soviet Red Army in the suburb of Praga and along the west bank of the Vistula River, the Polish Home Army surrendered after sixty-three days of house-to-house and floor-to-floor fighting. Although perhaps ill advised, the 1944 Warsaw Uprising demonstrated what an inspired, well-led insurgent organization could accomplish against a mechanized army equipped with tanks and artillery. Yet for all its successes, the Polish Home Army failed to liberate its beloved Warsaw, because inadequate supplies and moral exhaustion forced it to admit defeat.

In most discussions of city fighting, the battle of Stalingrad almost always comes to mind. Without question, the battle in Stalin's City offers a prime example of two conventional armies locked in bitter urban combat. In today's world, however, the probability of two large states engaging each other in a major city is less likely than a battle between a modern army and an insurgent force. The 1944 Warsaw Uprising provides an instructive example of how contemporary city fighting might transpire. Unlike the armies at Stalingrad, the Polish Home Army was an irregular force, not a conventional one. This difference in belligerent status affected not only how the Poles chose to fight, it affected how the Germans chose to subdue the insurrection. A present-day conventional army would do well to examine Warsaw, not only as a case study of how to combat an irregular force in an urban environment but of what happens when an army loses control of its soldiers.

Following Poland's surrender in late September 1939, the Polish army scattered throughout Europe to continue the fight against Germany. Many Poles made their way south through the Carpathians before continuing west to gather in France and England. Others found themselves prisoners of war (POWs) of the Soviet Union, and those lucky enough not to lose their lives at the hand of the NKVD (People's Commissariat of Internal

Affairs, otherwise known as the Soviet Secret Police) remained incarcerated for the next two years.[2] Upon those few regular army soldiers and officers remaining in Poland fell the task of organizing the growing numbers of Poles who volunteered to continue the fight against the Germans in some fashion.[3] By 1943 the Poles had several underground groups located throughout their country that were conducting operations against the occupying Germans.[4] The first band in Warsaw to strike at the Germans on a large scale was not the Home Army, however, but the Jewish Fighting Organization (Zydowska Organizacja Bojowa, or ZOB), a group located in the Warsaw Ghetto.

In keeping with their racial policies, the Germans deported or executed more than 300,000 Jews during the summer of 1942, leaving between 55,000 and 60,000 people in the Warsaw Ghetto. Witnessing the devastating effects of what the Germans called an *Aktion* (campaign or operation), many of the Ghetto's remaining Jews formed the ZOB to preclude the Germans from conducting further deportations.[5] The organization did not have long to wait before going into action. As expected, the Germans attempted a small *Aktion* in January 1943, but it met resistance from ZOB members armed with pistols. Surprised by the opposition and suffering several casualties, the Germans withdrew from the Ghetto to regroup their forces and reevaluate the situation.[6]

Although initially shocked by the possibility that the Jews would arm themselves and react violently to another round of deportations, the Germans returned in force in April to liquidate the Ghetto completely. On April 19, 1943, at six in the morning, 16 officers and 850 men of the Waffen-SS, police, and Wehrmacht units, under the command of SS Obergruppenführer Ferdinand von Sammern-Frankenegg, police commander of the Warsaw district, moved into the Ghetto to conduct the *Großaktion* (grand operation). To preclude a repeat of the embarrassing January incident, von Sammern-Frankenegg sent along a tank and two armored cars to provide additional security, as well as maintaining another two thousand troops in reserve. After entering in columns through the Ghetto gates, the German soldiers began to fan out to round up the inhabitants. Shortly after moving into the buildings, the ZOB, under the direction of Mordecai Anielewicz, struck with pistol fire, homemade hand grenades, and Molotov cocktails. Just as in January, the violence of the resistance caught the Germans by surprise, and within two hours they had withdrawn from the Ghetto area after taking several casualties.[7]

Receiving reports that the *Großaktion* had thus far failed, SS Brigadeführer Jürgen Stroop, von Sammern-Frankenegg's superior, arrived to take command of the operation. Stroop sent his troops back into the Ghetto, where they focused their fire onto the rooftops to force the resisters off the roofs of the buildings. Armed with pistols, the ZOB members could not return the German fire effectively. Retiring to the sewers, basements, and bunkers that they had built in preparation for the uprising, the fighters transformed the *Großaktion* into a protracted urban struggle. By the afternoon of April 20, the police chief's troops resorted to a systematic approach of clearing bunkers with flamethrowers and explosives. Worried that he was suffering far too many casualties, Stroop sought a means to expedite the *Großaktion*. Having received permission from SS Reichsführer Heinrich Himmler to use whatever means necessary to liquidate the Ghetto, Stroop resorted to the only technique that had worked thus far in forcing the Jews out of the buildings and bunkers: burning. Beginning on April 21, the Germans set about systematically destroying each building in the Ghetto with explosives and fire. Aware of the possibility that the trapped Jews might try to escape their fate through the sewers, Stroop ordered them flooded with water or gas. The Jews who managed to escape a fiery death often died from asphyxiation or drowning.[8]

Despite employing an average of more than two thousand troops in the Ghetto per day, Stroop was unable to bring the *Großaktion* to a rapid conclusion. Besides trying to convince German industrialists who had factories within the Ghetto to evacuate their equipment, the police chief found that although the fires forced many unarmed Jews from their bunkers, the ZOB fighters continued to roam the streets, particularly under the cover of darkness. By early May, Stroop, while still employing the technique of systematic destruction through demolition and fire, also initiated nine-man night combat patrols within the Ghetto. Through the use of these patrols, the Germans ambushed several ZOB units as they moved from one bunker to another or shot those who had left the safety of the bunkers to breathe fresh air. Despite the Germans' nocturnal tactics, in Stroop's words, "Setting fires still remain[ed] the best and only method for destroying the Jews."[9]

In spite of the Germans' overwhelming superiority in personnel and equipment, the *Großaktion* dragged on into the second week of May, and even the dynamiting of the ZOB's tactical headquarters on May 8 had little direct bearing on bringing the uprising to an end. Increasingly frustrated by his units' inability to subdue the Jewish resistance completely, Stroop ordered the destruction of the main synagogue as a signal that the reduction of the Ghetto was at an end. On May 16, the SS brigadeführer declared the operation complete when Warsaw's main synagogue collapsed into a pile of rubble at 10:15 P.M., but sporadic fighting continued as small bands of ZOB fighters persistently engaged the German troops.[10] Looking back over his experiences during the *Großaktion*, Stroop observed that units required significant stockpiles of explosives to reduce bunkers. Although not admitting as much in his final report, the police chief must have been at least somewhat impressed with the tenacious resistance of poorly armed and supplied fighters. For all that the Germans might have learned from the Warsaw Ghetto Uprising of 1943, particularly against a clandestine and irregular foe, one cannot help but wonder why they repeated several of the same tactical errors during the following year's insurrection.

Although some members of the Home Army assisted the ZOB during the Ghetto uprising, the majority did not participate in the fighting, waiting instead for their own planned revolt. Since the formation of organized resistance units in 1940, the Poles had conducted limited sabotage operations against the occupying Germans. Remembering their treatment at the hands of the Soviets in 1939, the occupied Poles suggested to their exiled government in late 1942 that in the case of a German withdrawal from Poland, the Home Army should resist the Red Army and prevent a Soviet occupation. Concerned about the political ramifications and the ongoing negotiations with Josef Stalin's government, the Polish commander in chief, Gen. Wladyslaw Sikorski, settled the matter once and for all by directing that the Home Army treat the Red Army as an ally. Pursuant to this directive, Sikorski also ordered that the Home Army units conduct military operations against the Germans only. The timing of these attacks would coincide with the imminent collapse of the German forces within Poland.[11]

After several months of wrangling between the government in exile and the AK leadership over the timing and purpose of the uprising, Gen. Tadeusz Komorowski, commander in chief of the Home Army, issued instructions in late 1943 that outlined the parameters for Operation Burza (Tempest). In the event that the Germans conducted an organized retreat through Poland, thus making a national uprising impracticable, the AK would conduct "intensified diversionary activity" against the German armed forces. Charged with demonstrating the Home Army's resolve to engage the Germans openly and preclude the retreating army from taking out its frustration upon the Polish civilians, Burza would occur in stages, from east to west, matching its tempo with that of the German retreat. To reduce civilian casualties in the capital, Warsaw was to participate in Burza only in the case of a general uprising. As the senior AK officer in Poland, Komorowski retained the authority to order Burza when he believed that the situation presented the Poles with the best possible opportunity to succeed.[12]

By the summer of 1944, the time to conduct Burza seemed imminent. Massing some 1.2 million men with another 1.3 million in reserve, the Soviets launched Operation Bagration on June 22, 1944, the third anniversary of the German invasion. Caught completely unaware by the Red Army's attack, the Germans found their front line penetrated by several Soviet columns that plunged on to the west. Having completed the encirclement of Minsk some two weeks later on July 3, the Soviets continued on to the Vistula, capturing thousands of German soldiers in the process.[13] For the AK leadership in Poland, Burza was not a question of "if" but "when."

As July waned and the Soviets rapidly approached Warsaw, the AK changed its plans for the role of the Polish capital, which, by this point of the war, had between 1 million and 1.5 million inhabitants and covered some 140 square kilometers.[14] At some point between July 14 and 21, Komorowski came to believe that a German collapse in Poland was imminent. Instead of waiting for the Red Army and protecting Warsaw, the AK would now attack the Germans and occupy the Polish capital before the arrival of the Soviets.[15] This decision appeared to contradict Komorowski's earlier desire to minimize civilian casualties and prevent further destruction of the already damaged city, but the increasingly optimistic reports about German setbacks and disorganization allayed the Home Army commander's fears of a long struggle. The memory of 1939 also still weighed heavily upon the AK leadership, and Varsovians firmly believed that if the

Home Army failed to seize Warsaw before the Red Army, a Soviet-sponsored government, not the Polish government in exile, would become Poland's postwar political leadership. With these factors in mind, Komorowski decided to liberate the capital before the Red Army crossed the Vistula.

This abrupt reversal of the capital's role had serious repercussions and adversely affected the conduct of the uprising, particularly with regard to availability of weapons and munitions. Over the next ten days, the Home Army leadership conducted several meetings to assess both the German and Soviet capabilities. By the end of the month, the Red Air Force had sent several patrols over the city, and Varsovians had heard regular Soviet artillery fire to the east. Despite a report that help from the western Allies was not forthcoming and that the Polish Parachute Brigade was not available to reinforce the Home Army, optimism among the senior AK leadership was high. Receiving a report on July 31 from Col. Antoni Chrusciel, the AK commander of Warsaw, that Soviet tanks were entering Praga, a suburb of Warsaw, Komorowski issued the following terse statement: "*Tomorrow, at 1700 hours precisely, you will start operation 'Burza' in Warsaw* [original emphasis]."[16] Within twenty-four hours, on August 1, 1944, Warsaw would rise to meet its German oppressors after almost five years of occupation.

Despite his soldiers having trained and rehearsed their missions for limited visibility conditions, Komorowski set H hour for 5:00 P.M. for two primary reasons. The first had to do with deceiving the Germans as to the AK's intentions. Throughout the month of July, Varsovians had taunted their occupiers with the statement, *"Dzien sie zbliza"* (the day [of reckoning] is coming).[17] Although raising Polish spirits, these comments served to heighten German fears of an uprising. By setting the operation's start at the height of rush hour, the AK commander sought to hide his units' movements for as long as possible and increase their chances of assembling without interference. The second reason was practical as well. By beginning the uprising at five in the afternoon, the Home Army units had some four hours of daylight to conduct their missions before nightfall, hopefully enough time to achieve all their objectives before dark.[18]

For all its pent-up emotions and fervor brought about by five years of occupation, the Home Army faced serious challenges in seizing the Polish capital, a complex urban setting, as illustrated by the Warsaw 1944 map. Although massing three divisions in the city (the 8th, 10th, and 28th Infantry) numbering between 25,000 and 28,000 insurgents, the Poles had only approximately 2,500 men who were properly armed. Because Komorowski did not envision Warsaw to be part of Burza, in July alone the AK commander authorized the shipment of almost 1,000 submachine guns and 4,400 rounds of ammunition to the eastern part of Poland for the coming operations there. Worse, the Germans had captured a Polish cache of 40,000 homemade hand grenades *(filipinki)* only a few days before the uprising was to begin. Of the 15,000 to 16,000 German soldiers stationed in and around Warsaw in late July, almost all were equipped with their basic weapons and well supplied with ammunition and food. Expecting the uprising to take no more than seven to ten days, and hoping for only three or four, the AK leadership did not allow their meager logistical capabilities to influence postponing the operation.[19]

Supply was not the only potential challenge; timing and coordination were also serious issues. Although Komorowski was the senior AK officer in Warsaw, Chrusciel, as Warsaw commandant, was responsible for planning and executing the uprising itself. Recognizing the inherent difficulties of controlling a complex operation in an urban environment, the commandant offered a

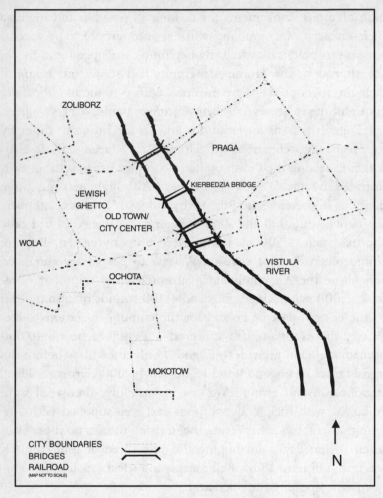

Warsaw 1944

simple plan. As his chief of staff later described the intent of the
operation, Chrusciel expected his divisions "literally to sit down
across the main arteries of Warsaw. The Germans would then be
disorganized and disarmed and we would take the city."[20] Simultaneously attacking in six different districts—Old Town/City Cen-

ter, Zoliborz (north), Wola (west), Ochota (southwest), Mokotow (south), and Praga (east)—the AK chose to rely upon speed and surprise rather than mass to achieve its objectives.[21]

By 5:00 P.M. on August 1, 1944, the AK units successfully assembled at their jump-off points. Despite indications from informants that the uprising was imminent, the Germans were again caught off guard by the resistance, just as they had been the previous year in the Ghetto. It did not take them long, however, to recover their senses enough to sound the alarm. Within fifteen minutes, columns of tanks and armored cars moved into the capital city. Although scoring initial successes against the armored columns, the Poles were soon in trouble. At the end of the first day, Chrusciel summarized the AK's gains in his first report, which declared that "[t]he most important objectives [were] . . . not seized. . . . I have no hope to seize the objectives that by this time have not been won."[22] Even worse, the attempts to liberate the suburb of Praga on the Vistula's eastern bank failed completely within five hours of their beginning. Placing more stock in surprise than preparation, the AK found itself lacking several of the key locations deemed necessary for overall success.

Yet all was not lost for the Home Army on the first day. By the evening of the following day, the Poles controlled several regions of the city, to include the gas, electric, and water works, and had destroyed at least twelve tanks.[23] The German garrison of Warsaw was in a state of chaos, causing Dr. Hans Frank, the governor general of Poland, to consider relocating his Cracow headquarters farther to the west to avoid being caught up in the insurrection. Seeing his opportunity to erase Warsaw once and for all, Himmler petitioned and received permission from Adolf Hitler to handle the situation in the Polish capital by himself. Promising his Führer that "Warsaw . . . will be erased," the reichsführer dispatched almost the entire Posen police force with some artillery and two brigades (Dirlewanger and Kaminski Brigades, named for their commanders) to bring the uprising under control. Himmler placed the units under the command of SS Gruppenführer Heinz Reinefarth and conveyed simple instructions: "I have given the order to destroy Warsaw completely. . . . [S]et fire to every block of houses and blow them up."[24] What began as an attempt by the AK to liberate the city from seemingly disorganized German forces rapidly became an all-out struggle for its survival.

On the morning of August 5, Reinefarth's units began their assault into the city. Striking from the west through Wola and the southwest through Ochota, the Germans attempted to cut Warsaw into two parts, seize at least one bridge across the Vistula, and reestablish communications with the suburb of Praga, on the eastern bank. The attacks along both axes rapidly degenerated into what one historian called "Dantean scenes of orgy and destruction," a result that should not have been a surprise, given the character of the SS units involved.[25] Along the northern axis was the Dirlewanger Brigade, a unit composed of condemned criminals and political prisoners whose commander had spent time in jail for molesting a minor. The Kaminski Brigade, to the south, was not much better. Although not exclusively convicted criminals, the undisciplined Ukrainians and Soviets had gained a horrific reputation for excesses while conducting antipartisan operations elsewhere in the Soviet Union and the Balkans. By the evening of the fifth, several thousand Poles lay dead in the streets. Besides losing momentum and failing to reach the Vistula, the German attacks on the fifth had a tremendous, and unpredicted, secondary effect. Outraged at the German conduct, the Poles fought with renewed vigor. Five years of occupation were bad enough; wholesale atrocities, particularly against the civilians, were infinitely worse. The desire for revenge, coupled with the knowledge that they could not expect those rights extended to combatants, caused the Poles to fight with a near fanatical resistance. It would take several weeks for the Germans to reverse what had happened at the outset; in some cases, they were never entirely successful at dispelling the images of the Ochota and Wola crimes.[26]

As the Kaminski and Dirlewanger Brigades committed their unspeakable acts against the Varsovians, Hitler's chief of antipartisan combat units, SS Obergruppenführer Erich von dem Bach-Zelewski, arrived on the scene to take command. Although initially under the impression that Reinefarth would be able to quell the uprising in a short period of time, Himmler dispatched a man he felt capable of bringing the insurrection under control. Characterizing him as "one of the cleverest persons," the reichsführer reiterated his instructions for Warsaw's fate. As von dem Bach related after the war, not only did Himmler direct that all captured insurgents be shot, regardless of their compliance with the Hague Convention, the Germans were to kill all noncombatants, women and children alike. Further, the entire city that was Warsaw was to cease to exist. All buildings were to be razed to the ground, either during the course of the operation or afterward. In short, the antipartisan chief had carte blanche to use whatever means necessary to end the uprising.[27]

Driving through the outskirts of Warsaw on the evening of August 5, von dem Bach witnessed the results of his units' handiwork. Despite his wide-ranging authority, the obergruppenführer chose not to follow his superior's instructions concerning the uprising. Believing that "a military force which loots and massacres ceases to fight," he ordered the immediate cessation of the executions. Von dem Bach was more a pragmatist than a humanitarian, and his experiences in antipartisan warfare had taught him that quelling an insurrection required a "plan . . . [with] a political and a military part." To that end, he decided that he "would have to suppress the uprising by all military means," which meant restoring discipline to his units. Relieving Kaminski, whom the Gestapo later executed for war crimes, and placing his brigade under an effective officer, von dem Bach slowly brought about the end of arbitrary executions, a process that took almost until the middle of August. Coupled with the military program was the obergruppenführer's belief that "from the first moment I had resolved if at all possible to put down the uprising by political means." Granting the Home Army combatant status, von dem Bach began a program of enticing the Poles to surrender that included leaflets and radio broadcasts.[28] Disorganized at first, just as they had been during the Ghetto uprising the year before, the Germans gradually abandoned an ad hoc approach to putting down an uprising for one that was more systematic and organized.

Von dem Bach's reorganization of units and enforced discipline began to pay dividends. By the evening of August 7, the Germans had pushed into Wola, causing Komorowski to relocate his headquarters from that district to the Old Town, farther to the east. Shortly after establishing his new headquarters, the Home Army commander received an even more troubling report. Blasting through the center of both Wola and the Old Town, the Germans had succeeded in capturing the Kierbedzia Bridge across the Vistula. Having reestablished communications across the river, the Germans now had the ability to reinforce and resupply their units on both sides. Capitalizing upon his gains, von dem Bach set about further dividing the Home Army into smaller pockets of resistance, away from the Vistula and the possibility of Soviet assistance. To the north, Reinefarth continued his attacks into the Old Town, while Maj. Gen. Gunther Rohr attacked through Mokotow in the south. Intending for his columns to meet in the middle of Warsaw, von dem Bach initially allowed the AK to reinforce its positions in the City Center, believing it better to advance block by block than to attempt to fight throughout the city in a series of unrelated, disjointed, small-unit actions.[29]

Polish logistical problems also contributed to the German successes in early August. As early as the fourth, Komorowski, concerned with ammunition expenditures, ordered that his subordinate commanders enforce "rigid economy in the use of ammunition." This directive, primarily a result of the AK's failure to build sufficient stocks of arms and ammunition stemming from the almost arbitrary decision to include Warsaw in Burza, had monumental consequences. At least for the remainder of the month, the AK would take the offensive only "in cases of tactical necessity." The Home Army commander recognized the potential danger in transitioning to the defense, particularly with an army that garnered its strength not from training but from the desire to exact revenge. By restricting ammunition usage, he risked dampening the fervor of his soldiers. This potential problem with morale would only get worse as the AK supply situation became more critical. Within eleven days of the uprising's start, short of ordnance and divided into pockets of resistance spread throughout Warsaw and its environs, the Poles abandoned any hope of defeating the Germans on their own. Focused strictly on the defense, all the AK's "efforts and plans, all . . . tactics and actions, had to aim at one thing: to hold out until the Soviets renewed their offensive on a large scale."[30] Polish expectations for success no longer lay exclusively with the Home Army but now were tied inextricably with the advance of the Red Army.

As the Polish government in London struggled to gain outside logistical and military support for the uprising, the lightly armed Home Army soldiers achieved varying levels of success against their better-equipped opponents. Some of the greatest threats faced by the Poles in the early stages of the insurgency were the fortified German positions scattered throughout Warsaw. Headquarters buildings, barracks, and magazines dotted the city. Often constructed of reinforced concrete and surrounded by barbed wire, these positions were formidable obstacles to the Poles' movement. An example of one of the better German positions was the notorious Pawiak Prison. Surrounded by pillboxes armed with heavy machine guns and overwatched by twelve machine-gun towers, Pawiak housed an entire battalion of German police and SS soldiers. Armed with only one small mortar, the AK unit assigned to capture Pawiak on August 1 was unable to overcome its defenses, and the prison served as a thorn in the Poles' side for the remainder of the uprising.[31] Lacking sufficient explosives and heavy weapons, the Home Army failed to capture or destroy the heavier German defensive positions, a dilemma that severely restricted Polish tactical and logistical movement throughout the city.

Another primary threat early on for the Poles was the sheer number of heavily armored Panther and Tiger tanks located in and around Warsaw. Although possessing some British PIATs (projector infantry antitank), an antitank weapon capable of launching a hollow charge projectile approximately a hundred meters, the Poles relied primarily upon their homemade *filipinki* and Molotov cocktails to disable the German tanks. Given the strength of the Panthers' and Tigers' armor, the Home Army soldiers found that the best method for disabling a tank was to tape several grenades together and throw them toward the vehicle's tracks. In most cases, a single *filipinka*'s explosion was sufficient to detonate the other grenades. If the cluster landed close enough to a tank's suspension, the force was sufficient to damage or destroy the track. In several instances, the Poles captured Ger-

man tanks using this method, allowing them to form the 1st Insurgents' Armored Squadron.[32]

Another effective method for disabling tanks was the employment of the Molotov cocktail, a bottle containing inflamma-
ble liquid that, once ignited and broken, would set the vehicle
on fire. Although some cocktails relied upon a burning rag as a
means to ignite the liquid, most used gasoline. Some used a tis-
sue containing a chemical compound that detonated upon striking the target. One drawback to this exceedingly simple weapon
was its bulkiness. In most cases, the AK soldiers used several
against one vehicle to increase the chances of setting it afire. As a
result, the insurgents had to carry several with them at a time, a
difficult proposition at best that was exacerbated by the tendency
of the liquid to slosh out. In at least one portion of Warsaw, an
enterprising group of Boy Scouts devised a solution to this problem. By prepositioning filled bottles at the barricades and along
known vehicle routes, the Home Army soldiers needed to carry
only the detonators, thus allowing them to move more quickly
about the battlefield and preventing the wastage of precious gasoline. Between using *filipinki* and Molotov cocktails, the Poles
disabled or destroyed some fifty tanks within the first few days of
the uprising.[33]

Explosives and inflammables were not the only techniques
the Poles used to reduce the effectiveness of the German armored columns. As long as German vehicles had unrestricted
access to Varsovian streets, the Home Army would be at a significant disadvantage. To counter the enemy's mobility, the Poles
set to erecting barricades to prevent their opponents from reinforcing their isolated strongpoints throughout the city. In the
early stages of the uprising, the barricades were hastily erected
but grew in complexity as the Poles had time to improve
them. Materials ranged from abandoned vehicles and furniture

to paving stones reinforced with filled sandbags.[34] With barricades springing up almost immediately throughout Warsaw, German access to the smaller streets was near impossible, even for the heavily armored Panthers and Tigers.

No strangers to city fighting, the Germans soon implemented effective methods for dealing with the tactical challenges that the Polish Home Army presented them. Before the barricades significantly reduced the Germans' mobility, the tanks fired their machine guns at the insurgents to suppress them while the column moved. Unable to fire accurately on the move, the armored vehicles would fire only their main guns at short range from a complete stop.[35] In some instances, unsupported tanks, relying solely upon shock effect to neutralize the defenders, attempted to rush the barricades, with little success. With the tanks moving unsupported by infantry and stopping often to fire, it is not surprising that the Poles inflicted heavy losses against the German armored columns early on.

By the second week of August, however, the Germans had assembled the equipment necessary to reduce the barricades. The preferred method was the use of the Goliath, a small, remotely controlled tracked vehicle packed with explosives. Upon closing with a barricade, the lead tank stopped outside the throwing range of the Poles manning the obstacle. Responsible for directing the Goliath, the lead tank's driver would guide the explosives to the barricade and detonate them. With a clear path ahead, the lead tank would then shoulder its way through and continue to the next obstacle. The Poles, realizing the importance of the umbilical cord between the lead tank and the Goliath, often focused their *filipinki* against the control cable in an effort to disable the smaller tank. In many instances, the insurgents were not only successful in stopping the Goliath and forcing the following tanks to withdraw but also benefited from the five hundred kilograms of explosives the Germans left behind.[36]

Another effective, although more barbaric, technique was the use of civilians to shield the German approach to the barricades. In many instances, the Germans herded Polish civilians in front of their tanks in the belief that the Poles guarding the obstacles would not fire on their own people. Most of the time, the Germans were correct in their estimate of the Home Army's reaction and managed to overrun the Polish positions. Not all of these attempts, however, had the desired outcome for either the Poles or the Germans. During the first week of the uprising, an AK machine-gun crew guarding a barricade along Powazkowska Street saw a large number of civilians moving toward them, in front of a German military police unit. After firing a warning burst, the AK crew saw why the civilians did not disperse: Each person was tied to a ladder that stretched across the width of the street. Fully aware of the stakes, the Polish machine-gun crew fired into their countrymen, effectively halting the German advance.[37] Although this method was cheap in German lives in the short run, it had significant repercussions throughout Warsaw. Just as the Poles sought vengeance for the crimes perpetrated in Ochota and Wola, the reports of the Germans using civilians as shields only served to enrage the already inflamed Home Army and strengthen its resolve to continue the fight.

In keeping with von dem Bach's systematic approach, the Germans also brought in artillery and aircraft to assist in the reduction of the barricades and the Polish points of resistance. Within the first few days of the fighting, German artillery and aerial bombardment began to rain down upon the beleaguered city. Although some of the rounds supported the tanks and infantry as they worked against the barricades, most seemed to be intended for the simple destruction of the Polish capital. Aerial incendiary and high-explosive bombs, artillery ranging from 105 to 420mm, mortars, and rockets all took their toll. Unable to control the railroad lines that ran in and around Warsaw, the

Poles were powerless to prevent the Germans from bringing into the capital two armored trains bristling with artillery pieces. Cognizant of their capabilities, the Germans used the trains as mobile firing platforms, moving them through the city at will and employing them in support of the various attacking columns.[38] For all the damage brought about by tanks, infantry, and engineers, the artillery and aviation clearly did the most damage to the city's structures.

As it became increasingly difficult to move above ground, the Poles soon took to using the sewers to send messages, move units, and conduct resupply operations throughout Warsaw. Inexplicably, despite their experiences fighting the ZOB the previous summer, the Germans did not immediately seek to prevent the Poles from using the subterranean avenues. It was only after the Germans accidentally discovered that the AK was using the sewers to its advantage that they began to focus their efforts below ground. Soon after, the struggle in the sewers matched the intensity of what was transpiring on the streets above and quickly changed the nature of the fighting. Control of the sewers' access points rapidly became more important than controlling the sewers themselves, resulting in heavy fighting around the manholes.[39] What were before only mundane access covers became critical objectives for the Poles; loss of a manhole meant the inability to receive messages, replacements, or resupply or, worse, to retreat.

The Germans did not restrict themselves to fighting above ground to prevent the Poles from using the subterranean passages. In many cases, they packed barbed wire into the passages, forming an impenetrable barrier to individual movement. Another technique involved floating fuel down the sewers and igniting it, thus incinerating or asphyxiating those within the passage. Booby traps in the sewers were common. Often armed hand grenades were strung with wire across the width of the pipes; their detonation affected not only the person who tripped them but those farther up and down the way as well, for in such a confined area, the resulting concussion often caused more damage than the fragments.[40] Despite these hazards, the AK continued to use Warsaw's subterranean passages for the duration of the uprising.

As the Germans slowly destroyed those buildings offering resistance and sought to deny the Poles use of the sewers, both belligerents also relied upon snipers to restrict movement between buildings and strongpoints. At first, the Germans believed that rubbling and burning buildings as they advanced provided the best security against Polish snipers, but they soon found that the AK snipers easily infiltrated to their rear. Areas believed safe soon degenerated into deadly kill zones for unassuming German soldiers. Frustrated, the Germans at times resorted to bricking in windows rather than creating rubble as a method to prevent sniping, but this technique met with varying levels of success given its time-intensive nature. Once again, the Germans discovered what they had found to be most effective against displacing ZOB squads in the Ghetto the previous year: small combat patrols. Unable to maintain a continuous front, given the rubbled buildings, destroyed vehicles, and barricades, the Germans fell back upon small *Kampfgruppen* (combat groups) to provide security and root out any AK snipers who managed to slip by the German positions. Although unable to ensure complete security against isolated snipers, the patrols, coupled with German snipers equipped with dum-dum bullets, significantly reduced the threat of harassing fires along main communications routes.[41]

Given the nature of the Home Army's plan to strike throughout the capital simultaneously, communications between the subordinate units was, without exaggeration, a nightmare. Possessing almost no portable radio sets, the Poles relied mainly

upon a system of runners to carry messages among the various
smaller units and strongpoints. To maximize the number of men
in combat roles, runner duties almost always fell to women and
older children, who accomplished their missions with dedica-
tion and efficiency, in some cases spending several hours in the
sewers and emerging exhausted and slime covered to deliver
their messages. Maintaining radio contact was not much easier.
Although many of the larger radio sets could contact and receive
messages from London throughout the uprising, they were unable to communicate directly with other sets in Warsaw, sometimes located only blocks or streets away. As a result, London
became a relay station for the Home Army units located
throughout the capital, transmitting anything from status reports to sewer directions. Despite the cumbersome arrangement,
using the London relay at least offered the Poles a way to supplement their messenger efforts. Having seized the telephone exchange, the Poles also had the capability to communicate with
the Red Army on the eastern bank of the Vistula, but the Soviets
never established that line of communication.[42]

The inability to communicate was one of the primary reasons why Komorowski relocated his command post from Wola
to the Old Town, but he soon found that his new location was
becoming untenable. Within a few days, the fighting with the
advancing German columns was adjacent to his headquarters
building. Again faced with the possibility of losing his entire
staff, the AK commander relocated his command post, this time
to the City Center, the strongest area of Polish resistance. Despite Chrusciel's presence in the Old Town, the Poles were unable to counter the Germans' advantage of possessing the main
thoroughfare through Warsaw and the Kierbedzia Bridge across
the Vistula. By September 1, the German advances had forced the
Poles out of the Old Town completely. Once again failing to

block the sewers, the Germans attacked into the Old Town on the morning of the second, only to find that the entire Polish garrison had withdrawn the previous night.[43]

Despite the Germans' gradual closing of the noose around the Home Army, the loss of the Old Town did not result in a Polish collapse. The AK still retained the City Center, Zoliborz, and Mokotow, and the Germans had not yet forced the Poles away from the Vistula south of the city. Morale among the Poles remained high, but the logistical situation was becoming increasingly serious, both in terms of stocks on hand and resupply efforts for the far-flung insurgent units. Komorowski, recognizing that resistance could continue only if his units received food and ammunition, issued orders for AK units to conduct diversionary attacks to attract attention, thus allowing Polish resupply columns to slip through the German lines.[44] Polish attacks no longer focused on gaining ground; their primary purpose was to facilitate resupply efforts. Both the Home Army headquarters in Warsaw and the Polish government in exile redoubled their efforts to gain outside assistance from the Allies. With the commitment of the Polish Parachute Brigade no longer a possibility, the Poles pleaded for aerial resupply of food and ammunition, with varying levels of success.

Because the Poles failed to take any of Warsaw's surrounding airfields, airdrops were the only possible means of delivery. Although some Allied bomber crews stationed in southern Italy managed to parachute supplies throughout August and September, the primary American and British effort took place on September 18. After finally securing clearance from Josef Stalin for the aircraft to land in the Soviet sector, 110 B-17s, escorted by 62 P-51s, delivered almost 1,300 containers. Unfortunately by this time, the Germans had occupied the areas surrounding Warsaw, and only 288 containers found their way to the Home

Army. Worse, in order to avoid the antiaircraft fire, the bombers flew at between 14,000 and 17,000 feet, thus making accurate delivery almost impossible.[45] Soviet efforts were more accurate but not necessarily more effective. Using small spotter aircraft, the Red Air Force flew at low level to avoid the German antiaircraft defenses. At such a low altitude, the Soviets were more accurate than the western Allies, delivering almost 55 tons of supplies. Unfortunately, the gains in accuracy were more than offset by the Soviet failure to use parachutes for the bundles. Poles consistently recovered weapons and ammunition that sustained damage in the drop, thus rendering them useless.[46]

As September wore on, the Poles continued to resist, firmly believing that a Soviet crossing from the now-occupied suburb of Praga was imminent. In the vicinity of the Polish lodgment on the Vistula south of the city, the river was only some 250 meters across in places, a result of the unusually dry summer. Although the Soviets eventually sent two battalions across the river, the crossings were a hollow gesture. Both battalions comprised recently conscripted Poles from the Lublin area who were almost completely untrained. Worse, though well armed, the AK units on the western bank were hesitant to entrust their new additions with independent fighting positions. Considered by the Home Army soldiers to be of questionable use, these new Polish reinforcements soon became liabilities when their ammunition and food ran out.[47]

Von dem Bach, also concerned with the possibility of a Soviet crossing in force, redoubled his efforts to force the Poles away from the river, while at the same time seeking to negotiate surrender. He had offered terms earlier, in August, to no avail, primarily because the Poles refused to believe that the Germans would actually permit them the rights due combatants. As September wore on, and it became increasingly clear that the Allies were either unwilling or unable to assist them with materiel and forces, Komorowski began to consider the German offers seriously. Negotiations dragged on through the latter part of September as the AK leadership attempted to stall the talks while at the same time sought to persuade the Soviets to cross the Vistula. With almost no food or ammunition on hand, Komorowski finally accepted the fact that a Red Army crossing was not forthcoming when he failed to receive response to his pleas from Marshal Konstantin Rokossovsky, the senior Soviet commander. The armistice was signed at 10:00 P.M. on October 2, and organized resistance in Warsaw ceased on the fourth. The Home Army units marched out of the Polish capital to meet their fate in a German POW camp the following day.[48] Although reports vary, approximately 200,000 Polish Home Army soldiers and civilians became casualties in the rubble that was Warsaw. The German cost for putting down the uprising was not inexpensive; loss estimates range between 20,000 and 26,000 soldiers.[49] After sixty-three days, the Germans were once again masters of Warsaw.

Although the Warsaw Uprising was perhaps destined to fail, several factors contributed to the Poles' ability to resist for more than two months against a well-supplied, mechanized army. More than any other factor, Polish morale ensured that the struggle continued despite overwhelming odds. Five years of occupation, coupled with the unspeakable atrocities of early August, ensured that the Home Army fought with an unparalleled ferocity. Knowing that they could expect no quarter from the Germans, Poles fought to the death rather than surrender or give ground. As one young insurgent wrote toward the end of August, "Death is not to be feared, we know how to die."[50] Von dem Bach's offer of combatant status did not have an immediate effect on the Poles' will, primarily because the insurgents refused to believe that such terms were possible.[51] Despite the increasingly tenuous supply situation, the Soviet capture of Praga served to bolster Polish morale. It was only after it became clear to the Poles that Allied resupply efforts were insufficient and the Soviets had no intention of crossing the Vistula that they began to consider seriously the German terms for surrender. Had the Germans employed disciplined troops capable of pushing through Warsaw in a short period of time at the beginning of the insurrection, the Polish will to resist may have eroded more rapidly.

After five years of occupation, the Poles had developed a significant clandestine infrastructure that also aided the uprising immeasurably. After gaining control of a district, the Polish shadow government took over almost immediately and began to coordinate the civilians' efforts. In most cases, building commanders knew their roles and their reporting chain before August 1. As casualties took their toll, the Home Army consistently appointed new leaders to ensure continuity and unity of effort. The underground armaments industry, responsible for producing the *filipinki* as well as other weapons systems, both built and repaired weapons systems throughout the uprising. Komorowski knew well the revolutionary character of his army and benefited immensely from the contributions of the women and children who acted as runners, pack mules, guides, and, in many cases, combatants.

The long duration of the uprising, although primarily a function of Polish capabilities, was also partly due to the German inability to remember and to apply its experiences from the previous year in the Warsaw Ghetto. Overconfident in their abilities, the Germans failed to acknowledge that their opponents were capable of putting up a spirited defense. Once presented with resistance, multiple columns with little support and an ad hoc approach was a recipe for disaster. In both cases, it was only after employing a systematic approach to building clearance that the Germans were able to make significant gains.

Yet the systematic approach was not the only solution to their problems. Rubbling and burning buildings did little in the long term if there was insufficient security present to preclude individuals and small units from circling back and occupying positions behind the lead units. Although requiring significantly more artillery and aerial bombardment than the previous year due to the larger area, it was not until the Germans employed combat patrols between the units that they were successful in reducing the sniper threat. Goliaths provided the tanks with the capability to breach the Polish barricades, but not until the accompanying infantry moved up could the tanks be assured that the Home Army soldiers who overwatched the barricades would not engage them with grenades and Molotovs.

Inexplicably, the Germans more readily identified the sewers as avenues of movement during 1943 than in 1944. The discovery of Polish movement under Warsaw's streets was a coincidence stemming from a German effort to tunnel into a Polish center of resistance and was not the result of an intelligence analysis. Even after finding the opportunities that the sewers presented, the Germans contented themselves with halfhearted attempts at blocking or booby-trapping the passages. Although focusing their aboveground efforts on capturing manholes throughout the city, they never mounted a coordinated effort to deny the subterranean avenues, allowing the Poles to withdraw units on several occasions. Believing in the inevitability of their success, the Germans did not seem to take advantage of all their opportunities to bring the uprising to a rapid conclusion. Although they did triumph in the end, they lost more than 20,000 soldiers in the process, almost two divisions that might have served them better against the Red Army.

Despite the technological advances in weapons and communications equipment over the past fifty years or so, today's soldiers can expect to fight an urban battle in much the same way as the Poles and Germans did on and under the Varsovian streets in 1944. As the Home Army demonstrated, a poorly equipped but inspired insurgent force can hold off a modern army for an indeterminate amount of time in an urban environment. The Germans eventually ended the Warsaw Uprising, but they did so only after they denied the Poles the ability to resupply themselves, persuaded them that surrender was a viable option, and convinced them that continued resistance was not worth the human cost. The uprising might have ended sooner had the Germans been more successful at disrupting Polish resupply efforts or dispelled their belief that Allied assistance was imminent: two techniques of defeating an urban opponent that are still available to today's armies.

ENDNOTES
    1.   Tadeusz Komorowski, *The Secret Army* (New York: The Macmillan Company, 1951), 239.
    2.   Allen Paul, *Katyn: Stalin's Massacre and the Seeds of Polish Resurrection*, rev. ed. (Annapolis, MD: Naval Institute Press, 1996), 41 passim.
    3.   Komorowski, 21–23.
    4.   By far the largest organization was the Association for Armed Struggle (Zwiazek Walki Zbrojnej), renamed the home army (Armia Krajowa) in 1942, and was a subordinate unit of the Polish armed forces and the exiled government. Other groups included the People's Guards (Gwardia Ludowa), renamed the People's Army (Armia Ludowa) in 1944, and the National Armed Forces (Narodowe Sily Zbrojne). Jan Ciechanowski, *The Warsaw Rising of 1944* (New York: Cambridge at the University Press, 1974), 81, 84–85, 89.
    5.   Israel Gutman, *Resistance: The Warsaw Ghetto Uprising* (New York: Houghton Mifflin Co., 1994), xvii, 132, 176.
    6.   Ibid., 180, 182.
    7.   Ibid., 184; Dan Kurzman, *The Bravest Battle: The Twenty-eight Days of the Warsaw Ghetto Uprising* (G. P. Putnam's Sons, 1976), 94–100; Jürgen Stroop, *The Stroop Report: The Jewish Quarter Is No More,* trans. Sybil Milton (New York: Pantheon Books, 1979), report 516/43, April 20, 1943.

8.   Gutman, 209–10; Kurzman, 145, 171; Stroop, reports 527/43, April 21, 1943; 530/43, April 22, 1943; 549/43, April 25, 1943.

9.   Kurzman, 204, 222; Gutman, 270; Stroop, report 616/43, May 7, 1943.

10.   Gutman, 241; Stroop, report 652/43, May 16, 1943; Kurzman, 336.

11.   Ciechanowski, 138.

12.   Ibid., 167–71, 212–13.

13.   Robert A. Doughty, et al., *Warfare in the Western World*, Vol. II, *Military Operations Since 1871* (Lexington, MA: D. C. Heath and Co., 1996), 768–70.

14.   J. K. Zawodny, *Nothing but Honour: The Story of the Warsaw Uprising, 1944* (Stanford, CA: Hoover Institution Press, 1978), 16.

15.   Ciechanowski, 212–15.

16.   Ibid., 234, 239–40. The Varsovian Poles' optimism concerning the uprising's success was not shared by Lt. Jan Nowak, an emissary from the Polish government in exile. When asked by Komorowski what he believed to be the result of Burza, Nowak prophetically responded: "I don't know the details of the military situation . . . but if you . . . consider Operation TEMPEST to be a political and military demonstration, it will not influence the policy of the Allies in the least. As far as public opinion in the West is concerned, TEMPEST will be, literally, a tempest in a teacup." Jan Nowak, *Courier from Warsaw* (Detroit, MI: Wayne State University Press, 1982), 334.

17.   Richard Lukas, *The Forgotten Holocaust: The Poles under German Occupation* (Lexington, KY: University Press of Kentucky, 1986), 186.

18.   Komorowski, 215.

19.   Lukas, 186, 189; Ciechanowski, 212–13; Komorowski, 237.

20.   Zawodny, 16.

21.   Ibid.; Lukas, 189.

22.   Komorowski, 223, 228; Zawodny, 16.

23.   Lukas, 189; Komorowski, 228.

24.   Lukas, 193–94.

25.   Joanna K. M. Hanson, *The Civilian Population and the Warsaw Uprising of 1944* (New York: Cambridge University Press, 1982), 85.

26.   Ibid., 85, 87; Lukas, 196–99, 204.

27.   Lukas, 195; Hanson, 85–86.

28.   Lukas, 204–6.

29.   Ibid., 206–7; Komorowski, 251.

30.   Komorowski, 239, 262.

31.   Zawodny, 16–17; Komorowski, 248, 250–51.

32.   Komorowski, 229–30; Nowak, 352.

33.   Waclaw Zagorski, *Seventy Days,* trans. John Welsh (London: Frederick Muller, Ltd., 1957), 73–74; Komorowski, 241.

34.   Zawodny, 58; Zagorski, 27.

35.   Komorowski, 229.

36.   Ibid., 254–55; Julian E. Kulski, *Dying, We Live: The Personal Chronicle of a Young Freedom Fighter in Warsaw (1939–1945)* (New York: Holt, Rinehart and Winston, 1979), 256.

37.   Kulski, 221–22; Hanson, 81; Zagorski, 61; Komorowski, 232–33.

38.   Komorowski, 238, 253, 274 passim; Kulski, 240.

39.   Komorowski, 297–301; Lukas, 209.

40.   Komorowski, 301–302.

41.   Ibid., 253; Zawodny, 59; Zagorski, 29.

42.   Zawodny, 47–48; Nowak, 363; Komorowski, 276, 300, 345.

43.   Komorowski, 313–17.

44.   Ibid., 285.

45.   Neil Orpen, *Airlift to Warsaw: The Rising of 1944* (Norman, OK: University of Oklahoma Press, 1984), 77 passim; Komorowski, 349–50; Lukas, 216.

46.   Lukas, 214; Kulski, 250; Stefan Korbonski, *Fighting Warsaw: The Story of the Polish Underground State, 1939–1945,* trans. F. B. Czarnomski (London: George Allen & Unwin, 1956), 388.

47.   Komorowski, 341, 348.

48.   Ibid., 361–69, 377–78. The Soviet failure to render assistance to the Polish Home Army remains a contentious issue and is beyond the scope of this work. To this day, Poles still consider the Soviet halt at the Vistula nothing short of criminal. Despite the Germans' belief that their attacks, and not Stalin's orders, halted the Red Army, the Soviet unwillingness to allow Allied aircraft to stage from Red Air Force bases and the ease with which they crossed the two Polish battalions to the western bank of the Vistula suggest otherwise. Heinz Guderian, *Panzer Leader,* trans. Constantine Fitzgibbon, rev. ed. (New York: Da Capo Press, 1996), 358–59; Ciechanowski, 250–52; Zawodny, 69–78.

49.   Lukas, 219; Hanson, 203.

50.   Ibid., 288.

51. Reflecting after the war, Komorowski was uncertain what prompted von dem Bach to avoid suppressing the uprising in the manner that both Hitler and Himmler encouraged. Acknowledging that granting combatant status to the Home Army was most likely a function of wishing to end the insurrection as quickly as possible, the Polish commander also speculated that perhaps the SS general was hoping that by recognizing the Home Army as a legitimate force, the Western Allies would recognize the newly formed Volkssturm units in the same manner. Komorowski, 369–70.

FOUR

Arnhem, 1944:

Airborne Warfare in the City

by Lt. Col. G. A. Lofaro

The lessons of 1940 and '41 were clear enough. Airborne tactics depended for success upon the exploitation of surprise; upon really intimate cooperation between the air force—both troop-carriers and fighter-bombers—and the airborne soldiers; upon the ability of the commander to influence the outcome by committing reserves to meet the needs of the battles; and upon the fighting qualities of the troops. And one further, sombre fact was evident. Against an experienced, determined enemy, especially in terrain where he could use his tanks, the whole concept of airborne warfare was hazardous in the extreme.[1]

—Maurice Tugwell

At 12:40 P.M. on Sunday, September 17, 1944, Maj. B. A. "Boy" Wilson, commander of the 21st Independent Parachute Company, led his 5 officers and 180 men into action near Arnhem, Holland.[2] Having flown from England in twelve Stirling bombers from No. 38 Group, Royal Air Force (RAF), Wilson's men were pathfinders whose task it was to mark the drop zones (DZs) and landing zones (LZs) for the gliders and paratroopers of the British 1st Airborne Division, due to arrive twenty minutes later.[3] Wilson's pathfinders landed without sustaining any injuries; they quickly set up their marking panels, smoke canisters, and Eureka transmitting beacons, then took up defensive positions along the edge of the open ground. In the process, they captured fifteen Germans who had been eating lunch when the aircraft appeared and were too stunned to offer any serious resistance.[4]

Ten miles north of Arnhem, at Hoenderloo Barracks, SS Standartenführer Walther Harzer, commander of the SS 9th Panzer Division, was likewise sitting down to lunch in the officers' mess of the divisional reconnaissance battalion, having just decorated the commander of that unit, SS Capt. Viktor Eberhard Graebner, with the Knight's Cross.[5] Though Harzer also saw the paratroopers, he later stated, "It could not be deduced . . . that a large-scale operation was under-way."[6] He could not have been more wrong, for what Harzer was witnessing was the beginning of the largest airborne operation in history.

Operation Market-Garden was a combined airborne ("Market") and ground ("Garden") offensive designed to catapult Field Marshal Bernard Law Montgomery's 21st Army Group across the Rhine and into the Ruhr, Germany's industrial heartland. The plan called for the creation of a sixty-four-mile-long corridor by three airborne divisions through which an armored spearhead would pass, leading Montgomery's forces over the Lower Rhine at Arnhem. The corridor, running in a northeasterly direction, comprised, from south to north, Maj. Gen. Maxwell D. Taylor's U.S. 101st Airborne Division, which was to drop near Eindhoven; Brig. Gen. James M. Gavin's U.S. 82d Airborne Division, dropping near Nijmegen; and Maj. Gen. Robert E. "Roy" Urquhart's British 1st Airborne Division, reinforced by Maj. Gen. Stanislaw Sosabowski's Polish 1st Parachute Brigade, dropping outside Arnhem. Commanding the northernmost airborne task force, Urquhart had as his primary mission to "capture the ARNHEM bridges or a bridge," with the secondary mission of establishing "a sufficient bridgehead to enable the follow-up formations of 30 Corps to deploy NORTH of the

NEDER RIJN [Lower Rhine]."[7] Key to Urquhart's success was the capture of a highway bridge situated in the heart of Arnhem, thereby necessitating that his forces fight through the city to their objective. Finally, Lt. Gen. Brian Horrocks, commander of XXX Corps, the ground component of Market-Garden, expected "to pass 20,000 vehicles over the highway to Arnhem in sixty hours."[8] During the operation, which ran from September 17 to 26, the Allies dropped 20,190 paratroopers, landed 13,781 glider-borne infantrymen, and air-delivered 5,230 tons of equipment, 1,927 vehicles, and 568 guns.[9]

Montgomery conceived this daring plan in the full flush of victory. Allied intelligence reports stated that "the August battles have done it and the enemy in the West has had it."[10] A week later, these intelligence reports added that the German army in the west was "no longer a cohesive fighting force but a number of fugitive battle groups, disorganized and even demoralized, short of equipment and arms."[11] As late as the first week of September, the Combined Intelligence Committee predicted that "no recovery is now possible" for the German army in the West."[12] In light of these reports, and having been granted operational control of the newly created First Allied Airborne Army (FAAA) as well as the U.S. First Army by Supreme Comdr. Gen. Dwight D. Eisenhower, Montgomery broke with his usual cautious demeanor and ordered the immediate mounting of Market-Garden.[13] But in the seven days it took the Allies to plan, coordinate, and execute Market-Garden, the German situation changed dramatically, especially around Arnhem.[14]

Though Montgomery's army group had taken Antwerp on September 4, it had failed to secure the islands commanding the Schelde Estuary to the west. This oversight not only negated use of the port at Antwerp, it allowed the Germans time to evacuate elements of nine divisions, comprising 65,000 men, before they could be cut off and destroyed.[15] Hitler had meanwhile tasked

Gen. Kurt Student, Germany's airborne pioneer, to form from this inchoate mass the First Parachute Army, whose mission it was to stop the British advance.[16] Student's army was to form part of Field Marshal Walther Model's Army Group B, which had as its reserve the SS II Panzer Corps, commanded by SS Gen. Wilhelm Bittrich. Having fought a series of delaying actions since the Allied invasion in June, Bittrich's corps was in desperate need of rest. On September 3, Model ordered Bittrich to withdraw the SS II Panzer Corps, consisting of the SS 9th and 10th Panzer Divisions, to a relatively quiet sector of the front where it could refit. Model selected Arnhem as Bittrich's center of operations.[17]

On September 17, the first day of the battle, the SS II Panzer Corps was posted in several encampments scattered north and east of Arnhem and, at only 20 to 30 percent of its establishment, was in the process of refitting.[18] However, once over the initial shock, Bittrich assumed operational control of a variety of other Wehrmacht units in the area, to include an SS panzer-grenadier training school, and thereby quickly built up superior combat power. Urquhart's troopers were likewise surprised by the presence of crack SS troops in Arnhem. Private James Sims of the 2d Parachute Battalion best summed up the intelligence picture the British troopers had on entering the battle: "Intelligence told us we had nothing to worry about. There was no armor in the area and only second-rate line-of-communications troops and Luftwaffe personnel—a piece of cake in fact."[19] But a "piece of cake" it was not, and the British soon found themselves outgunned and outnumbered, engaged in a ten-day street fight that cost them dearly.

By dawn on September 26, when the survivors of the 1st Airborne Division were withdrawn from the fight without having secured any of its assigned bridges, the butcher's bill was astounding: More than 10,000 men had been dropped into the target area; fewer than 4,000 returned.[20] German casualties are generally estimated to have been approximately 3,300; an additional 453 civilians lost their lives.[21] Only one battalion, Lt. Col. John Frost's 2d Parachute Battalion, along with remnants from a variety of other units, succeeded in making it to the Arnhem bridge. Comprising fewer than 750 men, Frost's force held out for three days and four nights before being overrun. [22]

After being taken prisoner, Maj. C. F. H. "Freddie" Gough, commander of the 1st Airborne Division's Reconnaissance Squadron, was sent for by a young German major. After exchanging salutes, the German officer asked Gough to join him in a meal. "Now please don't misunderstand," said the German major, "I'm not trying to interrogate you, but I should like to ask you about one thing, because it is obvious that the British airborne troops must have had a great deal of experience in street fighting." When Gough asked the major why he would think that, the German replied that he and many of his soldiers who were fighting at Arnhem had learned a great deal about street fighting in Russia and they assumed, from the way in which the British fought, that they had had similar experiences. "Oh no," replied Gough, at his most urbane, "as a matter of fact, this is our first experience—none of us has ever been involved in street fighting before."[23]

Though the operational and strategic goals of Market-Garden were not realized—Montgomery's army group could not "catapult" over the Rhine because the Arnhem bridges were not secured—a close study of the British fight at Arnhem reveals many poignant insights about urban combat. For example, Urquhart's failure to accomplish his mission can be directly attributed to several factors: having insufficient mass with which to fight through or around resistance, a breakdown in command and control, and the failure of intelligence compounded by the waste of reconnaissance assets. Furthermore, enemy snipers stymied the British, as did the breakdown of the resupply plan and insufficient artillery and close air support. Conversely, the stand by Urquhart's lightly armed troopers against seemingly overwhelming odds is testament to the staying power of defenders in the city.

As stated earlier, not only were the German units in the area stunned and momentarily paralyzed by the appearance of the 1st Airborne Division in their midst, they were scattered in small detachments throughout Arnhem and its environs and were thus unable, for several desperate hours, to effectively mass forces against the threat. In a postwar debriefing, General Student commented that the Germans at Arnhem were taken "completely by surprise," having "never considered the possibility of an airborne attack in the area."[24] Unfortunately for the British, decisions they made *before* the battle negated what may have been a decisive, albeit temporary, advantage and resulted in the severe dissipation of British combat power.

The first such decision, made during an Allied air planning conference on September 11, concerned the problem of having to deliver 35,000 men to three separate areas despite having sufficient airlift for only 16,500. Because the American airborne divisions were larger than their British counterparts, and because any effort at Arnhem would be for naught if the bridges to the south were not taken first, Lt. Gen. Lewis H. Brereton, FAAA commander, decided to allocate more aircraft to the U.S. 82d and 101st than to the 1st Airborne.[25] This meant that Urquhart would be unable to insert the whole of his division and the attached Polish brigade in one lift, and Maj. Gen. Paul Williams, whose U.S. IX Troop Carrier Command was to transport the 1st Airborne, would not agree, for reasons of crew rest and maintenance, to make two trips in one day.[26]

A second decision, this one by Lt. Gen. F. A. M. "Boy" Browning, the British I Airborne Corps commander and overall commander of the Market portion of the operation, concerned the allocation of lift aircraft for his corps headquarters element. This was Browning's first battle as a corps commander, and he proposed to command from Groesbeek Heights, an area southeast of Nijmegen in the 82d Airborne Division's sector. To get there, Browning's headquarters required thirty-eight Horsa gliders, all of which went in with the first lift, and all of which were subtracted from the 1st Airborne Division's account. Had Urquhart been allocated these gliders, he could have inserted the equivalent of another infantry battalion.[27]

All told, the 1st Airborne Division was left with 161 parachute aircraft and 320 gliders for D day.[28] Urquhart apportioned his aircraft in such a way as to deliver the three battalions of Brig. G. W. Lathbury's 1st Parachute Brigade, Brig. P. H. W. "Pip" Hicks's 1st Airlanding Brigade (minus two companies), his (Urquhart's) divisional reconnaissance squadron, his regiment of 75mm howitzers (minus one battery), and various other medical and engineer troops.[29] Yet, as several students of the battle have pointed out, despite the airlift constraints under which it was already operating, the 1st Airborne's load planning left much to be desired. Given an airlift component comprising primarily gliders, it seems that Urquhart's planners "allowed their units the luxury of all the jeeps, motor cycles and heavy gear that the gliders could carry, disregarding the imperative needs of battle—a small number of carefully selected heavy loads and lots and lots of fighting soldiers."[30] Moreover, despite British claims that they were being shortchanged regarding lift aircraft, "Because the British force was primarily gliderborne, and because British gliders had nearly double the carrying capacity of US gliders, the British lift capability, either total manpower or total tonnage, exceeded the lift capability of either of the American divisions."[31] Had the 1st Airborne planners been more discerning in their use of aircraft space, Urquhart could have had three full parachute brigades on the ground on D day; as planned, Urquhart ended up with "less than two-thirds of his potential [infantry] lift capability" on day one, and consequently spread the delivery of his entire force over a three-day period.[32]

Finding sufficient lift space with which to deliver his division was not the only planning problem that Urquhart encountered; finding *any* space on which to deliver it once it arrived in Holland proved equally exasperating. Ideally, Urquhart would have liked to drop his division as close to the Arnhem bridge as possible and, to facilitate its capture, on both sides simultaneously. Map and aerial reconnaissance suggested two prime locations: one immediately south of the bridge and another four miles north of town. However, intelligence reports indicated that the southern location was swampland crisscrossed with ditches and therefore dangerous ground on which to land gliders. The area north of town was also ruled out, for by dropping there, the lift aircraft would be forced to fly over an airfield thought to be heavily defended, and Allied airmen were unwilling to risk the casualties.[33] Hence, Urquhart was forced to use LZs and DZs situated eight miles from his objective on the western outskirts of Oosterbeek, Arnhem's affluent suburb.

Because his force would land so far from its objective, Urquhart conceived an unusual ground tactical plan. Immediately upon landing, Major Gough's reconnaissance squadron, comprising thirty-one gun jeeps, was to rush to the bridge to effect a coup de main. Meanwhile, the three parachute battalions of Brigadier Lathbury's 1st Parachute Brigade would follow on foot, taking three separate routes to the bridge, where they would link up with Gough's squadron. Brigadier Hicks's airlanding brigade would remain in the vicinity of the LZs and DZs in order to secure them for the follow-on lifts, scheduled to arrive the next day.[34]

Light infantry forces derive a considerable advantage from

defending on terrain through which vehicular traffic is restricted, such as swamps, jungles, and cities, but the key is to *get sufficient mass to the area to be defended in the first place*. Unfortunately for Urquhart, the combined effect of the prebattle decisions described above militated against his getting to the Arnhem bridge quickly enough and in sufficient numbers to hold until the XXX Corps arrived.

Though Brereton and Browning restricted the quantity of airlift assets available to the 1st Airborne on D day, the effect of their decisions was compounded by faulty load planning, resulting in the diminution, by one-third, of the infantry force the British could have delivered to the objective area. Urquhart's decision to retain his airlanding brigade at the LZs and DZs further exacerbated the situation by reducing, by one-half, the amount of combat power being sent to the objective.[35] Finally, by splitting his parachute brigade in thirds and sending it to the bridge along three separate routes, Urquhart fragmented this force, allowing the Germans, once they recovered from the initial surprise, to defeat each in detail. The end result was that only 750 of the more than 10,000 troops delivered to the area around Arnhem even made it to the objective area. As one participant-turned-historian wrote many years afterward, "The plan as produced effectively negated Brereton's admonition that the bridges [Arnhem bridge as well as those farther south in the American sector] must be grabbed with 'thunderclap surprise.' "[36] He went on to state that "if Frost could succeed in holding the north end of the Arnhem bridge with his small force for three days, there is small doubt that two parachute brigades . . . could have seized and held the bridge until XXX Corps arrived."[37]

After briefing the plan to the officers of his 4th Parachute Brigade, due to arrive at Arnhem on day two, Brig. J. W. "Shan" Hackett stated, "You can now forget all that. Your hardest and worst casualties will not be in defending the [bridge], but in trying to get there!"[38] Hackett was correct, and it is to a discussion of the difficulties that the 1st Airborne had in mounting its attack through the streets of Oosterbeek and Arnhem that the story now turns.

Though the leading elements of the 1st Airborne sustained minimal casualties and encountered only light resistance while landing and assembling, it was not long before Urquhart's plan quickly began to unravel. Major Gough's reconnaissance squadron, the coup de main force, assembled twenty-eight of its thirty-one jeeps and began moving toward the bridge by 3:40 P.M. Less than half a mile from its start point, the squadron made contact with SS Capt. Sepp Krafft's SS 16th Panzergrenadier Depot and Reserve Battalion, a scratch force of three companies supplemented with mortars, antitank weapons, and flamethrowers.[39] The squadron's lead element, C Troop, took seven casualties; the remainder of the squadron backed off, dismounted, and subsequently never made it to the bridge.[40] More importantly, this action denied Urquhart his battlefield "eyes and ears." Major Gough had previously questioned the use of his squadron as a coup de main force. He felt that the greatest asset his unit provided the division was battlefield intelligence on enemy dispositions. Gough argued that, by proceeding ahead of the three parachute battalions bound for the bridge, his unit could find the open routes and relay this information to higher headquarters, which could, in turn, adjust unit axes of advance with an eye to avoiding enemy contact en route to the objective.[41] This was especially important given the nature of the terrain through which the parachute battalions were advancing—narrow and confining streets that were easily blocked by even the smallest of forces. As one participant stated, the fighting through the streets "was unlike any other action. We had spent months and months practising [*sic*] battalion attacks on a 400– to 600–yards fronts [*sic*], and the battalion finished up attacking up a street no more than fifty yards wide."[42] Hence, as a result of the first significant contact with the enemy, not only did the *heaviest* force at Urquhart's disposal fail to get to the objective area, the division lost the one asset that could quickly find the gaps in the enemy defenses through which the attacking parachute battalions might have advanced.

Urquhart's command and control was also hampered by lack of effective radio communications. The 1st Airborne had at its disposal four different types of radios: 68 sets, 22 sets, 19HP sets, and 76 sets. The "76 sets" were jeep-mounted radios capable of Morse transmissions of more than three hundred miles but could not be operated on the move. Only two jeep-mounted "19HP sets" were landed at Arnhem due to space limitations. These had a range of twenty-five miles and were used to coordinate with XXX Corps artillery once it got within range. Hence, Urquhart had only the jeep-mounted "22 sets," with a range of five miles, and the man-portable "68 sets," with a range of three miles, with which to maneuver his division.[43] Given the fact that the bridge was eight miles from the LZs and DZs, and transmission ranges were degraded due to the buildings, it is no wonder that Urquhart often found himself out of touch with his subordinates.

Although there was an alternative means of communication available to Urquhart—the local telephone system—he and his staff did not take advantage of this despite the failure of their radios. Shortly after landing, members of the Dutch Resistance approached the British and explained to them that they could still use this system, despite the fact that the Germans had occupied the local Arnhem exchange and cut many of the private telephone lines.[44] As one writer explains:

[I]n addition to this public telephone system, there was an entirely separate network belonging to the Gelderland Provincial Electricity Board (Dutch initials PGEM).

Every transformer sub-station in the province of Gelderland was connected to this network, which in turn was linked to similar networks in other provinces of Holland. Moreover, it was possible to obtain access to the public telephone system from the PGEM network by dialling [*sic*] a secret number.[45]

Since the German occupation, the Gelderland Provincial Electricity Board (PGEM) management had been cooperating fully with the Dutch Resistance. Hence, this telephone network could not only have augmented or even replaced British communications, it would have served as another means by which the British could collect information about German troop movements and dispositions. The Germans, conversely, did make extensive use of the telephones. Immediately upon learning of the British attack, Bittrich used the local phones to contact his subordinate units and get them moving.[46] Additionally, an SS 10th Panzer Division war diary entry noted, "The existence of a first-class telephone service in Holland was a tremendous advantage at Arnhem. We had only a few wireless sets . . . and the Dutch telephone network enabled us to dispense with radio communications."[47]

The failure of communications caused Urquhart to quickly lose control of the battle. In an attempt to regain control, Urquhart went forward to see for himself how his parachute battalions were progressing. While accompanying Brigadier Lathbury's brigade headquarters element, moving behind the 3d Parachute Battalion along the middle route to the bridge, Urquhart was cut off, pinned down, and incommunicado for thirty-nine critical hours. His designated replacement, Lathbury, was with him, a fact that caused considerable confusion at the division's main tactical operations post about succession of command. As Brigadier Hackett later wrote, "By the time Urquhart got back to his HQ and resumed control . . . it was too late for critical decisions which he alone could [make], while indecision and procrastination had dispersed the last chance of a co-ordinated drive to get through to Frost."[48]

Meanwhile, Frost's 2d Battalion did get through to the bridge, where it succeeded in forming a defensive perimeter in the houses around the northern ramp. The other two battalions, moving blindly in the same direction but along two separate routes, were not as fortunate. Each of the battalions, though, encountered circumstances for which they were unprepared; these circumstances greatly hindered their movement through Oosterbeek and Arnhem.

In the early stages of the attack, before the battle reached its full intensity, Dutch civilians, overjoyed at the appearance of their liberators, proved a great hindrance. As they came out to greet the British advancing on the Arnhem bridge, the lead companies brushed them aside, but the trail elements in each battalion received considerable attention, a phenomenon that resulted in several breaks in contact.[49] Furthermore, as Urquhart later commented, a British soldier's "respect for the property and the houses of the people over whose land he fights" also served to slow the progress of the parachute battalions.[50] In the opening stage of the battle, Urquhart's paratroopers "were even knocking on the doors of the houses of [the] hospitable and welcoming Dutch folk, politely asking them for permission to search the buildings for Germans."[51]

Once the paratroopers entered the built-up area, the "wire fences along the roadside and between each house—all about four feet high—limited any deployment off the road."[52] As a result, explained Urquhart, "when troops were fired upon during the move into town they tended to gravitate to the nearest ditch or to take cover where they could, and if the firing was prolonged they got into the closest houses and stayed there as long as there was opposition."[53] Additionally, during the early stages of the fight, when speed was most essential, Urquhart found his paratroopers paying "too much attention to the odd bullet."[54] General Kurt Student concurred when he noted in his after-action review that "the foremost British parachute brigade . . . lost too much time whilst overcoming resistance by weak German garrison [units]."[55] And finally, as an unnamed British soldier remarked about the advance through town on day one: "It was a slow job getting along. . . . We were kept being told to lie low. . . . There didn't seem much out in front. Anyway I was glad. I didn't like walking down them streets [*sic*]. You felt Jerry was very close and watching you all the time."[56]

The combined effect of the failure of communications, the misuse of the reconnaissance assets, the caution with which the parachute battalions advanced, and the breakdown of command and control as a result of Urquhart's being separated from his headquarters was that the battle evolved into a series of uncoordinated attacks, none of which alone was strong enough to overcome the increasing German resistance. Furthermore, it was not until the afternoon of the second day that Brigadier Hicks assumed command of the division, unaware up to that point that Urquhart was missing. In the interim, the 1st and 3d Parachute Battalions were still fighting their way to the bridge. They had not sustained heavy casualties, but the warren of streets through which they were advancing served to disperse the units and decrease their combat power. As the lead company commander of the 1st Parachute Battalion explained: "We kept losing people, a few here and a few there, and by the end of this phase I was down to twenty or thirty men. What happens in close country is that people have a go at this and that and you never see them again. It was a bash-bash-bash sort of business. The missing men weren't all killed or wounded. The idea is that you meet up again somewhere, but it didn't often happen."[57]

Meanwhile, after the arrival of the 4th Parachute Brigade

with the second lift on day two, Hicks committed four more battalions to the fight: the 2d Battalion, South Staffordshire Regiment; the 10th Parachute Battalion; the 11th Parachute Battalion; and the 156th Parachute Battalion. However, lacking an overall commander, these battalions failed to coordinate their efforts, and the battle in the streets leading to the Arnhem bridge became increasingly chaotic. At one juncture on day two, four battalions—the 1st, 3d, 11th, and the South Staffordshires—were "all in the same area and available for a co-ordinated attack."[58] But there was no overall commander, and "the difficulty of moving among the houses . . . produced a bottleneck and terrible confusion. Company and platoon commanders were separated, the wireless failed, and there was a lack of firm control and local tactical planning."[59] As a result, "the conditions were such that the best part of four battalions [ceased] to exist."[60]

On Tuesday morning, September 19, day three of the battle, Urquhart finally broke out of his hiding place and made it back to division headquarters. What he found was a battle that had spun out of control. The German defenders had sealed off Frost's battalion at the bridge and were slowly squeezing it into a smaller and smaller perimeter. They had also started to form a second box around the remaining British units, forcing them away from the bridge and into the Oosterbeek suburb. Finally, the Germans were pouring more and more armor into the fight. By Tuesday evening, the 1st Airborne casualties were staggering. Of the four battalions (1st, 3d, and 11th Parachute, and the South Staffordshires) that had been fighting on the outskirts of Arnhem in an attempt to break through to the bridge, some 2,300 men, there remained but 500.[61] Hackett's 4th Parachute Brigade (the 10th and 156th Parachute Battalions with the 7th Battalion, King's Own Scottish Borderers attached), fighting north of Oosterbeek, was down to less than 50 percent strength.[62] Only one battalion, the 1st Battalion, Border Regiment, was anywhere near full strength. As a result, Urquhart decided to consolidate his forces (minus Frost's battalion) into a second perimeter in Oosterbeek, trusting in XXX Corps to come to their rescue. For the British, the offensive phase of the battle was over.

Writing after the war, Urquhart stated "a built-up area is hell for the attacker and an asset for those in defence."[63] That the lightly armed paratroopers and glider men of the 1st Airborne were able to hold out for as long as they did, despite overwhelming odds, while defending their two perimeters is testament to the truth of Urquhart's observation. Frost's stand at the Arnhem bridge, which began at approximately 9:00 P.M. on day one, when his lead elements seized control of the northern exit, lasted until the early morning of day five, Thursday, September 21, when the last remnants of his force were overrun. During that stand, Frost's band fought back attack after attack, including a major assault by the SS 9th Reconnaissance Battalion, comprising twenty-two armored vehicles with supporting infantry, destroying twelve of the enemy vehicles in the process.[64] When it came, the final German assault consisted of more than a thousand panzergrenadiers, supported by armor, including Tiger Is and IIs. By that time, Frost's fighting strength was well below two hundred.[65] Alfred Ringsdorf, an SS section commander in the SS 10th Panzer Division, said of the fight at the bridge: "This was a harder battle than any I had fought in Russia. It was constant, close range, hand-to-hand fighting. The English were everywhere. The streets for the most part were narrow, sometimes not more than 15 feet wide, and we fired at each other from only yards away. We fought to gain inches, cleaning out one room after the other. It was absolute hell!"[66]

The defensive fight for the remainder of the 1st Airborne began the evening of day three, Tuesday, September 19, when Urquhart decided to cease all attempts to break through to the bridge in order to consolidate his remaining forces into a perimeter in Oosterbeek, where they would hang on until the XXX Corps arrived. This defensive stand lasted until early morning, Tuesday, September 26, when the last ferry load carrying evacuees to the south bank of the Lower Rhine completed its run. This second perimeter fight, which the Germans labeled *der Hexenkessel*, the witches's cauldron, was even bloodier than that conducted at the bridge. One participant, SS Capt. Hans Moeller, who commanded an assault pioneer battalion during the battle, described the fighting as "bitter isolated and hand-to-hand fighting, as my men fought their way from room to room, from garden to garden and from tree to tree. . . . The Red Devils still fought back and battled for every room and every house, for every piece of ground or garden, no matter how small it was— like cornered tigers."[67]

As the quotes indicate, the street fight in which the British and Germans were locked involved a great deal of very close combat. Because of this, grenades quickly became the weapons of choice by both sides, especially because the closed nature of the urban terrain enhanced their effects. Staff Sergeant Les Frater, a glider pilot fighting in Oosterbeek, described an attack during which Germans attempted to dislodge his unit from a house. Frater said he could "see them through the iron grille on the front door and [I] fired up the hallway at pointblank range." Amazed that he survived, Frater added that what tipped the balance in his unit's favor was "the action of the lieutenant who had dashed upstairs and . . . dropped grenades on our adversaries from the bathroom window."[68] An unnamed soldier fighting at the Arnhem bridge described a scene in which a group of Germans stuck their machine gun through the window he was defending. He responded by shooting the gunner; he then grabbed the German machine gun and turned it on the attackers. The Germans threw grenades through the windows, forcing the British to evacuate the building. Once outside, the British responded in kind, driving the Germans away with their own fusillade of grenades.[69]

Another difficulty with which both sides had to contend was the identification of friend and foe. Louis Hagen, another glider pilot fighting in Oosterbeek, was manning a Bren gun in an attic position when he saw movement in a house next door. He rushed to the window and lobbed several grenades on his supposed adversaries before realizing that the people he was engaging were British soldiers. They survived only because Hagen, in his haste, had failed to cook off his grenades, giving the British enough time to retrieve them and throw them out the window.[70] Lieutenant Colonel R. Payton-Reid, commander of the 7th Battalion, King's Own Scottish Borderers, had an experience "typical of those of many others in the division. More than once as he inspected his positions [in the Oosterbeek perimeter], he came across Germans instead of his own men."[71] One method increasingly adopted by the British as a means to identify themselves was to shout the 3d Parachute Battalion's battle cry, "Woho Mahomet," because "the Germans seemed unable either to comprehend the nature [of the cry] or to imitate it."[72] But generally the fighting was at such close quarters, and so confused, that, in the words of one 3d Battalion soldier, "It was a bloody shambles. I never knew what was going on and don't think any of my mates did either."[73]

When defending in houses, especially in the fight around the Arnhem bridge where the buildings were connected, both sides adopted the technique of mouse-holing, which consisted of removing "bricks from the internal dividing wall between the house in occupation and the one next door. The purpose could be either offensive or defensive, providing for either access to or escape from the enemy."[74] But where possible, the British eschewed defending from inside buildings, preferring instead to dig positions in gardens. Brigadier Hackett explained that it was better to be in the garden; inside the building, not only was there the danger from high explosives but an additional hazard from falling bricks and timbers.[75]

Whether inside or out, the British could do little against the increasing amounts of armor that the Germans committed to the battle. At first the British held their own, skillfully employing their limited number of 6– and 17-pounder antitank guns, along with their PIATs and Gammon bombs.[76] Lance Corporal Bob Thompson of the reconnaissance squadron commented that without supporting infantry, the German self-propelled guns would not press home their attacks and "as a result, the gun would come to the crossroads, fire a few shots and then retreat."[77] Another writer commented that the Germans always made their tank attacks very carefully, that they "were particularly reluctant to go as far as a corner around which there was likely to be an antitank gun," but despite this fear the biggest tank killer was the PIAT.[78] However, casualties and an ammunition shortage eventually negated British antitank capabilities, and the Germans closed in for the kill.

The defenders at the Arnhem bridge were the first to experience the devastating effect of German armor. After the few antitank guns brought by the defenders were destroyed or out of ammunition, the German armor would simply stand off and use their main guns to demolish buildings, room by room. Eventually the Germans switched from high explosive to phosphorus shells in an attempt to burn the British out. This use of phosphorus and other flame weapons was one of the primary reasons why Colonel Frost surrendered his position, for without the ability to evacuate his wounded, who were being housed in the cellars of the few buildings that the British held, Frost would not risk having his men burned alive.[79] Trooper Jimmy Cooke, fighting in the Oosterbeek perimeter, recalls Saturday, September 23, with particular dread: "That was the day . . . when they [the Germans] brought the flame-thrower up, and I think it was that which frightened me more than anything else. It fired out of the wood, and those great tongues of flame, about twenty feet long, travelled [*sic*] over our slit trenches and landed at the back of us. We knew it was going to be used, because they had it on a tank, and we used to listen for the tracks coming up. These things struck fear and terror into everyone."[80]

Along with their use of armor, the Germans relied increasingly on indirect fire, especially against the Oosterbeek perimeter. According to SS Cpl. Wolfgang Dombrowski, "We achieved much success with our mortars. Most prisoners claimed the "whump-whump-whump" of the "moaning minnies" [15cm Nebelwerfer rocket launchers that fired rockets from their six barrels at two-second intervals] was their most frightening experience. Many of them emerged from cellars with their nerves shot to pieces."[81] By the end of the battle, the Germans had concentrated 110 artillery pieces and mortars against the Oosterbeek perimeter, relying on firepower instead of manpower to finally put paid to the British defenders.[82]

The use of armor and indirect fire succeeded in tearing holes in the thinly held Oosterbeek perimeter, and it was through these holes that the Germans would infiltrate snipers, a threat that dogged the British throughout the fight. Urquhart noted that each night the Germans would stop their indirect fire in order to move their snipers into positions from which they could take the British under fire.[83] Captain Jim Livingstone of the King's Own Scottish Borderers noted:

The worst thing was the snipers. You couldn't pinpoint them. You would have some men in a certain position and the next thing you knew they were gone—snipers! My batman, an elderly man by airborne standards, being in his thirties, was hit by a sniper in our slit trench and badly wounded. He stood up and said, "Now you'll have to get your own bloody food," before leaving for treatment. Another time, I had a sergeant with me in the slit and he wouldn't wear his helmet. I told him to put it on, but he said it was too uncomfortable. It wasn't long afterwards that I found his head in my lap, the top of it shot off—killed at once.[84]

One participant, Tom Angus, wrote that the snipers were taking a steady toll of the leadership because they could spot the badges of rank sewn on the sleeves of the airborne smocks. He consequently issued an order "for all officers and NCOs to remove their badges of rank and throw away their map cases; maps should then be stuffed into pockets and binoculars pushed inside the necks of smocks."[85] Of course, the British had their own snipers, but their use became much more limited as the battle continued due to lack of ammunition. Eventually orders were issued telling the British defenders to conserve their ammunition and fire only when necessary to repel assaults. This allowed the Germans much more freedom to maneuver, whereas the British were increasingly made to turn their positions into strongpoints, because their own movement between positions became untenable.[86]

The dismal failure of the Allied aerial resupply effort has received much attention. Plans, of course, had been made for the delivery of supplies to the 1st Airborne, but the overrunning of the designated drop zones by the Germans, combined with the failure of communications that precluded Urquhart from adjusting his DZ locations, resulted in fewer than 200 of the 1,488 tons of supplies delivered to the Arnhem area being recovered by the British.[87] Besides ammunition, the most pressing need was water. The Germans cut the main water supply to Oosterbeek on the first day of the battle, so as the British drained their canteens, the search for water became paramount. One writer notes that "storage tanks, central-heating systems, even fish bowls were drained."[88] German snipers would target locations where water could be found. One pump, sixty yards from the British aid station in the home of Kate ter Horst, had a path leading to it lined with the bodies of the dead.[89] But the failure of the resupply effort cannot be laid at the feet of the pilots. All told, British and American aircrews flew 629 resupply sorties, losing 66 aircraft and 540 men in the effort.[90]

What was noticeably absent in the skies above Arnhem was Allied close air support. After escorting the lead elements of the 1st Airborne on day one of the operation, Allied close air assets did not reappear until day eight.[91] This occurred as a result of technical difficulties associated with combined air operations. Not only were the procedures for requesting close air cumbersome, there were severe restrictions against using British and American tactical aircraft in the same airspace at the same time. Hence, whenever U.S. Eighth Air Force assets were in the battle area, which was most of the time during daylight hours, RAF close air was prohibited from carrying out missions.[92] Only after the Arnhem aerial resupply effort was abandoned on day seven due to prohibitively heavy casualties did the RAF reappear. Urquhart stated that he was disappointed in the close air support he received throughout the battle: "The re-supply boys' gallantry had been magnificent, but our fighters were rare friends."[93]

One asset that did aid the British was their own artillery. In the early stages of the battle, fire support from Lt. Col. W. F. K. Thompson's 1st Airlanding Light Regiment of 75mm howitzers helped break up many attacks by German infantry against Frost's position.[94] Once the bridge force fell, Thompson's guns sustained the defensive effort at Oosterbeek by carrying out both indirect and direct-fire missions against massing German formations. Fortunately for the British, just as Thompson's ammunition began to run short, radio contact was made with XXX

Corps's 64th Medium Regiment of 4.5-inch and 5.5-inch guns. Beginning on day five, Thursday, September 21, this unit, shooting from eleven miles away, engaged targets as close as a hundred yards ahead of British positions. On two occasions, the 64th also brought accurate fire inside the perimeter on parties of infiltrating Germans. So impressed was Urquhart by the accuracy and responsiveness of this unit that after the battle he petitioned the War Office to grant the 64th the right to wear the Pegasus arm badge (the request was denied).[95]

But this last-minute fire support was not enough; because of the defensive effort of Student's First Parachute Army, XXX Corps was not going to arrive in sufficient force to save the 1st Airborne. Even the arrival of Sosabowski's 1st Parachute Brigade, south of the river, on day five provided insufficient reinforcement to Urquhart's force on the opposite bank.

From a tactical perspective, much can be gleaned from a careful study of the 1st Airborne's fight at Arnhem. A superficial reading of the battle would simply admonish never to send light infantry against tanks, but such superficiality would also obscure deeper, more relevant lessons. Some of these can be summarized as follows.

Light infantry forces possess tremendous defensive power in cities. Frost's battalion held out for more than three days, with little support and no reinforcement, against incredible odds. Likewise, the remainder of the 1st Airborne held out for approximately six days against what approximated two full enemy armored divisions.

Conversely, offensive action in built-up areas by light infantry forces, unsupported by armored vehicles, is bound to fail unless carried out with speed and complemented by accurate intelligence and competent reconnaissance. There must also be sufficient numbers of infantrymen to exploit gaps in the enemy defenses and overcome weak resistance. Probably the best offensive technique would be to employ an offensive defense: to quickly seize key terrain or buildings, then set up a strong defense, thereby compelling the enemy to move in the open, where he can be engaged and destroyed. It does not take much to stop a light infantry column in the city; hence, if the mission is to seize key terrain, enemy contact en route to the objective must be avoided or quickly reduced. Finally, troops should be inured to the "odd bullet," which, echoing through the streets, so stymied the British advance to the bridge during day one. Procedures for dealing with civilian noncombatants should also be rehearsed and enforced.

Command and control is essential. Radios must work so that commanders at all levels can maneuver forces, which, due to the nature of street fighting, will invariably be split up, especially when in the attack. The use of indigenous telephone systems should not be overlooked, especially if unit equipment is failing. Additionally, some method of marking friendly buildings is essential.

Supply operations are critical. City fighting consumes large amounts of ammunition, especially grenades. Infantrymen can carry only so much ammunition; therefore, some system by which ammunition and grenades can be resupplied is essential. Casualty evacuation is also critical, as is water resupply. Unlike fighting in forests, where lakes and streams can often be found, cutting off water in a city is relatively easy.

Defending from inside buildings may be hazardous, especially if the enemy has no qualms against destroying them. As already stated, the 1st Airborne troopers preferred defending from outside buildings once the Germans began their campaign of methodical destruction.

Snipers are a significant threat in a city. Buildings provide innumerable vantage points, and the streets are natural kill zones. Countersniper techniques require much ammunition as well: another reason why resupply is critical. Smoke may have been useful, though it seems that the only smoke available to the 1st Airborne was that used to mark LZs and DZs. In a sniper-rich environment, conspicuous trappings of rank are best made less so. In the modern age, night operations and thermal imagery may make snipers less of a threat because they might be identified more easily.

Effective antitank weapons are essential. The Germans could make full use of their armor only after the British antitank weapons were destroyed or ran out of ammunition. Light infantrymen should also be prepared to engage tanks at very short ranges. As stated above, the British antitank guns had a significant deterrent effect against German armor, but the Germans lost more armor to shoulder-fired PIATs and Gammon bombs.

Finally, fire support is critical, and gunners should be prepared to deliver fires dangerously close to friendly troops. Gunners should recognize that those calling for fire have limited fields of vision and therefore may be incapable of identifying targets at distant ranges and may find it difficult to locate precisely their own positions relative to the enemy. The accurate delivery of close air support will encounter the same challenges.

ENDNOTES

1. Maurice Tugwell, *Arnhem: A Case Study* (London: Thronton Cox, 1975), 13–14.

2. Martin Middlebrook, *Arnhem 1944: The Airborne Battle, 17–26 September* (Boulder, CO: Westview Press, 1994), 96.

3. Tugwell, 56. See especially appendix 2, "1st Airborne Division's Allotment of Aircraft and Gliders to Units, by Lifts."

4. Middlebrook, 96–97.

5. Robert J. Kershaw, *It Never Snows in September: The German View of MARKET-GARDEN and the Battle of Arnhem, September 1944* (New York: Hippocrene Books, 1994), 61. The previous commander, Brigade-

führer Sylvester Stadler, had been wounded during the fighting withdrawal from France, and Harzer assumed command and remained in command of the division throughout the fight at Arnhem.

6. Harzer as quoted in Kershaw, 66.

7. Robert Elliot Urquhart, *Arnhem* (London: Cassell, 1958), 209. Portions of Lt. Gen. F. A. M. Browning's order to Urquhart detailing the 1st Airborne's role in the operation are reproduced at appendix I. Urquhart's order to his subordinate units is reproduced at appendix II.

8. Horrocks as quoted in Cornelius Ryan, *A Bridge Too Far* (New York: Simon and Schuster, 1974), 166.

9. Middlebrook, 13.

10. Quoted extract from "SHAEF Weekly Intelligence Summary 23," August 26, 1944, in Forrest C. Pogue, *The Supreme Command* (Washington, DC: Office of the Chief of Military History, 1954), 244–45.

11. Quoted extract from "SHAEF Weekly Intelligence Summary 24," September 2, 1944, in Pogue, 245.

12. Quoted extract from "Report of Combined Intelligence Committee, Prospects of a German Collapse and Surrender as of 8 September 1944," dated September 9, 1944, in Pogue, 245.

13. Martin Blumenson, *Breakout and Pursuit* (Washington, DC: Office of the Chief of Military History, 1961), chapter xxxi passim. The First Allied Airborne Army (FAAA), commanded by Lt. Gen. Lewis H. Brereton, was activated on August 2, 1944, and constituted Eisenhower's sole reserve in September 1944. The FAAA consisted of two corps, the U.S. XVIII Airborne Corps and the British I Airborne Corps. At the time of Market-Garden, only the U.S. 82d and 101st, the British 1st Airborne Division, and the Polish brigade were available. The U.S. 17th Airborne Division was still assembling, and the British 6th Airborne Division was reorganizing after a long spell in Normandy. See Middlebrook, 10.

14. Montgomery first proposed the plan to Eisenhower on September 10 during a contentious meeting aboard the latter's plane at Brussels airport. See Ryan, 82–89.

15. Kershaw, 24.

16. Ibid., 21.

17. Cornelius Bauer, *The Battle of Arnhem,* trans. D. R. Welsh (New York: Stein and Day, 1967), 67.

18. Figures for the SS II Panzer Corps are as of September 7. Kershaw, 38–39.

19.   Sims as quoted in Peter Harclerode, *Arnhem: A Tragedy of Errors* (London: Arms and Armour Press, 1994), 64.

20.   There has never been a completely accurate accounting of either the numbers engaged or the number of casualties. Harclerode quotes figures of 2,398 men withdrawn and 7,212 casualties (p. 153). Ryan gives 10,005 as the number engaged, with casualties totaling 7,578 (p. 599). Urquhart writes that 10,005 landed in Arnhem and 2,163 came out (pp. 181–82). Middlebrook, who gives perhaps the best accounting, writes that 11,920 men took part in the action around Arnhem and 3,910 returned (pp. 438–39).

21.   Civilian casualties are given in Middlebrook, 440. German casualties are estimated at 3,300 in both Middlebrook (p. 440) and Ryan (p. 599).

22.   Like the casualty figures, the number of soldiers at the bridge is in dispute, though figures of 700 to 750 are those generally given. The best accounting is perhaps Middlebrook's, who estimates there were 739 British soldiers with Frost at the bridge. Middlebrook, 287–88.

23.   Incident recalled in John Fairley, *Remember Arnhem: The Story of the 1st Airborne Reconnaissance Squadron at Arnhem* (Aldershot, Hampshire, England: Pegasus Journal, 1978), 131.

24.   Student as quoted in Christopher Hibbert, *The Battle of Arnhem* (London: B. T. Batsford, 1962), 55.

25.   Harclerode, 48–49.

26.   Ibid., 49. Williams's command had recently been doubled in number of aircraft but had not received a concomitant increase in the number of ground crews. Williams was also concerned about his pilots' lack of night flying experience.

27.   Harclerode, 163–64.

28.   Tugwell, 56.

29.   Harclerode, 55.

30.   Tugwell, 27.

31.   William Thomas Johnson, *Cracks in the Coalition: Anglo-American Cooperation During the Planning of Operation Market-Garden, 1944* (M.A. thesis, Duke University, 1981), 71.

32.   Johnson, 72.

33.   Hibbert, 31–34.

34.   Middlebrook, 124.

35.   This decision is even more peculiar when considering the relative size of airlanding versus parachute battalions in the 1st Airborne Division. Lewis Golden, a member of the divisional signals section during the battle,

states in his book *Echoes from Arnhem* (London: William Kimber, 1984) that the size of airlanding battalions was almost double that of parachute battalions (p. 24). Middlebrook writes that the average size of the parachute battalions at Arnhem was 548 all ranks, whereas the average size of the airlanding battalions was 773 all ranks (pp. 23–29).

36. Geoffrey Powell, *The Devil's Birthday: The Bridges to Arnhem, 1944* (New York: Franklin Watts, 1985), 235. Powell was a company commander in the 156th Parachute Battalion, which arrived on day two of the battle.

37. Ibid.

38. Hackett as quoted in Harclerode, 63.

39. Kershaw, 36.

40. Action described in Middlebrook, 123–26. The squadron consisted of three line troops, a headquarters troop, and a support troop. One of the line troops was to remain behind to bolster the defense of the LZs and DZs while the remainder made for the bridge. The support troop had two 20mm antiaircraft guns and two 3-inch mortars. Each jeep had a Vickers K machine gun. Fairley, 13–16.

41. Harclerode, 165.

42. Sergeant Norman Howes of the 2d Battalion, South Staffordshire Regiment (1st Airlanding Brigade) as quoted in Middlebrook, 200.

43. Golden, 140–41.

44. Bauer, 127–28.

45. Ibid., 128. Gelderland is the Dutch province in which Arnhem is located.

46. Powell, 94.

47. Quoted in Janusz Piekalkiewicz, *Arnhem 1944,* trans. H. A. and A. J. Barker (New York: Charles Scribner's Sons, 1976), 68.

48. Hackett as quoted in the foreword of Tugwell, 12.

49. Hibbert, 88; Middlebrook, 130.

50. Urquhart, 45.

51. Powell, 66.

52. Middlebrook, 130.

53. Urquhart, 199–200.

54. Ibid., 56.

55. Student as quoted in Powell, 96.

56. Quoted in Hibbert, 87–88.

57. Major J. Timothy as quoted in Middlebrook, 140.

58. Middlebrook, 189.

59.   Urquhart, 200.

60.   Ibid.

61.   Middlebrook, 216.

62.   Ibid., 280.

63.   Urquhart, 200.

64.   Kershaw, 129–31.

65.   Ibid, 217. See also Appendix B, "The German Order of Battle During Operation Market-Garden 17–26 Sep," 323–38. See also Tugwell, 16.

66.   Ringsdorf as quoted in Kershaw, 127.

67.   Moeller as quoted in Kershaw, 239.

68.   Frater as quoted in Middlebrook, 357–85. It is interesting to note that British glider pilots were trained to fight as infantry once on the ground. This was not the case with U.S. glider pilots.

69.   Tugwell, 39.

70.   Louis Hagen, *The Arnhem Lift* (New York: Pinnacle Books, 1945), 103.

71.   Urquhart, 159.

72.   Fairley, 104. This cry was adopted by the British paratroopers when they were fighting in the hills of North Africa, and it seemed that every message shouted by the Arabs from one village to the next began with these words. Hibbert, 122.

73.   Hibbert, 121.

74.   Fairley, 185.

75.   Ibid., 163.

76.   The 6– and 17-pounders were standard towed antitank guns. The PIAT (projector infantry antitank) was a shoulder-fired weapon that discharged a 3–pound shape charge capable of penetrating 75mm of armor. The Gammon bomb was a bag filled with plastic explosive and fitted with a contact fuse. When thrown against a tank, the bomb detonated, causing splintering inside the tank.

77.   Thompson as quoted in Fairley, 144.

78.   Middlebrook, 363–64.

79.   John Frost, *A Drop Too Many* (London: Cassell, 1980), 230–31.

80.   Cooke as quoted in Fairley, 168.

81.   Dombrowski as quoted in Kershaw, 265.

82.   Kershaw, 291.

83.   Urquhart, 117.

84.   Livingstone as quoted in Middlebrook, 356.

85.   Tom Angus, *Men at Arnhem* (London: Leo Cooper, 1976), 80–81. Tom Angus is a pseudonym; from the description of events, the author is most likely Maj. Geoffrey Powell, C Company commander, 156th Parachute Battalion.

86.   Fairley, 92; Powell, 205.

87.   Middlebrook, 400.

88.   Hibbert, 160.

89.   Ibid., 163.

90.   Middlebrook, 398.

91.   Fairley, 180.

92.   Johnson, 74–75.

93.   Urquhart, 106.

94.   Tugwell, 47–48.

95.   Middlebrook, 350–51, 376–77; Powell, 170; Urquhart, 122, 183–84. Middlebrook notes that besides receiving calls for fire, the 64th also served as the 1st Airborne's main communications link with XXX Corps.

FIVE

Troyes, France, 1944:

All Guns Blazing

by Col. Peter R. Mansoor

General Wood came in to state that the 4th Armored had just captured Troyes. This capture was a very magnificent feat of arms. Colonel, later General, Bruce Clark brought his combat command up north of the town, where a gully or depression gave him cover, at about three thousand yards from the town. The edge of the town was full of German guns and Germans. Clark lined up one medium tank company, backed it with two armored infantry companies, all mounted, and charged with all guns blazing. He took the town without losing a man or a vehicle. Later, it was necessary to re-attack to get him out, because the Germans closed in behind his small force.[1]

—Gen. George S. Patton, Jr.

The 4th Armored Division's summer campaign of 1944 demonstrated the versatility of the training received by the divisions of the U.S. Army prior to their entry into combat. Prepared for long, sweeping movements across great distances, the 4th Armored Division proved its abilities in close combat as well, both in the hedgerows of Normandy and the urban confines of the city of Troyes. Armored units do not customarily elect to fight in cities; rather, the choice is forced upon them by circumstances. When this happens, units must be prepared to do battle even in the tight confines of the urban morass, for more often than not, there is little or no time to adjust tactics, techniques, and procedures as events rapidly unfold. Such was the case with the U.S. 4th Armored Division after the breakout from Normandy and during the pursuit of the German army to the West Wall in the late summer of 1944. As the tankers and armored infantrymen of Combat Command A (CCA) fought to cross the Seine River, they unexpectedly found themselves enmeshed in city fighting as they struggled to gain and maintain control of the vital bridges in Troyes. Their battle was ultimately a successful one, but in it one finds numerous lessons of value to the military professional interested in exploring the recurring characteristics of urban warfare.

Perhaps the most important of these lessons is that urban warfare, although unpleasant, is often necessary to achieve important military or political objectives. In this case, the 4th Armored Division's mission to seize Troyes was predicated on the need to secure its vital communications nodes, especially bridges and the road network that led across the Seine River and into the interior of central France. Other lessons are of tactical value. As the 4th Armored Division discovered in Troyes, fighting in cities is distinctly different from fighting in the open countryside. Fighting in the former situation is best done by small, combined-arms groupings capable of negotiating the closed spaces of the urban jungle and dealing with the unexpected presence of enemy forces in three dimensions. Units can quickly become disorganized and lose track of themselves, their comrades, and the enemy. Combat forces must develop or train for specific tactics, techniques, and procedures to overcome these challenges. One technique employed by the 4th Armored Division in Troyes, for instance, was to use tracer rounds fired from machine guns to locate adjacent friendly positions within the city. Furthermore, enemy units bypassed during an advance through a city can quickly reemerge in a unit's rear. Charging into the center of a city, as the American task force that entered Troyes discovered, is not the same thing as clearing it.

The 4th Armored Division was exceptionally well prepared for combat in open terrain, but not for combat in the closed spaces of towns and cities. Activated on April 15, 1941, at Pine Camp, New York, the division spent two and a half years training in the United States and Great Britain prior to its deployment to Normandy in July 1944. This training included participation in the 1942 Tennessee maneuvers, six months at the Desert Training Center in California and Arizona, and several months of training on Salisbury Plain in England. Regrettably, but perhaps predictably, given the U.S. Army's lack of experience in urban warfare, the only training the division received in city fighting was a short village assault course administered at Camp Bowie, Texas, prior to the division's preparation for overseas movement.[2]

The breakout of the U.S. First and Third Armies from Normandy after the success of Operation Cobra in July 1944 gave the 4th Armored Division the opportunity to put to use the lessons it had learned during its long period of preparatory training. Long, sweeping armored movements distinguished the division's operations in Brittany. By early August it was clear to Maj. Gen. John S. Wood, the commanding general, that Cobra had broken German defenses beyond repair. He chafed at the order that pulled his division into the Brittany peninsula in accordance with an operations plan that no longer fit the circumstances of the evolving campaign. The success of Operation Cobra, Wood correctly reasoned, now made that plan irrelevant. If the Third Army were to swing east, it could cut off the German forces in Normandy, and France would then belong to the Allies. "We're winning this war the wrong way," Wood chafed to his superior at VIII Corps, Maj. Gen. Troy H. Middleton. "We ought to be going toward Paris."[3] For the moment, however, the 4th Armored

Division stepped out of the spotlight as the crucial battle developed in the Falaise Gap.

On August 13, the 4th Armored Division was reassigned to XII Corps and ordered to concentrate for an attack toward Orleans. Wood was about to get his wish to advance east, albeit somewhat late. He had pushed his men aggressively to take advantage of the fluid situation after the breakout from Normandy. These advances were not foreign to the division, for they resembled the lengthy movements performed during army maneuvers in Tennessee, at the Desert Training Center in California, and on Salisbury Plain. Combat Command A commander Bruce C. Clarke later recalled: "Everything we did in battle we practiced. We practiced on Salisbury Plain. We practiced these breakthroughs. We'd go down and run an operation, break through, and go into exploitation . . . From then on all I had to do was to say, 'Remember what we did at Salisbury Plain that day?' "[4]

The 4th Armored Division was in its element and thoroughly trained for the task at hand, its commander finally satisfied with the direction of the attack.

The pursuit of the broken German armies to the Seine River was swift and sure. By August 21, CCA had taken Sens, less than a day's march from the Seine River. There the combat command rested, performed maintenance, and awaited the provision of gasoline that would allow it to continue the advance eastward. On August 24, CCA received its new orders to attack Troyes the next day and secure its vital bridges over the Seine River.[5] Colonel Clarke ordered D Troop, 25th Reconnaissance Squadron, to move at nine that night and conduct a route reconnaissance toward the city. At 9:30 P.M. the commanders of the 35th Tank Battalion, Lt. Col. Delk M. Oden, and the 10th Armored Infantry Battalion, Maj. Arthur L. West, Jr., huddled with Colonel Clarke in his command post to receive their orders.

Clarke split CCA into two columns for the attack. Task

Force (TF) Oden consisted of two medium tank companies and a light tank company of the 35th Tank Battalion, a company of armored infantry from the 10th Armored Infantry Battalion, a company of tank destroyers from the 704th Tank Destroyer Battalion, a company (minus one platoon) of combat engineers from the 24th Armored Engineer Battalion augmented by elements of a treadway bridge company, and supported by the self-propelled howitzers of the 66th Armored Field Artillery Battalion reinforced by a battery of 155mm self-propelled howitzers from the 191st Field Artillery Battalion. Task Force West consisted of a medium tank company of the 35th Tank Battalion, two companies of armored infantry from the 10th Armored Infantry Battalion, a platoon of combat engineers from the 24th Armored Engineer Battalion, and supported by the self-propelled howitzers of the 94th Armored Field Artillery Battalion reinforced by the 155mm self-propelled howitzers of the 191st Field Artillery Battalion (minus one battery). The plan, which sounded simple, was for TF West to conduct a frontal assault on Troyes while TF Oden crossed the Seine River eleven miles to the north to envelop the city from the northeast.[6] As so often happens in war, what sounded simple in planning became much more difficult in execution.

The German defenders of Troyes, although a formidable force on paper, were hastily organized, woefully underequipped, and poorly trained. The task of defending the upper reaches of the Seine fell to the German First Army, whose mission was to delay the American advance long enough for reinforcements to form a coherent line of defense behind the river. The Troyes Military Administrative Headquarters, a garrison organization, was in the city proper. The troops under its command consisted primarily of the 1009th Regional Defense Battalion. To its north was the 1010th Security Regiment, which had been severely depleted in fighting west of the Seine. These units were organized for security operations in rear areas. Their personnel were on the whole overage and equipped with inferior French-made weapons; they lacked antitank guns, entrenching tools, and steel helmets.

Also present in the area were elements of the SS 51st Panzergrenadier Brigade, a newly formed organization intended for the activation of the SS 27th Panzergrenadier Division but pressed into service early in a vain effort to reconstitute the battered SS 17th Panzergrenadier Division. This unit consisted of a weak infantry regiment made up of school troops without any collective training. Antitank weapons were limited to a few 20mm antiaircraft guns and handheld panzerfaust antitank grenade launchers. The regiment had been formed in early August 1944, only a couple of weeks before the battle of Troyes, and would be destroyed before it had the opportunity to become a cohesive, trained fighting unit.[7]

The attack by CCA began at seven on the morning of August 25 when TF Oden crossed the initial point (IP) at Les Clarimois and advanced to Fontaine, eleven miles north of Troyes. The task force destroyed numerous vehicles and several 88mm antitank guns, and killed or captured a large number of enemy personnel. The column reached the Seine River at Savieres by early afternoon. Lieutenant Colonel Oden sent C Company, 10th Armored Infantry Battalion, across the river to establish an outpost while the combat engineers began work on a bridge. The bridging operations were much more extensive than the initial engineer reconnaissance had determined would be necessary, and additional bridging equipment had to be brought up from CCA reserves. The bridge across the Seine was completed by 8:30 P.M., but Oden's column was forced to halt again while the engineers constructed another bridge across a canal that ran parallel to the river on the far side. By 2:30 A.M. on August 26, TF Oden was across both water obstacles and coiled into an assembly area waiting for dawn.[8]

Task Force Oden's delay due to the necessarily extensive bridging operations across the Seine barrier meant that TF West would attack Troyes alone. Task Force West's advance began at eight in the morning. By using secondary roads and cross-country routes to avoid enemy roadblocks, it managed to arrive at the high ground, in the vicinity of the village of Montgeux, approximately three miles west of Troyes, by one that afternoon. There Major West deployed his forces, sent out patrols from the attached platoon of the 25th Cavalry Reconnaissance Squadron and the Intelligence and Reconnaissance Platoon of the 10th Armored Infantry Battalion to reconnoiter the enemy positions, and contacted Colonel Clarke for orders.[9]

Colonel Clarke was now faced with the decision of whether to wait for TF Oden to complete its bridges or have TF West attack Troyes without support. He decided on the latter course of action to take advantage of the element of surprise, hoping that the German defenders would be caught unprepared by the speed of CCA's advance. Clarke ordered TF West to attack alone at 4:30 P.M.[10]

Sporadic enemy artillery fire throughout the afternoon delayed preparations. Colonel Clarke arrived at Montgeux to assess the situation and conduct a leader's reconnaissance upon the high ground overlooking Troyes. After discussing the situation with Major West and the supporting artillery commanders, Clarke ordered the attack to commence at 4:30 P.M. Patrols had reported that the enemy defenses seemed to be concentrated outside the city perimeter. The terrain between the American and German positions was a broad, flat plain that sloped gently downhill. Clarke decided on a bold, frontal assault using an open "desert" tactical formation that the 4th Infantry Division had perfected during its time at the Desert Training Center in California. Tanks would lead, followed by infantry mounted in half-tracked personnel carriers. The force was to move at maximum speed to increase the shock effect on the defending enemy forces.[11]

Major West assembled his company commanders and battle staff on the high ground overlooking Troyes to issue the necessary oral orders.[12] "As you know," West began, "there is enemy artillery falling on this ground and to our left front. The artillery observers have been unable to determine the course of this enemy fire." He continued:

The enemy occupies the roads and fields to our front toward the city. Roads to the edge of the city are not mined. As stated this morning, enemy artillery pieces are located at various positions on the main road leading into the city itself and the city is believed to be occupied by 300 to 500 enemy personnel. Explosions can be seen in Troyes. It is believed that the enemy are destroying ammunition dumps and equipment in preparation to leave the city.

You know the mission of CCB [Combat Command B] is to take the town to our right. Oden's column is now held up repairing a bridge across the Seine River at Seveeres [*sic*]. The 94th and 191st are in position in that draw. They will support our attack on Troyes. A forward observer will go with each company to the attack. This task force attacks the town at 1630— line of departure—this high ground we are now on—left boundary RR track, right boundary that highway leading into the city. We will attack in column of companies, companies on line, deployed on a wide front . . . Our most dangerous ground is that open ground between here and the city, a distance of approximately 3½ miles. Our best security can be obtained by moving fast across that area to get into the protection of the town. The companies will follow each other in successive distances of 100 yards. The first phase line for reorganization will be about 500 to 600 yards inside of the town proper. The 2nd phase line will be the RR track at the RR station. We will then attack in column down the street until we reach the Seine Canal. At that time further orders will be issued. No town plans are available. You will have to feel your way after we get into the town. The battalion CP [command post] will be in the rear of A/10.

All companies . . . turn on SCR [Signal Corps Radio] 300 and 536 in addition to vehicular radios, now. When necessary to dismount, take them with you. The time is now 1600—are there any questions?

The company commanders asked for more time to issue their order and prepare, so West agreed to postpone the attack until 5:00 P.M., and CCA was notified of the change in plans.

At five o'clock, the Sherman tanks of C Company, 35th Tank Battalion, roared down the hill toward Troyes, followed closely by the half-tracked vehicles of A and B Companies, 10th Armored Infantry Battalion. Enemy artillery and small-arms fire raked the formation. The task force moved directly into and through the area where the artillery concentrations were impacting, which forced the enemy forward observers to make corrections to the target location. The German fire support system, however, could not react quickly enough to the frenzied pace of the American attack. Task Force West thus missed being hit by the lethal fires.[13]

Heavy small-arms fire hit the formation from the right flank. Two tanks and a squad of infantry destroyed several machine-gun positions in that direction. A platoon of infantry dismounted to kill or capture approximately fifty Germans defending from individual fighting positions. Task Force West moved over a railroad embankment and picked up speed, and ran head-on into an antitank ditch across its front. This was a critical point in the battle. Had the ditch been constructed properly, the American forces would have been forced to halt and maneuver to seek a bypass. They would then have been vulnerable to massed artillery and antitank fires. Instead, poor construction of the obstacle enabled the American tank drivers to gun their engines and jump the ditch to the far side, where the tank treads fought to gain a foothold in the loose soil. By this method the tanks broke down the far wall of the ditch, allowing half-tracks and jeeps to follow in their wake. A lane was soon discovered to allow wheeled vehicles to cross the ditch more efficiently, albeit in single file. Enemy forward observers in the ditch were quickly killed, further reducing the effectiveness of enemy fires.[14]

The American formation lost cohesion as it neared the outskirts of Troyes. One group of two tank platoons and an infantry platoon, under the command of Captain Miller (commander of C Company, 35th Tank Battalion), made its way to the city square, a four-block, parklike area near the bridges on the Seine River. This force was followed by Major Elwell, the battalion executive officer, with the battalion headquarters, the intelligence and reconnaissance (I&R) platoon, mortar platoon, and an additional platoon of infantry. Upon reaching this area, the Americans outposted the streets leading into the perimeter, cleared numerous snipers from buildings overlooking the square, and sent patrols to locate the bridges across the Seine. The remainder of the force followed Major West into the city.

Lacking adequate maps, the force found navigation difficult if not impossible. Upon reaching the railroad station, the force under Major West became lost. Fortunately, it soon regained radio contact with Major Elwell's element. As a field expedient measure, both forces fired .50–caliber machine-gun tracer ammunition into the air to locate each other's position. Major West then regrouped his units and attacked to rejoin the elements near the objective, all the while coming under intense artillery, small-arms, and antitank grenade fire.[15]

Upon linking up with Major Elwell's force, Major West issued orders to secure the town and clear a route for supplies and medical evacuation. Lieutenant Abe Baum, the battalion S-2, located a town plan, which greatly helped clarify the situation. Two platoons of Sherman tanks covered by an infantry company were broken into small groups and used to guard approaches to the square. Another infantry company, supported by the battalion assault gun platoon, guarded the bridges across the canal along the east side of the perimeter. The I&R and engineer platoons pushed to the Seine River to reconnoiter the condition of the bridge and routes leading across to the east side. The I&R platoon took fire as it neared the bridge across the river, which was then blown as American forces approached it. The Headquarters Company commander, Captain Seavers, was appointed temporary provost marshal and civil affairs officer, and one of his immediate tasks was to clear the area of civilians, both for their own protection and to prevent information of American dispositions from falling into enemy hands.[16]

For all intents and purposes, TF West had conducted an old-fashioned cavalry charge into the center of Troyes, only to find itself cut off and surrounded by hundreds of disorganized enemy troops. German vehicles wandered into the perimeter, only to be destroyed by tank, assault gun, or small-arms fire. Snipers were silenced individually, at least one in a church steeple being eliminated by fire from the 75mm gun of a Sherman tank. Early the next morning, an enemy ammunition convoy was intercepted and destroyed, resulting in explosions that boomed periodically.[17]

Medical care was the most critical need, for the task force had incurred at least thirty casualties that required assistance. The battalion aid station, however, did not make it into the city square with the remainder of the task force. In fact, the bodies of the battalion surgeon and several medics were later found, apparently shot after capture by the enemy.[18] Captain Seavers improvised by contacting local authorities, who gathered a small group of French doctors and nurses to attend to the wounded soldiers.

At 8:00 P.M. Major West sent a platoon of infantry, supported by a tank platoon, back along the route leading into the city from the west. They advanced approximately one mile before being forced to turn back by heavy small-arms and machine-gun fire. The force was recalled into the perimeter. For at least the rest of the night, TF West was isolated from outside support, although radio contact was maintained with CCA headquarters. Gasoline, water, and ammunition all began to run low (the battalion trains also failed to make it into the city with the attacking elements).[19]

Major West gathered his commanders and battle staff together at 1:00 A.M. on August 26 to exchange information and issue orders. Combat Command A had decided to launch a relief force, consisting of a medium tank company (A Company, 35th Tank Battalion), at 6:00 A.M. This force would fight into the city from the west, while TF West would launch a simultaneous attack to effect linkup with two infantry platoons and a tank platoon starting from their positions in the city square. Major West also planned attacks designed to clear the areas along two major routes into the city while the I&R platoon attacked to seize the area between the canal and the Seine River.[20]

The relief operation began at six as planned. All forces were successful in achieving their objectives. The I&R platoon overran an artillery battery that was withdrawing from its position to the east of the canal. Near the city square, tanks and half-tracks destroyed a column of enemy trucks and dozens of enemy personnel, which were later confirmed to be the headquarters of the SS 51st Brigade. Its commander, a general officer, was taken prisoner. The local Gestapo headquarters was turned into an inferno by the fire of a tank platoon, after which armored infantrymen cleared the building. German losses were fifty-eight dead and fifty prisoners, with the Americans suffering no losses. By 8:00 A.M., linkup was made with A Company, 35th Tank Battalion, and a resupply route was cleared into the city from the west.[21]

Meanwhile, at 7:00 A.M., TF Oden began an advance from its bridgehead and soon seized positions on the high ground in the vicinity of Vailly. Caught between the forces of TF West in Troyes and TF Oden on the high ground to the northeast, pummeled by artillery fire, and strafed by American fighter-bombers, German forces suffered heavily attempting to escape the jaws of the American vise. An estimated seventy-five to a hundred enemy vehicles were caught in the open attempting to withdraw from the trap and were destroyed.[22] By the end of August, the German First Army would rate the remnants of the SS 17th Panzergrenadier Division as "split up and heavily battered even during assembly, poorly strengthened and not always reliable unit of low combat strength. Relief from front line service for reconditioning and stabilization urgently necessary."[23]

At eleven that morning, the 53d Armored Infantry Battalion moved into Troyes to relieve TF West and mop up the remnants of enemy forces in the city. Its mission complete, TF West moved at 12:50 P.M. to join TF Oden on the east bank of the Seine River. Their short experience with city fighting over, the soldiers of TF West could once again look forward to combat on the rolling hills and valleys of central France. At the cost of three vehicles destroyed, 15 men killed in action, and 65 wounded, TF West had destroyed fifty-three enemy vehicles and eight artillery pieces, had killed 533 enemy soldiers, and had taken 572 prisoners.[24] One history of the battle concludes, "From the viewpoint of the Combat Command and also apparently from that of the Corps commander there were no flaws in this operation. In fact, the Combat Command was commended by the Corps commander for the boldness and efficiency of the operation, and it was considered by many to be a classic example of an attack of a city by armor."[25] But was it?

Task Force West initially utilized the speed, firepower, and shock effect of its armor to overwhelm the disorganized enemy defenders of Troyes. Utilizing reconnaissance by fire and "marching fire," the task force was able to continue to move at a high rate of speed, bypassing a few pockets of enemy resistance and destroying others. This battle, however, took place on the outskirts, as opposed to the interior, of the city, against an enemy that was not prepared for a full-scale assault on its positions. Once the American formation moved into Troyes proper, its operations became much more difficult to organize and control. The task force became split up until quick-thinking soldiers used the expedient method of firing tracers into the air to locate one another's positions.

Once the task force was consolidated in the heart of the city, its problems had just begun. Major West quickly reorganized his forces for the decentralized nature of urban combat. He formed small tank-infantry teams that guarded every street leading into the task force perimeter in the city square and cleaned out enemy snipers and pockets of resistance. Lack of supplies and medical care, however, were matters of some concern and could have been more costly to the task force had the battle lasted for more than twenty-four hours. The task force asked for and received some medical assistance from the local population. This technique was available to the Americans because they had attacked the city as liberators from the viewpoint of the French citizens.

The most vital contribution of the local French population to the battle was in the provision of intelligence to the American forces. Before the battle, Major West had only a 1:50,000 scale map on which to plan the advance. This map proved insufficient when the task force actually entered Troyes. The densely built-up city could not be navigated effectively using such a crude tool. The task force S-2 finally asked for assistance and found an accurate map of the city, complete with a listing of enemy installations and billeting locations, from a baker who supplied the German forces in the city with bread.[26] Other French patriots guided American platoons along unguarded routes to specific points in the city where they would kill or capture German elements in small, successful raids.[27]

Besides the skill and courage of the American troops who attacked Troyes, the next most important determinant of the battle's outcome was the lack of organization and training of the defending enemy forces. On paper a formidable organization of SS warriors, the enemy forces defending Troyes were in actuality a polyglot collection of rear area security and school troops hastily assembled for the purpose of delaying the attacking American forces long enough to allow a more effective defense to be arrayed along the Moselle River, farther to the east. German command and control was insufficient to orchestrate the operations of the forces in the city, which fought disjointedly and were destroyed piecemeal by the outnumbered, but better trained and equipped, soldiers of the U.S. 4th Armored Division. Had the German commanders arrayed their forces to defend the interior of Troyes and enticed the American force into a city fight, the outcome would undoubtedly have been markedly different. German infantry could have used the cover of buildings to engage American tanks and armored infantry at close range with panzerfausts and machine guns. By defending the rural outskirts, the Germans gave up any advantage the city offered for their protection. This is somewhat surprising, given the German experience with urban combat at Stalingrad, Cherbourg, and elsewhere.

The battle of Troyes shows the greater flexibility of the American army in the late summer of 1944 vis-à-vis its German opponents. Inexperienced in urban warfare, TF West had nevertheless succeeded by forming small, combined-arms groups capable of dealing with the uncertainties of combat in the closed spaces of the city. Major West formulated plans that allowed his forces to retain the initiative. On the other hand, the poorly organized defenders of Troyes, though superior in numbers to the American task force, failed to use the advantages offered by the streets and buildings and their superior knowledge of the urban terrain in the city. Perhaps the point is a moot one. The German defeat was inevitable due to the impending envelopment from the north by Combat Command B after its successful crossing of the Seine River. A short delaying action was about all the German First Army could expect under the circumstances.

The brief struggle for Troyes was but a small weave in the larger tapestry of the Allied pursuit of German forces across France in the late summer of 1944. The superbly trained and well-led soldiers of the 4th Armored Division accomplished their assigned mission there and quickly moved on to another and far more significant battle farther east along the Moselle River near the city of Nancy. Lost in the larger sweep of the U.S. Third Army advance across France, the battle of Troyes faded into relative obscurity, except in the memories of the soldiers involved and the grateful citizens of a liberated city. Perhaps that is monument enough for the soldiers of TF West, who established a well-earned reputation for excellence by their deeds alone.

ENDNOTES

1. George S. Patton, Jr., *War as I Knew It* (Boston: Houghton Mifflin, 1947), 118–19.

2. Fourth Armored Division, "Division History," 604–0.1, Record

Group 407; Diary, 37th Tank Battalion, July–September 1943, 609–TK (37)-0.2, Record Group 407, National Archives II.

3.   Frank J. Price, *Troy H. Middleton* (Baton Rouge: Louisiana State University Press, 1974), 188.

4.   Bruce C. Clarke, Oral History, The Bruce Cooper Clarke Papers, U.S. Army Military History Institute, 129.

5.   HQ, Combat Command A, "After Action Report for July and August 1944," 604–CCA-0.3, Record Group 407, National Archives II.

6.   Ibid.

7.   Albert Emmerich, "The Battles of the 1.Armee in France from 11 Aug to 15 Sep 1944," MS #B-728, Record Group 338, National Archives II, 5–8; Georg Tessin, *Verbände und Truppen der deutschen Wehrmacht und Waffen SS im Zweiten Weltkrieg 1939–1945* (Osnabrück: Biblio Verlag, 1977), 173; Kurt Hold, "Organization and Order of Battle of First Army between 11 Aug 1944 and 14 Feb 1945," MS #B-732, Record Group 338, National Archives II, 13–14.

8.   HQ, 35th Tank Battalion, "Battalion History, 15 August to 31 August 1944," 604–TK(35), Record Group 407, National Archives II; HQ, 25th Tank Battalion, "After Battle Report," November 1, 1944, 604–TK (35)-0.3, Record Group 407, National Archives II.

9.   Unit Diary, 10th Armored Infantry Battalion (AIB), 604–INF (10)-0.2, Record Group 407, National Archives II, 44.

10.   4th Armored Division Association, *The Legacy of the 4th Armored Division* (Paducah, KY: Turner Publishing, 1990), 23.

11.   10th AIB Unit Diary, 44; Brig. Gen. Arthur L. West, Jr., and Col. Crosby P. Miller, "Troyes—An Armored Attack," *Armor*, LXXII, No. 6 (November-December 1963), 4–9.

12.   The following account is taken from the 10th AIB Unit Diary, 45. A similar account is given by West and Miller in "Troyes—An Armored Attack." Because the unit diary was written immediately after the event, I have chosen to follow its account.

13.   10th AIB Diary, 46; "Troyes—An Armored Attack," 7.

14.   Ibid.

15.   10th AIB Diary, 47; "Troyes—An Armored Attack," 7.

16.   10th AIB Diary, 47; "Troyes—An Armored Attack," 8.

17.   Ibid.

18.   "Troyes—An Armored Attack," 9; Kenneth Koyen, *The Fourth Ar-*

mored Division from the Beach to Bavaria (Munich: Herder Druck, 1946), 40.

19.   10th AIB Diary, 48–49; "Troyes—An Armored Attack," 8.

20.   10th AIB Diary, 48–49; "Troyes—An Armored Attack," 8–9.

21.   10th AIB Diary, 49; "Troyes—An Armored Attack," 9.

22.   HQ, Combat Command A, "After Action Report for July and August 1944," 604–CCA-0.3, Record Group 407, National Archives II.

23.   Albert Emmerich, "The Battles of the 1.Armee in France from 11 Aug to 15 Sep 1944," MS #B-728, Record Group 338, National Archives II, 16.

24.   10th AIB Diary, 50; *The Legacy of the 4th Armored Division*, 24.

25.   *The Legacy of the 4th Armored Division*, 24.

26.   10th AIB Diary, 50.

27.   *The Legacy of the 4th Armored Division*, 23.

SIX

Budapest, 1944–45:

Bloody Contest of Wills

by Col. Peter B. Zwack

The true contempt of an invader is shown by deeds of valor in the field.

—Hermocrates of Syracuse, 415 B.C.

In April 1992 the late Col. Will Densberger took his officers of the U.S. Army's Phantom Brigade from Aschaffenburg, Germany, to the top of Gellert Hill, overlooking the great Hungarian city of Budapest. Many of the officers had just returned from the ideal armor conditions of Desert Storm. From this vantage point the experienced armor veteran mused on how his mechanized infantry brigade, one with more than fifty M1 Abrams tanks and a hundred M2 Bradley fighting vehicles, would fare in combat within a complicated and massively built-up urban complex such as Budapest. He dismissed the U.S. stock answer that we would avoid it and concentrated instead on the realization that this formidable combat brigade with the equivalent fighting power of several World War II divisions would quickly become diffused within a few city blocks of a large, well-defended city. Without adequate dismounted infantry, or any systemic preparation in the army's leader development system regarding the command and control of large forces in an urban environment, any large-scale city fight involving U.S. forces would be a dangerous and bloody exercise in "ad-hockery." It was an eye-opening visit for this heavy brigade and its leadership.

The Siege of Budapest

The siege of Budapest was the longest, most sustained siege battle of World War II fought to conclusion in the midst of a major civilian population. It was one of the most vicious as well, because both sides, with the sobering experience of Stalingrad behind them, applied their grim craft to the built-up streets of Budapest.

City fighting always has been the most challenging and most daunting arena within the so-called "art of war." The decision to reduce a major city always has significance far beyond the number of soldiers committed to an urban battle. Major cities, especially capitals, are foremost political and economic prizes, which is why, in defiance of most logic, the decision to reduce them is occasionally made. This is precisely why Hitler skewered his Sixth Army in Stalingrad, yet, in apparent contradiction, balked at Leningrad the year before.

Budapest was both a political and militarily strategic prize. The historic city sat astride the main avenue of approach into the southern Reich and was the capital of Hitler's last operational ally. It was the main road and rail hub in the Danubian basin. The classic invasion route into Central Europe, used by countless armies and marauders throughout the centuries, extended from the eastern steppes, through the Danube's "Iron Gate" south of the Carpathians, and up to Budapest's proverbial walls via the broad Hungarian *puszta* (plain).

For an invading army approaching from the east, the ease of passage and trafficability ends at Budapest, which is bisected by the broad and important Danube River. An invader must first

cross this significant obstacle north and south of Budapest in order to bypass the city's massively built-up eastern section of Pest.
The great river flows from northwest to southeast, making a
riverine-supported assault from the Balkans difficult. However,
bypassing Budapest and leaving the city behind the army as it
travels west does the invader no good. Budapest's central position and control of all Hungarian lines of communication make
it mandatory that the city is reduced before an invader makes a
serious march on Vienna. Finally, west of the Danube and in
Buda, the terrain becomes hilly and very defensible, which is why
Budapest is the perfect place to make a defensive stand. It is no
small wonder that as an eastern outpost of Christendom for almost a thousand years, Budapest was besieged no fewer than
thirty times before 1944.[1]

Budapest is divided into two main geographical entities.
Pest, where the bulk of the population lived, is located on the
Danube's eastern bank. Though the approach to Pest is flat and
easy, the city's inner core is heavily built up with massive government buildings, municipal infrastructure, and apartment blocks.
In 1944 it was already equipped with all the amenities of a modern city: cobblestone or macadam roads, underground sewers,
subway tunnels, electric trams, train stations. All were assets that
made Pest convertible into an urban fortress. The bulk of Budapest's industry was also located in Pest, and on Csepel Island,
just to the south. Consequently, Pest was a thorny proposition
for any invading force. Its sister city, Buda, sat among hills on
the western bank of the Danube (both were incorporated into
the single municipality of Budapest in 1873). Even if invading
forces were to skirt Pest, they had to tackle the natural bastion of
Buda, which was linked to central Pest by five bridges. Any garrison could rapidly shunt its defenders back and forth to meet
various threats.

At the heart of Buda stood its prize, the imposing Royal Palace, located on Castle Hill. It was approachable only from the west, north, or south *after* crossing the broad Danube. Castle Hill was not a particularly dominating height at eighty-two meters above the Danube; however, any river crossing from the Pest side could be easily repelled from its stout seventeenth-century walls and parapets. The real key to the defense of Buda, and consequently the entire city, was the complex of hills encircling Castle Hill. From northwest to south they were Rose Hill, Schwabian Hill, Eagle Hill, and Gellert Hill. As long as the garrison retained strongpoints on these hills, any enemy attacks in the shallow valleys and saddles below could be contained. Eagle and Gellert Hills were particularly critical to the defense because they overlooked the entire Budapest area, and from their summits enemy artillery spotters could call accurate, observed fire on Castle Hill or anywhere else on the garrison.

The situation facing the resurgent Soviets in November 1944 gave Stalin significant ground for optimism. Since August 1944 the Second and Third Ukrainian Fronts had been inexorably advancing west toward Budapest after the triumphant Jassy-Kishenev Operation in Romanian Bessarabia in which the German's Army Group South Ukraine was destroyed, with its Sixth Army wiped out once again. Romania had fallen and opportunistically switched sides, providing troops and support to the Soviets that assisted their drive into Hungary and the Balkans. Despite a series of checks in eastern Hungary during October that involved some of the largest tank battles of the war, by November the Soviets were poised on the Tisza River just seventy miles from Budapest's eastern suburbs.

During this period Hitler declared a "Fortress Budapest," and troops were rushed from all over greater Germany's shrinking borders to shore up the defense of Hungary, which after the loss of Ploesti was the last source of refinable oil for the Reich. These reinforcements included a number of well-known formations, including the 1st, 3d, 6th, and 8th Panzer Divisions, which were desperately needed on other fronts as well.

Stalin, despite protestations, directed Marshal Malinovsky and his tired Second Ukrainian Front to seize Budapest within five days. Therefore on November 1, the Soviets launched a rapier-like thrust directly at Budapest and within a week managed to penetrate into Pest's southern suburbs, before being stopped by forces that had been deployed by city trams to the battlefront. Along the main axis of advance, hastily committed German and Hungarian armor and assault guns of all types battled mostly Soviet T-34s and lend-lease Sherman tanks in a stubborn attempt to stem the advance.

The Soviets, unable to push into built-up Pest, conducted local attacks and brought up their siege artillery. They methodically built their forces up to strength while Marshal Tobulkhin's Third Ukrainian Front, having "liberated" Belgrade, pressed on Budapest from the south. By early December both fronts were poised to resume the offensive, this time with the objective of totally enveloping strategic Budapest.

The German/Hungarians in the meantime reinforced their forces that were occupying a hard knob of a bridgehead covering Pest east of the Danube. To the north, weak forces hunkered down behind the Danube; to the south, a stronger line defended the factories and workshop on Csepel Island, around which the Danube forked into the main city. South of Csepel the so-called Margaret defense line veered southwest to Lake Velences and the huge Lake Balaton, which provided a major natural obstacle.

On December 18, the front exploded as both refitted Soviet fronts launched their major offensive to seize Budapest. South of Budapest, the Third Ukrainian Front, with nine rifle divisions compressed into an overwhelming breakthrough frontage, crushed

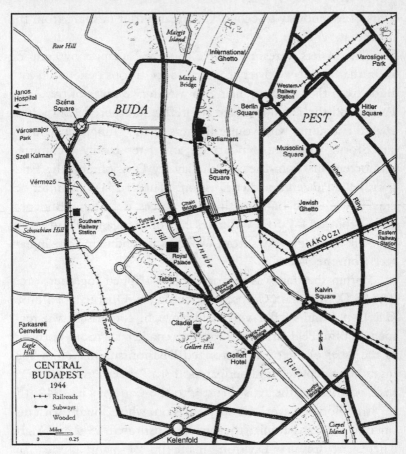

Budapest²

the undermanned 271st Volksgrenadier Division. To the north, Malinovsky's Second Ukrainian Front successfully crossed the Danube near Vac.³ Despite frantic German counterattacks west of Budapest with several panzer divisions shorn of their infantry support, armor from the exploiting XVIII Tank Corps was able to isolate Budapest by Christmas Day 1944. The armor linked up triumphantly the following day in ancient Esztergom with

units of Malinovsky's Second Ukrainian Front pushing from the
northeast.

The Soviets were nearly able to seize Budapest by coup de
main that first day. Soviet reconnaissance troops penetrated into
Buda from the west, advancing to within two miles of the Royal
Palace and the Danube River before being embroiled in a haphazard encounter with young fighters of the Hungarian University Storm Battalion, gendarmes, and later hastily committed
reinforcements from the SS 8th Cavalry Division and the Feldherrnhalle Panzergrenadier Division.[4] This crucial encounter occurred while the bulk of the Axis forces defending Budapest
were deployed five to seven miles east of the Danube and facing
the bulk of Malinovsky's front, which was conducting a fixing attack from the *puszta*.

Within the trap was a formidable if slapped-together force.
The SS IX Mountain Corps, commanded by Obergruppenführer
(Lt. Gen.) Karl Pfeffer von Wildenbruch, comprised two regiments of the Feldherrnhalle Panzergrenadier Division, born out
of the ashes of the 60th Motorized Division annihilated in Stalingrad; the depleted and peripatetic 13th Panzer Division, which
had spearheaded the Axis thrust into the Caucasus in 1942; the
SS 8th "Florian Geyer" Cavalry Division, which fought with distinction in Transylvania; the newly constituted SS 22d "Maria
Theresien" Cavalry Division, made up of many Hungarian-
speaking "Volksdeutsch"; the capable 10th Hungarian Infantry
Division; the weak 12th Hungarian Reserve Infantry Division;
the remnants of the 1st Hungarian Panzer Division; a Hungarian
assault-gun battalion; and some armored hussars. The defenders
had sufficient artillery to support a credible defense, including
two battalions of the formidable 150mm self-propelled Hum-
mels and numerous 88s, as long as rounds were available. Completing the defense were fifty to sixty tanks and assault guns,

including Panthers, Mark IVs, and the low-slung but dangerous Hungarian *Zrinyi* 105mm assault-howitzers (SP). Troop strength numbered approximately 76,000, of which about 37,000 were German.[5]

The Soviets encircling Budapest numbered close to 300,000 troops. While Tobulkhin worked quickly to build an outer ring of encirclement in the western Hungarian plain, Malinovsky received the assignment to reduce Budapest. Six infantry corps, including the VII Romanian Corps fresh from its volte-face from the Axis, supported by considerable artillery and armored assets, were assigned the mission to take Budapest.

The Soviets first pushed into the eastern Pest suburbs while in the west Tolbulkhin's outer encirclement line braced for likely German counterattacks. In a grinding, methodical attack, Malinovsky's forces gradually cleared the villages, small towns, and light industry ringing Pest. The garrison selectively withdrew when pressed to harder inner defense lines, reluctant to become decisively engaged outside the heart of the city. Losses were disproportionate and favored the defenders, a harbinger of the horrific street battles soon to come.

Along a built-up railway embankment that encircled much of central Budapest, the defense stiffened. Across Varosliget Park in Pest, German panzers traded rounds with Soviet armor in one of the last open areas of inner Pest. Soviet and Romanian infantry slogged down several axes toward the center, the Soviets toward the Western Railway Station and the Romanians toward the Eastern Railway Station. The deeper they drove, the tougher the defense became and thereby the more savage the fighting. The Romanians in particular were badly bloodied. The Hungarian 10th Infantry Division supported by Zrinyis from General Bilnizer's battle group fanatically defended the Eastern Railway Station, in contrast to other episodes when Hungarian resistance against the Soviets was often inconsistent and half-hearted. The Romanians after three weeks were withdrawn from the siege line by an incensed Malinovsky. Not only had they riled the local population and stiffened Hungarian fighting resolve everywhere they were committed, they lost more than 11,000 of their 36,000-man force.[6]

While the fighting intensified in Pest, the Germans launched a vicious counteroffensive with forces stealthily redeployed from Poland. On New Year's Eve, Obergruppenführer Herbert Gille's elite SS IV Panzer Corps, comprising the dreaded SS 3d Panzer Division "Totenkopf" and the SS 5th Panzer Division "Viking," crashed into Tobulkhin's overextended Soviet Seventh Guards Army near Tata. Supported by the III Panzer Corps, consisting of the veteran 1st and 3d Panzer Divisions, the Germans during the following five days drove more than thirty-five miles in difficult terrain up to the key junction of Bicske, just twenty miles from Buda's western suburbs. By skillfully shifting reserves from the south and off the Budapest siege ring, the Soviets barely managed to parry this thrust.[7] Blocked, Gille then redeployed the Viking Division north of Budapest and over narrow forest roads. In miserable weather a slender offensive tendril led by the SS Westland Regiment was driven south to the hill town of Pilis-szentkereszt, from which Budapest's distinctive skyline could be seen by its Scandinavian grenadiers.[8] Forced to withdraw by mounting pressure, the persistent Gille then redeployed his blood-ied but still lethal SS panzer corps by rail; it reappeared with the III Panzer Corps in the more trafficable south near the junction of Szekesfehervar. Soviet radio intercepts failed to track the redeployment.

On January 18 Germans once again achieved tactical surprise; with four panzer divisions abreast, they shattered Tobulkhin's southern line and brought the Soviets their last operational crisis of the war.[9] The 3d Panzer Division, recalling the earlier heady days of blitzkrieg, managed in just three days to advance a hundred kilometers to the Danube, where its lead elements shot up surprised Soviet river traffic plying the broad river. Tobulkhin's Third Ukrainian Front was split, forcing the Soviets to consider the previously unimaginable: Pull back behind the Danube, thereby relinquishing their hold on Budapest. Stiffened, however, by Stalin's will, Tobulkhin decided to stand fast and battle it out, while reinforcements brought up from the south began to pound at the long southern flank that the Germans had exposed with their rapid advance. Faced with a rapidly declining correlation of forces, the German counteroffensive ended a mere fourteen miles from Budapest.

Throughout this drama the German-Hungarian garrison could hear the fighting and exchanged ghostly flares throughout the evening. Morale rose as the prospect of relief became real. The spearhead element, Kampfgruppe Phillipp of the 1st Panzer Division (attached to SS Totenkopf), received the message from the hard-bitten eastern front veteran Oberführer (Col.) Helmut Dorner, commanding the SS Police Regiment: "Warm wishes toward your success and our liberation, 10,000 of our wounded await you."[10] Therefore, Gen. Hermann von Balck's order to Army Group South to pull back its overextended forces was a crushing blow to both the relief force—the spearheads of which felt they could actually punch into the pocket—and the surrounded garrison, which had been forbidden by Hitler to attempt a breakout.

The failure of Budapest's relief seemingly did not diminish the will or capability of the garrison's defenders. Venerable Ju-52 transports and converted He-III bombers parachuted supplies as well as pulled heavily laden gliders flown by Hitler Youth and crash-landed onto a converted six-hundred-yard-long airfield (appropriately named the Vermezo, or "Bloody Meadow") under Castle Hill. Additionally, barges and small ships filled with ammunition attempted to navigate the Danube by night and in fog until heavy ice and increased Soviet awareness choked off this approach. Inside the city the garrison rapidly devoured the more than 32,000 horses, both local draft animals and the approximately 20,000 brought into the city by the two SS cavalry divisions, and foraged among the approximately 1 million inhabitants for added foodstuffs. By mid-January the typical ration of frozen horsemeat, fodder, and some flour was reduced to 250 grams. Most of the garrison by then suffered from "blood-guts," uncontrollable diarrhea, which made fighting outside in the freezing cold almost more preferable than sitting in the over-crowded, stinking dugouts, bunkers, and cellars. Although food was difficult to find, there was no shortage of alcohol, which helped to mitigate the effects of the frigid weather.

From early January until the siege's end, the Soviet and Axis forces were locked in a no-holds-barred urban meat grinder. Entire battalions were mangled while seizing single buildings. The streets were swept clear in daylight by machine guns emplaced in key corner buildings. Both sides resorted increasingly to moving troops and supplies among the densely packed buildings by blowing holes through their sides rather than braving the streets. Sharpened spades, grenades, and combat knives became more important than bayonets as many of the combatants hefted sub-machine guns instead of rifles. Throughout the grisly close-quarter fighting, hundreds of thousands of civilians cowered in their basements.

Though the Soviets employed hundreds of large-caliber guns, howitzers, and Katyusha multiple rocket launchers, it was the simpler infantry and crew-served weapons that the defenders respected most. Observed mortar fire was the deadliest of indirect fires, because it was high volume, responsive, and mostly un-

heard and could reach behind city blocks and land almost verti-
cally in dugouts, foxholes, and revetments. Its shrapnel effect,
bad enough on soil, was devastating on cobblestones or stone
buildings, because the light rounds shattered like glass with a
terrible splintering effect on the hard surfaces.

Whereas mortars wreaked the most havoc, snipers were the
most unnerving. Although both sides employed snipers effectively, it was the Soviets who proved more adept, having developed sniping to an art form by Budapest. Most Soviet snipers
were armed with the same efficient and deadly Moisin-Nagant
bolt-action rifle with scope that later killed many Americans in
Vietnam.

In Budapest, Soviet snipers, many born hunters from the Si-
berian taiga, seeped through the loose perimeters and sited
themselves behind German-Hungarian lines to pick off officers
and key personnel. Following such a sniper back through Soviet
lines was one measure the Germans used to infiltrate the lines
minutes before the breakout of February 11.[11] In open terrain,
such as wooded but leafless Varosmajor Park, snipers would brave
the cold to pin down entire units during daylight. One well-
placed shot managed to nail a Hungarian officer from at least
three hundred meters away through the eyepiece of his binoculars that he was using from a protected dugout.[12]

Soviet writer S. Smirnov best captures this "hunt" in his
1947 narrative *In the Struggle for Budapest*:

> Early one morning Afonyin found a good position in the
> fourth story of a house near the main battle line. He
> soon spotted a German officer who was moving care-
> fully down the side of a neighboring street. The officer
> glanced around and attempted to dart across the street.
> Afonyin sighted carefully and felled him with a round
> through the leg. The German collapsed in the middle of

the street. The Master Sniper did not kill the officer with his first shot. He waited. He guessed right. Soon a German soldier moved out from a nearby house to help the wounded officer. He barely reached the street when Afonyin shot him dead. The officer then tried to drag himself to safety however the Russian put another round into him. The officer stopped moving but lay still moaning. After several minutes another German soldier emerged to help him. Afonyin also shot him and then administered the officer a coup-de-grace shot, killing him.[13]

Though armies have made great strides in weapons technology since Budapest, the well-trained sniper will always remain an uncertain, morale-crushing, and deadly factor in the built-up urban arenas of present and future urban combat.

As in all city fighting, innovation played a major role in Budapest. One unit in particular, the Hungarian Vannay Battalion, was constituted just weeks before the siege from a mix of older World War I and World War II veterans pulled from Budapest's public utility and transportation departments. This assemblage of firemen, sewer workers, and utility men proved to be particularly adept at fighting within the large city's urban battlefield. Assisting them were Hungarian officer cadets and young volunteers who were attached to the older fighters in a field-expedient "buddy system" nicknamed Uncles and Pups. This unit held Buda's important Varosmajor Park front for seven weeks, repulsing several determined regimental-size assaults that included in the process the point-blank destruction of several Soviet T-34s.[14]

Vannay's grenadiers worked closely with civilians to ascertain the locations of Soviet soldiers within buildings. The grenadiers would often snake in under a building via the sewers or cellars and communicate with civilians sheltering underground by tapping through the walls. Armed with information as to the Soviets' whereabouts, they would then enter from both underground and the roofs, usually catching the occupying Soviets off guard. Several major apartment buildings were recaptured this way. One technique used in the stand-alone villas and houses of residential Buda was to withdraw from a contested building and leave substantial amounts of spirits behind. The grenadiers would wait a few hours until the early morning, then counterattack while the Soviets predictably were intoxicated and lethargic from the alcohol.[15]

Survival was initially tougher for the civilians living in Pest than in Buda. Pest was mostly industrial in its outskirts and commercial downtown. Much of its population consisted of workers and commercial employees living in apartment flats and small houses. Displaced early in the siege, and with limited foodstuffs, many had to rely on civil and military organizations for survival and assistance. Living in shelters, or overcrowded apartment blocks near Pest's center, thousands perished in the shelling and cross fire. Mercifully those who did not make the dangerous trip across the Danube bridges into Buda were "liberated" by the Soviets on January 18. Those in Buda, site of the garrison's "last stand," had to endure intense shelling, bombing, and house-to-house fighting for another three weeks.

From Csepel Island, Hungary's industrial heart, several thousand workers and families were brought to Castle Hill and permitted to take shelter in the vast, miles-long complex of limestone tunnels that interlaced the height. They joined close to 20,000 citizens and soldiers packed into the dank, fetid environment. Entire Buda neighborhoods occupied certain portions of the tunnels, which had been in use since the first Allied bombing raids in April 1944. The residents were so well organized that almost to the end the Hungarians managed a postal and telephone service in the tunnels that linked section to section. Throughout these medieval cellars and natural cavities that laced Castle

Hill were also numerous makeshift emergency hospitals with thousands of wounded. The stench, already difficult due to the packed humanity, was unbearable near these hospitals. By the end of the siege, more than 10,000 wounded filled the tunnels, many dying from suppurating wounds unable to heal in the pervasive heat and dampness. Children born in the tunnels almost invariably died due to the poor light, heavy air, and malnourishment. Though food was scarce, with civilians receiving even smaller rations than the starving garrison, water was plentiful due to an extensive system of natural and man-made cisterns and wells.[16]

It was difficult for the garrison to manage their allied civilians. Some, fearing looting and destruction, refused to tear themselves away from their homes and villas. Others strove to cling to some semblance of routine and normalcy. One SS 8th Cavalry Division officer, whose company was defending the important Farkasreti (Wolf's Meadow) Cemetery, was bemused to observe for several weeks an elegant, older Hungarian woman in full furs brazenly walking her dog in broad daylight among the combatants.[17] Others attempted to defend the sanctity of their homes and property. A Hungarian officer cadet related how he and his squad occupied an upper-story position in a strategically placed corner building overlooking Italian Avenue, planted their rapid-firing MG-42 on a grand piano, and tore up white bed linens for winter camouflage. A bizarre pillow fight ensued between the young soldiers during which the elderly landlady appeared, recognized the officer cadet, and shrieked that she was going to tell his grandfather about the squad's misbehavior. The young soldiers forcibly ushered her downstairs; minutes later the apartment was demolished by direct artillery fire after the squad opened fire on the Soviets below.[18]

The defenders also had to contend with managing the last substantial surviving Jewish population in Europe west of Spain. More than 120,000 Jews were in Budapest during the siege;

they were the survivors of Adolf Eichmann's horrific 500,000-person roundup for Auschwitz the summer before. More than 68,000 were compressed into an enclosed ghetto within the heart of inner Pest. Although the Germans were not particularly sympathetic to the plight of the Jews, they made conscious efforts to limit the worst depredations of the Hungarian Nazis, the Arrowcross. Several thousand Jews were nonetheless butchered by the Arrowcross, whose favorite technique was to shoot the hapless Jews into the frozen Danube from the Pest Embankment near the Chain Bridge. This was during the time when the valiant Swedish emissary Raoul Wallenberg saved countless thousands of Budapest's Jews by challenging the Germans and Hungarians at every turn and by providing legal and counterfeit safety passes to many of the beleaguered citizens. He disappeared at the siege's end, whisked away by the Soviets to a lonely death somewhere in Stalin's vast gulag.

By January 17 it became evident that the defense of Pest was futile. The Soviets had penetrated the inner ring road, entered the still-occupied Jewish ghetto, and were several hundred meters from splitting the defense near the Eastern Railway Station. Accordingly, Hitler finally authorized the abandonment of the eastern bridgehead over the Danube. That night and the following day, more than 30,000 defenders crossed the Chain and Elisabeth Bridges into Buda under constant artillery and air attack. Sturmovik ground attack aircraft roared low along the Danube raking the bridges while German and Hungarian antiaircraft firing from Buda's heights created terrible incidental damage to Pest's beautiful and historic waterfront. The evacuation, though bloody, was successful, except that several Hungarian units were left behind in the confusion and forced to surrender.

Though geographically the bulk of Budapest had been captured, the seizure of Buda provided the Soviets with an extremely thorny proposition. Augmented by the Pest garrison, the now primarily German defense was tightly concentrated into a one-by-three-kilometer box. Though there had been heavy fighting in Buda, Soviet efforts up to January 26 had been distracted by Gille's incessant relief attacks from the west and the main effort to clear Pest. The Germans still held all the inner hills and valleys. Notably the tenacious defense of Eagle Hill by the SS 8th Kampfgruppe Portugall and the Hungarian Berend Battle Group stymied the repeated Soviet attempts to seize this key position. Below the critical height another SS 8th Battle Group's macabre fight among the gravestones and mausoleums of Farkasreti Cemetery, and the tough resistance put up by the Vannay Battalion in Varosmajor Park, helped the defense coalesce in the west while crisis engulfed the eastern Pest garrison.[19]

In northern Buda tough back and forth fighting swirled across Rose Hill and lower Schwabian Hill. Here, young volunteer university students backed by SS 8th Cavalry Division troopers fought off several sharp probes by Soviet infantry attempting to seep down into the valley leading to Castle Hill. Self-propelled artillery supported one counterattack with direct high-explosive (HE) fire, blowing the defending Soviets out of the villas they had temporarily occupied.[20]

By early February the garrison was down to its last artillery rounds and, despite the brave air supply efforts, had little ammunition for its weapons. Fuel for its small armored reserve was carefully husbanded for any breakout, and by this juncture it was impossible to routinely employ tanks in hilly, obstacle-strewn Buda except in a static role. Many in the garrison now carried captured PPsH Soviet submachine guns, because as long as Soviets were slain or captured and positions retaken, small-arms ammunition would be abundantly available.

On February 6, after repeated assaults from three sides, Kampfgruppe Portugall was pried off Eagle Hill, which outflanked the stubborn defenders in Farkasreti Cemetery. Buda's defense quickly began to unravel. Shortly thereafter the Soviets captured the Southern Railway Station after three days of furious fighting and began to infiltrate into the Taban sector directly under the southern base of Castle Hill. This development threatened to cut off the defense force on Gellert Hill from the remainder of the garrison and made any breakout south from Castle Hill untenable. Simultaneously, the Soviets finally annihilated the Vannay Battalion in Varosmajor Park except for remnants who holed up for a final stand in the stout "Postal Palace" on Szell Kalman Square, directly west under Castle Hill.

On February 11, contrary to Hitler's directive to stand fast, Obergruppenführer Karl Pfeffer von Wildenbruch gave the order to break out. After hurried preparations that included the destruction of most remaining armor, approximately 30,000 German and Hungarian troops, including gendarmes, Arrowcross, and civilians, were assembled in the narrow streets that laced Castle Hill. At 8:00 P.M. a mixed SS 8th Cavalry Division and Hungarian assault group infiltrated along a preplanned breakout route northwest of the shrunken pocket. The alarm was raised as the assault group penetrated the main Soviet line. The Soviets, initially slow to react, began to fire star shells and rain heavy mortar and artillery fire on the main body, now exposed in bright light on the streets and boulevards under Castle Hill. It was a massacre. Though perhaps 10,000 actually broke away from Castle Hill, an estimated 5,000, including the commanders of the SS 8th and 22d Cavalry Divisions and the 13th Panzer Division, were killed during the initial breakout attempt. Never in World War II had so many division commanders of any army perished so quickly. The command group also failed to make it to safety. Pfeffer-Wildenbruch and his entire staff were caught the following morning holed up in a villa several miles from Castle Hill after successfully infiltrating under the Soviet front line in a large sewer main.[21]

More than 5,000 broke out into the wooded hills and began a desperate race to reach German positions near Zsambek, about twenty-five miles away, before the Soviet net could haul them in. In daylight German aircraft tried to airdrop supplies to the breakout groups as they emerged from the relative safety of the heavily wooded hills onto open terrain. Soviet combat groups converged on the many small bands trudging west in the heavy snow; most perished in little firefights along the breakout route. Many others, short of ammunition and physically exhausted, abjectly surrendered to their pursuers. Hundreds, especially Waffen SS, were executed on the spot. By February 18 the last survivor reached German lines. Of more than 30,000 in the breakout groups, only 785 survived—an absolute catastrophe.[22]

By morning the Soviets were mopping up the Castle Hill area despite a die-hard platoon-size defense in the rubble of the Defense Ministry composed of fanatical young students of the University Battalion. They routed out the tens of thousands of civilians and Axis wounded in the tunnels and labyrinths of Castle Hill. Hundreds suffocated to death, especially those in underground field hospitals, when Soviet troops set fire to portions of the labyrinth. Many civilians were raped in the aftermath.

The fifty-one-day siege of Budapest and the battles that raged around the city delayed the Soviet drive on Vienna and the southern Reich for four months, from November to February. The sustained fight to capture the huge metropolitan area exacted a gruesome toll on the Soviets; more than 100,000 were killed or wounded while all but 785 of the garrison were killed or captured.[23]

Lessons learned were numerous, especially the challenges of assaulting or defending in the midst of a huge civil population. Heavy artillery, although effective, brought terrible incidental damage to structures and people; mortars were more effective. Armor was useful primarily in a support role; both sides learned this costly lesson earlier in the war. Rarely were armor and artillery employed unsupported by infantry. Snipers ruled the streets in the daytime, which forced much of the action underground, inside and between buildings, and at night. In short, combined-arms tactics prevailed when they were synchronized.

An active defense was essential to identify enemy concentrations and mask weaknesses; both sides actively patrolled at night. Command and control was extremely difficult; regimental-size and higher assaults rapidly diffused into numerous individual platoon and squad actions within Budapest's complicated maze of streets, buildings, and alleys. These lessons are similar today. The only significant difference is the ability to turn night into day with today's new generation of night vision devices and improved communications with lightweight tactical radios.

Epilogue: MOUT Déjà Vu:
The 1956 Hungarian Revolution

A scant eleven years after the 1945 siege battle for Budapest, the free world was riveted by another urban battle in Budapest. On October 23, 1956, several thousand Hungarians, mostly students and members of the patriotic Petofi Circle, rallied below the Josef Bem statue in Buda and marched across the rebuilt Margaret Bridge to Budapest's Radio Building. Fighting soon broke out between the crowd and the AVH, Hungary's reviled Stalinist political police. That evening large crowds moved on to a giant bronze monument of Stalin off of Varosliget Park (Millennium Square). They savagely tore down the monument, leaving the despot's man-size boots remaining, and shortly were engaged in running gunfights across the city with the AVH.

The Soviet army was promptly called in from their camps in the countryside to restore order. Already garrisoned in Hungary, some of these soldiers became sympathetic to the rebel cause, which had grown to include most of Budapest's population and much of the countryside. Tempers flared, however; shots were exchanged and soon the Soviets were deeply enmeshed in a vicious urban battle with Budapest civilians representing all social strata. Seemingly ignorant of the bitter lessons learned in Budapest city fighting just a decade prior, several Soviet armored columns arrogantly entered Budapest along major boulevards with minimal infantry support. All were stopped or fragmented before reaching the city center. One column, on Pest's Ulloi Boulevard opposite the Corvin Theater and Killian Barracks, was virtually annihilated in a well-laid ambush. More than twenty armored vehicles, including a number of modern T-54 tanks and huge Su-152 assault guns, were immolated under a hail of fiery gasoline-stuffed Palinka and Unicum bottles, and direct fire from antitank weapons captured from a Soviet assault minutes prior.

The fighting became indiscriminate and brutal. Soviets fired tank rounds and rained artillery on anything that moved. Losses on both sides mounted rapidly. Hungarian army units, trained by the Soviets, either remained in their barracks or joined the rebels; sturdy workers, supposed poster children for the Communist Party proletariat, joined the rebels en masse. After four days of confused fighting, the Soviets withdrew on October 29, leaving an ecstatic city to the revolutionaries.

After an ephemeral six-day respite, during which Budapest's citizens began to dare believe that the Stalinist yoke had truly been lifted, the Soviets returned with a vengeance on November 4, reinforced by significant forces from outside Hungary. In textbook fashion the Red Army systematically reduced the stubborn resistance, using direct fire and artillery without regard for civilian casualties. Within a week the revolution was brutally snuffed out and the city retaken. Losses were heavy for both sides; the Soviets suffered more than 3,500 casualties, with several hundred armored vehicles knocked out. More than 20,000

Hungarians were killed or wounded, many of them civilians caught in the cross fire. Several hundred were later executed by the regime after order was restored.[24]

There were many interesting parallels between the revolution and the 1944–45 siege. Some of the Hungarians who fought in the revolution were young soldiers from the 10th and 12th Infantry Divisions, the University Storm Battalion, and other ad hoc units that had experience fighting Soviets in urban combat from the urban siege. The core of the resistance was made up of young students, reinforced by older workers from Budapest's industrial suburbs and Csepel Island, teamed with current and former soldiers who loathed Stalinism. Ideology played little part here; a number of fighters were formerly ardent World War II communists, particularly those who served in the 2,500-strong Buda Volunteer Regiment, which assisted the Soviets in the final 1945 reduction of Buda.[25] The defense minister for President Imre Nagy's Hungarian revolutionary government, Col. Pal Maleter, was a Hungarian army lieutenant during World War II who became in 1944 an anti-German partisan in Transylvania. During the siege, he led the epic rebel defense of the massively built Killian Barracks, which was reduced by direct-fire artillery and an infantry assault on the main gate. Never disavowing his belief in socialism, Maleter nonetheless became a key revolutionary figure in the drama. Betrayed during truce negotiations, he was summarily executed after the siege.

The Soviets in turn probably had a number of senior NCOs and officers who fought in the 1945 siege and returned again in 1956, mostly in the second wave. Again urban lessons painfully learned from World War II were poorly applied or outright forgotten, just as during the initial phase of the 1995 Russian debacle in Grozny. Brute firepower ruled the day.

And unfortunate Budapest, partially rebuilt after the 1945 devastation, was once again wrecked, especially along the key access points and arteries leading to the center. Damage was particularly extensive around Moscow Square (Szell Kalman Square), the Eastern Railway Station (Keleti), Ulloi Boulevard, and the Radio Building (near the Astoria Hotel and National Museum). Parts of Csepel Island were also heavily damaged, because its factories and workshops were the sites of the freedom fighters' final resistance.

In retrospect, the greatest casualty of this brief but savage city fight was the image of the Soviet Union and the Warsaw Pact as a monolithic, unified entity. The fierce, well-publicized Hungarian resistance, and the heavy-handed manner in which it was suppressed, forever exposed Soviet-inspired communism for the lie it was and presaged a thirty-three-year-long ideological erosion that contributed directly to the Warsaw Pact's demise in 1989. It also revealed what a motivated, albeit ill-trained, force of civilians and military can do in an urban MOUT environment against the best-equipped conventional forces available, which the Soviets were in 1956. This is the most important lesson learned when considering MOUT today, which will in the not too distant future assuredly embroil U.S. forces despite our greatest efforts to the contrary. We had better be ready, or the butcher's bill will be high.

ENDNOTES
    1.   Delia Meth-Cohn, "Flow East" in *Budapest Art and History* (Florence: 1992), 18.
    2.   Map from Peter Zwack, "The Siege of Budapest," *Military History Quarterly,* Vol. XI, No. 2 (Winter 1999), 21.
    3.   Colonel David Glantz, ed., *Soviet Military Deception in the Second World War* (London: Frank Cass & Co. Ltd, 1989), 179.
    4.   Laszlo Hingyi (Hungarian military historian), interviews, 1993–94.
    5.   Peter Gosztony, *Der Kampf um Budapest* (Munich: Ungariches Institut, 1963). Interviews with Dr. Istvan Ravasz and Dr. Hingyi, both Hungarian historians.

6.   Mark Axworthy, *Third Axis, Fourth Ally* (London: Arms and Armour Press, 1995), 209–10.

7.   Colonel David Glantz, ed. *Art of War Symposium, 1986: From the Vistula to the Oder* (Carlisle Barracks, PA: Center for Land Warfare, Army War College), 670.

8.   Peter Gosztony, *Endkampf An Der Donau* (Wien: Verlag Fritz Molden, 1969), 127.

9.   *Art of War Symposium,* 1986, 670–74.

10.   Erich Kern, *Die Letzte Schlacht* (Oldendorf: Verlag K. W. Schutz KG Preuss, 1972), 183–84.

11.   Hingyi interview.

12.   Ervin Galantay, Hungarian Vannay Battalion veteran and historian, eyewitness account, 1993.

13.   S. Smirnov, *V Boax za Budapest* (In the Battle for Budapest) (Moscow: Armed Forces Military Publishers, 1947), 112.

14.   Galantay interview.

15.   Ibid.

16.   Mrs. Laszlo Hingyi interview, 1993. Lived in tunnels during siege.

17.   Hauptsturmführer Joachim Boosfeld (squadron commander, SS 8th KD), interview, 1994.

18.   Galantay.

19.   Hauptsturmführer Kurt Portugall (commander, SS 8th KD 88mm Flak Battery), *Memoirs,* 1993.

20.   Erich Klein (commander, Feldherrnhalle Division, 150mm SP "Hummel" Battalion), interview, 1993.

21.   Personal interviews with historians Dr. Istvan Ravasz, Dr. Ervin Galantay, Christian Unvary, and Laszlo Hingyi as well as numerous German veterans, including Knight's Cross winner Joachim Boosfeld. Information on breakout both sketchy and contradictory. Very little about it is cited in Soviet sources.

22.   Gosztony, *Endkampf am Der Donau,* 155.

23.   Conflicting numbers of casualties. Range fluctuates for Soviets between 70,000 and more than 150,000. "Over 100,000" is a good average estimate based on numerous sources and interviews.

24.   Peter Fryer, "Hungarian Tragedy" in *Eyewitness in Hungary,* ed. Bill Lomax (Nottingham, England: Spokesman Press, 1980), 14.

25.   Gosztony, 151.

SEVEN

Aschaffenburg, 1945:
Cassino on the Main River
by Mark J. Reardon

*Hand grenades and bayonets were used as the principal
weapons in house to house fighting.*
—45th Infantry Division history

In the final weeks of World War II, American soldiers in the European theater of operations found themselves thrust into urban combat with regular frequency. Intense fighting often ignited at a crossroad village, rural town, or strategically positioned city even though organized resistance within Germany was gradually decreasing. In many cases, urban combat flared up when advancing Allied columns encountered retreating German troops. In other instances, these clashes were the result of Hitler's attempts to trap Allied forces in an urban area. The battle of Aschaffenburg in March–April 1945 provides an example of the consequences of Hitler's decision to defend "fortress cities" to the last man. The intense fighting earned that city the nickname of "Cassino on the Main River," alluding to the battle for the town and Abbey of Monte Cassino that took place in Italy during 1943–44.

An examination of this battle illustrates how a nation's political leadership deliberately used a city in an attempt to trap an attacking force. Having seized nearby bridges over the Main River, the Americans were unwilling to permit the German garrison of

Aschaffenburg to remain in a position to threaten these crossing sites. The U.S. Seventh Army decided to eliminate the German force rather than bypass the city. This decision was precisely what the Germans had hoped for. They wanted to provoke the Americans into assaulting Aschaffenburg in order to tie up large numbers of U.S. troops and inflict significant losses on the attackers. However, when confronted by a well-equipped American force employing proven doctrine and combined-arms tactics, the Germans were unable to successfully use the perceived close-combat advantages of urban terrain to achieve their aims.

The Germans failed because they relied solely on urban terrain to negate the synergy of the U.S. combined-arms team. The city's complex topography, however, did not have a decisive influence on the battle. By employing tanks and infantry in close cooperation, the Americans achieved an overwhelming victory despite an unfavorable 1:1 ratio of attacker versus defender. The U.S. infantry consistently shielded their supporting armor against German short-range antitank systems. In turn, the American tanks effectively suppressed the defenders at decisive points on the battlefield, allowing the U.S. infantry to close with and destroy the enemy.

Although supporting air and artillery fires proved to be effective when harassing, isolating, and interdicting the German garrison, they were not the decisive factor in this battle. More prisoners were captured by U.S. infantry prior to the city's capitulation than fell into American hands after Aschaffenburg surrendered. The American combined-arms approach had proved more than a match for unsupported German infantry hoping to gain a decisive tactical advantage by fighting in urban terrain.

The bridges over the Main River acted as a magnet to draw the advancing Americans toward Aschaffenburg. Although U.S. doctrine called for cities to be avoided whenever possible, the attackers would find it difficult to bypass Aschaffenburg due to the hilly terrain and numerous villages surrounding it. Additionally, the major road networks leading east into the heart of Germany ran through the center of the city. From a purely military standpoint, Aschaffenburg had to be seized to protect the bridges over the Main from a German counterattack.

Any attacking force looking at the geography of the Aschaffenburg area would not see a reassuring picture. To the north of the city were the villages of Damm, Glattbach, and Goldbach, as well as the Aschaffenburg rail yards. To the southwest, a steeply wooded ridge ran from the outskirts of the city to the suburb of Schweinheim. The towns of Haibach, Grunmorsbach, and Gailbach straddled the southeastern and eastern avenues of approach. The Germans devised a plan that combined the advantages offered by a positional defense of the city and surrounding area with their own strongly held perception that American foot soldiers were unwilling or unable to attack without overwhelming support from tanks and artillery.

The Germans truly believed that their own infantry was better trained and more aggressive than their American counterparts. The defenders intended to use urban and natural terrain to separate the attacking infantry from their supporting tanks, artillery, and airpower, thus permitting the German infantry to fight the Americans on favorable terms. The defenders counted on the urban terrain to allow them to take advantage of their perceived "man versus man" superiority in infantry combat.

The City

Aschaffenburg lay forty kilometers northeast of Frankfurt and astride a major highway leading toward Wurzburg and Nuremberg. The Main River to the west and the Spessart Mountains to the north and east border the town. Within the city, dominant features include Schloss (Castle) Johannesburg; the Stiftskirche,

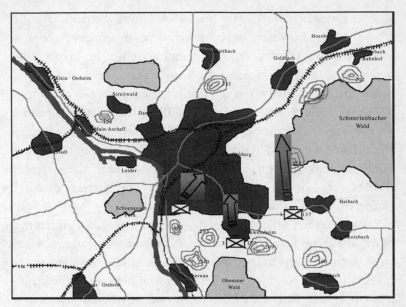

Aschaffenburg, 1 April 1945

a large tenth-century Roman Catholic Church; and five military barracks. Although not intended to serve primarily as fortifications, the barracks boasted heavy masonry walls and strategically placed firing slits.[1]

Because the city had physically expanded in response to various economic and social factors rather than to a central urban plan, its physical makeup featured a large variety of older buildings, modern residential housing, warehouses, parks, rail lines, and industrial facilities. The densely packed city center, with its imposing castle and church, winding alleys, and numerous businesses, would prove significant obstacles to any attacker.

Hitler was convinced that urban areas offered a significant advantage to the defender at the operational level of war. His beliefs were borne out by German experiences on the eastern front, where improvised "fortress cities" had successfully held out against overwhelming Soviet forces for lengthy periods of time. These tactics, however, were often borne of necessity, because nonmotorized German troops sought refuge in urban areas when surrounded by rapidly advancing Soviet armor and mechanized forces. Unable to avoid encirclement, the Germans took up all-round defensive positions within an urban area to protect themselves against the Soviet tanks. If the Soviets chose to attack the urban area, the defenders would be able to use their short-range antitank weapons to good effect. Although the attacking Soviets were normally able to overcome these "fortress cities," it often cost them considerable time and casualties.

The German officer charged with the defense of Aschaffen-burg, Maj. Emil Lamberth, did not fit the stereotype of a "fortress city" commandant. Bespectacled and grayish, he was credited by his American opponents with being "a firm believer in the principles of Nazism and one of the most noteworthy adversaries . . . ever encountered."[2] As the commander of the 9th Engineer Replacement Battalion, Lamberth had exhibited remarkable professional abilities in the past. His demonstrated loyalty to the Nazi cause, even in the last days of the Third Reich, coupled with his military credentials earned him a direct appointment from Hitler as the commandant of Aschaffenburg in February 1945.

Major Lamberth hoped to gain a tactical advantage over the Americans by employing a modified version of the urban defense developed in Russia. However, he sought to maximize his own slender resources at the onset by employing a linear, vice perimeter, defense. Lamberth hoped to accomplish this by integrating his garrison with the conventional units defending along the Main River. In this manner, Lamberth would not be forced to spread his units along Aschaffenburg's entire perimeter.

The defensive plan initially employed a line of pillboxes along the Main River that overlooked the most likely American avenues of approach. Once this line of pillboxes was penetrated,

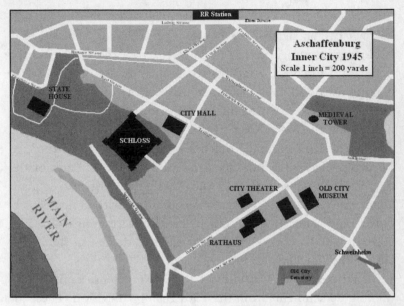

Aschaffenburg inner city

the defenders would concentrate their efforts on defending the villages just beyond the city limits. When Aschaffenburg's outer defenses were overcome, Lamberth intended to transition to a perimeter defense by pulling his troops back into an inner bastion centered on the five *kaserne*s (military posts). If the *kaserne*s fell, the surviving defenders would infiltrate through the rubble to occupy positions around Schloss Johannesburg.

In early March 1945, SS inspectors were sent to Aschaffenburg to check on the preparations being made for the city's defense. Fortunately for Lamberth, his ongoing efforts met with their approval.[3] The SS, however, did not depart upon completion of their inspection. Several officers remained to monitor Lamberth's political loyalty as the advancing Americans approached Aschaffenburg. On Lamberth's orders, most of the 30,000 civilians in Aschaffenburg were evacuated in mid-March 1945.

Armee Gruppe G also hoped to utilize Aschaffenburg within its own overall defensive scheme. The Germans believed they could defeat any American attempt to cross the Main River if they could force the attackers to accept combat under adverse conditions. As soon as the Americans began a deliberate assault on the city, two German infantry divisions would occupy positions along the Main River to the south of Aschaffenburg while another division occupied defensive positions north of the city. By deploying strong infantry formations to either flank of the city, the Germans hoped to turn Aschaffenburg into a giant "tank trap" that would negate Allied superiority in armor, airpower, and artillery. If the city's defenses were eventually overcome, it would occur only after a prolonged defense at significant cost to the attackers.

The manpower available for the city's defense consisted of training detachments from the 15th Infantry Division. These included the 106th Replacement Battalion, the 9th Engineer Replacement Battalion, and the 10th NCO Training Battery, Light Artillery Regiment. The instructors and staff of the Reserve Officers Training School, as well as recovering wounded assigned to the 483d Convalescent Company, were also drafted into taking an active part in the defense. In addition to the regular troops, the commander of Aschaffenburg, Major Lamberth, also integrated the 15th Volkssturm Infantry Division, 1st Battalion, composed of local civilians armed with rifles and panzerfaust antitank rockets, into his forces.[4]

Despite the key role envisioned by Hitler for Aschaffenburg, the city's 3,200 defenders did not possess sufficient weapons, equipment, or ammunition to carry out his plan. Major Lamberth could rely only on some fire support provided by the city's fixed and mobile flak defenses, as well as the mortars and light howitzers organic to artillery training units. There were also several refurbished panzers in a tank repair facility within Aschaffenburg that could be used for the defense. Lamberth's direct chain of command to Hitler served primarily only as a means to monitor the political steadfastness of the garrison, not to provide the defenders with significant aid, either in the form of materiel or reinforcements, from outside the city.

The Assault on Aschaffenburg

The Americans followed their urban combat doctrine when they launched their initial assault on Aschaffenburg. The U.S. Third Army had ordered the 4th Armored Division to conduct a hasty attack on the city in hopes of capturing an undamaged bridge over the Main River. Although armored units were normally discouraged from conducting combat operations in urban areas, U.S. Army field manuals stated that tanks could be employed en masse against an urban area if it was weakly defended. Prisoner of war interrogations and aerial reconnaissance did not provide the 4th Armored Division with any indication that the Germans would fight for the city. On the contrary, the Americans had been advancing farther into Germany against scattered resistance for the past two weeks.

When the interarmy boundaries were changed on March 27, the U.S. Seventh Army took responsibility for the Aschaffenburg sector. Because the 4th Armored Division had encountered strong resistance when it tried to secure the city, the Seventh Army followed approved standard doctrine by employing infantry-heavy forces supported by tanks to capture Aschaffenburg.

The Seventh Army dispatched XV Corps to Aschaffenburg. In turn, XV Corps tasked the 45th Infantry Division to relieve Combat Command B's 4th Armored Division and expand the bridgehead across the Main River. The army commander could not afford to permit the Germans to retain Aschaffenburg. Not only did the city lie almost astride the interarmy boundary, he was concerned that the urban area would provide the Germans with a base of operations to attack XV Corps elements crossing the Main River south of Aschaffenburg.

Knowing that his mission was to capture the city, the commanding general of the 45th Infantry Division planned to secure the dominant terrain surrounding Aschaffenburg with two regiments while seizing a foothold in the outlying suburbs with a third infantry regiment. When the city was completely isolated from outside aid, the Americans would continue to enlarge their foothold until they had penetrated the enemy's main defensive line. As soon as the city's defenses had been pierced, the attackers would methodically mop up the defenders until the remaining Germans chose to surrender or were wiped out.

The attacking force in the initial phase of the battle consisted of CCB, 4th Armored Division. Major subordinate units belonging to CCB included the 10th Armored Infantry Battalion, the 37th Tank Battalion, and the 3/104th Infantry Regiment, which was temporarily attached from the 26th Infantry Division. Combat Command B was also supported by an armored cavalry troop, a tank destroyer company, and an armored field artillery battalion.

As the battle progressed, the 157th Infantry Regiment of the 45th Infantry Division took over the fight from CCB. The 157th Infantry Regiment, commanded by Col. Walter P. O'Brien, was task organized as a regimental combat team (RCT) comprising three infantry battalions, the 158th Field Artillery Battalion, C/2d Chemical Mortar Battalion, B/645th Tank Destroyer Battalion, A/191st Tank Battalion, and an engineer company.

Although only a single RCT was committed to the fight for Aschaffenburg, the 45th Infantry Division did provide it with ample fire support. Although the 157th Infantry Regiment could normally call upon its own direct support (DS) field artillery battalion as well as C Company of the 2d Chemical Mortar Battalion (4.2-inch mortars), division also allocated to Colonel O'Brien's regiment a battalion of 155mm howitzers and 240mm howitzers, as well as a battery of 8-inch guns from XV Corps artillery. In addition to the corps artillery, during the initial phase of the attack the 45th Infantry Division had arranged for fire support to be provided by two 105mm howitzer battalions belonging to the neighboring 44th Infantry Division.[5]

The opening shots of the battle for Aschaffenburg were fired on March 26 when CCB, 4th Armored Division, attempted to seize several of the local bridges spanning the Main River. A hasty attack by the Americans on the road bridge at Obernau, a suburb southwest of Aschaffenburg, ended in failure when the Germans destroyed the lead tank as it crossed the span. As the American armored force paused briefly in the face of this setback, the intelligence and reconnaissance (I&R) platoon of the 10th Armored Infantry Battalion (AIB) radioed news of an undefended railroad bridge three kilometers to the south of the road bridge. The I&R platoon swarmed over the railroad bridge, cutting visible demolition wires and throwing demolition charges into the river. By noon, three companies of the 10th AIB had crossed the bridge, accompanied by M4 medium tanks of the 37th Tank Battalion.

The Americans quickly expanded their bridgehead to eight square kilometers as additional elements of CCB crossed over to the east bank of the Main River. Despite their success at increasing their holdings on the east bank, CCB was unsuccessful in its initial attempts to secure the nearby town of Schweinheim. After losing a pair of Shermans to handheld antitank weapons, the American tankers pulled back for the night.

On March 27, the Americans renewed their efforts to establish a lodgment in Aschaffenburg's outlying suburbs. Combat

Command B had hoped to create a corridor south of the city allowing it to bypass Aschaffenburg. Later that afternoon, however, CCB received a change in mission delivered personally by one of Lieutenant General Patton's aides. The Third Army representative carried instructions for CCB to send a raiding force behind German lines to free some U.S. prisoners held in Hammelburg. Patton's son-in-law, Lt. Col. John K. Waters, was among the POWs held at that camp. In turn, CCB instructed the 10th AIB to send a tank-infantry force under Capt. Abraham Baum to free the prisoners.

Captain Baum's task force began its journey to Hammelburg by roughly shouldering its way past the German defenders of Schweinheim. Once he learned that the Americans successfully penetrated Aschaffenburg's outer defensive ring, Major Lamberth sent more troops to Schweinheim in an effort to prevent CCB from exploiting Baum's success. Lamberth did not suspect that the Americans had no intention of continuing the fight for Schweinheim. The 4th Armored Division was ordered to shift to the north to conform to the newly revised boundary between the U.S. Third Army and Seventh Army. The XV Corps of the Seventh Army now had responsibility for attacking Aschaffenburg.

When informed of his new mission to secure Aschaffenburg, Maj. Gen. Robert Frederick assigned the task to the 157th Infantry Regiment. Frederick informed Colonel O'Brien that his regiment's first priority was to relieve the units that CCB left behind to secure the bridgehead until the 45th Infantry Division arrived.[6] Once the relief in place was completed, he explained, the attack on Aschaffenburg would begin. O'Brien's troops had complete priority crossing the railroad bridge until the next morning, March 29. At that time the remaining regiments of the 45th Infantry Division would begin crossing the Main River before advancing to the south to link up with the 3d Infantry Division.

Colonel O'Brien's tactical plan called for Maj. Gus M. Heilman's 2d Battalion to launch a frontal assault while Lt. Col. Felix L. Sparks's 3d Battalion moved through Schweinheim to outflank Aschaffenburg from the east. Lieutenant Colonel Ralph M. Krieger's 1st Battalion would remain in reserve until needed. The 3d Battalion would be supported by two platoons of medium tanks and M-36 tank destroyers (TDs), and Major Heilman's troops were assisted by a platoon each of medium tanks and TDs. Equipped with M5 and M24 light tanks, Company D, 191st Tank Battalion, would also become available to support the assault once it arrived.

At ten on the morning of March 28, the lead elements of the 157th Infantry, consisting of Companies I and L of the 3d Battalion, arrived at Gross Ostheim, a small village located southwest of the recently captured railroad bridge. With the exception of a few men who had ridden borrowed half-tracks, both companies endured a two-hour road march perched atop tanks and tank destroyers. Lieutenant Colonel Sparks quickly ordered both companies to cross over the railroad bridge to the east bank of the Main River.

As soon as the 45th Infantry Division troops appeared, troops belonging to CCB began withdrawing from the bridgehead. Lieutenant Colonel Sparks's remaining rifle company, Company K, 157th Infantry, arrived as the relief in place was being completed. By 6:30 P.M., the 3/157th Infantry completed crossing over the Main River. The Americans concentrated on preparing for the assault against Schweinheim the following morning while dodging an occasional mortar barrage.

The commander of the cavalry troop supporting CCB stopped by to update Sparks on the situation; German civilians had informed him that there were several thousand German troops defending the Schweinheim-Aschaffenburg complex. Sparks immediately sensed that his troops would be in for a rough time when they attacked the city.

The 2/157th Infantry also began crossing to the east bank of the Main River at 1:23 P.M. Once the entire 2d Battalion made it safely across the railroad bridge, Major Heilman sent F Company to sweep the riverbank running from the bridge to the western outskirts of Aschaffenburg. F Company's right flank was protected by E/157th Infantry as it moved along the river, while G Company followed in reserve. Augmented by the M5 light tanks of D/191st Tank Battalion, the 2/157th Infantry continued on, entering the outskirts of Aschaffenburg at dusk. However, the Americans did not remain there for long. Colonel O'Brien instructed Heilman to pull back to avoid being hit accidentally by air and artillery strikes scheduled to support the regiment's attack the next morning.[7]

Lieutenant Colonel Krieger's 1/157th Infantry crossed the river to take up positions between the 2d and 3d Battalions. At 7:20 P.M., Colonel O'Brien told Krieger to remain in his present location until the 3/157th Infantry captured Schweinheim. Once the town was secure, the 1st Battalion would seize the high ground to the northwest. Although the 1/157th Infantry was echeloned slightly to the rear, it drew the heaviest share of indirect fire that evening. Several mortar barrages fell on B and C Companies, wounding a total of fourteen men.[8] The Americans replied by shelling the suspected location of German artillery batteries throughout the night of March 28–29.

Following a preparatory barrage, the 157th Infantry Regiment launched its assault on Schweinheim at 6:20 A.M. Moving along a valley with L Company on the right and on the left, the 3d Battalion's advance provoked a storm of mortar fire from the Germans. The Americans continued advancing another four hundred yards when they were pinned down by intense machine-gun fire.[9] Assistance provided by the 1/157th Infantry temporarily silenced the opposing heavy weapons.

After reorganizing his battalion, Lieutenant Colonel Sparks

once again led them against Schweinheim. By 9:30 A.M., the 3d Platoon of I Company occupied several houses on the outskirts. Soon after entering the town, Company I encountered civilians taking an active role in the defense. This was to be the only instance of German civilians fighting alongside Lamberth's garrison. Once the battle began, most of the remaining local populace remained inactive and hid in their basements or in a nearby quarry.

Once the 3d Battalion entered the town, the supporting American armor outside of the town drew the attention of the German artillery. Shells rained down on the TDs and Sherman tanks, causing them to shift positions to avoid being destroyed. One M-36 from B/654th TD Battalion mired itself after throwing a track while trying to evade incoming artillery. The 3d Platoon leader of A/191st Tank Battalion was killed when a direct hit blew off the turret of his Sherman.[10] With the platoon demoralized by the loss of their lieutenant, the tank company was forced to temporarily pull them out of the fight.[11]

Frustrated at the lack of progress in Schweinheim, Colonel O'Brien committed a company from the 1/157th Infantry to reinforce Lieutenant Colonel Sparks. At 10:18 A.M., the 1st Battalion's commander personally led C/157th Infantry against Schweinheim. As it approached the town, C Company came under increasingly heavy fire from mortars, machine guns, and snipers. Pinned down by the incoming fire, C Company was unable to enter the fight for Schweinheim.[12]

After shelling the town for several hours, the 3/157th Infantry renewed its advance at 2:30 P.M. This time the 3d Battalion met with success, reaching the center of Schweinheim before it halted. Lieutenant Colonel Sparks decided to outflank the defenders by sending K/157th Infantry to work around the eastern side of town. K Company was reinforced with a platoon of the new M24 light tanks from D/191st Tank Battalion.[13] At the same time, C/157th Infantry entered the northwestern portion of Schweinheim.

As the Americans tried to outflank the town, the defenders sent tank-killing parties to knock out the Shermans that were shooting up German strongpoints inside Schweinheim. Two panzerfaust teams were decimated by machine-gun fire before a third team managed to hit one of the Shermans, setting it on fire.[14] Moments after scoring this success, soldiers from I/157th Infantry killed the panzerfaust team that had knocked out the American tank.

By late afternoon, the 3d Battalion's assault had finally ground to a halt. Company I was spread thinly amongst eighteen houses. With the U.S. infantry spread out across the town, the Germans quickly discovered that it was not difficult to infiltrate troops back into the houses lost earlier. During the course of the day, the 3d Battalion suffered three men killed and fifty-six wounded, including one officer in L/157th Infantry and two officers from I Company. Sniper fire hampered the evacuation of the wounded, prompting Lieutenant Colonel Sparks to order a smoke screen laid by the 4.2-inch mortars of C Company, 2d Chemical Battalion, to conceal the movement of stretcher bearers entering and exiting Schweinheim. During this intense engagement, at least eighty to a hundred Germans were killed or wounded and six others taken prisoner.[15]

Both Aschaffenburg and Schweinheim took a tremendous pounding from American artillery on March 29. Field artillery units supporting the 157th Infantry during the twenty-four-hour period ending at midnight expended approximately 5,000 rounds.[16] The American shelling was intended to continually impede the movement of German units, destroy communications nets, and demoralize the defenders. The intense shelling of Aschaffenburg by U.S. guns would continue for the remainder of the battle. Direct-fire weapons, such as tanks, TDs, and self-propelled howitzers, which possess greater accuracy than artillery or mortars, were employed by the attackers against frontline German positions.

The tough resistance did not deter the Americans from planning to renew their assault the following morning at 7:30.[17] Colonel O'Brien believed that Schweinheim constituted the key position in Aschaffenburg's outer defensive ring. Accordingly, he planned to concentrate his maneuver forces against the town in an effort to bring about the defeat of the Germans by overwhelming their strongest position. As soon as Schweinheim was secured, the 1st Battalion would widen the hole blasted in the German defenses. The 2d Battalion would also aid the 1/157th Infantry by sending a company to seize the high ground northwest of Schweinheim.

Before the 157th Infantry could jump off on March 30, the 36th Volksgrenadier Division launched a spoiling attack against the Americans.[18] The German assault, however, did not unfold exactly as planned. The 165th Grenadier Regiment started the battle by stumbling into K/157th Infantry at 12:40 A.M. The attackers fared poorly after their commander was shot in the opening stages of the fighting. The K Company command group killed several Germans who were trying to emplace a machine gun near their position. Confusion reigned as both sides shot at each other's muzzle flashes in the dark.

Several hours later, a second German company began filtering into a wooded area beyond the perimeter of L/157th Infantry. The Americans brought 81mm mortar fire on the unsuspecting Germans, killing and wounding a number of their assailants.[19] As this was taking place, a German patrol made its way behind the L Company command post, and more Germans appeared on both flanks of L Company. Virtually surrounded, L Company drew the mortar barrage in a tight ring around its entire perimeter. Unable to stand the punishment, the Germans retreated out of range.

At 3:05 A.M., K/157th Infantry experienced another counterattack, considerably better organized than the first German assault. The 158th Field Artillery Battalion broke up this assault with a barrage of high explosives. Following a two-hour firefight, the attackers drifted sullenly away into the darkness. The attacks launched by the 36th Volksgrenadier Division failed to overwhelm the American bridgehead. In fact, the Germans had not accomplished anything other than delaying the 3/157th Infantry's scheduled jump-off time by forty-five minutes.

After one in the morning on March 30, the 3d Battalion's 81mm mortar platoon began firing in support of yet another attack against Schweinheim. The Germans responded with a heavy barrage that sent the soldiers of L/157th Infantry diving for their foxholes. Disregarding the incoming fire, I/157th Infantry began pushing east through the ruined town. When the German artillery finally subsided, L Company also started moving forward, only to quickly run into a roadblock. To reduce the enemy position, M-36 tank destroyers were brought forward, which allowed L/157th Infantry to begin advancing once more.

The Germans launched a daylight counterattack against the 3/157th Infantry at 1:10 P.M. with the 165th Grenadier Regiment. The force, numbering approximately 260 men, slammed into the right flank of K and L Companies. K Company soon got the upper hand in a firefight, forcing the Germans to retreat. Part of the German force went to the northeast, where it encountered the American 179th Infantry. The other half of the withdrawing German force passed directly in front of L Company as it headed for safety. Presented with an unbelievably lucrative target, the GIs opened fire with machine guns, mortars, and artillery. Pelted with bullets, the Germans quickly scattered in all directions. L Company captured thirty prisoners, in addition to the killed and wounded suffered by the enemy force.[20]

The defeat of this German counterattack signaled a significant reduction in the resistance encountered by the 3d Battalion in Schweinheim. The Americans continued moving forward steadily until they secured both the southern and eastern portions of the town. By 4:15 P.M., I Company reached the northern edge of Schweinheim opposed only by a few snipers and machine-gun nests.

Once the attack of the 3d Battalion gained momentum, Lieutenant Colonel Krieger ordered C Company to seize the western edge of the town. Just as C/157th Infantry began moving, new orders arrived from Colonel O'Brien. These resulted from a visit by Major General Frederick to the 157th Infantry command post. After being briefed, he told O'Brien that his regiment was attacking on too narrow a front. Frederick ordered him to change the plan by sending the 1st Battalion around the right flank of the 3/157th Infantry.[21]

When word of the change reached the 1/157th Infantry command post, Lieutenant Colonel Krieger scrambled to comply with his new instructions. C Company halted until the 2d Battalion executed a relief in place. The rest of the 1st Battalion disengaged to the south before heading to a new assembly area. Once C Company rejoined, the 1/157th Infantry headed northeast to cut the roads leading out of Aschaffenburg.

The 1st Battalion soon encountered elements of 165th Grenadier Regiment defending a wood line just beyond Schweinheim. Backed up by A/157th Infantry and supporting armor, B Company cleared the Germans from the woods.[22] The 1st Battalion continued moving until 4:45 P.M., when it was stopped by machine-gun fire from a well-sited pillbox. Even as B Company began maneuvering to reduce the pillbox, another set of orders arrived for Lieutenant Colonel Krieger. The latest instructions from Colonel O'Brien ordered the 1st Battalion to hold in place. As the 1st Battalion began digging in for the night, B Company extended its lines until it made contact with L/157th Infantry in Schweinheim.

When the 2/157th Infantry was informed at 11:15 in the morning of the change in the original attack plan, Major Heilman dispatched G Company to relieve C/157th Infantry. From its positions southeast of Aschaffenburg, G/157th Infantry made its way toward Schweinheim. Arriving at 3:25 P.M., G Company occupied twelve houses to the left of I/157th Infantry. The rest of the 2d Battalion continued to trade fire with the Germans in southern Aschaffenburg. At 5:27 P.M., Major Heilman's battalion command post was hit by two mortar rounds, one of which passed through the roof and second floor before coming to rest without exploding. In response, a forward observer directed the 8-inch howitzers against Schloss Johannesburg. Wracked by numerous hits, the portion of the castle above ground was reduced to shattered wreckage.[23]

Both sides began waging a war of words after seventy-two hours of fighting. Although the 157th Infantry's S-2 believed that any attempt at psychological warfare would prove ineffective, Colonel O'Brien sent an artillery spotting plane over the city with a note addressed to Major Lamberth. The regimental adjutant dropped a mimeographed ultimatum into Aschaffenburg offering the Germans an opportunity to save their lives. The garrison was instructed to signal its acceptance of the surrender offer by raising a white flag on the engineer *kaserne*. If the Germans refused to capitulate, the U.S. troops "would be forced to level Aschaffenburg."[24]

Major Lamberth watched the garrison closely for signs of wavering morale. Anticipating the impact that continuous bombing and shellfire might have on the determination of the defenders, he executed one of his officers for failing to carry out instructions as an example to others. Lamberth also hoped to reinforce the determination of his garrison to fight to the end by issuing the following proclamation:

> Soldiers, Men of the Wehrmacht, Comrades:
> The fortress of ASCHAFFENBURG will be defended to the last man. As long as the enemy gives us time we will prepare and employ our troops to our best advantage. This means—Fight! Erect Dugouts! Make barriers! Get Supplies! And Win! As of today, everyone is to give to his last. I order that no one shall rest more than three hours out of 24. I forbid any sitting around or loafing. Our belief is that it is our mission to give the cursed enemy the greatest resistance and to send as many as possible of them to the devil.
> —Signed, Lamberth, Major[25]

The 157th Infantry Regiment prepared for renewed fighting on March 31 when Major Lamberth failed to respond to Colonel O'Brien's surrender demand. Between 6:30 and 7:25 A.M., four flights of fighter-bombers dropped high explosive and napalm on the city. Led by B/157th Infantry, the 1st Battalion began moving toward Haibach at 6:45. Incoming artillery fire dispersed one platoon from B Company, resulting in a two-hour delay. At 9:30, an air strike requested by the 3/157th Infantry against Haibach forced Lieutenant Colonel Krieger to halt his battalion's advance.

Once the planes departed, the 1/157th Infantry continued advancing until 2:45 in the afternoon, when reports of German troops and artillery in nearby Gailbach brought the Americans to a standstill. Because the 1/157th Infantry was temporarily operating in the 179th Infantry Regiment's zone of operations, it could not freely use supporting fires. The 1st Battalion's only alternative was to continue advancing even though it could not do so without being exposed to German flanking fire from Gailbach. As a result, Lieutenant Colonel Kreiger's battalion had to wait until the 3/179th Infantry cleared Gailbach.[26]

At 7:10 A.M., Lieutenant Colonel Sparks's 3d Battalion began operations designed to mop up the remaining defenders of Schweinheim. Supported by two platoons of medium tanks, K Company pushed forward to secure the remainder of the shattered village. The U.S. infantrymen made some progress when enemy troops in nearby buildings were suppressed by machine-gun and cannon fire from accompanying Sherman tanks. The medium tanks, however, were unable to move forward until the narrow streets were cleared of rubble.

The 3d Battalion made an unpleasant discovery as it advanced that morning. The Germans had dug underground tunnels from one cellar to another, allowing them to retreat unseen whenever a defensive position was rendered untenable. As soon as U.S. troops departed a building to continue advancing, the defenders would return via the tunnels. Soldiers from K/157th Infantry were ambushed several times by Germans firing from houses that had been cleared out earlier.[27] The 3/157th Infantry finally solved the problem by stationing guards in every intact cellar.

Although Schweinheim was officially cleared, an unceasing barrage of mortar shells pinned down the 3/157th Infantry that afternoon. At least 1,200 to 1,500 rounds struck Schweinheim, with 200 shells landing in a fifteen-minute period ending at 6:15 P.M. The 3d Battalion's leadership took several casualties as a result of the shelling. Two staff officers had been wounded at 10:55 that morning when the 3d Battalion forward command post was hit.[28] Lieutenant Colonel Sparks also lost his battalion operations officer to mortar fire several hours later.[29]

Once the mortar barrage subsided, Sparks ordered K Company, reinforced with tanks, to assault the artillery *kaserne* located on the southeastern edge of Aschaffenburg. The American attack fell apart, however, when the lead tank struck a mine.[30] Direct fire support of the assault was limited to the 57mm antitank guns of the 3d Battalion antitank platoon. The 57mm guns had been able to work their way forward using a newly bulldozed route through Schweinheim. Despite the support of the antitank platoon's guns, K Company failed to make significant headway in the face of this severe German opposition.

Major Heilman's 2/157th Infantry attacked the southern outskirts of Aschaffenburg at 8:00 A.M. Supported by two platoons of M5 light tanks from D/191st Tank Battalion, E and F Companies methodically cleared out each building as they worked their way toward the center of the city. A platoon was assigned to clear each house, repeating the process again and again as the 2d Battalion moved deeper into the city.

The advancing U.S. troops encountered numerous delays in the form of fallen rubble, fleeing civilians, and extensive roadblocks at critical choke points. The Germans adopted the tactic of allowing the lead elements of American units to pass through their defensive positions, then open fire on the trail elements. Dodging machine-gun fire from the U.S. light tanks, troops from the German 106th Replacement Battalion tossed grenades on the Americans from the upper stories of houses.

At one point, a Sherman tank adorned with a German Cross suddenly appeared from behind a row of buildings as the 2d Battalion continued to advance. The renegade M4 opened fire on an M5 Stuart from D/191st Tank Battalion moving up to support G Company.[31] The U.S.-made tank was able to avoid being hit by darting behind a shattered house. Following that brief contact, the enemy-manned U.S. medium tank again vanished from sight. Major Heilman called for M-36 tank destroyer support to be brought forward in case the enemy tank appeared again.

When several soldiers from G Company stepped into the open to accept the surrender of a group of Germans, the enemy-operated Sherman reappeared, opening fire on the Americans. Fortunately for G/157th Infantry, an M-36 tank destroyer from B/645th TD Battalion was in a position to quickly knock out the enemy Sherman. The M-36 then engaged German infantry accompanying the enemy tank, killing and wounding a number of them.[32] This unusual clash between opposing American vehicles served to mark the end of the day's fighting in the 2d Battalion sector.

In sharp contrast to the initial phases of the battle, each of the attacking U.S. battalions took some prisoners. Hungarian POWs captured by the 2/157th Infantry reported that more troops wanted to surrender but their German officers would not permit them to do so.[33]

The 3d Infantry Division to the south captured 1,700 prisoners over the previous twenty-four hours.[34] As information from other units flowed into his command post, Major General Frederick became convinced that the Germans would not be able to keep his men confined to the narrow strip of land they currently occupied bordering the Main River. Reports of collapsing resistance were also received from the 106th Cavalry Group to the north. Frederick responded by ordering the 179th and 180th Infantry Regiments to bypass Aschaffenburg while Colonel O'Brien completed the reduction of the city. When the rest of the division moved out, Colonel O'Brien's regiment lost the support of D/191st Tank Battalion. It would retain two 105mm artillery battalions, two 155mm artillery battalions, and one 8-inch howitzer battery.[35]

As the 179th and 180th Infantry Regiments prepared to move

east, the 157th Infantry started forward before dawn on April 1. Led by two platoons of K Company, the 3d Battalion infiltrated German lines. Within thirty-five minutes, one platoon reached the artillery *kaserne* undetected. As more Americans moved forward, however, K Company received 88mm and mortar fire. At 6:15 A.M., the Germans launched a counterattack against K Company's left flank. German soldiers from the 120th Convalescent Company isolated the American platoon that had penetrated into the artillery *kaserne*. Now being pressured on both flanks, K/157th Infantry by midmorning suffered at least seventeen casualties requiring urgent evacuation.[36]

The desperate situation was not remedied until 9:45 that morning, when I/157th Infantry moved up to aid K Company. Supporting tanks and tank destroyers also hurled dozens of high-explosive shells into the buildings on either side of K/157th Infantry, killing or wounding many of the defenders. Enemy opposition withered under the accurate American fire, permitting the Americans to evacuate their wounded and move up reinforcements.

As the 3d Battalion's assault gathered momentum, I Company advanced through K/157th Infantry. A platoon that remained behind to search the ruined barracks collected 125 prisoners, 23 of whom were wounded. The remainder of K Company moved forward and joined I Company.[37] Lieutenant Colonel Sparks's goal was to capture the Bois Brule *kaserne* strongpoint before the Germans could reestablish a cohesive defensive line.

The assault by the 3/157th Infantry against the *kaserne* was delayed slightly as friendly artillery fire fell on I Company. Once the fire was turned off, both I and K Companies moved forward. Supported by tanks, the U.S. riflemen blasted away at any likely pocket of resistance. The sheer volume of American fire inflicted serious casualties on the defenders at little cost to the attackers.

By 7:00 P.M., L Company moved to the left flank of I/157th Infantry while K Company reverted to battalion reserve. The ruined barracks of the *kaserne* were subsequently mopped up by a platoon from L Company.

The *kaserne* yielded a total of 475 prisoners. As darkness approached, Lieutenant Colonel Sparks decided to halt his attack. K Company suffered the bulk of the twenty-four killed in action and twenty-five wounded in action lost by the 157th Infantry on April 1. Sparks ordered the 3d Battalion to consolidate its positions around the ruined *kaserne* in anticipation of renewed operations the following morning.

Earlier on April 1, the 2d Battalion launched its own attack on Aschaffenburg at 7:45 A.M. Moving forward cautiously, E and G Companies methodically cleared each house. The 2d Battalion's advance suffered an early setback when G Company was pinned down by heavy fire near the city cemetery. After a prolonged fight, the Americans were finally able to push the defenders out of the cemetery at 12:20 that afternoon, capturing seventy-one POWs in the process.

As the 2d Battalion moved forward once again, a German Red Cross nurse entered the American lines under a flag of truce. The nurse claimed that the defenders wanted to quit fighting. Elated by the prospect of avoiding continued street fighting, Major Heilman halted his battalion before reporting to Colonel O'Brien that "the commandant of Aschaffenburg has sent a German nurse to effect the surrender of the town."[38] Hopes that the fighting would end soon were quickly dispelled when U.S. interrogators discovered that she was only an emissary from an isolated group of German troops facing the 2d Battalion, not a representative of Major Lamberth.

At 1:40 P.M., Major Heilman asked for permission to remain in his current positions and blast the heavily defended engineer *kaserne* with artillery and close air attacks. All three of his rifle companies were in excellent positions on high ground overlooking the barracks. Heilman's request was granted, and the 2d Battalion spent the rest of the day digging in as fighter-bombers and self-propelled 155mm howitzers pounded the *kaserne* with high-explosive shells.[39]

Like the 3d Battalion, the 1st Battalion had planned to attack before daylight and cross the open ground near Haibach without being detected. Unfortunately for Lieutenant Colonel Krieger, his battalion would have to wait until 8:00 A.M. to coordinate his attack with the neighboring 179th Infantry Regiment. Despite concerns about moving across the open terrain, the 1st Battalion attacked in daylight and pushed forward against scattered German opposition. By 11:40 that morning, A Company reached the southwestern outskirts of Haibach. The remainder of the battalion joined A Company soon afterward. As the Americans searched Haibach, they discovered several hospitals filled with German wounded, and captured 238 Germans.[40]

Orders arrived at 8:30 P.M. from Colonel O'Brien instructing the 1st Battalion to immediately cut the Wurzburg-Aschaffenburg road. Lieutenant Colonel Krieger decided to check out the area before committing his entire battalion, dispatching two patrols to locate any Germans to his front. Both of the patrols ran into serious opposition, prompting the 1st Battalion to cancel plans for an assault later that evening. Lieutenant Colonel Krieger also informed Colonel O'Brien that the 1st Battalion would not be able to cut the Wurzburg-Aschaffenburg road prior to first light on April 2. Krieger did not want to get involved in a night action without armored support, because most of the 1st Battalion's supporting tanks and tank destroyers were scattered about due to the hard fighting that occurred during the course of the day.

At 6:30 on the morning of April 2, the 157th Infantry Regiment renewed its attack against the visibly crumbling defenders of Aschaffenburg. The previous night, Colonel O'Brien had been informed that the 106th Cavalry Group had cleared the high ground north of Schloss Johannesburg without meeting any resistance. The main body of the 45th Infantry Division was advancing rapidly in a northeasterly direction against scattered resistance. Due north of the city, the 44th Infantry Division had also pushed past Aschaffenburg. [41] It seemed as though the city would soon be completely encircled by American troops.

The regimental command post received heartening reports from all three battalions as the assault progressed. True to Lieutenant Colonel Krieger's word, the 1st Battalion cut the road to Wurzburg soon after it started moving. Leaving C Company to establish a roadblock astride the route, the 1st Battalion secured Goldbach by early afternoon. Loss of the road and railroad line that ran through Goldbach meant that the last avenue of escape for the garrison of Aschaffenburg was sealed off. For the remainder of the day, tanks and artillery supporting the 1st Battalion engaged German troops attempting to leave the city. None of the retreating enemy made it past the American roadblocks.[42]

The 2d and 3d Battalions were steadily pushing forward, albeit against stiffening resistance. Lieutenant Colonel Sparks attacked with I Company in the lead at 8:00 A.M. By nine, the 3d Battalion gained its initial objectives, but more German troops appeared as K and L Companies moved up to reinforce I Company. The Americans responded with artillery and small-arms fire, precipitating a firefight that lasted until midafternoon.

Mustering his battalion for another attack at 5:15 P.M., Sparks requested a white phosphorus barrage from the 2d Chemical Mortar Battalion to screen his assault. Moving behind the smoke, the U.S. troops were able to gain a foothold in the industrial park along the northeastern section of the city. The only serious resistance encountered by the 3d Battalion came from a German 20mm antiaircraft gun, which was eventually silenced by U.S. tank destroyers within ten minutes after the German gun opened fire.[43]

In the center of the city, the 2d Battalion's attack began with a thirty-minute artillery preparation on the engineer *kaserne*. At 7:30 A.M., E, F, and G Companies moved out in line abreast, picking their way downhill through blasted houses. The 2d Battalion captured seventeen shell-shocked German soldiers as it advanced toward the north-south railroad running through Aschaffenburg. The railroad served to mark the halfway point to the *kaserne*.

Accompanied by tank destroyers and an M12 self-propelled gun, the 2d Battalion reached the railroad at 10:50 A.M. The foot soldiers and tank destroyers paused briefly at the rail line to reorganize themselves. Rather than continue on toward the barracks, E Company headed back to clear the southwestern outskirts of Aschaffenburg while the rest of the 2d Battalion resumed the advance.

As E Company departed, F Company began receiving small-arms fire from its right flank. The Americans faced toward the threat, plastering the German positions with machine-gun and mortar fire. After a short exchange, enemy resistance collapsed. By 1:00 P.M., F Company had gathered up 250 prisoners, including a full colonel. Leaving one platoon behind to secure the prisoners, F Company hurried to rejoin the rest of the battalion.

By 1:45, the 2d Battalion established itself around the engineer *kaserne*. The tank destroyers and M12 self-propelled gun were brought forward to soften up the Germans. The armored vehicles poured high-explosive shells into the barracks for thirty-five minutes. The American soldiers watched as 155mm shells blew away entire sections of building walls, revealing German soldiers scrambling for their lives amidst the falling masonry. After each salvo of high explosive, however, German machine gunners blazed away at their attackers.

When the defiant machine-gun crews grew silent, the U.S. infantrymen cleared the remaining Germans from the shattered *kaserne*.[44] The Americans soon discovered that there weren't many survivors. One POW claimed that the defenders suffered at least four hundred killed in the immediate vicinity of the barracks. The 2d Battalion had just shattered the final German line of defense.

As the 157th Infantry girded itself for a fifth day of combat in Aschaffenburg, a German Volkssturm captain, accompanied by a captured American soldier, entered the 2d Battalion's perimeter at 7:10 in the morning on April 3. The German carried a letter signed by Major Lamberth stating that he wanted to surrender. Lamberth also requested that the emissaries be permitted to return to the Schloss to escort him into captivity. Accompanied by two American officers, the German captain was permitted to return to Major Lamberth with word that his surrender offer had been accepted.

By 7:45, white flags were seen flying from atop Schloss Johannesburg. A small column of troops, comprising Lamberth's staff and headquarters defense platoon, marched out of the castle into captivity.[45] Major Lamberth accompanied the Americans to various parts of the city, convincing the last die-hard defenders to surrender. A total of 1,325 Germans, representing the surviving members of the garrison, were taken prisoner on April 3. The battle for Aschaffenburg, which eventually left the entire city in ruins, was finally over.

Analysis

The battle in the city of Aschaffenburg is a noteworthy example of how an attacking force can employ combined arms to negate the traditional advantages enjoyed by the defense. The fighting that took place demonstrated that U.S. forces achieved success by utilizing superior information, fire, and maneuver on a complex urban battlefield. Despite adverse urban terrain and fanatical defenders, over the course of four days the 157th Infantry Regiment killed or wounded 700 German soldiers and captured 2,536. United States losses were 193 killed and wounded.

It is interesting to note that both the attacker and defender planned to fight in the city from the onset of the battle. The Americans, however, were able to execute their plan because they presented the Germans with an unanticipated challenge at the tactical level. The complex terrain of the city did not degrade cooperation between the attacking tanks and infantry as the Germans believed it would. Because the Americans were able to maintain the integrity of their combined-arms teams at company and battalion level, they were consistently successful in executing their plan, whereas the German plan failed. Tank-infantry cooperation was the key element of success. Suppressive fire provided by tanks permitted the American infantry to maneuver against the defenders with great success while suffering relatively low losses in return. When the situation required heavier firepower, the Americans employed 155mm self-propelled artillery pieces in the direct fire role.

The Germans were also proven wrong in their belief that urban terrain would deny effective air support to the Americans. In spite of the difficulty that pilots face when trying to locate targets in a city from the air, the Americans successfully employed fighter-bombers to strike high-value targets on the periphery of Aschaffenburg, to physically isolate the defenders within the city by reducing buildings to rubble, and to unhinge the morale of the German garrison. Realizing the considerable difficulty involved in tracking all of the attacking units, American commanders employed airpower on targets beyond the front lines for the purpose of interdicting movement.

The lessons of the battle of Aschaffenburg offer key insights into the nature of combat in cities. In addition to failing at the tactical level, the Germans failed at the operational level. Hitler's hope that the garrison of Aschaffenburg could buy time went unrealized. Although 3:1 odds are considered optimal for an attacker, the 45th Infantry Division employed only a single infantry regiment against the 3,200 German troops defending the city. The perceived superiority of the German infantryman in close combat was also not apparent. At relatively low cost to the attacker, American combined-arms tactics consistently overcame German defenses based on interlocking machine-gun fire and man-portable antiarmor weapons, despite the complex urban terrain.

ENDNOTES

1.   Quentin Schillaire, *The Battle of Aschaffenburg: An Example of Late World War II Urban Combat in Europe* (Fort Leavenworth, KS: U.S. Army Command and General Staff College, 1989), 33.

2.   NARA, RG 407, Entry 427, Box 11062, The Adjutant General Records, World War II Operations 1940–48, 45th Infantry Division, History-Narrative From 157th Infantry Regiment April 1945, 1. His name is consistently misspelled by the 45th Infantry Division G-2 as "Lambert" instead of "Lamberth."

3.   Schillaire, 47–49.

4.   National Archives and Records Administration, RG 407, Entry 427, Box 10976, The Adjutant General's Office, G-2 Periodic Report, Headquarters, 45th Infantry Division, dated March 31, 1945, through April 1, 1945.

5.   NARA, RG 407, The Adjutant General's Office, Entry 427, World War II Operations Reports 1940–48, Box 10977, 345–3.2 (45th Infantry Division) G-3 Journal and File (German Campaign) March 1–May 10, 1945, folder April 1–3, 1945, 45th Division Artillery Field Order #9 dated 010300 April 1945.

6.   NARA, Record Group 407, The Adjutant General's Office, Entry 427, WW II Operations Reports 1940–48, Box 11061, 345–INF (157)-0.7, folder entitled 157th Infantry Regiment Operations Journal March 1945, log entry dated 3:30 P.M., March 28, 1945.

7.   NARA, RG 407, Box 11074, 345–INF (157)-0.7(2d Bn), folder

entitled 2/157th Infantry Regiment Operations Journal March 1–31, 1945, log entries dated 1:23 P.M., 4:05 P.M., and 4:45 P.M. on March 28, 1945.

8.   NARA, RG 407, Box 11073, 345–INF (157)-0.7(1st Bn), folder entitled 1/157th Infantry Regiment Operations Journal March 1–31, 1945, log entry dated 8:00 P.M. on March 28, 1945.

9.   See endnote 6. S-3 journal entries dated 6:41, 6:50, and 8:15 A.M. on March 29, 1945.

10.   See endnote 6, log entries dated 8:20, 9:00, and 9:16 A.M. on March 29, 1945.

11.   NARA, RG 407, Records of the Adjutant General's Office, World War II Operations 1940–48, Box 16645, ARBN-191-3.2, 1–1–45 to 3–31–45, S-3 journal for the 191st Tank Battalion March 1945, summary comments for March 29, 1945 (sheet 603–a).

12.   See endnote 9, 1st Battalion log entries dated 10:18 and 12:30 A.M. on March 29, 1945.

13.   NARA, RG 407, Records of the Adjutant General's Office, World War II Operations 1940–48, Box 11075, 345–INF (157)-0.7(3d Bn), folder entitled 3/157th Infantry Regiment Operations Journal March 1–31, 1945, log entry dated 1:45 P.M. on March 29, 1945.

14.   See endnote 12.

15.   See endnote 13. S-3 journal entries dated 4:35 and 9:50 P.M. on March 29, 1945.

16.   NARA, RG 407, the Adjutant General's Office, Entry 427, World War II Operations Reports 1940–48, Box 11030, 345–FA (158)-0.7, S-3 journal and file (German Campaign) March 1–May 10, 1945, fire mission log for March 1–31, 1945, entries from March 28 to April 2. This log includes missions fired by reinforcing field artillery (FA) units.

17.   See endnote 10; log entries dated 5:13 and 7:16 P.M. on March 29, 1945.

18.   See endnote 5, MS B-183, 11.

19.   See endnote 14, 3d Battalion S-3 journal entries dated 12:40, 3:00, and 3:15 A.M. on March 30, 1945. Also see endnote 6, IPW report from 157th Infantry Regiment dated 3:00 P.M. on March 30, 1945, which is included in the 45th Infantry Division G-3 journal and file.

20.   See endnote 13. S-3 journal entries dated 2:41 and 2:45 P.M. on March 30, 1945.

21.   See endnote 6. 157th Infantry Regimental S-3 journal entry dated 10:55 A.M. on March 30, 1945.

22.　See endnote 9. 1st Battalion S-3 journal entries dated 10:45 and 11:05 A.M. and 3:25 and 4:45 P.M. on March 30, 1945.

23.　See endnote 8. 2d Battalion S-3 journal entries dated 11:15 A.M. and 1:25, 3:45, and 5:27 P.M. on March 30, 1945. Also see endnote 6. Regimental S-3 journal entry dated 9:45 A.M. on March 30, 1945.

24.　See endnote 7. 2d Battalion S-3 journal entry dated 11:10 P.M. on March 31, 1945. Also recounted on page 11 of March 1945 Regimental Monthly History.

25.　Leo V. Bishop, et al., *The Fighting Forty-Fifth: Combat Report of an Infantry Division,* undated, 164.

26.　See endnote 8. 1st Battalion S-3 journal entries dated 1:30 and 2:50 P.M. on March 31, 1945.

27.　Monograph by Capt. Harold B. Henderly, *The Operations of Company D, 191st Tank Battalion at Aschaffenburg, Germany, 28 March–3 April 1945 (Central Europe Campaign) (Personal Experience of a Company Commander),* Advanced Infantry Officer Course, 1948–49, The Infantry School, Fort Benning, GA, 9.

28.　See endnote 6. 157th Infantry Regiment S-3 journal entry dated 10:55 A.M. on March 31, 1945.

29.　See endnote 13. 3d Battalion S-3 journal entry dated 3:20 P.M. on March 31, 1945.

30.　See endnote 5. Enclosure to 45th Infantry Division G-3 journal and file, 191st Tank Battalion S-3 periodic report dated 312400A March 1945.

31.　Henderly monograph, 12.

32.　See endnote 5. Enclosure to 45th Infantry Division G-3 journal and file, 645th TD Battalion Tank Destroyer Daily Report dated April 1, 1945.

33.　See endnote 6. 157th Infantry Regiment S-3 journal entry dated 3:10 P.M. on March 31, 1945.

34.　See endnote 7. 45th Infantry Division G-3 journal and file, 45th Infantry Division G-2 Periodic Report No. 193 dated April 1, 1945, covering the period 302400 to 312400 March 1945.

35.　See endnote 2, 45th Infantry Division G-3 journal and file entries dated 6:05, 7:20, and 10:10 P.M. on March 31, 1945.

36.　See endnote 13. 3d Battalion S-3 journal entries dated 5:35, 6:45, 7:15, and 9:45 A.M. on April 1, 1945.

37.　Ibid., journal entry dated 2:45 P.M. on April 1, 1945.

38. See endnote 7. 2d Battalion S-3 journal entry dated 12:58 P.M. on April 1, 1945.

39. Ibid., journal entry dated 1:40 P.M. on April 1, 1945.

40. See endnote 8. 1st Battalion S-3 journal entry dated 12:20 A.M. on April 2, 1945.

41. Ibid., journal entry dated 12:01 A.M. on April 2, 1945.

42. Ibid., journal entries dated 11:15 A.M. and 1:50, 2:35, and 3:30 P.M. on April 2, 1945.

43. See endnote 13. 3d Battalion S-3 journal entries dated 8:00, 9:10, and 10:55 A.M. and 5:15 P.M. on April 2, 1945.

44. See endnote 7. 2d Battalion S-3 journal entries dated 7:30, 9:45, and 10:50 A.M. and 1:45 and 2:20 P.M. on April 2, 1945.

45. Ibid., journal entries dated 7:10, 7:45, and 8:20 A.M. on April 3, 1945.

EIGHT

Manila, 1945:

City Fight in the Pacific

by Col. Kevin C. M. Benson

It seemed like a never ending house-to-house and room-to-room fight . . . By comparison, Dante's Inferno would have seemed like a weekend at the Waldorf.[1]

—B. C. Wright

Introduction

The fighting in the Pacific theater of operations during World War II invokes thoughts of island hopping, beach assaults, and close-quarter fighting in dense jungle. Overlooked in those bitter encounters is the fact that the U.S. Army fought a city battle for Manila in the Philippines that was as bloody as Aachen or Arnhem in the European theater. In this essay we examine the three distinct stages of the battle as well as the tactical-level techniques used during the fighting. The troopers of the 1st Cavalry Division made the transition from jungle fighters to city fighters, and won victories in the streets as well as in trackless jungles.

In February 1943, after the unit had surrendered key leaders to fill the ranks of another division in the U.S. Army's expansion effort, the remainder of the 1st Cavalry Division was alerted for overseas movement. It was the only division in the U.S. Army to retain and fight in the "square" structure of two brigades of two regiments each. The division was not as robust as a regular infantry division, the regiments having but two squadrons and none of the cannon or heavy weapons companies that were organic to infantry divisions. The division artillery was reinforced with a 155mm battalion. The division also was reinforced with a medium tank battalion. The 1st Cavalry Division retained its cavalry table of organization but fought dismounted throughout the campaigns in the Pacific.

The invasion of the Philippines, and the redemption of MacArthur's pledge to return, initially focused on the island of Leyte. In October 1944 the 1st Cavalry Division attacked the island to seize airfields. Seizure of the airfields on Leyte would extend the coverage of land-based aircraft and allow the American armies as well as fleets to operate under the umbrella of air superiority. On Leyte, the division met the Japanese in the close quarters of the jungle and grassy plains of the central portion of the island. The Japanese made a major effort to disrupt MacArthur's plans for the Philippines by holding on to Leyte. They transferred precious forces to defend the island and defeat the American invasion. The attempt failed. MacArthur was able to destroy a large portion of the Japanese Fourteenth Area Army on Leyte while keeping his focus on the real prize of the campaign, the island of Luzon and the capital city of Manila.

Operationally, the defeat of the Japanese forces on Leyte was the beginning of the end of Japanese control of the Philippines. On the tactical level, the fighting for the 1st Cavalry Division was tough and slow. The division secured the northeastern portion of the island where the Japanese were firmly dug into the hills. From these positions, the Japanese threatened the airfields and beachheads. The division was committed, therefore, to destroy the pockets of Japanese resistance near the beachheads to secure the flank of the Sixth Army. Meanwhile, MacArthur prepared to launch the Sixth Army against the main island of Luzon.

The Japanese

The Japanese forces in the Philippines were in some disarray following the fighting on Leyte. General Yamashita, commanding general of the Fourteenth Area Army, directed the defensive operations on Luzon. He had no intention of defending the city of Manila. Field Marshal Count Terauchi, the Southern Army commander, disrupted Yamashita's careful plans for protracted war by deciding to make a larger fight against MacArthur on Leyte, thereby slowly reducing any operational mobility left to Yamashita. In essence, Yamashita planned to delay MacArthur as long as possible outside Manila and deny American air forces the use of the extensive airfields and hangars at the Clark Field complex. Yamashita intended to do this by withdrawing as many Japanese forces as possible from Manila, then tying down MacArthur's forces in the Philippines by fighting in the mountains north and east of Manila.

The commander of Japanese naval forces, Rear Admiral Iwabuchi, was not under the command of General Yamashita. Iwabuchi, having decided to defend Manila, established ad hoc battalions from Japanese naval forces ashore; they ranged from supply units to naval defense gun battalions.

The Japanese army and navy commanders clashed over the relative importance of the city. Yamashita did not want to feed the nearly one million inhabitants, deciding that the Americans would be delayed more by having that responsibility. Iwabuchi believed that defending the city would buy more time for homeland defense and for the Imperial Japanese Navy to rebuild for fleet action against the American forces around the Philippines.

Japanese army forces were divided into groups for the defense of regions around Luzon. The Kembu Group was responsible for the defense of Clark Field. The Kobayashi Group, or Manila Naval Defense Force, was responsible for the delay of American forces into the Manila area and the recovery of supplies and stores vital to the overall Japanese campaign to tie up MacArthur in the Philippines. This group was subordinate to the Shimbu Group, the force built around the Forty-first Army, which would conduct operations in the mountains to the north and east of Manila.

The Japanese naval forces under Rear Admiral Iwabuchi established a Manila Naval Defense Force, which was not under the command of General Yamashita. The naval defense force established sectors in the city for the overall defense. The naval troops were not as well trained in land combat operations as Japanese soldiers, but, defending from strongpoints with machine guns and artillery, they were enough to slow down American operations in the city.

The Japanese, therefore, prepared two different defenses of the Philippines and Luzon. The army troops directly under General Yamashita prepared and improved defenses outside the city with the view toward the protracted struggle or delaying action. Naval forces under Rear Admiral Iwabuchi prepared positions within Manila to hold the city to the bitter end, with the view toward a battle of attrition within the city that would break the American forces' combat power. To try to make the best of this bad situation for the defense, a defense depleted by the unsuccessful defense of Leyte, army troops within the city were placed under the operational control of Iwabuchi.

Because of this tension, the organization of the defense of the city was haphazard. The heart of this defense was based in the Intramuros, a Spanish fort and the oldest part of the city, and took advantage of the modern, steel-reinforced-concrete government buildings that lined the approaches to the center of old Manila. The central feature of the Japanese defense was the improvisation displayed by the naval and army troops in fortifying the buildings in the city. Hallways were barricaded, and entrances were fortified with sandbags. Tunnels were dug connecting basements of adjacent buildings and bunkers outside buildings. The standard defense relied on improving positions within existing buildings. In addition, the streets of the city leading into engagement areas were strewn with obstacles of all types. The Japanese used wire, oil drums filled with cement, rails set at an angle into the pavement, ditches, even automobiles, trolley cars, and heavy machinery dragged from factories. The streets and buildings were mined with standard antipersonnel and antitank mines. The Japanese improvised mines using naval depth charges, beach mines, naval cannon ammunition, artillery, and mortar shells. In order to cover all obstacles with fire, the Japanese used a great number of automatic weapons in the defense. The Japanese naval troops were not well trained in the use of rifles, but even naval troops could be trained to sit in well-built bunkers and fire machine guns down a prescribed line. These methods would exact heavy casualties on Americans forces throughout the battles in the city.

Tactical Setting

The battle for Manila encompassed the fighting from the beachhead line to the city itself. The entire battle lasted from February 3 to March 3, 1945, thirty days of grim combat from tropical jungle to the complex urban setting of Manila. After establishing a beachhead on Luzon, Lieutenant General Krueger disposed his troops for a deliberate drive on Manila. The Americans established within the expanding beachhead contained sufficient manpower to conduct a deliberate advance on the city of Manila. Nevertheless, Krueger kept an eye on the rugged mountains to the east as his units approached the city. He feared that the Japanese forces on the island would strike his vulnerable flanks. MacArthur, however, had other ideas. He had a special regard for Manila and wanted to save the city and its population from the Japanese. He directed the 1st Cavalry Division to organize for a rapid advance to Manila to disrupt the Japanese defenses, free the captives of the earlier Japanese conquest of the islands who were held in prisoner-of-war camps, and prevent the destruction of the city.

Based on an incomplete picture of the Japanese defense, and expecting that Yamashita would not defend Manila, MacArthur visited the division shortly after it landed on Luzon. He directed the organization of flying columns to speed on to liberate Manila. The flying column, not a doctrinal term, was used to convey MacArthur's intent to speed to the city and not be delayed by a preoccupation with open flanks. Major General Verne D. Mudge, commanding general of the 1st Cavalry Division, organized two such columns to lead the dash to Manila. He used the 2d Squadrons of the 5th and 8th Cavalry Regiments, and augmented these forces with tanks from the 44th Medium Tank Battalion, the division's own tank troop, and the motorized cavalry reconnaissance troop, as well as motorized elements from the division's combat support and combat service support units.[2] The columns carried only four days' worth of supplies. Brigadier General William C. Chase, commander of the 1st Cavalry Brigade, led the columns.[3] The remainder of the 1st Cavalry Division followed as quickly as it could on foot. The division relieved column elements in place and kept open the lines of communication back to the beachhead.

The tactical focus and constraints placed on the division and all other divisions fighting in Manila were unique in that they were not in place in any previous combat during the island-hopping fights in earlier campaigns. "For the first time in the Pacific War, American forces were faced with the task of capturing a large, well-defended metropolitan area."[4] Field artillery and close air support would have to be carefully controlled. In short, city fighting was unfamiliar to the troopers of the division.

Manila was largely untouched by Allied bombing before the battle for the city began. In an effort to spare the city and its population from unnecessary destruction, MacArthur's headquarters issued extremely stringent restrictions on the use of indirect fires and close air support. MacArthur personally forbade any air attacks within the city. All artillery fires had to be observed and on pinpointed Japanese positions.[5] As the fight for the city progressed, the restrictions on the use of field artillery would be loosened, but the restrictions on air bombardment would remain in place.

There were three distinct phases of the 1st Cavalry Division's fighting in Manila: the flying column drive to Santo Tomas University, the division's fight to close the outer ring of forces around Manila and isolate the city, and the fighting that completed the destruction of Japanese defenders of the city in the Intramuros.

The Drive to Santo Tomas

A voice cut the darkness: "Where the hell is the front gate?" The Americans had arrived for sure.[6]

The advance on Manila began on February 1, 1944, with the movement of the columns on separate routes to the city. The fights en route were short and sharp, and consistent with a penetration. The Japanese forces were not sure of where the Americans were; nor were the Americans certain of the disposition of Japanese forces. Thus, the advance toward the city was actually a series of meeting battles and attempts at hasty demolition to slow the advance of the cavalry. Typical of these types of actions was one on the opening day of the advance. On February 3, 1944, Lt. (jg) James P. Sutton, U.S. Naval Reserve, assigned to a Seventh Fleet bomb-disposal unit attached to the 1st Cavalry Division, dashed onto a stone arch bridge across the Tuliahan River and cut a burning fuse from a dynamite charge. He disregarded the heavy Japanese fire and heaved other mines and dynamite charges off the bridge into the gorge beneath it. This action enabled the flying column of the 8th Cavalry to continue its advance. He was awarded the Distinguished Service Cross for gallantry in action.[7]

Due to heroic efforts such as these, the lead elements of the 2d Squadron, 8th Cavalry, entered Manila at 6:35 P.M. on February 3, 1944.[8] The flying columns of the 1st Cavalry Division covered more than a hundred miles in sixty-six hours and entered Manila.

The fights en route to the university and the expected liberation of American internees held there since 1941 gave hints to the type of desperate action that would typify the overall battle. A prime example of these actions occurred in the initial drive to a prisoner-of-war camp. On February 3, 1945, as elements of the 2d Squadron, 8th Cavalry, drove into the city toward Far Eastern University, they ran into a murderous cross fire from well-positioned Japanese troops. The streets of the city were so narrow that the column had to back out of the cross fire. In the midst of this fight, one Pfc. Thomas R. Luper of Service Troop distinguished himself by staying with his truck, although it had been hit and was set on fire, and in spite of his wounds he drove it and the wounded men on board to safety. He refused medical care until all others were treated. Luper was awarded the Silver Star.[9]

As troopers of the division drove toward the university, Filipinos living in the city guided them. Upon arriving at the university, there was some confusion regarding the location of the main gate and the number of Japanese troops in place around the site. The argument was settled in a direct fashion. A tank named Battlin Basic smashed through the front gate of Santo Tomas University. The flying columns arrived to liberate the 3,700 prisoners of war and the 276 American civilians who had been held by the Japanese since 1942.[10]

The fighting inside the university grounds was short and sharp, until Brigadier General Chase realized that the Japanese guards were holding nearly three hundred hostages. The cavalrymen traded fire with the Japanese inside the education building of the university until it became apparent that the fire was placing American civilians at risk. Chase now was faced with Japanese forces moving to counterattack him as well the hostage situation at the university. He appointed the executive officer of the 1st Cavalry Brigade, Col. Charles E. Brady, to negotiate with the commander of the remaining Japanese forces in the university for the release of the American hostages. At first, Brady used intermediaries to make contact with the Japanese. The camp commander, Lt. Col. Toshio Hayashi, demanded that all of his men be provided protection from any attack, and be able to retain all weapons, machine guns, and equipment. Negotiations went on throughout the day of February 4 and into the evening. Brady and Hayashi met on the night of February 4 and agreed on final terms. In order to save the American hostages, the Japanese were allowed to depart American lines and retain their personal weapons.

On the morning of February 5, Brady and men of E Troop,

5th Cavalry, met the Japanese troops at the door of the education building and escorted them to a point approximately one mile from the gates of the university complex. The Japanese troops were released without incident. These negotiations were the last act in the drama that was the flying column. The remainder of the division arrived to relieve the columns, and the battle to isolate the city from Japanese forces holding positions in the mountains began. The battle for the suburbs of Manila would come next.

The Stadium

In accord with existing doctrine, Lieutenant General Krueger directed the isolation of the city of Manila. The 37th Division formed the inner ring of encircling forces and the 1st Cavalry Division formed the outer ring. The 37th Infantry Division was a stronger force, having three robust infantry regiments to the 1st Cavalry Division's two brigades. The completion of the outer ring surrounding the city effectively cut off the remaining Japanese forces from the command and control of General Yamashita.

Once the outer ring was in position, the division attacked through the outlying suburban area of greater Manila. The first objectives were to secure the dams and reservoirs that supplied the city with water. This drive also separated the Japanese naval forces inside the city from the Japanese army forces outside the city and to the north.

This fight was not easy. As the division fought its way into the New Manila subdivision area and the Rosario Heights, overlooking a major reservoir, the lead patrols of the regiments found their way blocked by mines, numerous naval guns, 20mm antiaircraft cannon, and heavy machine guns. The troopers of the division found almost every open space mined. Every building and wall was a strongpoint, and the streets were barricaded.

The Japanese naval forces manning the guns were not well trained in offensive tactics, but they could hold fixed positions and lengthen the campaign by buying time as the American offense was slowed down. Nevertheless, the division fought through the outlying subdivision area of Manila. In these fierce actions, as historian Stanley Falk wrote, "Almost every major structure in Manila became a minor fort as the Japanese blocked entrances, put barricades on the stairways and in the corridors, cut firing slits in the walls, and dug connecting tunnels to nearby buildings."[11]

Manila was a modern city with mixed architecture, ranging from modern structures to turn-of-the-century Spanish structures to barrios of the homes of poor Filipinos. The suburbs of the city reflected the desires of the government to put forth a "modern" picture of a metropolis. There were numerous parks and baseball fields; the newest, Harrison Park, was a large athletic complex of baseball and football fields and gymnasiums. The Japanese turned the area into a strongpoint. During the attack into the complex, E Troop, 5th Cavalry, was ambushed. The Japanese dug in machine guns and rifle pits along the bleachers of the first-base side of the main baseball field. The troop was well into the middle infield when the Japanese opened fire. During the ensuing fight, Pvt. Ernest E. Pittman went to the aid of a fellow trooper, dashing into Japanese fire to recover him. As he administered first aid, Pittman was wounded. Although exposed to Japanese fire, he refused first aid till his fellow trooper was cared for, and he continued to return fire against the Japanese dug in near the dugouts of the baseball field. Seeing this action, Major General Mudge directed members of his staff to follow him. Mudge was the first to reach Pittman. He reached into his pocket and pinned a Silver Star on Pittman, then took Pittman's rifle and provided covering fire for the members of his staff as they evacuated both the wounded trooper and Pittman.[12] This was the kind of leadership exhibited by all leaders, from corporal to major general, and the type required by the brutal fighting the division faced as the battle for Manila continued.

As the division turned to the heart of the city, the men found themselves faced with a grueling battle. They had to fight from building to building. The steps would become standard practice. First, every artillery piece within range would fire on known targets. Then the combined-arms team of infantry would advance slowly behind tanks, under fire until closing to flamethrower and demolitions range, then blast a hole into the walls of the building being assaulted. Once inside, the infantry would clear room by room, killing the Japanese defenders every step of the way. Larger buildings would consume entire companies, with the fight to clear a building lasting up to a day. At night any surviving Japanese defenders would slip away while the cavalry troopers consolidated their gains. It was grim fighting. Still ahead lay the Intramuros.

Intramuros

The Intramuros area was the most formidable portion of Manila. Most of the city was now in ruins, and the Japanese were still in position to continue the battle. The following constraints placed by MacArthur remained as the Japanese force contracted into the Intramuros:

> The use of air on a part of a city occupied by a friendly and allied population is unthinkable. The inaccuracy of this type of bombardment would result beyond question in the death of thousands of innocent civilians. It is not believed moreover that this would appreciably lower our own casualty rate although it would unquestionably hasten the conclusion of the operations. For these reasons I do not approve the use of air bombardment on the Intramuros district."[14]

Thus, the weight of airpower was denied to the commander of XIV Corps, Lt. Gen. Oscar Griswold, and the commander of the 37th Infantry Division, Maj. Gen. Robert Beightler. Both of these men then planned for the use of massive artillery fire to assist in the reduction of Japanese fortifications within the Intramuros. The effect of the artillery fire was as devastating to the city's structures and population as the use of airpower would have been. The 37th Division concentrated the fires of twenty-one artillery batteries ranging from 105mm to 240mm and 8 inch, as well as two companies of 4.2-inch mortars and five platoons of tanks and tank destroyers.[15]

The fight for Manila was now concentrated in the Intramuros. To simplify the command and control of the fight, the 1st Cavalry Brigade, 5th and 12th Cavalry Regiments (less the 2/12 Cavalry), was placed under the operational control of the 37th Infantry Division. For the remaining two weeks of February, the 1st Cavalry Brigade fought its way through the Intramuros. The combat seemed never-ending. The cavalrymen battled through the rooms of the Army-Navy Club, the Manila Hotel, the Philippine General Hospital, and other government buildings. The pattern of tactical operations continued: concentrated fire on a portion of the building, blasting an entry point, then bitter room-to-room combat. The two weeks of continuous fighting reduced the buildings to rubble. Dead Japanese soldiers and Filipino civilians decomposed in the sun. The constant fighting, as well as the heat and dust, took a toll on the troopers of the 1st Cavalry brigade combat team.

As always there were moments of terror and tremendous courage. Typical of this was one such action on February 23, 1945. Private First Class William J. Grabiarz, a scout with E Troop, 5th Cavalry, was advancing down a Manila street when the troop was taken under intense fire from concealed Japanese positions near the customs building. The fire wounded the troop commander and pinned him down in the middle of the street. Grabiarz ran from the cover of a tank to rescue him. The private was wounded in the shoulder but continued to attempt to drag his troop commander out of the range of enemy fire. Unable to do so, he deliberately placed his body on top of his officer while calling for a tank to maneuver into position between the two men and the Japanese position. Before the tank could complete its move, the Japanese concentrated fire on the two men. Private First Class Grabiarz succeeded in saving the life of his commander at the cost of his own. For this action he was awarded the Congressional Medal of Honor.[16] The fighting in Manila continued until March 3, 1945, when XIV Corps and the Sixth Army declared the city free of Japanese forces.

The Cost

Japanese losses during the battle were high, and led to the greater loss of tactical and operational freedom of action for General Yamashita. He was unable to continue his defense as he had hoped. Although the overall campaign continued, MacArthur was able to use the Philippines for a staging area and air operations against the home islands of Japan. Japanese losses in the fight for Manila were estimated at more than 16,000. Almost no Japanese defenders survived the battle for Manila, and no organized Japanese units remained in the greater Manila area.

The loss of the city and control of the major portion of Luzon had a far-reaching effect on future Japanese operations in the campaign. General Yamashita's long-range strategy for Japanese forces in the Philippines was to embark on protracted warfare. He intended to tie down significant American forces for months—or years, as he told Tokyo. This protracted campaign would wear down American will and delay or suspend land operations against the Japanese homeland. The fractured command

and control structure in the region, a lack of an effective overall commander in chief of naval and army forces, and Field Marshal Terauchi's transfer of his headquarters to Saigon after the disastrous operation in Leyte all prevented any effective land-sea-air campaign against MacArthur. This inefficient control system doomed the Japanese forces to a forlorn hope, as much as the total air and sea supremacy held by MacArthur, William F. "Bill" Halsey, and George Churchill Kenney over the Southwest Pacific Area. Japanese forces remaining throughout the Philippines withered on the vine or fell to follow-on operations to liberate the entire island chain. Although formidable on paper, the Shobu Group, a force of more than 50,000 men, could do little more than sustain itself. The Shobu Group and General Yamashita could not affect any ongoing American operations in the Philippines or from the Philippines that were directed at the home islands of Japan.

American losses during the campaign were heavy but could be made up by replacements. Total U.S. losses were 1,010 killed and 5,565 wounded in action. The 1st Cavalry Division lost 250 men killed and 1,250 wounded. The fight for the city and the casualties suffered in the city fighting also affected future U.S. operations in the campaign. The 1st Cavalry Division, indeed all of the American forces in the U.S. Sixth and Eighth Armies, began the Luzon campaign understrength after a hard fight on Leyte. MacArthur's forces continued operations to liberate the remaining islands of the Philippines. Although bitter fighting remained on these islands, they were not the draining delay hoped for by the Japanese. The 1st Cavalry Division remained on Luzon at the conclusion of operations on that island, and trained for the invasion of Japan.

The most grievous losses of the battle were borne by the Filipino people. The human costs of the battle were enormous. Estimates of civilian losses were up to 100,000. The city of Manila, once called the Citadel of Democracy in the East, lay in ruins. The sewage and water systems needed extensive repair. More than a third of the bridges were destroyed, as were a majority of government buildings. The public transportation system was ruined. The electrical power grid was knocked out.[17] In short, the entire city was decimated. Its social, political, and economic life would have to be rebuilt from scratch.

Lessons Learned

At the end of the battle for Manila, the army conducted analyses of the battle and operations. The official U.S. Army history of the campaign, Triumph in the Philippines, stated that the U.S. Army doctrine for city fighting in effect at the time was sound. Although there were no official "lessons learned" during the operation, there were in reality lessons remembered by all ranks.[18] The fact that the cities of Japan remained to be taken by force of arms was in the back of the minds of all troopers. Although indeed sound, American doctrine for city fighting was grinding in nature. American forces continually used overwhelming fire to get to a point of penetration in a strongpoint or building, make a penetration in the building, then painstakingly clear the building room by room. The combined-arms team of engineers, infantry, tanks, and artillery could get the force to and through the walls of a building, but to clear the building itself required infantry. It was a brutal form of warfare. The realization of this, based on the results of fighting for Manila and the Philippines, as well as Saipan and Okinawa, led the senior leaders in the Pacific theater to request additional infantry divisions from the European theater upon the successful conclusion of campaigns there.

The Filipino population assisted the American forces by directing convoys, treating wounded soldiers, and providing information on Japanese dispositions. However, the Filipino civilians suffered greatly as the battle for the city raged; the Japanese used them as shields and hostages throughout the fighting in the city. The Japanese were not signatories of the Geneva-Hague conventions and used hospitals and churches as strongpoints. The initial efforts by the Americans to limit the destruction of the city, however well intentioned, gradually gave way to the need to overwhelm the defending Japanese forces. American forces and leaders concluded that the fights that inevitably lay ahead on the Japanese home islands would also be marked by the use of civilians as shields and a disregard, from a western point of view, of the laws of land warfare.

Looking at the battle for Manila through the lens of history, we can draw some lessons on the use of the modern weapons at our disposal for future combat in cities. In Manila, the U.S. forces faced restrictions on the use of airpower and field artillery, and also faced desperate enemy forces taking hostages. The use of airpower today faces many of the same constraints. Today there are a multitude of precision-guided munitions that can be used to effect strategic shock on an enemy's command and control, as well as his land, sea, and air forces. Given this dominance held by U.S. air forces, potential enemy forces may well choose to negate this advantage by seeking to fight in close terrain or in urban terrain. The "CNN factor" of seemingly never-ending news reports that characterizes our modern era must also be taken into account if we use precision munitions in populated areas. We saw this during the latest U.S. and NATO actions in Serbia, as well as the Russian operations in Chechnya. The results of the bombing are broadcast into American homes, as well as homes around the world. This is also true of the effects of a ground campaign into an enemy city or a friendly city held by enemy forces.

In campaigns such as the fight for Manila, American ground

forces used the strengths of the combined-arms team to direct overwhelming fire to a point of penetration in a building. Once the infantrymen were inside, it was up to them to clear the rooms of the building. Airpower may be able to get American land forces to the city with relatively minor fights en route, but once faced with the necessity of taking a city, or a portion of a city, we may be confronted by the same dilemma as Generals Griswold, Beightler, and Mudge: The use of airpower or bombardment may be proscribed due to civilian casualty considerations and media considerations.

The U.S. Army used field artillery to great effect during the operations in Manila. Assuming that, in the future, American forces will not be allowed to reduce a city to rubble for either defense or offense, the use of artillery may be strictly controlled in any future fight. Precision artillery rounds would be useful in destroying point targets during offensive operations in a city, but mostly on the outskirts of a city or small town. The technical problems of gun-target line and the scatter effect of tall buildings on the laser designator could limit the effectiveness of many precision artillery shells. Artillery, as a member of the combined-arms team, will serve to cover the approach of any American force to the edge of a city. But depending on the size of the city itself and the structures within the city, artillery may not be able to play a large role once the fight inside the city is joined. Depending on the risk we wish to assume, we can use artillery in a direct-fire role to assist in the advance of the infantry by blowing holes in the walls of buildings. This was done with certain effectiveness during the battle for Manila. Where artillery cannot be used, tanks and other pinpoint, direct-fire weapons will have to be used.

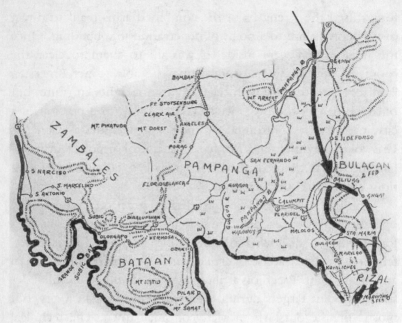

1st Cavalry Division approach to Manila[19]

Conclusion

The 1st Cavalry Division fought three distinct battles as part of the overall operations to liberate Manila: a penetration to free hostages and an attempt at a coup de main to seize the city, a series of attacks to isolate Manila from outside reinforcements, and attacks to annihilate the remaining Japanese forces within the city.

All of these fights required operations in built-up areas. The tactics, techniques, and procedures used in the Pacific were largely the same as the ones used in Europe. The grim nature of the fights caused the American and Allied high command to think about the impending Japanese defense of their home island after Manila was destroyed.

From trooper to general, it did not take much imagination

to envision the savage battles that lay ahead. The tactics used in the street fighting reinforced the requirement of using the combined-arms team. The focus of the combined arms was to make an entry point to allow the infantry to finish the job inside enemy-held buildings. However, contemporary conditions have changed.

Today, military forces fight under the immediate glare of television cameras reporting live from near the tip of the spear, or at least from a five-star hotel nearest the fighting. There is a greater density of urban terrain around the world, so city fights will become more frequent. Also, weapons have evolved since 1945. The power of the combined-arms team has increased, whereas the basic tactics of fighting in cities have not changed. There is one constant: Troopers must get to a point of penetration in a wall and begin the grim task of killing an enemy force inside.

ENDNOTES

1. B. C. Wright, *The 1st Cavalry Division in World War II* (Tokyo: Toppan Co. Ltd., 1947), 139.

2. The two flying columns were made up of the following units. The 2/5 Cavalry: Reconnaissance Platoon; Antitank Platoon; and Medical Detachment, 5th Cavalry. A Battery, 82d Field Artillery. A Company, 44th Tank Battalion. 3d Platoon, A Troop, 8th Engineers; and 1st Platoon, A Troop, 1st Medical Squadron. 2/8 Cavalry: Reconnaissance Platoon; Antitank Platoon; Maintenance Section, 8th Cavalry. B Company, 44th Tank Battalion. B Battery, 61st Field Artillery. 1st Platoon, C Troop, 8th Engineers; and 1st Platoon, B Troop, 1st Medical Squadron.

3. Robert R. Smith, *Triumph in the Philippines. The War in the Pacific: United States Army in World War II* (Washington, DC: Office of the Chief of Military History, 1963), 215; Wright, 126.

4. Stanley Falk, *Liberation of the Philippines* (New York: Ballantine Books, Inc., 1971), 107.

5. Smith, 249–50.

6. Wright, 125.

7. Smith, 220.

8. Wright, 128.
9. Ibid., 131; Smith, 252.
10. Wright, 132; Smith, 251–52; Falk, 103, 107.
11. Falk, 107.
12. Wright, 138–39.
13. Reproduced and modified from Smith.
14. Smith, 294.
15. Ibid., 294–97.
16. Wright, 140.
17. Falk, 109; Smith, 306–7.
18. Smith, 250.
19. Reproduced and modified from Smith.

NINE

Berlin, 1945:

Backs Against the Wall

by Maj. Mike Boden

History shows that there are no invincible armies.
—Joseph Stalin, 1941

In the early-morning hours of April 16, 1945, a tremendous artillery barrage rained down on German positions across the Oder River. This storm of steel signaled the final campaign of World War II on the eastern front and culminated on May 2 with the collapse of Adolf Hitler's Third Reich. The Berlin campaign provides a number of different perspectives on the nature of fighting in the closing stages of the war. At the same time, the campaign demonstrates the serious problems both sides faced in urban, city combat.

Leadership was also tested in the fierce battle for Berlin. A surprising element of the campaign was the degree of sloppiness that characterized fighting by both armies, and the decisions made by their commanders. On the Soviet side, generals and marshals led operations poorly. On the German side, the leadership was somewhat better, although no degree of war fighting excellence could compensate for the overwhelming disparity in numbers and firepower. One of the reasons that the final campaign of World War II was so complex is because of the different types of combat that occurred. The varied terrain provided diverse challenges to leaders at all levels. The first part of this campaign occurred in the open plain to the east of Berlin, whereas the final two weeks consisted of close-quarter, no-holds-barred, urban warfare in the labyrinth of Berlin. The battle for Berlin yields many important lessons concerning the challenges of urban warfare when a determined enemy has his back against the wall in a desperate city fight.

The Opening Stages

For the Berlin campaign, the Soviet Union mustered more than 2.5 million troops in three fronts along the Oder River.[1] By comparison, the combined forces of Great Britain and the United States on the western front, including the elements stationed in England, did not comprise 2.5 million troops.[2] In addition to the huge numbers of men, the general headquarters of the Soviet high command, Stavka, also allocated half of the entire Soviet army's armor forces and a third of its artillery for the assault. More than 7,500 combat aircraft supported the attack as well.[3] The Wehrmacht formations facing this imposing force consisted of between 250,000 and 340,000 German troops and 850 tanks belonging to Army Group Vistula, under Col. Gen. Gotthard Heinrici. With a reputation as a skillful defensive fighter, Heinrici took command of the army group on March 20.[4] The numbers do not include German elements inside the Berlin city limits. Estimates indicate that the city's defenders numbered between 100,000 and 225,000 men, most of whom possessed questionable combat worth.[5] By depleting all remaining personnel resources, including the last reserves of Volkssturm (Home Defense) and Hitlerjugend (Hitler Youth) forces, city administrators possibly could have raised another 75,000.[6]

As if the German situation was not bleak enough, shortly before the offensive began, at Hitler's insistence the German high command in Berlin transferred four of Heinrici's panzer divisions—half of his available armor—south to Army Group Center under Field Marshal Ferdinand Schörner. Hitler was convinced that the Soviets would direct their main effort in the impending offensive against Prague.[7] As compensation for Army Group Vistula, Hitler personally promised Heinrici 150,000 men. The German high command also created a new army near Magdeburg, the Twelfth Army, under Gen. Walter Wenck, to assist in the eastern defenses. Of the promised troops, only 30,000 untrained conscripts eventually arrived on the Oder, a mere 1,000 of them with weapons. Wenck's Twelfth Army eventually reached a strength of five divisions and 55,000 men and played a considerable role in Heinrici's operations.[8]

Command and Control

Although much of the German problem of unity of command can be traced directly to Hitler, other agencies within the German civil and military apparatus cannot escape blame for the ominous situation that developed before the beginning of the campaign. From its inception, the German command structure within Berlin possessed serious flaws. An initial question existed as to whether or not the city should be defended at all. For Hitler, the necessity for the city's defense was never in doubt. In early February 1945, the Führer proclaimed Berlin a *"Festung"* (fortress), ordering the city to be defended to the last man. Unfortunately, neither the Führer nor any of his subordinates in the armed forces general headquarters (Oberkommando der Wehrmacht, or OKW) under its chief, Field Marshal Wilhelm Keitel, actually dedicated or earmarked any troops or supplies to be used for this defense.[9]

Only after the third commander of the Berlin Defense Area, Lt. Gen. Helmuth Reymann, took charge on March 8 were any plans actually drawn up for the defense of the city. Part of this

shortcoming stems from the fact that the military leadership of
Germany outside the OKW felt that the city should not be defended at all. General Heinrici developed his army group's operational concept with the primary purpose of saving as many
soldiers and civilians as possible from the Soviets, allowing them
to flee westward into the arms of the British or Americans. With
this as his main consideration, upon the city being threatened,
troops inside Berlin would occupy prepared defensive positions
to the east of the city. Once there, if forced to fight they would
join with elements of the German Ninth Army under Gen.
Theodor Busse and retreat to the northwest, around the city,
into Mecklenburg, facilitating surrender to the British.[11]

The command situation would not improve for the Germans. Between early February 1945 and the fall of the city, no
less than five different officers commanded the Berlin Defense
Area.[12] Additionally, none of these commanders retained independent responsibility for the defense, each of them having to
answer to the Führer for all decisions, crippling their ability to
enact any changes or modifications to the already piecemeal defense plan. In addition to this rapid succession of leadership,
many different military organizations had responsibility for some
aspect of the defense. Few of these, however, had any jurisdic-
tion over other agencies conducting concurrent tasks necessary
for the defense. At the center of this web was Hitler himself, who
never relinquished personal command of the city until hours before his death. The emasculated OKW served primarily as a
mouthpiece for Hitler and was unwilling or unable to voice any
dissenting opinion concerning military operations. As a result,
the high command failed to prepare any plans for the defense of
the city, relying alternately on either Hitler's assurances or their
own beliefs that the city should not be defended.[13] Army Group
Vistula actually did develop plans for the defense of the Berlin

area, but these were designed to avoid battle for the capital entirely.

Complicating the already complex situation, organizational responsibility for the city's defense changed just as frequently as actual military command. The Wehrmacht Area Headquarters held initial responsibility as the Berlin garrison headquarters but transferred this mantle to Army Group Vistula on April 19 when combat became imminent. Hitler revoked this transfer only three days later, and placed Berlin's defense directly under the OKW—for all practical purposes, under himself. Two days later the army high command fled Berlin, driven out by strong pressure from Marshal Ivan S. Koniev's advancing armored spearheads. After a day of confusion, command reverted to LVI Corps of the Ninth Army, under Gen. Helmuth Weidling. This unit had occupied defenses to the east of Berlin and withdrawn into the city under Soviet pressure.[14] Each of these command authorities held different objectives and goals regarding Berlin, objectives often at cross-purposes with one another.

Inside the city, among the nonmilitary forces, similar problems with command existed. Regardless of the differing opinions concerning the fate of the city itself, the focus of military groups remained on fighting the Soviets. The primary function of the civilian agencies still in the city was to support this activity. To accomplish this task, inside Berlin the civilian bureaucracy could draw upon Wehrmacht and Waffen-SS troops, military police units, Hitlerjugend detachments, Volkssturm units, and various other party mechanisms and officials. The most important person in this bureaucracy was the *Gauleiter* of Berlin, Joseph Goebbels, who was directly responsible for organizing the city's defenses.[15]

Goebbels had extensive resources at his disposal. Although the prewar population of Berlin had shrunk during the war years from nearly 4.5 million to just over 2.5 million, even in April

1945 there was still considerable industrial activity in the capital. Sixty-five percent of Berlin's factories still functioned, utilizing more than 600,000 workers.[16] Goebbels also served as Reich defense commissioner for Berlin, taking responsibility for all measures not of a purely military nature more than ten kilometers behind the front. His area of responsibility included such activities as preparing bridges for demolition and preparing field fortifications using civilian labor.[17] To add to this convoluted process, Goebbels and the Reich defense commissioner for Brandenburg, Steurz, did not get along.[18] The animosity contributed to the fact that none of the commanders of the Berlin Defense Area had any direct control, or even any input into prioritization or execution, over any of the non-army troops or activities in Berlin. This included Volkssturm units, SS troops, flak units (under the control of Reichsmarshal Hermann Göring's Luftwaffe, not answerable to the army), Hitlerjugend forces, the Todt labor organization, and any labor services. Even some regular Wehrmacht units remained unavailable to the army commanders until the last days of the fighting. As one contemporary German officer wrote, "It was not incompetence—apart from individual instances—nor sabotage that led to the downfall of Berlin, but the disorganization of the command system, brought about by Hitler."[19]

On the Soviet side, the same degree of confusion in command did not exist. Only one person directly controlled military operations for the Berlin campaign, and that was Joseph Stalin, general secretary of the Soviet Union's communist party. The problems the Soviet armed forces faced in the campaign stemmed from Stalin's delineation of powers among his subordinate commanders for the operation. The three front commanders leading the operations represented three different career trajectories among the Soviet senior leadership. Commanding the

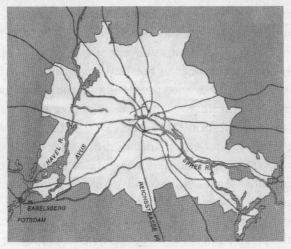

The districts[20]

1st Byelorussian Front, Marshal Georgi Konstantinovich Zhukov was the pure soldier who had managed to avoid Stalin's military purges of the immediate prewar years. His counterpart leading the 1st Ukrainian Front, Marshal Ivan S. Koniev, was a fiercely political officer who, although a gifted leader, owed his high command more to political loyalty than to military ability. Marshal Konstantin Rokossovsky, leading the 2d Byelorussian Front, was a talented commander who was imprisoned during the purges for three years on charges of sabotage and "crimes against the people." In 1940, following the Soviet debacle in Finland, Stalin released him from prison.[21] These were the three men who would lead Soviet forces against Berlin.

When Gen. Alexi I. Antonov, chief of the Soviet general staff, first developed the plan in Moscow at the beginning of April, the task of taking the city itself fell to Zhukov, arguably the Soviet Union's most able front commander in 1945. The plan called for the three Soviet fronts, attacking simultaneously along several axes, to pierce the German defenses and take Berlin by the twelfth to fifteenth day of the operation.[22] When Koniev received the task of conducting a supporting attack to the south of Zhukov, the commander of the 1st Ukrainian Front protested the demarcation line between armies. Upon reconsideration, and wishing to offer incentives to his competing commanders, Stalin deleted the frontal boundary beyond the town of Lübben, halfway between the Oder and Berlin, declaring, "Whoever breaks in first, let him take Berlin."[23] This action on the part of Stalin stimulated both Zhukov and Koniev to drive their fronts faster and harder to reach Berlin first, leading to certain rash decisions on the part of each. Rokossovsky, to the north of Zhukov and already involved in the destruction of German forces trapped in the Courland pocket, had to readjust his lines rapidly to the west in preparation for the operation and would not be a serious contender in the race for the capital.

Stalin's intentional vagueness in designating responsibility for the final capture of Berlin caused considerable problems for Soviet leaders at all levels during the drive to the city. Stalin was clear, however, on one particular point: The Reichstag building itself, although a burnt-out shell and unoccupied for twelve years, symbolized the heart of both Berlin and Nazi Germany to the attackers; all Soviet plans terminated with the capture of this one structure. Therefore, both Zhukov and Koniev, with no love lost between them, pushed their subordinates to the breaking point in order to reach the capital city first. The fact that Zhukov, normally an exceptionally capable commander, performed far below his normal standards during the campaign did not facilitate Soviet progress. Whereas his formations struggled against the German defenses in the opening days of the campaign, Koniev's troops found the going much easier in the southern approaches to the German capital. As early as 6:55 on the morning of April 16, a few hours after the campaign kicked off, the 1st Ukrainian Front was able to report that of the 150 crossing sites in its sector, 133 were secure and in use.[24] Zhukov tried to bull his way into Berlin by the shortest possible route, as indicated by his order of the day for April 16: "The enemy will be crushed along the shortest route to Berlin. The capital of Fascist Germany will be taken and the banner of victory planted over it."[25]

The fierce competition between Zhukov and Koniev was not unique within the Soviet leadership. Colonel General Vasili Chuikov commanded the Eighth Guards Army under Zhukov, and was best known as the hero of Stalingrad. In that epic struggle, Chuikov commanded the unit that had been redesignated as the Eighth Guards Army (the former Sixty-second "Stalingrad" Army). Although a gifted commander, he frequently disagreed with his superior on the conduct of the Berlin operation. Chuikov felt strongly that Zhukov prematurely halted the first Soviet offensive of the year, the Vistula-Oder Operation, in February. The hero of Stalingrad felt that Soviet forces could have taken Berlin easily had Zhukov kept pressing the offensive. For his part, Zhukov believed that Soviet logistics and fighting capabilities were worn out and stretched to the breaking point at the completion of this operation.[26] Some of the friction from this earlier disagreement remained between the two officers throughout the Berlin campaign, although it was not until after the war that this debate grew particularly heated. A second disagreement concerned the nature of the Berlin operation. Chuikov favored a "narrow" approach to take the city, concentrating forces along a tight front, whereas Zhukov decided upon a "wide" attack, hitting the defenses at many locations simultaneously.[27] After the costly, and for the most part futile, Soviet attacks during the first few days of the operation against the Seelow Heights, tensions remained high at the senior levels of the 1st Byelorussian Front.

The Developing Battle

The opening battle of the campaign began on the night of April 16 and, surprisingly, went reasonably well for the Germans. For a variety of reasons, the advancing armies of Zhukov's 1st Byelorussian Front made little to no headway against German defenders on the Seelow Heights, consisting of the Ninth Army. The Soviet time line called for Zhukov to break through the forward German defenses within twenty-four hours of the start of the offensive, but it was not until late on the evening of April 19 that Zhukov finally broke through these lines and began the open drive to Berlin.[28] This late penetration significantly affected the Soviet plan.

Although Zhukov achieved little success in the opening stages, his counterpart to the south, Koniev, cracked the German defenses south of Cottbus relatively easily and swiftly raced west and north to Berlin. In light of this success, Koniev readjusted his advance northward toward Berlin. Stalin approved of this move, much to the chagrin of Zhukov, who drove his forces harder in response on the seventeenth and eighteenth, in many cases reinforcing failure. A second development occurred: To the north of Zhukov, Rokossovsky's 2d Byelorussian Front accelerated its planning cycle and began its advance against the German Third Army, under the command of Gen. Hasso von Manteuffel, on April 19, earlier than originally planned.[29] Zhukov now faced the dilemma of lagging behind rivals on either flank.

Within the German command, this second development, coupled with the collapse of the German front on the evening of the nineteenth, caused Heinrici to set events into motion that would shape the coming battle for Berlin. Heinrici believed that it was imperative for the Ninth Army, facing Zhukov, to retreat from the Oder in order to remain intact, but such a decision rested in the hands of Hitler. The Führer's refusal to grant this request on the twentieth guaranteed the Ninth Army's destruction; after this, Heinrici concentrated his efforts to the north, where the Third Army still had a reasonable chance of conducting a fighting retreat and surviving.[30] Fulfilling Heinrici's fears, Zhukov's advancing forces pushed the bulk of the Ninth Army to the south in the course of the next few days of fighting, trapping it between his and Koniev's front.

The only element of the Ninth Army not caught in this trap was the LVI Panzer Corps, under Weidling. During the Soviet onslaught across the Oder, the corps directly faced Zhukov's main effort on the Seelow Heights and suffered heavy casualties. In this position, it was the Wehrmacht unit directly to the east of Berlin that had retreated due west when the German lines finally broke on the nineteenth. Upon completion of the first stage of the campaign, the unit was in position on the eastern outskirts of Berlin, battered but still intact and relatively dangerous. In a strange twist of fate, when Hitler heard of Weidling's "unauthorized" retreat from the Heights, he ordered the general arrested for desertion and executed. Weidling, becoming incensed upon receipt of this notice, called in his position to the Führer's bunker by public telephone, then hurried there to give a situation report in person. Hitler, visibly impressed with the commander known as "Smasher Karl" by his subordinates, not only removed the death warrant but placed Weidling in charge of Berlin's defenses, subordinate to Hitler alone.[31]

Once the 1st Byelorussian Front broke through the German defenses, its units were able to advance on Berlin as rapidly as the 1st Ukrainian Front was doing from the south. To the north, Rokossovsky was making slower progress against Manteuffel's Third Panzer Army. By the morning of April 21, elements of the Second Guards Tank Army, under Col. Gen. S. I. Bogdanov, crossed the autobahn ring northeast of Berlin, and Soviet heavy field artillery began shelling the city center by noon.[32] Beginning the next day, there was a brief lull in the battle as the Soviets prepared to attack the city. In general, although the advancing Soviet forces had not yet officially achieved encirclement, the escape routes open to the Germans trapped inside the city were few. Zhukov arrayed the bulk of his forces to the north and east of Berlin, roughly along the line of the Hohenzollern Canal and the River Spree. Three of his armies, along with two from Koniev's 1st Ukrainian Front, encircled Busse's 200,000 men trapped with the Ninth Army near Märkische Buchholz, southeast of the city.[33] The formal Soviet linkup between Zhukov's and Koniev's forces, completing the encirclement of Busse, occurred on April 24. At the same time in the north, Zhukov's Sixty-first Army, under Col. Gen. P. A. Belov, crossed the Oder-Havel Canal and separated the Third Panzer Army from German forces to the south, including Berlin and the other pieces of Army Group Vistula.[34]

Aside from LVI Panzer Corps, German formations within the city remained chaotic, particularly on April 21 as the lead Soviet elements closed on the city proper. The German forces opposing them faced impossible odds. Back on April 16, at the start of the campaign, Reymann, then commandant of the city, reported that forces within the city consisted of 41,253 men, mostly untrained Volkssturm. If necessary, a second call-up could be made that would theoretically mobilize another 50,000 conscripts of dubious quality. Even if such a call were successful, and this was a doubtful possibility at best, there were not enough weapons to man the force.[35] In addition to this, the leader of the Berlin Hitlerjugend, Reichsjugendführer Artur Axmann, created his own "Axmann Brigade," consisting for the most part of young boys, mounted on bicycles, armed with panzerfausts.[36] There were virtually no trained formations within the city.

When Weidling assumed effective command of Berlin's defenses on April 23, he solidified this shaky picture somewhat. Although the administrative and military confusion within the city made effective command and control problematic, a fair estimate of military formations by the time the Soviets encircled Berlin suggests approximately 60,000 men and fifty to sixty tanks within the Soviet ring. This includes the five divisional-size units within the city and the numerous smaller detachments at various locations throughout Berlin. The addition of LVI Panzer Corps added approximately 15,000 experienced and effective troops to the defense, and the realignment of the city defenses into six different zones added some semblance of organization to the picture. With the flight of the army high command on April 21 from Zossen, south of Berlin, command rested for all practical purposes with Weidling alone. Hitler did not leave his bunker again and, aside from ordering operational relief attempts and forbidding any breakout efforts, did not give any directives on the conduct of the defense.

Weidling simplified the existing defensive organizational structure when he reorganized the city's defenses upon his assumption of command. To begin with, he redistributed the city's nine defensive zones, putting experienced commanders in charge and using his veteran units to greatest benefit. The two divisions regularly assigned to LVI Panzer Corps were the 9th Parachute Division occupying Area A and the 20th Panzergrenadier Division at Zehlendorf in Area E. Weidling kept the 18th Panzergrenadier Division (previously the OKW reserve) as his reserve north of Tempelhof Airfield while he ordered two other army reserve formations, the "Müncheberg" Panzer Division and SS 11th "Nordland" Panzergrenadier Division, to occupy defensive positions at Karlshorst (Area B) and Tempelhof (Area C), respectively.[37] For artillery support, Weidling employed LVI Corps artillery in the Tiergarten, although ammunition shortages remained a serious problem during the final week.

In the east, Areas A and B fell under the command of Maj.

Gen. Werner Mummert, commander of the "Müncheberg" Panzer Division. In the southeast, SS Maj. Gen. Joachim Ziegler, commander of the SS 11th "Nordland" Division, assumed control of Area C. The LVI Panzer Corps chief of artillery, Col. Hans-Oskar Wöhlermann, commanded Area D at Tempelhof Airfield, and Maj. Gen. Josef Rauch, commander of the 18th Panzergrenadier Division, took charge in Area E to the southwest in the Grunewald Forest. Colonel Anton Eder led the defense in Area F, at Spandau and Charlottenburg, and Col. Harry Herrmann, commander of the 9th Parachute Division, was responsible for Areas G and H in the north. The final area, Z, was the "Zitadelle" and consisted of the area between the River Spree and the Landwehr Canal, including the Reichstag, under the command of SS Lt. Col. Siefert. Weidling intended this area to be the city's "last stand."[38] Although the defenses were now more organized, a new problem developed. Many of the replaced commanders in the new arrangement were Waffen-SS or political officers and deeply resented placement under Wehrmacht forces.[39]

Any pause in the fighting did not last long. Operations continued during this period, including the significant junction of Chuikov's and Rybalko's armored units at Schönefeld Airfield on the morning of the twenty-fourth, closing the ring around Berlin's defenders.[40] Colonel General Pavel Semenovich Rybalko was an outstanding commander, probably the Soviet Union's most innovative and successful armor commander of the war.[41] When the two armies of these commanders finally linked up at Schönefeld Airfield in the early-morning hours of April 24, the news came as a surprise to all commanders concerned. Zhukov at first did not believe Chuikov's report of a linkup with Rybalko, and there is some suggestion that this meeting was Zhukov's first indication that Koniev's forces were actually in the fight for the city itself.[42] Koniev beat Zhukov in the race for the city suburbs, reaching them on the twenty-second, but he severely depleted his forces in doing so. He had required a full day's rest and refitting (April 23) to prepare for the assault on the city, whereas Zhukov advanced more or less continually during the shift from maneuver warfare to urban fighting.[43]

This may have proved to be a fortuitous development for the commander of the 1st Byelorussian Front, because at 12:45 A.M. on April 23, Stalin at last had given final judgment on responsibility for the prize of the Reichstag. By directive number 11074, Stalin delineated the boundaries of Koniev's and Zhukov's armies eastward from Lübben to the Anhalter subway station in Berlin, less than two hundred yards from the Reichstag. The important building itself lay on Zhukov's side of the boundary.[44] On the morning of the twenty-fourth, the Soviets resumed the attack against the city on all fronts. To face Weidling's 60,000 men, the two Soviet fronts massed approximately 464,000 men, supported by 12,700 guns and mortars, 21,000 Katyusha rocket systems, and 1,500 tanks. Two air armies, the Sixteenth and the Eighteenth, supported the operation, often serving effectively as forward observers for Soviet artillery.[45] As the situation unfolded, the Soviets prepared to reduce the city with five rifle and four tank armies.[46]

Soviet completion of the encirclement ensured Berlin's ultimate fate. Final subjugation of the city, however, proved a hard task to accomplish. Between April 24 and 28, heavy fighting still raged in many of the outer suburbs, between the inner and outer rings of defense.[47] Even though Stalin's orders of the twenty-third denied Koniev's forces the honor of taking the Reichstag, the great advances of the twenty-fifth and twenty-sixth occurred in his command, particularly on Rybalko's front. After initial difficulties crossing the Teltow Canal on the twenty-fourth, his forces spent the next two days conquering the city districts of Zehlendorf, Lichterfelde, and Steglitz and the southern part of Grunewald. They finally cut the German defenses in half, trapping 20,000 defenders in Wannsee.[48] Potsdam fell on the twenty-seventh.

In the north, Zhukov's drive met a great deal of obstinate resistance, especially during the 1st Byelorussian Front's attempts to cross the Spree.[49] In the northeast, Col. Gen. V. I. Kutznetsov's Third Shock Army needed three days to advance three kilometers through the Pankow, Wedding, and Prenzlauerberg districts of Berlin. Farther to the west, elements of Maj. Gen. S. I. Perevertkin's LXXIX Corps of the Third Shock Army needed nearly the same amount of time to breach German defenses along the Hohenzollern Canal and advance to Moabit and the Tiergarten. The corps sustained particularly heavy losses in several failed attacks across the Westhafen Canal before finally succeeding on the twenty-sixth.[50] Also on the twenty-sixth, despite heavy resistance, Chuikov's army occupied Tempelhof Airfield by noon; then the army redirected its advance toward the Landwehr Canal.[51]

In addition to the difficult nature of the urban fighting and the fatigue of the Soviet attackers, other facts allowed defending German forces to stiffen their resistance. From the twenty-third to the twenty-sixth, Weidling was able to maintain relative stability and order within the city's defenses, even though the inevitable outcome of the fighting was apparent to most. The organization of the city's defenses proved as effective as could be hoped for, but the defenders were reaching the limits of their endurance. Cracks started to develop on the twenty-seventh, as witnessed by the loss of Tempelhof. Weidling had to continually adjust defensive lines and commanders.[52] By the end of April 27, the defense consisted of a long oval, stretching approximately fifteen kilometers east to west and five to six kilometers north to south. In addition to the constriction of the defensive lines, Manteuffel's Third Panzer Army finally succumbed to the repeated batterings of Rokossovsky's 2d Byelorussian Front and was in full retreat to the north of Berlin.[53] This collapse would cost Heinrici his job in the evening of the twenty-eighth, after a vitriolic exchange with Keitel.[54]

By the twenty-ninth, the German situation was desperate. Weidling, recognizing that the end was unavoidable, commented early in the morning, "By [tomorrow] morning the Russians will be able to spit in our windows."[55] The Soviets launched their final series of attacks against the remaining German resistance along three axes: first, from the east toward the Berlin center, conducted by the Fifth Shock Army; second, from the south toward the zoo via Tempelhof, then to Hohenzollernplatz, by units of the Second Guards Tank Army; and third, toward the zoo from the south and southeast through Charlottenburg by the Fifth Guards Tank Army and the Eighth Guards Army.[56] By the end of the day, Weidling's comment from the morning had proven prophetic: The German defenses in Zitadelle had been split into three parts.[57] Most of the defenders in these areas were either foreign auxiliaries fighting voluntarily for the Third Reich or die-hard members of the Waffen-SS. Hitler awarded the last Knight's Cross of the war on April 29 to Unterscharführer (Cpl.) Eugene Vaulto, the "Panzerfaust virtuoso," of the Charlemagne Battalion (French) for destroying eight tanks single-handedly on the twenty-seventh and twenty-eighth. After receiving his award, Vaulto returned to the fighting, where he perished.[58]

As Heinrici was losing his command of Army Group Vistula, Weidling, recognizing the futility of further efforts, drew up plans for a breakout from the city, to be conducted in three waves. The first wave would contain all mechanized assets available and two divisions, the 18th Motorized and the 9th Parachute Division. The second wave would consist of mostly administrative elements, including Hitler's staff, with some maneuver elements to provide security. The final wave would include the remaining combat formations, which by the evening of the twenty-eighth included only the "Müncheberg" Panzer Division, Maj. Gen. Erich Bärenfanger's garrison command,[59] the SS 11th "Nordland" Division, and a rear guard from the 9th Parachute Division.[60] On the evening of the twenty-eighth and twenty-ninth, Weidling proposed the breakout plan to Hitler. The German defenses within the city had been pushed back even farther, reduced to a long, narrow band, running close to ten kilometers on an east-west axis, but nowhere greater than one mile north to south. Within this oval, the remaining 30,000 German defenders fought on as food and ammunition rapidly diminished. Weidling estimated that his forces could hold out no more than another forty-eight hours. Regardless of the situation, Hitler, supported by numerous fanatical Nazi Party officials and soldiers, refused to grant permission for the breakout.[61] At the same time that the military leadership recognized the imminent end of the battle, the political leadership of the city and the Reich began last-ditch efforts to forestall complete and total surrender to the Soviets. On April 28 Heinrich Himmler, from his castle residence at Ziethen, attempted to discuss surrender/peace terms with Count Bernadotte of Sweden. Although these endeavors came to nothing, this betrayal of the Führer served to further depress the mood within the highest elements of the German government.[62]

German forces outside the city did not sit by idly while the offensive progressed. The Führer's staff in his bunker drew up plans for three separate relief attempts, although none of the commanders in the field would execute those plans with the dexterity or the will that Hitler envisioned. Hitler and his command group placed their greatest hope on the efforts of SS Obergruppenführer (Lt. Gen.) Felix Steiner, from the north. On April 22, Heinrici directed Steiner to organize an improvised task force in order to relieve pressure on Manteuffel's Third Panzer Army by conducting a spoiling attack in the north. In two days of hard fighting near the town of Oranienburg, Steiner first advanced about ten kilometers south, then retreated back under heavy Soviet pressure. But he did manage to gain three days for Manteuffel to better prepare his forces for the fighting withdrawal ahead.[63] The fact that Steiner, one of the most highly regarded SS generals in the German command, actually raised seven battalions and conducted a limited advance in the direction of the capital was surprising.[64] Although the attack ultimately failed, Hitler saw this as a golden opportunity for the relief of Berlin. The key to success, though, entailed providing Steiner with the necessary forces to conduct such an operation; the problem, one that neither Hitler nor any members of his staff would recognize, was that there were no forces available. Hitler ordered Steiner to conduct a relief of the city along the same line. Pressured by the advancing 2d Byelorussian Front, worn down by hard fighting, and with no reinforcing troops, any such attack was doomed from the start. Steiner recognized this, and never seriously attempted to advance, although both Hitler and Keitel looked and planned for its launching well into the twenty-eighth.[65]

The other two efforts were closely related. On April 23, Hitler ordered Busse and Wenck to bring their armies into Berlin to reinforce the garrison.[66] For Wenck, this meant beginning a counterattack into Koniev's western flank. Busse, limited by Hitler's "no retreat" orders of the previous week, had less ability to maneuver. Inability and unwillingness on the part of both commanders to reach the doomed city led to the operation developing into a breakout attempt by the Ninth Army in the direction of a relief effort by the Twelfth Army. Beginning on April 28, Busse attacked to the west with approximately 200,000 troops and tens of thousands more civilians in an attempt to reach Wenck's limited advance. The Ninth Army caught the encircling forces unprepared for such a maneuver and managed to pierce the Soviet ring along the Zossen-Baruth road and move west. This small crisis, however, brought a swift Soviet response, and Koniev's troops pounded Busse's column for the next forty-eight hours. Only 40,000 soldiers and one "Tiger" tank reached Wenck's lines on May 1.[67] Wenck, having advanced nearly fifty kilometers toward Busse, could not hold on to his advanced position near Beelitz for an extended period of time, and turned to the west in order to reach the Elbe as soon as the two armies joined. On May 7, he surrendered the 100,000 men of the Ninth and Twelfth Armies to American forces. With his troops were 300,000 civilians, many of whom had escaped with Busse's forces.[68] The actions of these two elements are among the most stirring of the operation, although they did not figure directly into the Berlin fighting. Koniev himself praised Busse's troops in his memoirs, commenting on their tenacity, fighting as they were for their very lives against hopeless odds.[69]

Early in the morning of April 30, Keitel informed Hitler that all relief efforts had failed. At 3:20 in the afternoon, after finally (and far too belatedly) authorizing Weidling to conduct a breakout from Berlin, the Führer and his bride, Eva Braun, committed suicide.[70] Weidling ordered the breakout to begin on the evening of April 30. Many different elements attempted to escape from the doomed city, but few succeeded. Most efforts ended in failure and capture or destruction by encircling Soviet forces. After accounting for casualties and the breakout attempts, on May 1 approximately 10,000 combat troops remained in the city center. Most of these occupied positions in the Reichstag, the Friedrichstrasse Railway Station, the Gendarmenmarkt, the Air Ministry, and the Reichs Chancellery. The units consisted primarily of a mixture of Volkssturm, Waffen-SS detachments (mostly foreign volunteers), the SS "Nordland" Division, the SS 15th

"Latvian" Fusilier Battalion, and one battalion of the SS "Anhalt" Regiment.[71]

By that time, however, the final Soviet assaults, entrusted to Perevertkin's LXXIX Rifle Corps, were under way. They began on the morning of the twenty-ninth, when elements of the 756th and 380th Rifle Regiments assaulted the Moltke Bridge, a few hundred yards from the Reichstag. After initial failure, Perevertkin committed his second echelon, the 207th Infantry Division.[72] Finally, after much effort, assault teams seized the bridge and Soviet forces assaulted government buildings on the immediate south side of the river, including the Gestapo headquarters (commonly known as "Himmler's House").[73] It took Soviet troops nearly twenty-four hours to complete the elimination of German forces within these few hundred square yards. Perevertkin's troops did not capture Himmler's House until 2:30 on the morning of the thirtieth, and the remainder of the morning consisted of preparation for the final assault on the Reichstag. Finally, around midday on April 30, the 150th and 171st Rifle Divisions assumed their positions and prepared to attack the Reichstag.[74]

Approximately 5,000 German troops defended the Reichstag building. Most of these, however, were fanatical SS or foreign auxiliaries, for whom there could be no surrender. The fight proved to be incredibly vicious. Adding to the intensity of the attack, the overriding concern among the Soviet leadership was to take the building in time for May Day celebrations, which meant that attacking units had less than twelve hours to storm the structure. Anticipating the ultimate success of the attack, the Military Council of the Third Shock Army produced nine special red banners (one for each rifle regiment in LXXIX Corps) to be placed on the Reichstag, signifying the capitulation of the building.[75]

At 1:00 P.M., Soviet artillery opened up on the Reichstag,

followed by a three-battalion assault. One of these battalions, the 1st of the 756th Rifle Regiment, planted its banner from a second-floor window but could not advance any further. A second assault followed at 6:00 P.M., which met with more success. As part of this attack, the 150th Infantry Division's "Red Banner Number 5," carried by a handpicked escort of Party and Komsomol members, flew from the roof at 8:50, just over an hour before Stalin's suspense elapsed.[76] Unfortunately for the attackers, although the banner flew atop the building, only 300 Soviet soldiers occupied the roof; a few thousand German troops still occupied the lower floors. Fighting continued for two more days before the last 1,500 survivors surrendered at 1:00 P.M. on May 2. The Red Army took 2,600 German prisoners in the Reichstag, and counted an additional 2,500 dead on the ground. The Soviet War Memorial on the Siegesallee holds the graves of 2,200 Soviet soldiers who died in the assault.[77] Although sporadic skirmishing continued around the city for another few days, the fall of the Reichstag marked the end of all organized resistance. In the early-morning hours of May 2, Weidling arrived at Chuikov's headquarters to formally surrender Berlin to the Soviets.[78]

Tactics

For the Germans, the defensive situation was always bleak. The city defenses themselves remained divided into three different sections: an outer ring, an inner ring, and the closest confines of the city itself, known as the Zitadelle, consisting for the most part of the area around the Tiergarten and the Reichstag building itself. The outer ring lay approximately thirty kilometers from the city center. This line rested at the farthest extent of the city proper; beyond this line the Wehrmacht Area Headquarters and the Commander, Berlin Defense Area, retained operations control and responsibility. Up to that point, the most significant obstacles to advancing Soviet forces were of the natural variety: woods, lakes, rivers, and canals. However, due to serious shortages in both mines and wire, defenses along this line, and continuing back to the inner ring, consisted mainly of barricades and gun emplacements at critical positions, such as major road intersections. When fighting actually reached these positions, German defenders (what few there were) offered little resistance. Only occasional antitank ditches served to prohibit the advance of Soviet armor, a product of the conflicting and confusing spheres of command and responsibility within the city. Taken as a whole, this outer line extended approximately a hundred kilometers. The inner ring ran for the most part along the city circuit railroad and consisted for all practical purposes of no more than a simple, continuous trench.[79] With a few notable exceptions, the defenses along the Teltow Canal being the most significant, neither of these two lines would factor into the fight for the city to any great degree.

German defensive tactics remained far from uniform and most often depended on the circumstances of the combat itself. Some factors, however, stand out as trends common to the German defense. First, as the German lines contracted, the defenders enjoyed a better ratio of soldiers per meter of front. In addition, the soldiers who occupied these increasingly narrow frontages belonged more often to troops of better quality, such as LVI Panzer Corps, and achieved a higher standard of ability and discipline than many of the ad hoc units in the city. The Soviets could not press their significant numerical advantage in such a situation either, and the ratio of attackers to defenders, although never approaching equality, gradually decreased as the fight progressed.[80]

Another factor that worked in the defenders' favor was their use of underground structures. German soldiers proved adept at using the city's underground transportation network for such support functions as care of the wounded, lines of communication, and sheltering of noncombatants. On May 1, by which time the only two pockets of German resistance lay in the Tiergarten and near Spandau, German messengers still used the subway tunnel system under the city to maintain contact, admittedly somewhat sporadically, between the two locations.[81] In many instances the tunnels flooded, inhibiting Soviet forces already leery about entering the subterranean passages of the city from using them to any great effect. Koniev recalled in his memoirs that the "enemy's use of underground structures caused a good deal of trouble . . . groups of submachine-gunners, snipers, grenade throwers and men armed with *panzerfausts* emerging from the underground communications fired on motor vehicles, tanks and gun crews moving along already captured streets, sever[ing] our lines of communication and creat[ing] tense situations behind our firing lines."[82]

Most of the German defenses consisted of individual strongpoints, with or without external support. The farther from the city center these lay, the less effective they usually were in repulsing assault parties. Some of this systemic failure can be attributed to low-quality troops manning these positions during the opening days of the street fighting. Volkssturm security detachments of fewer than forty manned most of these posts, frequently with obsolete or useless weapons. A German observer wrote, "There is no mention in any report of serious fighting for the forward defense position[s]."[83] The report of Major Komorowski, a battalion commander in the Gatow sector, conveys the inadequacy of the non-Wehrmacht troops facing the Soviets:

> The position consisted of a well-built, continuous trench. The battalion was composed of construction and *Volkssturm* troops, none of whom had had combat expe-

rience. They were armed with captured rifles and a few machine guns, and had only a limited supply of ammunition. The infantry was supported by an 88mm anti-aircraft gun battery and a heavy infantry gun platoon, although the latter unit had never fired its weapons . . . On the evening of the first day of battle all the *Volkssturm* troops deserted, and the gap was filled only by recruiting stragglers. In two days of fighting all the defenders were either killed or captured.[84]

The closer the Soviets came to the city, however, the stronger the bunker complexes became. German defenders fortified street-corner buildings by closing all entries so that only small firing ports remained. Barricades of wood, cement, and iron, up to four meters thick, secured the flanks of many of these strongpoints. The most massive of these were undoubtedly the three colossal flak towers of the city, six stories high, with garrisons approaching a thousand men serving the antiaircraft guns on the roofs of the buildings.[85] These three towers—"Zoo," "Humboldthain," and "Friedrichshain"—were located in the vicinity of the Tiergarten. In addition to their garrisons, each tower protected more than 40,000 wounded soldiers and civilians against Soviet assaults.[86] Other engineering projects, however, consisted merely of building tank ditches, often with neither any coordination with the units that would actually be defending those ditches nor any thought as to the best means of emplacement.[87]

It was not until General Weidling took charge of Berlin's defenses that the situation improved to some degree. By that time, April 23, it was already far too late. The appointment of Weidling did, however, facilitate a few important improvements to the German dispositions. First, there was now a single, gifted military commander in charge of the defense. Even though he still had to answer to the Führer, the departure of the OKW and the army high command (Oberkommando der Heeres, or OKH) on the twenty-first at least allowed Weidling to have uninhibited military authority within the city in placing the defenses.[88] Second, Weidling brought his unit, LVI Panzer Corps, an experienced unit that could be called upon to man and fight the most tenuous positions along the line. As the German defensive lines constricted, this meant that more often the experienced soldiers of this unit would face the Soviet attackers.[88]

Many of the tactical problems for the Soviet forces resulted from a number of different considerations. The simple fact that Zhukov himself, one of the great military minds of the Soviet Union, was not at his best during the campaign was a critical factor in its evaluation. Whether the result of Stalin's manipulation or other factors, the commander of the 1st Byelorussian Front exhibited many failures during the final weeks of April. After facing criticism for overestimating German forces during the Vistula-Oder Operation in January and February, he now overcompensated and did not credit the German defenses enough. This resulted in his flawed initial plans for the battle, including his orders for direct frontal assaults, and his subsequent use of the front's tank armies before exploitation was a reasonable possibility. His front's practice of shining searchlights directly at the enemy lines (instead of reflecting off the clouds) only served to silhouette his formations crossing the Oder. Finally, his inability to adjust to initial problems during the opening days of the campaign and his lack of flexibility in adapting his plans to the realities of the battlefield further slowed Soviet progress in this stage of the operation.[89] Stalin certainly did not mitigate these challenges by his calculated statements to Zhukov after the failed attacks of the sixteenth.[90]

Koniev called the Berlin operation as "the most complicated of all the operations I carried out during the war."[91] Part of his assessment concerned the fact that advancing Soviet armies had to contend with a variety of different geographical features during the operations. Brandenburg, and the terrain around Berlin, contained many hindrances to maneuver, such as woods, marshes, and many different water obstacles, both man-made and natural.[92] Once the advancing armies negotiated these obstacles and reached the city limits of Berlin itself, the terrain changed again. Now fighting in an urban environment, the advancing Soviet forces had to get through the city suburbs. In the outer reaches of the city, the terrain consisted for the most part of suburban neighborhoods, small garden plots, and a great number of canals, lakes, and waterways. Once beyond these outer suburbs, the advancing forces found themselves in the city center, where yet another type of landscape awaited them—the urban inner city, consisting mostly of large concrete, multistoried buildings.

April 22 marked the transition from the mobile campaign to the suburban battle of encirclement that would culminate in the city fight proper.[93] Before the start of the campaign, Koniev's plan designated his two tank armies, the Third Guards Tank Army, under Rybalko, and the Fourth Guards Tank Army, under Gen. D. D. Lelyushencko, to "cut loose" from their supporting infantry and rush to the southern suburbs of Berlin with all haste.[94] These two armies accomplished this task quite ably by the evening of the twenty-second, when some of Rybalko's tanks reached the Teltow Canal a dozen kilometers southwest of the Reichstag. The war of maneuver thus far proceeded so swiftly, in fact, that at one point on April 21 elements of Koniev's VI Guards Tank Corps, under Maj. Gen. V. A. Mitrofanov, in Rybalko's army, ran out of fuel near Baruth and were decimated by a detachment of Hitlerjugend armed only with panzerfausts. The German success, however, was short lived, because Rybalko's main body renewed the advance in the afternoon.[95] Koniev's operation had progressed well, but now it slowed down suddenly as the nature of the fighting shifted to the city environs. On the morning of April 24, Rybalko's units found themselves storming a fortified city, fighting from house to house.[96] Success came much slower from this point; successes were now measured in city blocks, not kilometers. Also on the twenty-second, the forces of Col. Gen. V. I. Kutznetsov (Third Shock Army) and Col. Gen. S. I. Bogdanov (Second Guards Tank Army), under Zhukov, attempted to take Berlin by a sudden and swift strike from the east. This attempt failed as the two attack prongs quickly became tied down in urban fighting.[97] Across the entire Soviet front, the transition between maneuver warfare and urban fighting presented a considerable problem of adaptation.

A final element influencing the slow progression of the campaign, at least from the Soviet perspective, was the fact that soldiers in the Red Army could see the war winding down. A significant dichotomy existed between the Red Army's senior leaders, driving their forces as fast as possible in order to secure the German capital by Stalin's deadline of May 1 (in time for the May Day celebrations), and the desire of the common foot soldier or tanker in the Soviet army to stay alive and make it home in one piece.

In preparation for the intense urban fighting, coming as soon as it did on the heels of a maneuver fight, the Soviets developed distinct methods to apply in Berlin. Both Koniev and Zhukov recognized the need for unique methods of attacking desperate German positions. The Soviet commanders outlined their concepts early in the campaign and ensured dissemination and rehearsal prior to the actual commencement of operations on April 16. There was no opportunity, however, to actually implement these tactics until a week later, well into the actual fighting for the city itself. By then casualties had worn out and significantly reduced Soviet forces. It was not until April 24 and 25 when these tactics finally secured widespread, consistent use among the attacking

Soviet forces. German defenders noted in retrospect that during the early urban assault, Soviet armor and infantry coordination appeared haphazard and left much to be desired, although the untrained defenders proved unable most of the time to resist a determined Soviet attack.[98] Chuikov himself described many mistakes the attacking forces made, even citing some elements of his own Eighth Guards Army sending tanks through city streets in column, where German troops armed with panzerfausts and panzerschrecks easily blocked the street at either end and wiped out Soviet columns piecemeal.[99]

One thing all Soviet commanders recognized in fighting for the city streets was the need for heavy firepower, particularly artillery, to subjugate the enemy. Chuikov remarked, "A battle within a city is a battle of firepower."[100] In theory, at least, Zhukov's tactics and methodology were more precise and thorough than those of his rivals in the other fronts. Koniev reported that his units set up special assault task forces for fighting in the city. These groups consisted of different combined-arms troops, including between a platoon and a company of infantry, a platoon of tanks, a section of self-propelled guns, a section of Katyushas, and a detachment of sappers.[101] The artillery detachments and the engineers were the most important elements in this situation, particularly the latter as the Soviets crept closer to the center of the city, where the Germans made good defensive use of the city's concrete buildings and subterranean passageways.

Assaults almost always involved the initial use of artillery forces that pulled up a close distance to the German defenses. The size of these guns ranged from 85mm all the way to large 203mm pieces and Katyushas, the latter incredibly powerful when used in a direct-fire manner.[102] Although the cost usually was devastating to the artillerymen who were left in the open and unprotected as they fired on the Germans from a few hun-

dred meters away, this tactic proved most effective in strongpoint elimination when combined with appropriate use of the
other element forces.[103] One Soviet war correspondent wrote
that the Soviet guns, in such circumstances, "sometimes fired a
thousand shells on to one small square, a group of houses, or
even a tiny garden."[104] Once the artillery softened up the defenses, Soviet armor and/or infantry attacked. Zhukov's forces
used armored units more frequently in initial attacks on the barricades as they tried to batter down the defenses before follow-
on infantry came through. Forces in the southern sections of
Berlin, facing the 1st Ukrainian Front, reported more instances
of infantry assaulting without armor support.[105] Nevertheless,
this ad hoc and almost surprisingly late-found reliance on combined arms at the small-unit level was a key ingredient in the
ultimate Soviet success. Chuikov reflected: "Comradeship in action, mutual assistance between infantry, artillery, engineers, signals, tanks and reconnaissance, became the decisive factor at this
stage."[106]

In other areas, the Soviets adapted rather well to fighting
within the city's boundaries. Sapper detachments often proved
extremely valuable to the attacking Soviet forces. In attacking a
fortified building or house, the attacking forces frequently discovered that the more effective way to eliminate the strongpoint
was to go through the cellar. While forces above ground kept the
defenders occupied, elements of the assault force attempted to
break into the building through holes made by antitank guns. If
a wall proved too thick for such a measure, as occurred more frequently the closer the attackers closed on the city center, the sappers were called on to break down the wall using a *faustpatron,*
or tank-busting charge.[107] German civilians, many of whom attempted to hide from the fighting in the lower reaches of their
dwellings, suffered high casualties in such attacks.[108] Although

the Soviet forces often attempted successfully to utilize the cellars of the buildings as a toehold or staging area for further attacks, they were somewhat hesitant to enfilade the German positions through the sprawling Berlin subway system.

As the fighting closed in on the city center, narrowing unit frontages once again forced the Soviets to change their approaches to the attack. By the morning of April 27, regiments attacked on a front as narrow as 175 to 225 meters. Zhukov deployed his forces so that "units and smaller elements were assigned specific streets, squares, and other objectives." Although he certainly painted a rosy picture through his observations that behind the chaos of street fighting was "a logical and well-thought-out system," there is ample evidence to suggest at least an attempt on his part to standardize the process.[109]

At this point in the fighting, as the attacking fronts penetrated to the city center by the twenty-seventh, the combined-arms teams mutated again. Infantry troops now rooted their way through individual buildings, usually with an assignment of one regiment per street, a battalion working its way down each side. Soviet light infantry employed their organic firepower through the buildings while artillery tried to progress through back alleys in order to get into position.[110] As the operation reached its climax, the Soviet forces deployed in these operations typically suffered severe casualties. In their haste to achieve the fall of the city, unit commanders spent little effort rotating fresh troops into the line, relying instead on hours of darkness for the forward elements' rest and recovery. The two-plus weeks of fighting reduced most front-line companies to twenty to thirty men; regiments could field only two battalions instead of the normal three.[111] One Soviet veteran recalls that by April 30, of the 104 men from his company who had survived the first phase of the operation, the penetration of the Oder line, only 20 were left inside the city.[112]

Lessons from Berlin

Losses on both sides were extremely heavy. Of the 2.5 million Soviet soldiers who participated in the campaign, the Soviet government awarded the Soviet medal for the capture of Berlin, specifically for those who fought within the city, to slightly more than 1 million men (1,082,000).[113] Official reports list Soviet casualties as 352,475, of which 78,291 were killed. In addition, the First and Second Polish Armies, which also took part in the operation, lost 8,892 soldiers.[114] The two air armies supporting the offensive lost 527 aircraft. As a testament to the determination with which many of the attackers conducted themselves, more than 600 of them received recognition as Heroes of the Soviet Union, 13 of them for the second time.[115]

On the German side, losses were catastrophic, not only for combatants but for civilians as well. The destruction of Berlin was so great that after the war estimates showed that the city contained one-seventh of the rubble in Germany.[116] Of the civilian population, at least 30,000 died and 40,000 occupied hospitals at the conclusion of hostilities. Nearly half of the houses in the city were destroyed and 20 percent of those remaining were badly damaged.[117] Casualties are much harder to determine for German military units during the operation. The Soviet fronts took approximately 480,000 prisoners during the campaign from April 16 through May 5, when the last column attempting to break out of Berlin (consisting of 17,000 combatants from the Ruhleben vicinity) was eliminated. This includes soldiers captured on the Oder line, during Manteuffel's retreat in the north, and during the breakout operations of Busse's Ninth Army. Koniev and Zhukov captured 134,000 Germans within the city itself. The grand total amounted to the equivalent of at least ninety-three German divisions destroyed in the operation.[118] In addition, the Soviets claim to have destroyed or captured 1,500 tanks, 8,600 guns and mortars, and 4,500 aircraft.[119]

In the end, though, the Soviet attack was far too great for the Germans to withstand. The fighting was so fierce that nearly twenty years after the battle, equipment from the fighting still littered certain areas around Berlin.[120] But the Soviet armies did not pause after the city capitulated. On May 3, Koniev left Berlin and continued the Soviet push south toward Dresden and Prague, in order to beat the Western Allies to those cities. In Berlin, the occupiers swiftly began to organize the new government. As early as April 28, Col. Gen. N. E. Berzarin took over as the Soviet commandant of Berlin, and within the week Walter Ulbricht flew in from Russia to take over as the leader of a new Germany. By May 11, the conquerors had renamed the streets.[121] For four years, the Soviet Union had suffered 29 million deaths in the struggle against German fascism. The fall of Berlin marked the close of that struggle and the dawn of a new one in which Berlin, again, would take center stage. The intensity of the fighting bore out the words of Lenin, who said in the early decades of the century, "Whoever controls Berlin will rule Germany; whoever controls Germany rules Europe."[122]

ENDNOTES
1.   Tony Le Tissier, *The Battle of Berlin, 1945* (New York: St. Martin's Press, 1988), 1.
2.   Stephen E. Ambrose, *Eisenhower and Berlin, 1945. The Decision to Halt at the Elbe* (New York: W. W. Norton & Company, Inc., 1967), 67.
3.   Le Tissier, *Battle of Berlin*, 1, 6.
4.   Ibid., 43.
5.   Tony Le Tissier, *Race for the Reichstag: The 1945 Battle for Berlin* (London: Frank Cass, 1999), 15.
6.   Erich Kuby, *The Russians and Berlin, 1945* (New York: Hill and Wang, 1968), 33; Anthony Read and David Fisher, *The Fall of Berlin* (New

York: W. W. Norton & Company, 1993), 328; Andrew Tully, *Berlin: A Story of a Battle* (New York: Simon and Schuster, 1963), 79, 128.

   7.   Kuby, 32; Read, 283.

   8.   Read, 287, 297.

   9.   Le Tissier, *Race*, 14; Wilhelm Willemer, *The German Defense of Berlin* (Historical Division, headquarters, U.S. Army, Europe, 1953), 7–8.

  10.   Map from Willimer.

  11.   Willemer, 11–12.

  12.   Early February, General von Kortzfleisch; February to March 8, Lt. Gen. Brunno Ritter von Hauenschild; March 8 to April 22, Reymann; April 22 to 23, Col./Lt. Gen. Ernst Kaether; April 23 to May 2, Gen. Helmuth Weidling.

  13.   Willemer, 10.

  14.   Ibid., 14.

  15.   Le Tissier, *Race*, 21–23.

  16.   Cornelius Ryan, *The Last Battle* (New York: Simon and Schuster, 1966), 16.

  17.   Le Tissier, *Race*, 18. In the city itself, 483 bridges were prepared for demolition.

  18.   Willemer, 20.

  19.   Ibid., 23.

  20.   Map from Ryan.

  21.   Richard Woff, "Rokossovsky" in *Stalin's Generals*, ed. Harold Shukman (New York: Grove Press, 1993), 181.

  22.   John Erickson, *The Road to Berlin: Continuing the History of Stalin's War With Germany* (Boulder, CO: Westview Press, 1983), 531.

  23.   Ibid., 533.

  24.   Read, 315.

  25.   Ibid., 309.

  26.   John Strawson, *The Battle for Berlin* (London: B. T. Batsford Ltd., 1974), 71; Georgi K. Zhukov, *Marshal Zhukov's Greatest Battles,* trans. Theodore Shabad (London: Macdonald, 1969), 276–79.

  27.   Vasili I. Chuikov, *The Fall of Berlin,* trans. Ruth Kisch (New York: Holt, Rinehart, and Winston, 1968), 11, 170.

  28.   Erickson, 573.

  29.   Ibid., 574.

  30.   Le Tissier, *Race,* 33; Erickson, 579.

31. Erickson, 591.

32. Le Tissier, *Race,* 40, 43.

33. Erickson, 592. The Soviets dedicated 277,000 men, 7,000 guns, and 280 tanks to this encirclement.

34. Read, 364–65.

35. Ibid., 328.

36. Ibid., 337.

37. Le Tissier, *Race,* 105–6.

38. Ibid., 15–16, 105.

39. Ibid., 105–6; Ryan, 397.

40. Erickson, 589.

41. Richard Woff, "Rybalko" in *Stalin's Generals,* ed. Harold Shukman (New York: Grove Press, 1993), 214.

42. Le Tissier, *Race,* 94–95; Chuikov, 170.

43. Le Tissier, *Race,* 58.

44. Erickson, 586.

45. Ibid., 595.

46. Erickson, 582. The armies were Kutznetsov's Third Shock and Bogdanov's Second Guards Tank from the north (Zhukov); Chuikov's Eighth Guards Tank and Col. Gen. M. I. Katukov's First Guards Tank from the east (Zhukov); Gen. N. E. Berzarin's Fifth Shock Army from the east (Zhukov); Lt. Gen. F. I. Perkhorovitch's Forty-seventh Army from the south (Zhukov); and Rybalko's Third Guards Tank Army, Lt. Gen. A. A. Luchinsky's Twenty-eighth Rifle Army, and Lelyushencko's Fourth Guards Tank Army from the southwest (Koniev).

47. Kuby, 145.

48. Read, 377; Erickson, 597–98.

49. V. Zubakov, *The Final Assault* (Moscow: Novosti Press Agency Publishing House, 1975), 24.

50. Le Tissier, *Race,* 88–89, 120.

51. Ibid., 124.

52. Ibid., 121–22.

53. Erickson, 598.

54. Le Tissier, *Race,* 152, 156–57; Read, 430; and Joachim Schultz-Naumann, *The Last Thirty Days. The War Diary of the German Armed Forces High Command From April to May 1945/The Battle for Reflections/ Reflections on the Events of 1945,* trans. D. G. Smith (New York: Madison Books, 1991), 35–41.

55.　Tully, 233.

56.　Kuby, 150.

57.　Read, 444. The commanders of each part were SS Maj. Gen. Wilhelm Mohnke, SS Maj. Gen. Gustav Krukenberg, and Lieutenant Colonel Siefert.

58.　Read, 447; Schultz-Naumann, 178. The SS Charlemagne Battalion was the last outside force to enter the besieged city, brought in by its leader, Major General Krukenberg, on April 24 with three hundred men. In eight days of fighting, the unit destroyed sixty Soviet tanks and was reduced to fewer than thirty men by the cessation of combat on May 2.

59.　Le Tissier, *Race*, 120. Bärenfanger was a political lackey of Goebbels, who received promotion and command within the city due to his party connections. In fairness, he acquitted himself well in the last few days of the siege.

60.　Erickson, 599.

61.　Le Tissier, *Race*, 152.

62.　Ibid., 38, 151.

63.　Willemer, 61; Read, 365. Hitlerjugend member Helmut Altner wrote about Steiner's action: "Most of us were killed by infantry fire, because we had to attack across open fields. Then the fighting in the town—two days of it. In two days and nights, Oranienburg changed hands four times. That finished another part of us. Then the Russians started bombarding the town with Stalin Organs, and when we wanted to finish and go home, we were stopped and made to join the escape across the canal. My platoon leader, who refused, was strung up on the nearest tree by a few SS and an SA man—but then, he was already 15 years old."

64.　Willemer, 61; Read, 395.

65.　Le Tissier, *Race*, 137–38.

66.　Willemer, 62.

67.　Le Tissier, *Race*, 154–55, 173–74.

68.　Ibid., 182.

69.　Ivan Koniev, *Year of Victory*, trans. David Mishne (Moscow: Progress Publishers, 1966), 182.

70.　Le Tissier, *Race*, 170.

71.　Ibid., 173.

72.　Tully, 253.

73.　Erickson, 601–3.

74.　Ibid., 604.

75. Le Tissier, *Race,* 168.
76. Erickson, 605–6.
77. Le Tissier, *Race,* 178.
78. Ibid., 190–92.
79. Willemer, 25–27.
80. Ibid., 31.
81. Ibid., 63.
82. Koniev, 176.
83. Willemer, 28.
84. Ibid., 31.
85. Koniev, 175–76.
86. Schultz-Naumann, 153.
87. Willemer, 27.
88. Ibid., 6.
89. Tony Le Tissier, *Zhukov at the Oder: The Decisive Battle for Berlin* (Westport, CT: Praeger, 1996), 252.
90. Erickson, 567.
91. Koniev, 124.
92. Ibid., 85.
93. Ibid., 131.
94. Erickson, 560.
95. Read, 347–49.
96. Koniev, 167.
97. Erickson, 582.
98. Le Tissier, *Battle of Berlin,* 79–81.
99. Le Tissier, *Race,* 80; Chuikov, 203. Chuikov writes that the Germans were "able to knock out our tanks only because the men in charge of the latter were guilty of tactical illiteracy: is it permissible to send machines into battle in column, along streets?" This particular incident occurred on April 28.
100. Read, 386–87.
101. Koniev, 168.
102. Read, 386–87.
103. Le Tissier, *Race,* 75.
104. Read, 386–87.
105. Le Tissier, *Race,* 79–84.
106. Chuikov, 193.
107. Vladimir Abyzov, *The Final Assault: Memoirs of a Veteran Who*

Fought in the Battle of Berlin (Moscow: Novosti Press Agency Publishing House, 1985), 51.

108.   Read, 386–87.

109.   Le Tissier, *Race,* 132–33.

110.   Ibid., 133.

111.   Erickson, 589.

112.   Abyzov, 67.

113.   Le Tissier, *Race,* 195.

114.   John Erickson, "*Poslednii Shturm:* The Soviet Drive to Berlin, 1945," in *The End of the War in Europe 1945,* ed. Gill Bennett (London: HMSO, 1996), 28–29; Le Tissier, Race, 195. Total official losses for Soviet land forces are as follows: 1st Byelorussian Front, of 908,500 men at the start of the campaign, 179,490 total casualties (19.7 percent), 37,610 killed or missing; 1st Ukrainian Front, of 550,900 men at the start of the campaign, 113,825 total casualties (20.7 percent), 27,580 killed or missing; 2d Byelorussian Front, of 441,600 men at the start of the campaign, 59,110 total casualties (13.4 percent), 13,070 killed or missing. The Soviets also admitted losing 2,156 tanks and self-propelled guns, as well as 1,220 guns of other types.

115.   Zubakov, 36.

116.   Alexandra Richie, *Faust's Metropolis: A History of Berlin* (New York: Carroll & Graf Publishers, Inc., 1998), 607.

117.   Martin Gilbert, *The Day the War Ended. May 8, 1945—Victory in Europe* (New York: Henry Holt and Company, 1995), 48; Ryan, 520. Ryan puts the number of civilian deaths at 100,000. Of these, 6,000 committed suicide and 20,000 died of heart attacks.

118.   Erickson, 621–22.

119.   Le Tissier, *Race,* 195.

120.   Koniev, 181.

121.   Read, 436–37; Gerhard Weinberg, *A World at Arms: A Global History of World War II* (Cambridge: Cambridge University Press, 1994), 825; Kuby, 240.

122.   Strawson, title page.

TEN

Jaffa, 1948:

Urban Combat in the Israeli War of Independence

by Benjamin Runkle

Men of the Irgun! We are going out to conquer Jaffa. We are going into one of the decisive battles for the independence of Israel. Know who is before you, and remember whom you are leaving behind you. Before you is a cruel enemy who has risen to destroy us. Behind you are parents, brothers, children. Smite the enemy hard. Aim true. Save your ammunition. In battle, show no more mercy to the enemy than he shows mercy to our people. But spare women and children. Whoever raises his hands in surrender has saved his life. You will not harm him. You will be led in the attack by Lieutenant Gideon. You have only one direction—forward. [1]

—Menachem Begin

With the words of their commander fresh in their minds, the Jewish guerrilla group Irgun Zevai Leumi (Irgun) launched a daring assault on the key Arab stronghold of Jaffa on the morning of April 26, 1948. In six days of intense street fighting, the outmanned and outgunned Jewish forces managed not only to dislodge the city's Arab defenders but subsequently withstand repeated counterattacks by the British army. In the end, as Begin predicted, the Irgun's conquest of Jaffa marked a significant turning point in the Israeli War of Independence.

However, for most modern military historians and strategists, the battle of Jaffa's true importance lies in its implications for contemporary urban warfare. Indeed, few engagements touched upon as many aspects of urban combat as did the Irgun's improbable victory. For the battle of Jaffa demonstrates how a numerically and technologically disadvantaged force can achieve success through a superior understanding of the unique principles of urban warfare. In particular, the battle illustrates the importance of combined-arms operations, tactical innovation, and small-unit leadership, and the effect of tactics upon civilian populations. Moreover, in a world where nonstate actors are becoming increasingly relevant militarily (for example, the former Yugoslavia, Somalia, Chechnya), the Irgun's success against the modernized British forces serves as a particularly poignant lesson for current U.S. military leaders.[2]

In this essay, therefore, I examine the key events of the battle of Jaffa and analyze how the Irgun's appreciation for the tactical complexities of urban warfare led to victory. I begin with a brief discussion of the strategic significance of Jaffa, as well as an overview of the Jewish, Arab, and British forces involved. I then proceed to distinguish the two separate phases of the battle: the Irgun's successful attack against Jaffa's Arab defenders, followed by the unsuccessful British counterattack to regain the city. I then analyze the battle's implications for modern urban combat. In particular, I examine the importance of combined-arms operations, tactical innovation, and small-unit leadership and the effect of tactical operations upon civilian populations. In the end, I argue that it was the Irgun's greater understanding of these unique variables that proved decisive in the battle of Jaffa.

Strategic Significance of Tel Aviv/Jaffa

Conventional military wisdom throughout the ages has been fairly consistent with regard to the undesirability of fighting battles in urban areas. Sun Tzu wrote, "The worst policy is to attack cities. Attack cities only when there is no alternative."[3] Similarly, a contemporary historian notes that for centuries Western military thinkers have held the deeply entrenched opinion "that cities are places where battles should not be fought."[4] And the American military's aversion to urban warfare is explicitly acknowledged on the first page of FM (Field Manual) 90–10, *Military Operations on Urbanized Terrain (MOUT),* stating that "Tactical doctrine stresses that urban combat operations are conducted *only* when required and that built-up areas are *isolated* and *bypassed* rather than risking a costly, time-consuming operation in this difficult environment."[5] However, cities often represent strategically vital centers of gravity that must be captured or controlled in order to gain the decisive advantage in a broader conflict. This was clearly the case with the city of Jaffa in Palestine before the 1948 Israeli War of Independence.

On November 29, 1947, the United Nations General Assembly voted thirty-three to nineteen to partition Palestine and establish a Jewish state. Over the next five months, Arab and Jewish forces engaged in a bloody civil war that would be an ominous foreshadowing of the ethnic conflicts that have plagued the post-Cold War era. More significantly, however, these armed clashes would determine the strategic position of the combatants when the British mandate ended on May 15, 1948. For the withdrawal of the remaining British forces from Palestine was immediately followed by an invasion of the newborn state of Israel by the surrounding Arab nations.

Perhaps no area was of greater strategic significance than the twin cities of Tel Aviv and Jaffa. Tel Aviv, with a population of 250,000, was the heart of the Jewish community in Palestine and its greatest source of manpower. Yet Tel Aviv was surrounded by a cordon of Arab villages and subject to constant harassment from its neighbor to the south. Jaffa, with its 100,000 Arab inhabitants, was the largest Arab city in Palestine and the second biggest port.[6] Snipers operating in the Manshieh quarter—a panhandle projecting from Jaffa into the heart of Tel Aviv—had inflicted nearly a thousand casualties, mostly civilians, in Jewish Tel Aviv during the months since the partition vote. The minaret of the Hassan Bek Mosque, from which the snipers operated, had become an especially obnoxious symbol of the irregular war. This constant sniper fire also tied down Jewish forces in defensive positions when they were needed for operations elsewhere in Palestine.

Yet these considerations were secondary to Jaffa's potential importance in an impending conventional war. Jewish leaders feared that the Arabs would drive a column from Jaffa to Jerusalem to cut off the Negev Desert, thereby splitting the Jewish territory and heralding the end of any Jewish state. Moreover, it was anticipated that the Egyptians could land by sea at Jaffa (or even the British intervening on behalf of the Arabs) to initiate a massive attack against Tel Aviv.[7] Arab control of Jaffa, therefore, was seen as a serious military threat to the viability of any Jewish state.

Forces Engaged in the Battle of Jaffa

The official Jewish defense force, the Haganah, decided against an invasion of Jaffa for several political and military considerations. Because the city fell within the Arab state under the United Nations (UN) partition plan, the Haganah did not want to risk antagonizing the world community while the Jewish state's security was still far from guaranteed. Although the British had withdrawn from all of the nearby Jewish towns, they continued to maintain a garrison in Jaffa as a clear hint of armed intervention in the event of a Jewish attack on the city. Thus, the Haganah chose to capture the Arab villages encircling the city on the assumption that the city itself would then inevitably fall.[8]

Unlike the Haganah, however, the Irgun was less concerned about the diplomatic dangers of a direct attack on Jaffa. Indeed, the underground militia thrived on direct action for its psychological effect on both the enemy and the Jewish population.[9] In a January 1948 planning session, the Irgun high command listed the conquest of Jaffa as one of its four strategic objectives, second only to Jerusalem in importance.[10] Thus, on April 21, 1948, the Irgun decided to shift away from partisan attacks against selected British targets and launch its first "aboveground" operation.

For the attack on Jaffa, six hundred officers and men were assembled in what would be the Irgun's largest operation to date. Menachem Begin appointed the Irgun's talented operations officer, Amichai "Gideon" Paglin, as commander of the attacking forces. The Irgun force was equipped with assorted small arms, two Bren gun carriers, a limited number of PIAT armor-piercing shells, and two 3-inch mortars. The Irgun would also be able to reap the benefit of a raid on a British ammunition train a week earlier, during which the Irgun confiscated twelve tons of mortar shells.[11] However, the Jewish forces would be attacking fortified defensive positions without the benefit of either armor or air support.

The Arab forces defending Jaffa consisted mainly of loosely organized militias that followed the leadership of the radical Grand Mufti of Jerusalem. The Mufti had named one of his best fighters, Sheik Hassan Salame, as commander of the Jaffa-Ramle-Lydda district. Salame, who had divided Jaffa into three sectors, each with a separate subcommander, controlled approximately eight hundred to twelve hundred soldiers. Additionally, three hundred Iraqi irregulars from the Arab Liberation Army (ALA) occupied defensive positions in Jaffa.[12] These Arab forces were entrenched, armed with Spandau machine guns of superior firepower to the Irgun's Brens, and well stocked with ammunition. Yet the economic effects of the months of street fighting with the Jews had left the Arab militias demoralized, and, as later events would show, the various Arab forces lacked unity of command.

The city's Arab defenders were also ostensibly supported by the sizable British garrison remaining in Jaffa under the command of Gen. Gordon MacMillan. The British regiments in Jaffa were part of the 1st Infantry Division and possessed organic armor in the form of the 4/7 Dragoon Guards, as well as a battery of the 41st Field Artillery Regiment.[13] These forces could also be supported by British Spitfires and a destroyer offshore. The heavy British military presence in the Mediterranean theater gave them an almost limitless supply of manpower. During the course of the battle of Jaffa, an infantry battalion, two Royal Marine Commando units, and a tank regiment would be deployed from Cyprus and Egypt.[14]

It appeared that the Irgun faced nearly insurmountable odds at the outset of the battle. With six hundred men, they would be attacking a numerically superior enemy occupying fortified defensive positions. Even if that initial attack were to prove successful, they were likely to face intervention by a modernized, experienced force with unlimited air support and armor at its disposal.

Phase I: The Irgun Offensive

Amichai Paglin planned a two-pronged attack for the conquest of Jaffa. The first group would launch an infantry attack westward toward the sea at the narrow bottleneck connecting the Manshieh quarter to the main part of Jaffa to the south. This attack would cut off the bulk of Manshieh from Jaffa. In the ensuing Arab panic, two motorized forces, utilizing nearly a hundred stolen or confiscated trucks, would attack from the northern end of the panhandle, race through it, and fan out into the heart of the town.[15]

On the evening of April 25, the Irgun forces gathered at Camp Dov in Ramat Gan, a northern suburb of Tel Aviv. At about 2:00 A.M., Begin and the Irgun leadership emerged from the headquarters and addressed the troops. Although Begin's identity was a closely guarded secret, and this was the first time his men had seen him, the troops instinctively knew it was their leader speaking to them. After Begin's remarks, Paglin added his instructions, emphasizing the need to conserve scarce ammunition. A little after 3:00 A.M., the men filed out onto the main road through Tel Aviv, establishing operational headquarters at the abandoned Alliance School in southern Tel Aviv.

Although Paglin had hoped for a night attack, dawn broke at 4:30, and a series of minor delays had thrown the Irgun behind schedule. Paglin considered postponing the attack until the next evening, but he knew that the Arabs in Manshieh had probably observed their movement and were aware of the pending attack. At 8:00 A.M. the Irgun's mortars opened up a heavy barrage, raining fire all over Jaffa, particularly in the center south of Manshieh. Inside Jaffa, the endless whine and explosions of the incoming rounds had a devastating impact on civilian and irregular morale but little effect on the direction of the battle in Manshieh.

At the bottleneck of Manshieh, an intense machine-gun duel developed, with attacking Irgun forces taking fire from both north and south. The Arab Spandaus provided greater firepower than the Irgun Brens and were being fired from fortified defensive positions among the rows of ruined buildings. In addition to this natural cover, the Arabs had constructed cement pillboxes at strategic street corners and on the roofs of several buildings. Arab fire quickly began to take its toll on the attackers, with few visible returns. Although the Irgunists were able to take some frontline positions, in most cases they were forced to retreat under heavy fire. The first day's fighting ended with no substantial gain for the Irgun, with four men killed and six seriously wounded.[16]

The Jewish forces renewed their attack on April 27 with another massive mortar barrage. This time the Irgun made limited advances, breaking into the first rank of houses and driving out or killing the Arab defenders in room-to-room fighting. At the same time, Arab civilians were reportedly boarding boats in Jaffa harbor, evacuating the city due to the intense mortar fire. Yet at the end of the second day of fighting, the actual defenses in Manshieh still showed no hint of weakness.

The Irgun's setback on the battlefield did not upset the official Jewish leadership in the Haganah and the Jewish Agency. In fact, many officials hoped that the Irgun's potential political power would be destroyed in the disgrace of defeat. Yet by the second day of fighting, the militarily pragmatic officers in the Haganah began to view the Irgun attack in a different light. They realized that if the Irgun broke off its attack, their own operation to isolate Jaffa by flanking attacks would prove more costly; consequently, they hoped the Irgun's attack would continue to tie down resistance within Jaffa. Thus, Yigal Yadin, the Haganah chief of staff, met with Begin and, under the terms of a March 8 Irgun-Haganah agreement to increase coordination between the two forces, approved the continuation of the attack.

At this point, however, Begin himself was highly skeptical of the Irgun's chances for success in Jaffa. Although his forces had captured several Arab positions, the attack was bogged down and seemed to offer little chance of a dramatic breakthrough. Begin told his military chiefs: "I do not think we should go on battering our heads against fortified positions, which in any case are covered by British tanks. We have done our best for two days. In these circumstances it is no disgrace—not even for the Irgun—to suspend the direct assault. We shall defend the line we have taken with a strong holding unit. The rest of our troops, we shall withdraw."[17]

Although a few commanders agreed with Begin's assessment, the Irgun's junior officers and men pressed him to renew the attack. Paglin himself made another reconnaissance of the front line to search for a way through the Arab defenses. He returned to headquarters breathless, covered in dirt and dust from crawling on his hands and knees. "I have found some weak points in the enemy's positions," he said. "I am sure we can break through." Begin was impressed by the spirit of his forces and reluctantly agreed to give Paglin twenty-four hours to reach the sea.[18]

Paglin immediately set out with his officers to develop a new plan of attack. He recognized that although the Irgun was poorly trained in conventional tactics, it possessed extensive expertise in the use of explosives. He recognized the urgency of adapting this skill to urban warfare, for it was useless to continue attempting to move over narrow roads that could easily be raked by fire from entrenched positions. Paglin therefore decided to drive a corridor to the sea by blowing a passage through the houses and constructing sandbag walls across the streets. Using picks and sledgehammers, the men would create "mouseholes" through the houses, with the outer walls providing natural cover until they reached the Arab lines. There they would place explosives near the Arab positions and blow them up. In this manner, the Irgun hoped to cover about three hundred meters in twenty-four hours.[19] In the face of the difficult operation that lay ahead, Paglin observed, "The operation will be backbreaking and slow, but it is the only alternative left."[20]

At approximately 4:00 P.M. on the third day, April 28, the Irgun started its attack. Again, a barrage of hundreds of mortar shells was loosed upon Jaffa as the Irgun's forces began the task of carving two jagged parallel "aboveground tunnels" through blocks of houses. Paglin's men dug and bombed their way forward a yard at a time. At some points, the sandbag walls had to be constructed by men lying on their backs under devastating fire, lifting one bag forward at a time.

By seven in the evening, the Jewish forces reached a row of houses only seventy yards from the Arab forward positions. However, a road ran between the lines, and the Arab defenders could cover every inch of the road from strategically placed cement pillboxes. Paglin immediately realized that neutralizing these strongpoints was necessary for any further advancement. He waited until darkness fell before deploying a sapper to the left flank along the Irgun side of the road to destroy a three-story building just across the street from one of the Arab positions. When the building exploded, the debris fell onto the Arab position, as intended, and knocked it out. At the same time, two men dashed across the road, mined buildings adjacent to the other Arab positions, and again toppled the buildings onto the Arab pillboxes. Groups of Irgunists took advantage of the explosions by dashing across the road, while others constructed sandbag walls to negate the heavy flanking fire. Once across in force, the Irgun continued to burrow through the Arab defenses.[21]

Finally, just at the break of dawn, the tunnel's point man looked up and saw the sea only two blocks away. After twenty-four hours of exhausting effort under relentless cross fire, their objective was in sight at last. A "mass hysteria" rose over the Irgun forces as without hesitation the men charged headlong into the final Arab positions. The Arabs, aware at last of what had happened, fled in panic. The joyful Irgunists dashed into the sea, firing their weapons in the air, shouting and screaming like boys. In just over twenty-four hours, Paglin had achieved his objective, and the Manshieh quarter was finally cut off.[22]

The Irgun began house-to-house clearance of the remaining Arab resistance within the Manshieh quarter. The group of militants occupying the Hassan Bek Mosque put up a particularly stubborn battle, but by midmorning the Zionist flag flew from the minaret. Meanwhile, the Irgun command tasked its two mortars to support the bogged-down Haganah attack on the outskirts of Jaffa. By April 30, the Irgun captured the Jaffa railway station and strengthened its positions along the Jerusalem road. Finally, the way into the center of Jaffa lay open.

Phase II: The British Counterattack

During the five months between the passing of the United Nations partition resolution and the outbreak of formal war in Palestine in May 1948, British policy toward its former territory was confused at best. Theoretically, British forces were supposed to remain neutral in the conflict between Jews and Arabs, which the British believed would inevitably result in an Arab victory.[23] Yet this neutrality was carried out in such a manner that both Jews and Arabs suspected the British of conspiring with and aiding the enemy.[24] As two historians observed, "What [Britain's Palestine policy] lacked in authority and precision it made up in variety and contradiction."[25]

However, the Irgun's success, which seemed to foreshadow the fall of the whole city to the Jews, caught the British by surprise. When the attack had started, the British sat back and waited for what they expected would be an Irgun defeat. But once the Irgun forces were on the verge of total victory, the British felt they could no longer stand aside. General MacMillan was primarily concerned with his evacuation from the Sarafand camp in Jaffa, as well as the safety of the route of withdrawal from Ramallah, Lydda, and Latrun. More importantly, Foreign Secretary Ernest Bevin was outraged by the Irgun's victory. The British had already been accused by the Arabs of having sold out Haifa to the Jews,[26] and now the Jews were about to capture an entire Arab city outside the partition boundaries. Bevin decided that the Jewish forces had to be ousted from Jaffa at all costs. Consequently, MacMillan received a signal from the War Office in London that read simply: "Recapture Jaffa, and hand it back to the Arabs."[27]

At 11:00 A.M. on April 30, British tanks moved out from the main sector of Jaffa along the three major roads toward Manshieh. Paglin, observing the advance from a rooftop, was surprised that the British would intervene directly on the Arabs' behalf so soon before their scheduled withdrawal from Palestine. Yet he responded immediately, dispatching a PIAT team to a position along the main road. When the lead British tank came into sight, they made a direct hit with the first round, disabling the tank and blocking the route of advance with the whole line stalled behind it. Similarly, when a tank came to a halt beside a tall building on a second road, a demolition team collapsed the facade of the building on top of the tank, thereby stopping the second convoy. Things progressed more smoothly for the third armor formation, whose lead tank knocked out the Irgun's armored Bren carrier, killing the four-man crew inside. However, upon seeing the two other attack routes blocked, the column leader withdrew and pulled his tanks back into central Jaffa.

The next morning the British launched an air strike against the Bat-Yam quarter of Tel Aviv, and MacMillan's twenty-five-pound guns began randomly shelling the Jewish city. Spitfires made strafing runs on the Irgun positions in Manshieh, and a

British destroyer appeared offshore. At the same time, an infantry battalion, two Royal Marine Commando units, and a tank regiment all arrived from Cyprus and Egypt, although MacMillan had not requested these reinforcements.

British tanks, this time supported by infantry, began moving out again from central Jaffa. Artillery fire, mortars, and machine guns raked the Irgun positions. With no antitank guns remaining, Paglin ordered his sapper teams to create blocks in front of and behind the first group of British tanks. The only way to do this was by toppling the houses literally onto the British tanks or between them to immobilize them. As the column stalled, the Irgun crept up to the tanks and tossed lit dynamite sticks at them. Although this method disabled several tanks, the heavy British firepower nevertheless tore isolated Irgun units to shreds. Still, the British found the going extremely slow, because the streets were clogged with smashed masonry, and the Irgun's return fire pinned down the infantry. Realizing after several hours that the Irgun was still resisting and the way out was in jeopardy, the tanks pulled up and began to retreat back into the center of Jaffa. For the second consecutive day, the Irgun had managed to hold their defensive line by the narrowest of margins.

Meanwhile, as the battle raged between the British and the Jewish forces, chaos spread among the Arab defenders of Jaffa. Captain Abdel Najim al-Din (ALA commander in Jaffa), infuriated by the news that he was to be replaced, withdrew, taking with him his three hundred men and all their weapons. Abdel Najim's rival, Hassan Salame, abandoned his command as well, evacuating the city with other Mufti supporters upset over increasing ALA domination. Each commander accused the other of treason before departing from the battlefield with his forces. With the whole structure of the Arab defense crumbling, Michael al-Issa, the new local ALA commander, cabled his superiors for instructions. He received no orders and, feeling abandoned, joined the exodus with his men. Thus, Jaffa was left virtually leaderless, and the remaining Arab resistance was completely broken.[28] As news of the latest British setback spread among the Arab population, streams of refugees poured out of the city by land and sea. Anarchy descended upon Jaffa as wild mobs of fighters and refugees looted, set fires, and settled vendettas in the debris-strewn streets.

General MacMillan was now in a hopeless position. London continued to bombard him with demands that he retake Jaffa at any cost and reestablish Arab control there. Yet even if he wanted to launch another direct assault against the Irgun's positions, there were virtually no Arabs remaining in Jaffa to whom he could "return" the city. MacMillan felt that retaking Jaffa by force would incur losses totally disproportionate to the limited and temporary gains to be achieved.[29]

MacMillan flew to the Suez Canal Zone to explain his dilemma to the British Middle East commander, Gen. Sir John Crocker. Crocker agreed to explain the actual situation to London and make the suitable recommendations. MacMillan returned to negotiate with the Jewish leadership on ways to stabilize the situation. The British wanted the right to send armored patrols through the Manshieh quarter, as well as to control the Manshieh police station. Menachem Begin opposed these conditions but agreed to let the Haganah take over the occupied area and deal with the British however they saw fit. With regard to the police station, the Irgun called a press conference to discuss the terms of the British proposal. At exactly 10:00 A.M., after the foreign correspondents arrived, the first question asked was whether the Irgun would accept the British terms. Paglin merely looked at his watch and waited. As he began to speak, a huge explosion shook the room. "That's our answer," Paglin said. "There is no Manshieh police station."[30]

In the end, only 5,000 of the original 100,000 Arabs remained in Jaffa. The Irgun had lost 42 killed in action and 400 wounded.[31] At 3:30 P.M. on May 13, as the last British forces left Jaffa, an agreement with the remaining Arabs went into effect, giving the Jewish forces complete control of Jaffa. On May 14, the State of Israel declared its independence, and the next day the armies of five Arab nations attacked the newborn state. However, because they were unable to use Jaffa as a port of entry, the Egyptian forces were required to attack along the Mediterranean axis. Consequently, the most powerful and most dangerous of the invading Arab armies was halted more than twenty miles south of Tel Aviv near the village of Isdud. With the exception of a few limited air strikes, Egypt's main objective was relatively untouched throughout the course of the war. Thus, the Irgun's heavy losses in Jaffa were justified as Begin's words on the eve of the battle proved prophetic. Indeed, the Irgun's victory at Jaffa proved to be one of the decisive battles in the Israeli War of Independence.

Lessons Learned

The Irgun's victory in Jaffa holds several important lessons about modern urban warfare. In fact, Jaffa may be a highly relevant case for America's future combat leaders, for unlike the many examples of urban combat drawn from World War II, the fighting in Jaffa illustrates the unique challenges that modern armies encounter when facing nonstate actors in less than total war. This is important to the U.S. military for at least three reasons. First, since the end of the Cold War, the large majority of armed conflicts across the globe have been *interstate* rather than *intrastate*. Thus, in the future, the U.S. military will be called upon more frequently to intervene against nonstate actors.[32] Second, nonstate actors tend to rely on tactics and strategies that are different from those of conventional armies. In particular,

nonstate actors can effectively utilize guerrilla warfare against
Western forces occupying their territory. In urban combat, these
militias can effectively blend into the civilian population, use
noncombatants to gain an intelligence advantage, and initiate
engagements at the time of their choosing.[33] Moreover, nonstate
military forces will be less tied to bureaucratic norms and standard operating procedures, thereby gaining increased tactical
flexibility in comparison to professional militaries. Finally, because they have fewer recourses to international law than sovereign states, nonstate actors will often have greater interests at
stake in the outcome of a military intervention. Whereas Western
militaries will feel constrained against causing unnecessary noncombatant casualties and collateral damage in situations falling
short of total war, nonstate actors may be willing to absorb greater
costs in order to achieve their objectives.

The battle of Jaffa's implications for modern urban warfare is
focused on the importance of combined-arms operations, tactical innovation, and small-unit leadership. The importance of the
effect of tactics upon civilian populations is also a major lesson
learned, and may often prove decisive in determining the outcome
of an engagement in an urban environment.

Combined-Arms Operations

Among the most significant lessons to be learned from the Irgun's victory in Jaffa is the importance of combined-arms operations. In particular, the battle illustrates several key lessons about
the utility and limitations of airpower, indirect fire, armor, and
engineer assets in an urban environment.

First, the engagement demonstrates the difficulty of using air
strikes to influence the urban battlefield. During conditions of
total war, with few or no rules of engagement, aerial bombard-

ment has been extremely useful. However, in fighting that falls short of total war, where the need to minimize collateral damage is a significant factor, airpower is not terribly effective.[34] Moreover, buildings can often interfere with aircraft engagements.[35] In Jaffa, the British bombings of Tel Aviv and Spitfire attacks on Irgun positions had little or no impact on the outcome of the fighting. Conversely, the Irgun was successful in both the offensive and defensive phases of the battle without any air support. Therefore, one can see how the advantage of U.S. airpower may be limited or negated in urban warfare.

Second, the fighting in Jaffa demonstrates some important constraints on the use of indirect fire support in urban warfare. When used in a direct-fire mode, artillery has proven useful in destroying well-fortified targets. Mortars, with their high trajectory, have proven especially useful in the urban environment. However, because of concerns about collateral damage, indirect fire may be counterproductive to contemporary Western forces.[36] Additionally, in the frequently vertical landscape of modern cities, direct observation of fires may be difficult, thereby impairing fire control and accuracy. Thus, indirect fire can produce mixed results in urban combat, a reality illustrated by the battle of Jaffa. For although the Irgun's constant mortar barrages were relatively ineffective against the Arabs' defensive positions, they did manage to disrupt the enemy's lines of communication and transport.[37] Also, the mortars had an invaluable psychological effect on noncombatants in Jaffa that eventually proved decisive. In contrast, the British artillery and mortars were limited to desultory shelling of Tel Aviv and Irgun positions. Thus, we can see that indirect fires are of limited utility in urban combat.

Third, armor played a critical role in the fight for Jaffa, especially during the British counterattacks on April 30 and May 1. Tanks and armored fighting vehicles can be a valuable asset in urban warfare. Their firepower can be used precisely; they can serve as troop carriers; and they can be useful for shocking opposition forces and less-than-friendly noncombatants. Yet in constrained urban environments, tanks are particularly vulnerable to rocket-propelled grenades, Molotov cocktails, and other munitions.[38] Many observers concur with Ralph Peters's assessment that "today's tanks are death traps in urban combat."[39] Hyperbole aside, tanks can be a battle-winning weapon in urban combat. However, the design of the vehicle is of secondary consideration to how it is used tactically. Specifically, tanks must be supported by dismounted infantry.[40]

This conclusion is clearly established by an analysis of the British counterattacks against the Irgun forces in Jaffa. On April 30, when British tanks attacked unsupported, the Jewish forces were able to halt their advance with relative ease. The next day, however, when dismounted infantry supported the British armor, the Irgun incurred significantly higher losses, and the British almost achieved a decisive breakthrough. Although armor's offensive capabilities in the urban environment are obviously impaired, armor is still a valuable asset in the defense. However, because the British did not enter the fray until after the Arab defenses were broken, one can only conjecture as to whether or not deploying armor in the defense would have proved decisive in Jaffa.[41]

Finally, the Irgun's utilization of its engineering assets for mobility, countermobility, and demolitions proved to be one of the critical factors in the battle of Jaffa. The creation of mouseholes through buildings and aboveground tunnels allowed the Irgun to avoid fire sacks on roads and alleys. The Irgun's sapper teams also provided vital countermobility support by demolishing buildings to block the British forces' avenues of advance. Similarly, the sappers acted as "living artillery," toppling buildings on key Arab strongpoints and on British tanks when their limited supply of antitank weapons was exhausted.[42] Indeed, the

Irgun's superior use of its sapper teams and engineers proved decisive to their victory at Jaffa.

In the end, although some observers argue that "urban combat is a peculiarly infantry skill," combined-arms operations are vital for success in urban operations.[43] The battle of Jaffa clearly shows that there is no single weapons system or technology that guarantees victory in urban combat. The unsuccessful British counterattacks demonstrate the limitations of airpower, artillery, and unsupported armor in the urban environment. Even when the British armor attacks were properly supported by infantry, their lack of engineering support caused them to lose the mobility/countermobility fight. Conversely, the Irgun achieved victory precisely because it was better able than the Arab and British forces to integrate its infantry, mortar, and engineer assets into its operations.

Tactical Innovations

Another key to the Irgun's success was its ability to develop innovative tactics during the course of the battle. As one veteran of urban warfare states the problem, "Every room is a new battle."[44] Rigid adherence to conventional tactics in urban operations may prove counterproductive when the situational environment can change from street to street. Thus, leaders conducting MOUT operations must be prepared to be tactically flexible, as the situation demands.

The Irgun's ability to adapt its tactics according to the situational needs was a crucial factor in the battle of Jaffa. It is a widely held belief that attacking forces are at a severe disadvantage in the urban environment, as illustrated during the first two days of the Irgun offensive, when the Jewish forces attempted ill-conceived frontal assaults that exposed them to intensive covering fire. Realizing that this tactic was futile, Paglin shifted his plan to take advantage of his men's expertise with explosives. Similarly, rather than mounting a conventional defense, the Irgun's forces developed tactics during the battle to take advantage of the urban environment. Conversely, the Arab forces never deviated from a static defense of their lines in Manshieh, and the British failed to adjust from their plan of a direct assault on the Irgun lines. Thus, the Irgun's tactical flexibility was a significant factor in its battlefield success.

Small-Unit Leadership

Urban warfare almost inevitably degenerates into a series of small-group battles. As the battle develops, "the streets and building-blocks of the urban physical morphology fragment urban warfare into conflict between units usually of squad or platoon size, with generally insufficient space for the deployment and maneuvering of larger units."[45] Leaders must position themselves well forward on the battlefield where they can experience and guide subordinate actions. The compartmentalized nature of built-up areas denies any semblance of direct control over a unit's operations to any but the forwardmost tactical leader. Sometimes junior leaders and individual servicemen may determine a force's success or failure in accomplishing a mission.[46] Therefore, it is imperative that forces have highly motivated, highly disciplined leadership at the front when engaging in urban combat.

Throughout the battle of Jaffa, the Jewish forces clearly demonstrated the value of this small-unit leadership. After the Irgun's initial attacks were unsuccessful, Paglin personally made the critical reconnaissance that enabled him to gain a firsthand appreciation of the situation and devise a new plan. Also, during the British counterattacks, Paglin was on the front line emplacing antitank weapons and sapper teams to halt the British advance. His leading by example inspired his subordinates to plead with Menachem Begin to continue the assault on Jaffa. Similarly, numerous other Irgun officers demonstrated remarkable bravery under heavy fire. Conversely, the Arab leadership was racked by strife, distrust, and poor coordination. The Irgun possessed a decisive advantage in leadership skills over the Arab forces, which, because of this factor's special significance in urban combat, enabled the Jewish forces to overcome numerous material disadvantages.

Influence of Civilian Population on Tactical Considerations

Civilians play an inherently more important role in urban warfare than in combat in rural or open environments. In almost every major urban battle in modern times, the presence of noncombatants has affected the course of the operation.[47] Tactics that are militarily successful but alienate the civilian population may ultimately prove self-defeating. Therefore, any discussion of future American MOUT doctrine must recognize that controlling noncombatant behavior is highly desirable to keep such personnel out of harm's way and to otherwise influence their actions in a manner favorable to achieving friendly force objectives.[48]

The impact of the noncombatants on tactical considerations was clearly a vital factor in the fight for Jaffa. The Irgun intentionally used its mortars to induce panic among the Arab inhabitants of the city, thereby crippling the morale of the Arab defenders and complicating their rear operations. (At the same time, however, the Irgun avoided direct attacks on women and children that would have increased the Arab forces' will to resist.) On the other hand, the British forces, who were ostensibly supposed to be maintaining order in Jaffa, did nothing to reassure the civilian population. Thus, the Arab flight from Jaffa rendered the outcome of the subsequent British counterattack irrelevant. For even if the British had obtained a decisive breakthrough of the Irgun's defenses, they no longer had any Arab population to whom the city could be returned. Thus, the British inattention to civil affairs proved to be a critical factor in the battle of Jaffa.

In conclusion, the battle of Jaffa provides an excellent case study of contemporary urban warfare. For the Irgun's victory clearly demonstrates how a numerically and technologically disadvantaged "militia" can defeat a modern army through the superior utilization of factors unique to urban combat. The fighting in Jaffa shows that no single weapon system or technology can guarantee success in an urban environment, but rather that tactics incorporating combined-arms operations are crucial for achieving military objectives. Also, the Irgun illustrated the special importance of tactical innovation and small-unit leadership for urban operations. Finally, the battle of Jaffa teaches the importance of taking into account the effects on the noncombatant population when considering tactical options. For in urban combat, the danger of winning a battle tactically but losing it strategically is a serious threat, particularly for American leaders constrained by concerns of collateral damage.

ENDNOTES
1. Menachem Begin, *The Revolt* (New York: Nash Publishing, 1977), 354.
2. For the purpose of this essay, I define nonstate actors as those military forces not under the direct control of an internationally recognized sovereign state. This can include independent militias supporting a quasi government, rebel forces, or terrorist organizations.
3. Sun Tzu, *The Art of War*, trans. Samuel B. Griffith (New York: Oxford University Press, 1982), 78.

4. G. J. Ashworth, *War and the City* (London: Routledge, 1991), 112.

5. Department of the Army, *Military Operations on Urbanized Terrain (MOUT)*, Field Manual 90–10 (Washington, DC: U.S. Government Printing Office, August 15, 1979), 1–1. Emphasis in original.

6. Aviezer Golan, *The War of Independence* (Tel Aviv: Ministry of Defence Publishing House, 1974), 81; Dan Kurzman, *Genesis 1948: The First Arab-Israeli War* (New York: World Publishing, 1970), 169.

7. Samuel Katz, *Days of Fire* (Garden City, NJ: Doubleday & Co., Inc., 1968), 218–19; Begin, *The Revolt*, 370–71.

8. Golan, *The War of Independence*, 81–82.

9. Kurzman, *Genesis, 1948*, 172. The question of whether the Irgun was a terrorist or guerrilla organization continues to be one of the more controversial issues of Israeli history. For the purposes of this essay, however, I will avoid this debate and refer to the Irgun as a militia or guerrilla force, because its actions during the battle of Jaffa were of a conventional military nature.

10. Begin, 348.

11. J. Bowyer Bell, *Terror Out of Zion: The Fight for Israeli Independence* (New Brunswick, NJ: Transaction Press, 1966), 299; Begin, 349, 355.

12. Kurzman, 180, 181.

13. General G. H. A MacMillan, "The Evacuation of Palestine," *Military Review*, June 1949, 75–76.

14. Kurzman, 182.

15. Ibid., 176.

16. Bell, 300.

17. Begin, 365.

18. Bell, 301; Kurzman, 177; Begin, 365.

19. Bell, 301.

20. Kurzman, 177.

21. Ibid., 178.

22. Ibid.

23. The General Officer Commanding (GOC) British troops in Palestine, General MacMillan, concluded by April 1948 that, in terms of troops, equipment, and geography, the combined Arab armies "would have no difficulty in taking over the whole country." Jon and David Kimche, *A Clash of Destinies: The Arab-Jewish War and the Founding of the State of Israel* (New York: Frederick A. Praeger, 1960), 114.

312   CITY FIGHTS

24.   See, for example, Katz, *Days of Fire,* 219–20; Begin, 356, 362, 366; Kurzman, 181.

25.   Kimche, 111.

26.   The British withdrew from the "mixed" city of Haifa on April 20, 1948, handing over their strategic positions to the Arab forces. Yet by April 22, the Haganah had managed to overwhelm the disorganized Arab defenders and capture the city.

27.   Kimche, 113.

28.   Kurzman, 181–82.

29.   In an almost simultaneous yet separate operation, the Haganah had tightened the ring around Jaffa by capturing the villages of Salameh and Yazur east of the city. Kurzman, 184.

30.   Kurzman, 185.

31.   Bell, 303.

32.   In 1994 alone, thirty-four out of thirty-five armed conflicts (those including more than a thousand deaths) were interstate wars. See Margareta Sollenberg and Peter Wallensteen, "Major Armed Conflicts, 1994," in Stockholm International Peace Research Institute (SIPRI), *SIPRI Yearbook, 1995* (Oxford: Oxford University Press, 1995), 21–35.

33.   The 1940 Marine Corps *Small Wars Manual* states that in warfare of this kind, "members of native forces will suddenly become innocent peasant workers when it suits their fancy and convenience. In addition, the Force will be handicapped by partisans, who constantly and accurately inform native forces of our movements. The population will be honeycombed with hostile sympathizers, making it difficult to procure reliable information." Similarly, Clausewitz notes: "An area may have long since been cleared of enemy troops, but a band of peasants that was long since driven off by the head of a column may at any moment reappear at its tail." See U.S. Marine Corps, *Small Wars Manual, 1940* (Manhattan, KS: Sunflower University Press, 1940), 14–16; Carl von Clausewitz, *On War* (Princeton, NJ: Princeton University Press, 1976), 479–83.

34.   William G. Rosenau, " 'Every Room Is a New Battle': The Lessons of Modern Urban Warfare," *Studies in Conflict and Terrorism,* October 1997, 387.

35.   Russell W. Glenn, *Combat in Hell: A Consideration of Constrained Urban Warfare* (Santa Monica, CA: RAND, 1996), 10.

36.   Rosenau, 388.

37.   Begin, 358.

38. Rosenau, 386.

39. Ralph Peters, "Our Soldiers, Their Cities," *Parameters,* Spring 1996, 47.

40. Colonel Michael Dewar, *War in the Streets: The Story of Urban Combat from Calais to Khafji* (London: David & Charles, 1992), 12, 85; Rosenau, 386.

41. Several Jewish sources allege that Irgun forces engaged British tanks in support of the Arab defenses as early as April 28. However, I have not found any substantiating accounts from credible third-party or British sources, whereas several Arab fighters actually believed that the British were aiding the Jews during the battle. See Begin, 356, 362; Katz, 219; Kurzman, 181.

42. Begin, 366.

43. Dewar, *War in the Streets,* 12.

44. Rosenau, 377, quoting an Israeli Defense Force brigade commander on his experiences in Beirut.

45. Ashworth, *War in the City,* 117.

46. Glenn, *Combat in Hell,* 12, 18.

47. Rosenau, 387.

48. Glenn, 40.

ELEVEN

Seoul, 1950:

City Fight after Inchon

by Maj. Thomas A. Kelley

No operation in military history can match either the delaying action where you traded space for time in which to build up your forces, or the brilliant maneuver which has now resulted in the liberation of Seoul. I am particularly impressed by the splendid cooperation of our Army, Navy, and Air Force and I wish to extend my thanks and congratulations to the commanders of these services . . .

—message from President Truman to
General MacArthur on September 30, 1950

The brilliant maneuver that President Truman refers to was Operation Chromite, the amphibious landing at Inchon and subsequent attack to liberate Seoul, the capital of South Korea. Much has been written about the Inchon portion of Operation Chromite but comparatively little about the battle to liberate Seoul. Considering how rapidly the situation changed in Korea in fall 1950, it is not surprising that this battle is often forgotten. On September 14, 1950, the UN forces in South Korea were defending the southern tip of the peninsula near Pusan along the Naktong River line after two months of repeated attacks by the North Korean Peoples Army (NKPA). The situation seemed bleak. With their back to the sea, the U.S. Eighth Army had barely managed to avoid disaster by rapidly shifting forces and counterattacking to plug dangerous gaps in the line caused by enemy attacks. However, by the end of September, through the successful combination of Operation Chromite and a breakout operation from the Pusan perimeter, the situation was completely reversed. The enemy line had been penetrated and collapsed. Most of the NKPA was in disarray. Tens of thousands surrendered and the rest were either fleeing back to the north or hiding in the hills. The UN forces reached the thirty-eighth parallel, which served as a boundary between North and South Korea, with little opposition to prevent them from unifying the Korean peninsula by force.

Many historians tend to focus on Inchon, then jump ahead to the decision to cross the thirty-eighth parallel and continue the attack into North Korea. This tendency can create the impression that the liberation of Seoul was achieved largely through maneuver, or that it was a rather simple and straightforward affair. It was neither. It was a hard-fought battle that warrants a closer examination. Many of the difficulties that U.S. soldiers and marines faced in their effort to capture Seoul are still relevant today. Practitioners of the art of war, and policy makers as well, can benefit from an appreciation for this historically important battle and its many lessons in the combined-arms nature and challenges of city fighting.

General MacArthur's decision to land at Inchon was both controversial and risky. Because of the seasonal tidal fluctuations at this small port on the coast eighteen miles west of Seoul, timing was critical. To be successful, the UN forces would initially have to seize a small island called Wolmi-do overlooking the harbor, then get enough forces ashore during high tide to stop any counterattack before the harbor became a mudflat at low tide. The high seawalls and generally poor port facilities made Inchon a difficult place to establish and expand a beachhead. For these reasons and others, several navy and Marine Corps senior leaders, as well as the Joint Chiefs of Staff, initially expressed concern, serious doubt, or outright opposition to the operation. However, MacArthur knew exactly what he wanted to achieve and how he wanted to do it. Where some saw risk, he saw opportunity. His vision was to use his significant advantage in naval, air, and maritime power to conduct a deep envelopment that would cut the enemy lines of communication and supply that flowed through Seoul while simultaneously conducting a breakout from the Pusan perimeter. He believed that the UN forces could achieve operational surprise, because the enemy, aware of the tidal and port conditions, would not expect a landing at Inchon. Cutting off the NKPA from their supplies, communications, and reinforcements would place them in an untenable position. The amphibious landing deep in the rear area of the NKPA would prevent the flow of fuel, ammunition, food, spare parts, and medical supplies to their divisions near the Naktong River. Taken together, this would allow the UN forces to seize the initiative and force the NKPA to retreat, surrender, or risk annihilation.

In order to accomplish this task, MacArthur began to assemble in Japan a two-division-size force composed of U.S. and South Korean soldiers and marines and put them under the command of the newly created X Corps. The force consisted of the 1st Marine Division, the 7th Infantry Division, corps artillery battalions, an engineer brigade, and an amphibious tank and tractor battalion. However, to guarantee surprise, the planning and preparation for the mission, to include bringing the divisions together, getting them up to strength, and preparing them for this operation, had to be carried out with the utmost secrecy. Meanwhile, the desperate situation of the U.S. Eighth Army near Pusan resulted in increased pressure from above and below

for General MacArthur to provide combat units and replacements to the forces in contact and forget about his amphibious
scheme. Through force of will and persuasion, MacArthur was
able to prevail.

The 1st Marine Division, commanded by Maj. Gen. Oliver
Smith, would consist of the 1st, 5th, and 7th Regimental Combat Teams (RCT). The 1st RCT, commanded by Lt. Col. Lewis
"Chesty" Puller, assembled from forces at Camp Pendleton,
California, had only a few days to stage in Japan before sea
movement began toward Inchon. In early September 1950, the
5th RCT, commanded by Lt. Col. Raymond Murray, was still
busy defending the Naktong perimeter. It had to be pulled from
the line to join the division at sea. The 7th RCT, commanded by
Col. Homer Litzenberg, was also formed after the outbreak of
the war. It would assemble in Japan, then ship directly to Inchon, but it wouldn't arrive until a week after the other two regiments were already ashore and pushing inland. The 1st Marine
Division was augmented by the Republic of Korea (ROK) 1st
Marine Regiment, with an estimated strength of 2,800 men.
Supporting the regiments were a medium tank battalion, an artillery battalion, engineer battalions and companies, an ordnance
company, and other combat service support units.

The 7th Division, commanded by Maj. Gen. David Barr, was
composed of the 17th, 31st, and 32d Infantry Regiments. Like
the 7th RCT, the 17th Regiment was not immediately available
to the division. During the embarkation and assault phase of the
amphibious landing, the 17th would still be serving as a reserve
for the U.S. Eighth Army. Supporting these regiments were a
medium tank battalion, several artillery battalions, an antiaircraft
battalion, an engineer battalion, and a reconnaissance company.
At the outbreak of the Korean War, the 7th Infantry Division
had been stripped of about 1,500 soldiers and 140 officers to fill

out other units. In August 1950, more than 8,000 South Korean soldiers, or KATU.S.A, as they came to be called, were integrated into the 7th Infantry Division to bring it up to strength. Although more fully manned and equipped than many of the units that were initially thrown into Korea at the outbreak of hostilities, this hastily assembled force still lacked the training, combat experience, and cohesiveness that are the hallmarks of great units. In a letter to his family while at sea on his way to Inchon, Lt. Jack Madison of the 32d Infantry Regiment wrote, "I certainly do wish we had the opportunity for more training. I feel sure we will get some when we arrive. It would be nothing but foolishness to commit us in this state of readiness."

Despite the concerns expressed by Madison and many others about the feasibility of landing at Inchon, things went remarkably well. The NKPA was surprised and unable to put together a large enough force to counterattack and contain the amphibious landing. Perhaps this is what led MacArthur, an inveterate optimist, to predict that X Corps would recapture Seoul within five days. Major General Ned Almond, MacArthur's chief of staff and X Corps commander, was confident in eventual success as well but told MacArthur he figured it would take two weeks. From September 15 to 18, the 1st Marine Division quickly overcame the forces defending Inchon and established a beachhead. With air support, naval gunfire, artillery, engineers, and armor, the men of the 1st and 5th RCT pushed inland along the Inchon-Seoul highway and overcame moderate enemy resistance to capture key objectives, including Ascom City, Sosa, and Kimpo airfield. The 90mm gun of the M26 tank was instrumental in knocking out enemy T-34 tanks and hardened positions. The secure port of Inchon, recaptured supplies at Ascom City, and the airfield provided the logistical base of support that the UN forces needed to sustain the X Corps offensive. Furthermore, Kimpo airfield provided a forward air base for more responsive and lasting close air support and aerial attack by the marine air wings and elements of the Far East Air Forces. Airpower facilitated both the advance of ground units through aerial reconnaissance and the seizure of enemy-held ground through intense aerial bombardment.

On September 17, the 7th Infantry Division began landing at Inchon. The 32d Infantry Regiment established an assembly area and prepared to move inland to secure the right flank of the marine 1st RCT. The 31st Infantry Regiment was not scheduled to come ashore until September 20. The mission of the 31st would be to push south to Suwon to establish a blocking position against NKPA attempts to counterattack or reinforce Seoul. On September 18, the 32d Infantry began fighting its way through sporadic contact with enemy tanks and infantry to cut the main roads and rail lines leading to Seoul and align with the right flank of the 1st Marine Division. By September 20, after seizing Kimpo airfield, the marine 5th RCT had crossed the Han River northeast of Kimpo airfield, cut the rail line leading to Seoul, and advanced against enemy resistance to seize several key hills. Meanwhile, the 1st RCT had seized a strongly defended position on the hills adjacent to the Inchon-Seoul highway west of Yongdungpo, a large industrial suburb south of Seoul across the Han River. The army 2d Infantry Regiment had finally managed to catch up to Puller's right flank. Meanwhile, the 17th Infantry Regiment continued to serve as a reserve force near Pusan for Gen. Harris Walker's Eighth Army. After five days of fighting, the 1st Marine Division of X Corps was within striking distance of Seoul.

From September 16 to 20, for a variety of reasons, the U.S. Eighth Army breakout from the Pusan perimeter had not materialized as planned. The enemy appeared either unaware or unconcerned that a large force was getting close to severing their main line of supply. The offensive that had taken place in the first two weeks of September failed to break the Naktong line. The NKPA continued to hold. Bridging and crossing the Naktong River was proving to be more difficult than anticipated. Aerial attacks on the NKPA lines of supply were accurate but were not having immediate effects on the enemy line. MacArthur was concerned. He had his planners begin looking at an option for an amphibious landing a hundred miles to the south of Seoul at Kumsan. This would present the NKPA defending near the Naktong line with units in their immediate rear area and force them to fight in two directions. However, before any detailed planning began for this option, the losses inflicted by Far East Air Forces and the pressure exerted by the Eighth Army finally caused the North Korean line to begin to crumble. By September 22, the NKPA resistance in some sectors had noticeably lessened. On the twenty-third, the southernmost NKPA units began withdrawing. The combination of the UN ground and air attacks with the amphibious envelopment caused the NKPA defense to collapse. Seizing this opportunity, General Walker ordered a pursuit.

Ironically, just as the Eighth Army was finally beginning to break out, the X Corps advance around Seoul was slowing. Enemy direct and indirect fire, the complexities of river crossing operations, and numerous minefields all combined to slow the advance of UN forces. Additionally, the marine division, which was designed more for amphibious landing and expansion of the beachhead, began experiencing some logistical and communication challenges as they pushed farther inland.[1] In addition, the North Koreans, having adjusted to the surprise of the landing, rushed several nearby units to the area to defend the western hills and southern suburbs of Seoul. Reinforcements from the NKPA 87th Regiment, under Colonel Pak, and the 25th Brigade, commanded by Major General Wol, brought enemy strength in the area to an estimated 100,000 soldiers. Up to this point, the 1st Marine Division had managed to inflict serious losses on the North Koreans and make steady progress. The plan was for the 5th RCT to press forward on the north bank of the Han River and gain entry to the city. The 1st RCT was to clear Yong-dungpo, then cross the Han River just north of the suburb and seize South Mountain. The South Korean Marine Regiment would then conduct a forward passage through the 5th RCT to liberate their capital. The 7th RCT had the mission of protecting the north flank and cutting off enemy escape. The 7th Division was to protect the southern flank and push a task force south to Suwon. But as UN forces closed on Seoul, the NKPA changed tactics from a delaying action to an entrenched defense of the hill complex west of Seoul and the suburb of Yongdungpo. Over the next several days, progress would be measured in yards, not miles, and casualties on both sides would increase dramatically.

After a couple of poorly coordinated NKPA predawn attacks on September 20 were defeated, the hills overlooking Yong-dungpo were secured and the suburb was subjected to a full day of artillery preparation and aerial attack. That evening, the 1st RCT repositioned its forces for the attack to clear the suburb. However, this opened a gap between the 1st RCT and the 32d Infantry. The boundary between these two units was also the boundary between the two divisions from different services. Failure to fully coordinate these adjacent unit details had already caused synchronization problems over the previous two days. During daylight, these problems could be easily remedied. But at night, inadequate flank coordination caused increased danger and confusion. It heightened the possibility of enemy forces getting between or behind units and the risk of fratricide. The U.S. forces quickly relearned the importance of coordinating such details as flank locations, scheme of maneuver, signals, challenge and passwords, and patrol plans. Furthermore, the U.S. forces were relearning valuable lessons in security and rest plans. Physical and mental fatigue began to have an effect on the small-unit soldiers and leaders, many of whom had never experienced combat. Exhausted, some soldiers fell asleep while they were supposed to be maintaining security. Others failed to issue the appropriate challenge, and fired upon anything that moved. This made patrolling at night a risky business.

On September 21, with the amphibious landing almost complete, X Corps assumed control of all forces ashore from the 7th Joint Task Force. Major General Ned Almond, the X Corps commander, was now officially in charge. Thus far, more than 50,000 troops, 250,000 tons of supplies and equipment, and 6,000 vehicles were ashore. Despite the impressive advance and logistical accomplishment, the NKPA defense showed no signs of weakening. In fact, the closer the marines got to Seoul, the greater the resistance they faced. The 5th RCT continued to attack NKPA defensive positions on a series of hills on the western side of Seoul. These hills provided mutually supporting positions that further slowed the 5th RCT advance. The 7th Infantry Division zone was mostly quiet on September 21. The 32d Infantry Regiment maintained its position securing the marines' southern flank while a task force of reconnaissance, infantry, and armor elements continued to push south toward Suwon and the nearby airfield.

September 21 was also another tough day of combat for Lt. Col. Chesty Puller's 1st RCT on the outskirts of the suburb of Yongdungpo. Both enemy and friendly casualties mounted throughout the day, but the well-sited defense held firm. Later in the day, supported by heavy artillery fire, Puller committed his 3d Battalion in an attack along the Inchon-Seoul road to unhinge the position. Withering fire forced back the marines. Captain Barrow, the A Company commander, was able to maneuver his unit around the flank and rear of the enemy and establish a blocking position on a dike. Unfortunately, radio problems prevented him from contacting his battalion and letting the men know his situation. The slightly elevated ground provided good observation, fields of fire, and defensible flanks. After Barrow ambushed and destroyed an NKPA column, the enemy responded by conducting repeated company-size and larger attacks against the isolated unit. Despite being out of communication and getting low on ammunition, the marines held their ground and inflicted several hundred losses on the North Koreans throughout the remainder of the day and night.

When the sun came up on September 22, the 1st RCT found that much of the enemy in Yongdungpo had retreated north across the Han River into Seoul. The bridge over the Han was destroyed and some pockets of enemy still remained. Pursuit was not an option. The 1st RCT spent the day in street-to-street fighting, systematically rooting out NKPA snipers and small units that were still defending from inside buildings and on the roofs. Major General Smith, the 1st Marine Division commander, decided that rather than having Puller's men attempt to cross the Han under what would most likely be heavy direct and indirect fire, he wanted them to go upstream and cross near the location of the 5th RCT. This would allow him to close the gap between the 1st and 5th RCT and coordinate his forces for the attack to recapture Seoul. Smith believed that having his division all on one side of the wide river would simplify command and control and logistics. It would provide him with the additional combat power necessary to break the NKPA defense on the hills west of Seoul. To prepare for the crossing, Smith had the 1st Marines reconnoiter several possible river crossing sites.

Meanwhile, the 5th RCT renewed its attack on the stubborn defenders. An ROK battalion of South Korean Marines joined them in the battle to capture a set of small hills that were heavily defended. General Wol, the NKPA commander in charge of the defense, had placed his highly trained NKPA 25th Brigade and the 78th Independent Regiment in blocking positions. With more than 5,000 infantrymen, artillery units, light engineers, air defense, and antiarmor weapons, the NKPA was capable of a tough defense. In all, the enemy had about 20,000 men available to hold the Seoul area.[2]

Machine-gun and rifle positions were entrenched laterally to provide interlocking fires and in depth to prevent penetration. The defense was tied in to the Han River and could not be easily bypassed to the north. Minefields, mortars, and artillery added to the difficulty of breaking the defense. The initial attack by Murray's 5th RCT was able to gain some ground in the north and south but was repulsed in the center. Casualties were mounting on both sides but were particularly high in the ROK Marine battalion that was attacking in the center. Dozens of sorties of close air support were flown to knock out enemy trenches. Despite the devastating air and artillery bombardment, the defenders refused to surrender or retreat. The NKPA casualties for the day were estimated to be a thousand. Given the forces available, the NKPA had little chance of victory but was managing to fight a tough delaying action.

On the morning of September 23, the 5th RCT resumed the attack. The ROK Marines tried again to break the center position but were beaten back. Later in the day, the 2d Battalion replaced the ROK Marines and continued the attack. They made some limited gains but also suffered high casualties and were unable to break the defense. Air and artillery strikes continued to rain down on the NKPA trenches. On the left, the 7th RCT arrived to secure the flank. This allowed the 5th to focus more combat power on the decisive point. On the right, the 1st RCT was completing the clearing operation and moving to the river crossing site.

Major General Almond, the corps commander, spent the day visiting units all around the battlefield to get a firsthand impression of the situation. He was not pleased with the progress being made to take Seoul. He and Major General Smith had different ideas on the best way to take the city. Almond favored attacking quickly from multiple directions and bypassing the enemy to maintain momentum. Smith favored using mass and firepower to systematically reduce the enemy positions and not bypass pockets of enemy resistance. Their conflict over tactics was one of several sources of tension between the two officers. Although Almond, an army officer serving as chief of staff for MacArthur, had been selected to be the corps commander, Smith's 1st Marine Division was doing the majority of the fighting. Furthermore, Almond had a tendency to visit units and give orders without notifying the 1st Marine Division command post. Based on what he'd seen, Almond strongly suggested to Smith that if he maneuvered some forces around Yongdungpo to the east, he could get into the city behind the NKPA defenders. Smith was not receptive to the idea. He favored a river crossing to bring his forces closer together, not spread them farther apart. Smith predicted that it would take one more day to overcome the stalemate. Almond relented and gave him another day but said that if there were no significant progress he would change the boundary and have the 7th Infantry Division attack Seoul from the south. Smith saw this as a lack of confidence in him and his marines. He chafed under the hands-on leadership style of Almond. In this case, the two officers were professional enough to continue to perform despite their differences and the growing tension between them.

Almond wanted results; he wanted to capture Seoul as quickly as possible. He didn't think it wise to continue to batter away at the same toughly held position and sustain such high casualties. He knew that giving the enemy more time to prepare defenses within the city would make the job of taking Seoul even harder. Some believe that he was fixated on liberating Seoul by September 25 so it could be said that exactly three months after the North Koreans took Seoul, the UN forces liberated it. Others assert that he was pushing hard because he wanted to fulfill a promise made to MacArthur, or that he was being pressured to push harder. What is clear is that although Smith and Almond did not fully agree on where to press the attack and how hard, they put aside their differences and focused on winning the fight at hand.

On September 24, Murray's 5th RCT continued to attack to seize the low hills along the western approach to Seoul. The 2d Battalion sent two companies to seize a critical position on Hill 56. The companies tried to set a base of fire with one company and maneuver with the other but were unable to get close enough to overwhelm the position. The enemy bunker system was a well-developed network of interlocking positions. Trenches and caves dug into the back side of forward positions were used to shelter troops and ammunition. Concrete-hardened caverns and machine-gun nests could withstand heavy bombardment. In order to break the enemy positions, the marines were forced to resort to direct infantry assaults from the front and flanks using rifles, grenades, demolition kits, and knives while being subjected to a hail of bullets and shrapnel. Even when the marines were successful, the North Koreans often counterattacked immediately or at night to regain fallen positions. It was not unusual for trench lines to change hands several times and for bodies of fallen soldiers to become intermingled in piles of carnage.[3]

The marines continued to hit the bunkers and trenches with field artillery and from the air with the venerable Corsair. By now, however, the NKPA defenders were expecting it and managed to destroy two aircraft and damage five more. Casualties were mounting on both sides and little progress was being made, so that afternoon Almond met with his division commanders and key staff officers in Yongdungpo. Almond shifted the boundary between the 1st Marine Division and the 7th Infantry Division to the north and ordered the 32d Infantry Regiment and the 17th ROK Regiment to cross the Han River at the Sinsa-Ri ferry and attack into Seoul to seize South Mountain. At the same time that this meeting was taking place, the 2d Battalion, 5th RCT, reinforced with every replacement it could find and working closely with the 1st Marine Air Wing, seized the critical hill mass in the center position and cleared the trenches in hand-to-hand combat. One of the marine companies involved sustained more than 80 percent casualties in the effort, including 36 dead. North Korean losses were staggering. The combined effects of the air, artillery, mortar, and close fight had killed an estimated 1,750 men and wounded thousands more. While this battle raged, Puller's 1st RCT, after having successfully crossed the Han without incident, came up on the right to support Murray's 5th RCT. The 7th RCT remained on the left providing flank security, and the U.S. Army 187th Airborne Regiment landed at Kimpo airfield and took over the mission of providing airfield security. Without this secure airfield, logistics and close air support would have been much more difficult. As it was, supplying enough ammunition was becoming a problem, until a large ammunition storage area in Ascom City that had been abandoned in June was found intact. This provided many types of ammunition that the ground forces needed to sustain the momentum of their attack.

From September 20 to 24, X Corps had been frustrated in its efforts to gain entry to Seoul. However, on September 25 the situation improved dramatically. The combination of the results of the attack on September 24 and the massing of the 1st Marine Division put the NKPA in a precarious position. If it continued to try to hold the western hills, it faced the risk of being enveloped from the flank and rear. Therefore, it apparently chose to continue its defense within Seoul. At 6:00 A.M., an artillery barrage commenced on likely enemy positions in the area near the 7th Infantry Division Han River crossing site. Thirty minutes later, the 32d Infantry Regiment began crossing the Han in marine amtracs. Under the cover of smoke and fog, G Company was the first to cross. Things went smoothly until the men reached the far bank and found that it was too steep for the amtracs to climb. Fortunately, there was no enemy resistance other than some inaccurate mortar fire, and the soldiers were able to enter the water and slog their way onto land. Once the lead battalions of the 32d were across, they pushed ahead and were able to take South Mountain without a major engagement. With the crossing site secure, the engineers set up a ferry to speed the crossing. The 31st ROK Regiment was also successful in crossing and seizing its objective, Hill 348 of South Mountain, with only sporadic enemy contact.

The 1st and 5th RCTs spent the day fully engaged in a street-to-street battle on the western and southwestern part of Seoul. Interestingly, there seemed to be no remarkable shift in tactics or undue considerations given to the nature of fighting in a built-up area. There were boundary changes but no special instructions were issued. This was not supposed to be an infantry-only fight. The combined-arms approach used up to this point remained in effect. Leaders continued to use basic squad and platoon cover and movement techniques to locate, gain contact, and defeat the NKPA that had taken up new positions at road intersections and within the buildings. They continued to effectively integrate tanks, engineers, and fire support to back the advance. When necessary, they improvised new techniques to deal with the tactical situation. Despite ten days of hard fighting that had taken a serious physical and mental toll on their ranks and leadership of the 1st and 5th RCTs, the marines continued to fight in a cohesive and effective manner.

The 1st and 5th RCTs focused their attack on the Ma-Po and Kwang Who Moon Boulevards, which led to the central business district. This portion of the city was highly defensible because the concrete and multistoried buildings provided additional protection from the effects of direct and indirect fire. Other key areas that would need to be cleared of NKPA forces in order to liberate the city included the railroad station, the U.S. Embassy, the Ducksoo Palace, the Government House, city hall, schools, and the prison. Complicating matters further, many South Korean civilians were trapped within the city. Some were in hiding out of fear of the North Koreans. Others were simply at a loss for a safe direction to turn from the horrors of war. Initially, UN forces put restrictions on aerial and artillery fires on the city to minimize the risk of civilian casualties. But as the battle began to rage on the streets of Seoul, providing support to forces in contact became more important, and the use of artillery and airpower increased.

On September 25, the UN forces, having gained entry to the city from the south and seizing South Mountain, began clearing Seoul of enemy forces street by street from the west and south. They did not try to use their flank units to encircle the city and cut off exits. In retrospect, this probably hastened the liberation of Seoul. Encircling the city would likely have caused the NKPA to collapse into a strongpoint defense and either fight to the death or until General Wol ordered a surrender. The UN forces wanted to liberate Seoul quickly. Surrounding the NKPA and attempting to annihilate them probably would have resulted in a longer and more destructive battle that likely would have caused even greater casualties for the UN forces. Leaving the enemy a route of egress while applying direct combat pressure from two directions and maintaining flank security put the NKPA in a position where they could fight a delaying action instead of an encircled defense. Overall, whether by design or luck, this may have allowed the UN forces to capture Seoul sooner than if they had encircled it.

Throughout September 25, the capital city came under devastating air, artillery, and small-arms fire as the UN forces sought to force out the NKPA. The North Koreans continued to fight a delaying action and pursued a scorched earth policy, burning and destroying much of the city as they were forced to give ground. At night, they counterattacked. As a prelude to their attack, they began shelling South Mountain. After midnight, several NKPA battalions launched an all-out attack on the 32d Infantry. From the top of the hill, G Company managed to hold off the attackers by launching its own counterattack. F Company, which was lower on the hill, was initially overrun. In the morning, Lieutenant Colonel Mount, the battalion commander, ordered a battalion counterattack. After a few hours of furious and desperate fighting, the North Koreans were forced off the mountain. Nearly 400 NKPA soldiers were killed and 170 were taken prisoner in this engagement.[4]

On the evening of September 25, the uncertainty, friction, and fog of war nearly caused a disaster for the UN forces. Early in the evening, before the counterattack on South Mountain, aerial reconnaissance reported that the North Korean army was fleeing to the north. General Almond, believing that the enemy was on the run, ordered a night attack to pursue them. This came as a surprise to the marines who had fought hard all day and had no indications that the enemy was pulling out. Something just didn't seem right about the report, so General Smith had his staff double-check the message and clarify the source of the order. The location reported for the enemy concentration was several miles northeast of Seoul. However, X Corps assumed that this indicated that the enemy in Seoul was pulling out. The 1st Marine Division reluctantly set about planning for one of the most difficult operations to conduct: a night attack through a city without a clear idea of where the enemy was located.

The report of fleeing enemy may have been accurate, but it wasn't the enemy in front of the 1st and 5th RCT. To prepare for the attack, units were being brought to full alert, local security was being upgraded, and orders were being issued. However, just as marines were about to launch their attack, the "fleeing" enemy beat them to the punch by launching their own night attack. Luckily, U.S. forces had not yet moved out and were able to quickly respond to the all-out assault. This posture and heightened local security allowed them to absorb the initial brunt of the attack and quickly mount a successful defense. North Korean tanks and infantrymen assaulted in company-size waves against the marines. Through well-sited positions, effective fire control, and rock-steady discipline, the marines held their ground and stopped the attack. The night battle was fierce. There were point-blank engagements between tanks and recoilless rifles. Barrages of artillery and mortars were called in nearly on top of friendly positions to slow the waves of NKPA infantry. The sound of automatic fire, rifles, mortars, and rocket launchers filled the night. The defense held and the NKPA pulled back, having suffered hundreds more casualties in the night.

To make matters even worse, after the report of the fleeing enemy and issuing the order for the night attack, X Corps, believing that the situation was well under control, sent a message to the UN command that the enemy was fleeing and Seoul was nearly in friendly hands. Shortly after the message was sent, the enemy counterattack began. Some have seized on this as evidence that the X Corps headquarters or Almond was inept, or speculated that this was part of a political ploy to influence the government in North Korea. The fact that X Corps and the UN command declared that Seoul had been liberated while heavy fighting continued on the streets for several days contributed to the rift between Almond and Smith. Smith saw the episode as another indication that the corps commander was not fully aware of the situation and what needed to be done. In any event, although victory seemed likely, the battle was not yet won.

On September 26 the fighting resumed. "The bitter street fighting was a house-by-house struggle that pitted marine and army tank-infantry teams against heavily defended barricades and buildings for several days. Progress was measured in blocks throughout the downtown and government areas."[5] These barricades were made from whatever was at hand: sandbags, vehicles, debris, and anything else that could provide some protection from the effects of direct fire and block the roads. The NKPA also incorporated minefields, snipers, and antiarmor weapons into the barricade defense. Reducing these positions while minimizing friendly casualties was a time-consuming, systematic process. It wasn't enough simply to have the tanks rumble down the streets blasting everything in their path, because NKPA soldiers could disable the tanks with satchel charges or by placing antitank mines in the streets. Also, the enemy could hide in buildings and behind walls and attack the infantry once the tanks had passed. Working together to clear the roads and buildings was a slow and dangerous process that required close cooperation among the infantry, armor, engineers, mortar, and artillery units.

As UN forces made their way across the city, it became increasingly evident that the NKPA had committed horrible atrocities. The UN forces found many trenches filled with the decaying bodies of hundreds of men, women, and children. Decapitated and mutilated corpses were found in many other locations, including the prison, where a large room with many tools of torture was discovered. Many South Korean government officials and their families had been rounded up and killed. The gruesome scenes were shocking and sickening to the marines and soldiers, who had not expected the war to be carried out against civilian noncombatants and innocent women and children.

Throughout September 26, the battle to clear the city continued. The searing heat and smoke from the burning buildings made it difficult for the men to keep their eyes open as they advanced in short bounds down the shattered boulevards. Damaged telephone poles lined the streets. Electrical power and telephone lines littered the road. Anguished cries of "Corpsman!" and "Medic!" followed the sounds of rifle fire and explosions of grenades and mortars with alarming frequency. Rising casualties and the need to provide litter bearers to evacuate the wounded from the rubble were sapping the strength of the marine and army units. While falling back, the NPKA positioned additional soldiers in depth to prevent flanking or maneuvering on the next series of barricades.

With a little practice, the marines developed an effective method of reducing these complex obstacles. First, navy and marine fighters conducted rocket and strafing attacks on the barricades and adjacent positions. Next, mortars and small arms provided protective fire while engineers went forward to detonate or disarm the land mines. Once a path was clear, tanks would move ahead and blast the enemy machine guns and antitank positions. If possible, they would smash through the barricade. Another technique was to use a flamethrower tank to burn down a position. While this was taking place, infantry riflemen would follow the tanks to give them protection from the suicidal satchel chargers.[6] Ammunition was being brought forward and casualties were being evacuated almost constantly. By the time the battle ended, more than 65 percent of Seoul had been reduced to a smoldering ruin. On September 28, marines of the 5th RCT were finally able to reach the capitol building and raise the American flag, which a short time later was taken down and replaced by a UN flag.

The physical destruction of much of Seoul in the name of liberating it caused some newspaper correspondents to wonder whether perhaps it might have been better to encircle the city, lay siege to it, and issue an ultimatum to the North Koreans. Was it really necessary to destroy so much of the city to defeat the NKPA? Couldn't the UN have taken back the city with infantry and done much less physical damage? Given where and how the NKPA chose to defend, this was not a feasible or desirable course of action. Even if it had been possible to isolate the NKPA in the city, there was no reason to believe they would have surrendered without a fight and every reason to believe they wouldn't. Laying siege to Seoul would probably have resulted in an even more prolonged battle, stronger defenses, and higher civilian casualties at the hands of the NKPA. It would have provided North Korea with time to organize forces for a counterattack or attempt a breakout operation. Finally, much of the physical destruction of the city took place in an effort to minimize UN casualties. Using the overwhelming firepower of fighter aircraft, tanks, artillery, and mortars destroyed many buildings but saved the lives of infantry soldiers and marines on the ground. Attempting to clear the city with infantry alone would have resulted in enormous casualties on both sides.

Matthew Ridgway, who commanded the U.S. Eighth Army in Korea after General Walker, had the following to say about the fight for Seoul: "The battle to retake Seoul, however, was bitter. Although, as he has reported, MacArthur had the city safe 'in friendly hands' by the twenty-fifth, the Marines still fought from house to house, from barricade to barricade, against enemy machineguns, anti-tank cannon, and sniper fire until the twenty-eighth, when the last North Korean was flushed out of his flaming refuge and smoke rose from every quarter."[7]

On September 29, in a brief ceremony punctuated by the sounds of falling glass and distant combat, General MacArthur formally returned Seoul to South Korean president Syngman Rhee. The triumph was complete. September, which had begun with a massive NKPA attack on the Pusan perimeter, was ending with the liberation of Seoul and the collapse and disintegration of the North Korean army. While the ceremony was taking place, elements of the 1st Marine Division were already pushing north to capture Munsan and Oijongbu.

In the special action report submitted several months after the battle, X Corps estimated that 14,000 NKPA soldiers were killed in action and another 7,000 were wounded. Reports from subordinate units indicated that the following equipment was captured or destroyed: fifty T-34 tanks, fifty-nine 14.5mm anti-tank rifles, fifty-six heavy machine guns, twenty-three 120mm mortars, nineteen 45mm antitank guns, eight 76mm guns, two 76mm self-propelled guns, and more than two thousand rifles. Additionally, a great deal of American equipment that was lost at the start of the war was recovered.

X Corps sustained nearly 3,500 casualties. The 1st Marine Division, which did the majority of the fighting, also sustained the majority of the casualties: 366 killed in action, 49 of which died of wounds; 6 missing in action; and more than 2,000 wounded. The 7th Infantry Division had 106 killed in action, 409 wounded in action, and 59 missing in action. X Corps Tactical Air Command flew more than 2,500 sorties in support of the liberation of Seoul, losing only 11 aircraft to ground fire.

Conclusions

The battle to recapture Seoul offers many useful lessons about fighting in and around a city. To even gain entry to a city may involve several battles. Lacking surprise and overwhelming force, the process of liberating a city is likely to be long and brutal. The liberation of Seoul was unusually fast for a city fight but still involved extensive destruction of the infrastructure. Technological advances in both the precision and lethality of many weapons and weapon systems do not necessarily mean that "destroying the city in order to save it" is a thing of the past. Extensive damage and destruction are unavoidable when fighting in a city. To win quickly involves the application of overwhelming force at decisive places. Targets should be carefully selected, but collateral damage cannot be completely avoided. Expecting the military to fight in a city without causing destruction and collateral damage is like expecting the fire department to put out a fire without getting the surrounding area wet.

We can expect fires to pervade the urban battlefield in the future. Soldiers will need to be mentally and physically prepared to fight in choking smoke and searing heat. An enemy may choose to use fire as a weapon to impede movement, to generate refugees, or simply to destroy facilities to prevent them from being taken. Additionally, the smoke could be noxious and require the use of protective masks. In their description of the battle of Seoul, several soldiers and marines commented on the difficulty of keeping their eyes open and getting enough water to satiate their thirst as they fought through blocks of burning houses and buildings. Burning buildings, rubble, and barriers also made it difficult to evacuate casualties using wheeled vehicles. The wounded were moved by litter until litters began to run out; then soldiers and marines had to improvise by using wooden doors and blankets as field expedient litters.

Fighting in a city is likely to be chaotic. Because most of the decisions will be in the hands of junior officers and noncommissioned officers and the action will be carried out by individuals and small units, commanders will find it difficult to control the flow of the battle and maintain a clear mental picture of the dynamic situation. Disciplined reporting procedures are essential so a commander can make timely and effective decisions. Commanders also need to ensure that subordinate leaders have a clear idea of the purpose of the mission and the commander's intent, so small-unit leaders are empowered to exercise their initiative in an environment of many simultaneous engagements. The difficulty of command and control is amplified when these engagements take place at night.

A major tactical lesson that should be learned from this battle is that fighting as a combined-arms team is just as essential in a city fight as it is on other types of battlefields. Taking advantage of the capabilities of different types of units will have a synergistic effect. Combining infantry, armor, engineers, fire support, and forward logistics creates greater combat power. It enhances force protection and thereby reduces casualties. A combined-arms approach to fighting in a city provides the range of capabilities needed to overcome complex defenses. As the street-to-street fighting in Seoul demonstrates, no single branch or type of unit can do it alone without facing extreme risk. Even if the enemy does not possess tanks or mines, the capabilities of armor and engineers would provide friendly forces with significant advantages in firepower, mobility, countermobility, and survivability.

The aftermath of this battle also pointed out several issues in dealing with enemy prisoners and civilian reprisals. Law and order will not simply emerge out of the rubble of war; it will have to be established. Enemy prisoners will need to be guarded to prevent retaliation by civilians or other parties that want to exact revenge. Furthermore, many people are likely to need medical care. The atrocities committed by the NKPA against the residents of Seoul may have contributed to the tendency to kill enemy soldiers rather than take them prisoner. Often, soldiers and marines are shocked and sickened by the murder and mutilation of noncombatants. Although it is probably not possible to prevent them from feeling this way, it is possible to let them know that they are likely to encounter barbaric acts and what they should do in such situations.

A final lesson about fighting in a city that is not readily apparent, but is important to consider, also deals with the post-conflict situation. The UN forces had it relatively easy for a time after the battle to liberate Seoul. The enemy continued to the north, and the government of South Korea was quickly returned to power. If the government had not been ready to take charge in the liberated city, the UN forces would have been faced with dedicating their manpower to prevent a humanitarian disaster by providing food, water, shelter, and medical care for refugees. As it was, the UN forces still assumed most of the logistical tasks involved in the relief effort for the short term. As the fight for Seoul demonstrated, the aftermath of almost any city fight is likely to be a complex humanitarian emergency.

ENDNOTES

1. *X Corps Special Action Report, Operation Chromite* (Quantico, VA: Marine Corps University Archives).

2. S. Stanton, *America's Tenth Legion: X Corps in Korea 1950* (Novato, CA: Presidio Press, 1989), 96.

3. Stanton, 98–99.

4. Maihafer, 89.

5. Stanton, 106.

6. R. Leckie, *Conflict: The History of the Korean War, 1950–1953* (New York: Putnam and Sons, 1962), 150–51.

7. M. Ridgway, *The Korean War* (Garden City, NJ: Doubleday and Co., 1967), 41.

TWELVE

Hue City, 1968:

Winning a Battle While Losing a War

by Maj. Norm Cooling

*Fighting house-to-house is the dirtiest of all fighting. . . .
Just as a rat must be drawn from his burrow to be
eradicated, an enemy soldier, burrowed in a building,
must also be pulled from his hiding place to be eliminated.
Normally, he will not come out without a fight. The
attacker must go in and dig him out.* [1]

—Maj. Ron Christmas, USMC,
company commander in Hue

The battle for Hue City during the Tet offensive of 1968 provides a useful case study for examining the nature of urban conflict as part of a major regional contingency. This twenty-six-day
fight for the cultural center of Vietnam was the largest U.S. battle in a city since that for Seoul during the Korean War. To date,
Americans have not conducted an urban battle since Tet 1968
that has exceeded the scale of fighting in Hue. At the operational
level, Hue was merely one operation in the American and South
Vietnamese campaign to counter the North Vietnamese and Viet
Cong Tet offensive. Viewed in this context, Hue demonstrates
the difficulty of shaping the battle space at the operational level
in response to a surprise attack in a built-up area.

Strategic Setting

Located in central Vietnam, Hue is the country's third-largest city, with a population of approximately 140,000. The city is actually two distinct towns separated by the Perfume River. The Citadel, built on the northern bank, is roughly eight square kilometers and once served as the residence for Annamese emperors. In 1968 the southern side, about half the size of the Citadel, consisted primarily of French-style residential areas along with the city's university and the French provincial capital. Located approximately a hundred kilometers south of the demilitarized zone (DMZ), Hue was the predominant cultural, spiritual, and educational center of Vietnam. Militarily, the city housed the headquarters of the 1st Infantry Division of the Army of the Republic of Vietnam (ARVN) as well as serving as a compound for I Corps' Military Assistance Command, Vietnam (MACV) advisors. The majority of Hue's populace, however, remained aloof from the war. With their imperial heritage, most of the city's religious and intellectual leaders advocated strong local autonomy with an emphasis on traditional national values. They largely distrusted both Ho Chi Minh's communist government in Hanoi and the U.S.-supported government in Saigon.[2]

The Vietnamese are an exceptionally homogeneous people. Their culture has been shaped by decades of Chinese oppression, French colonization, and, briefly, Japanese occupation. In this predominantly rural, agrarian country, the French succeeded in establishing a major commercial area in the southern part of Vietnam centered on Saigon. Although there is a strong Buddhist and Confucian heritage among the Vietnamese, French colonization also implanted a thriving Catholic tradition. Tet, or the lunar new year, is the largest annual Vietnamese holiday, and Hue, as the imperial city, hosts a prominent festival. By late January, several thousand visitors arrive in Hue to participate in the festivities.[3]

Vietnam[4]

Conflict History

Hue was located within the I Corps area of operations (AO) under ARVN control and was commanded by Lt. Gen. Hoang Xuan
Lam in Da Nang. Although the overall American theater commander was Gen. William C. Westmoreland, located in Saigon,
the senior operational commander in the AO was Marine Corps
Lt. Gen. Robert E. Cushman, commander of III Marine Amphibious Force (MAF). Also headquartered at Da Nang, III
MAF spread over 220 miles of eastern coastal plains as well as
western mountain ranges.[5] The 1st Marine Division, under the
command of Maj. Gen. Donn J. Robertson, was responsible for
the southern portion of the III MAF area of operations, which
extended from just south of Da Nang to slightly north of Hue.
This area was so large that Cushman divided the division and
established direct operational control over both halves. Accordingly, the 1st Marine Division (Forward) Headquarters, commanded by the assistant division commander, Brig. Gen. Foster
C. LaHue, was designated Task Force X-Ray and given responsibility for the area from the Hai Van Pass to the northern
boundary of the division's tactical area of responsibility (TAOR).

Task Force X-Ray's mission was to protect Phu Bai, located
just eight miles south of Hue, screen the western approaches to
the historic city, and keep Highway 1 open between Hue and the
Hai Van Pass.[6] LaHue located his headquarters in Phu Bai,
where he had the 1st and 5th Marine Regiments (each with just
two battalions) available to accomplish his mission. The marines
of TF X-Ray focused on gaining and maintaining the support of
the South Vietnamese residing in villages throughout the AO by
posting combined-action platoons (CAPs) to live in those villages as an ever-present security force.[7]

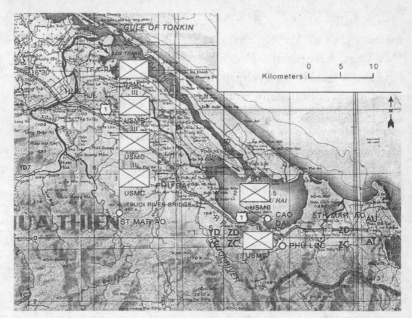

TF X-Ray dispositions[8]

Analyzing the American Campaign Plan

As in the earlier war in Korea, America's leadership viewed the situation in Vietnam in the context of their Cold War strategy of containment. Specifically, the United States feared that losing Vietnam to communism would lead to the loss of all Southeast Asia. Moreover, this loss would threaten Japan and South Korea while undermining U.S. influence throughout the Pacific region. The strategic objective for the United States in Vietnam, therefore, was to contain the spread of communism in Southeast Asia. This translated into an operational military objective of eliminating the effective North Vietnamese communist insurgency into the Republic of Vietnam.

Notably, Westmoreland and Cushman appear to have disagreed on the appropriate military strategy for reaching that operational objective. Westmoreland viewed the conventional forces of Gen. Vo Nguyen Giap's North Vietnamese Army (NVA) as the operational center of gravity. Westmoreland believed that the NVA's strength, relative to that of the U.S. forces, was Giap's critical vulnerability. In Westmoreland's mind, the key to victory lay in eliminating the NVA and the Viet Cong (VC) through search-and-destroy attrition tactics, a task he felt was well within the capability of the technologically superior U.S. forces. By the end of 1967, the highly touted strategic bombing campaign had not produced the promised results. The Johnson administration pressured Westmoreland to prevent further North Vietnamese infiltration. Westmoreland intended to accomplish this by placing the NVA forces in a position where superior U.S. firepower could destroy them. The U.S. forces would then attack west from Khe Sanh to interdict the communist supply route (the Ho Chi Minh Trail) in Laos.[9]

Unlike Westmoreland, Cushman viewed the Viet Cong insurgent forces as North Vietnam's operational center of gravity. He identified South Vietnamese support of the communists as the critical vulnerability to attack. Accordingly, he focused on small-unit pacification efforts in the village, believing that only the South Vietnamese themselves could truly expel the communists and eliminate the threat in the long term. The celebrated CAP program was a product of this approach. In time, the differences between these two operational commanders caused Westmoreland to grow increasingly concerned with the marines' ability to succeed in I Corps.[10] The friction between the two men would also complicate operational planning and execution throughout the Tet offensive.

Analyzing the North Vietnamese Campaign Plan

Ho Chi Minh and the communist leadership of North Vietnam had long suffered under the French and the Japanese during their quest for one strategic objective: Vietnamese self-government. Now, against the Americans and the South Vietnamese, the objective became a single Vietnamese government exclusively under their control. As part of a Maoist revolutionary war strategy, Ho employed rural insurgency and ambushes, complemented by an aggressive propaganda effort, to build a communist infrastructure among the South Vietnamese populace. By 1967, he felt the time had arrived to escalate his efforts to the conventional level. He believed that such an offensive would spark a simultaneous uprising among the peasantry of South Vietnam against its government. Ho knew quite well, however, that a conventional offensive was an all-or-nothing proposition with regard to fighting the Americans toe-to-toe. If the North Vietnamese failed, they would be forced to return to Mao Ze Dong's second phase (guerrilla warfare) and would not be able to fight the Americans as a conventional army again for several years, if ever.

Realizing that American public sentiment for the war was wavering, and aware that 1968 was an election year in the United States, Ho felt that an offensive was worth the risk. He recognized American confidence in the Johnson administration as a critical strategic vulnerability. If he could discredit Johnson and thereby cause the American public to lose confidence in the war effort, he could eliminate the U.S. operational center of gravity, its well-trained and technologically superior military power-projection capability. If he could not defeat the Americans in the field, he would defeat them indirectly. With the U.S. military out of the war, it would be only a matter of time before the ARVN government would collapse and he could secure his strategic objective.

Based on Ho's strategy, the military commander, Gen. Vo Nguyen Giap, planned an offensive operation for spring 1968. The first phase, scheduled to begin in fall 1967, would be a series of probing attacks to test American defenses and resolve. Phase Two, now known as the Tet offensive, would seek to simultaneously attack the weak points identified during Phase One. Because the Tet holiday was normally a truce period between the North and South Vietnamese, this would provide Giap with a greater opportunity for operational surprise. Finally, the third phase would consist of a "second wave," to reinforce victories achieved during the initial offensive. Counting on propaganda and terrorist tactics to manipulate South Vietnamese public opinion, the second and third phases would generate Maoist conditions known as the General Offensive and the General Uprising. Ho and Giap believed that this upsurge against U.S. involvement would cause the American public to withdraw its support for involvement in Vietnam.[11]

Hue played a significant role in the NVA campaign plan. The city was a key choke point along the critical U.S. and ARVN north-south line of communications (LOC), Highway 1. In addition, a railroad ran through Hue, and navy supply boats used the city as an embarkation and debarkation point for supplies moving to and from the ocean. Taking Hue would sever the American's LOC and prohibit the movement of supplies from Da Nang to the DMZ. The NVA viewed the city as a weak link in the allied defense of the two northern provinces, which were oriented against an anticipated attack along Route 9.[12] Accordingly, Giap directed two combined NVA and VC regiments, the 4th and the 6th, to infiltrate Hue during Phase One and attack the city during the Tet celebration. At the same time, other units would attack U.S. and ARVN installations throughout South Vietnam, to include Saigon. The NVA 6th Regiment's objectives included the ARVN 1st Division's Mang Ca headquarters compound, the Tay Loc airfield, and the imperial palace, all located within the Citadel. The NVA 4th Regiment's objectives were south of the Perfume River and included the provincial capital, the prison, and the U.S. MACV advisors' compound.[13] The VC would carry lists of "Enemies of the People" into Hue that included the names of various local and national government officials, intellectuals, and soldiers, and their families, with the intent of executing them.[14]

Campaign Execution

Phase One of the NVA campaign plan was executed almost flawlessly, so that as the NVA prepared for Phase Two, they were well aware of U.S. and ARVN force dispositions. Although allied intelligence noted NVA movements and knew that something was brewing, they were unable to discern the NVA's intentions. The Tet offensive kicked off on January 30, 1968, with approximately 74,000 communist troops streaming across the border into South Vietnam. Thirty-six provincial capitals, 5 of 6 autonomous cities, 64 of 242 district capitals, and more than 50 hamlets were all struck within 48 hours.[15] The battle for Hue began on January 31. Despite the one-day notice of the NVA attack, Hue and Saigon were largely unprepared when both were attacked on the second day of the communist offensive. The commanding general of the ARVN 1st Division, Brig. Gen. Ngo Quang Truong, however, did take the prudent steps of heightening his division's alert status and recalling his troops from Tet leave. In the long run, this decision likely saved Hue from being completely overrun by the communists. Truong expected the enemy to attack near Phu Loc in an attempt to sever Highway 1 south of Hue, and he deployed his battalions accordingly.[16]

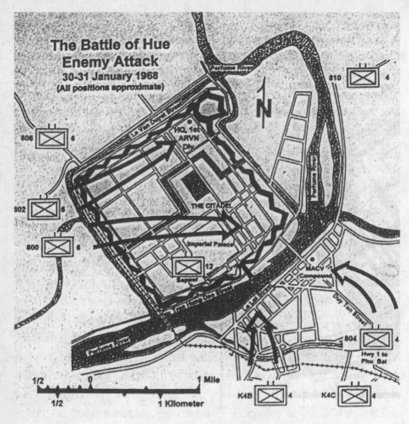

NVA/VC attack axes[17]

Viet Cong sappers infiltrated Hue on January 29 while the two NVA/VC regiments moved toward the city with 7,500 soldiers.[18] Around two in the morning of January 31, the NVA 6th Regiment linked up with its guides and at 3:40 A.M. seized a bridgehead into the Citadel. By 8:00 A.M. the NVA 4th Regiment had also entered the Citadel, and shortly thereafter the VC flag was waving over the imperial palace. The NVA and VC captured or killed isolated pockets of U.S. and ARVN servicemen throughout the city, but Truong's ARVN 1st Division continued to put up stiff resistance. Within a few hours, the communist forces seized control of the entire city with the notable exception of two key objectives: the ARVN's 1st Division headquarters, located in the northeast corner of the Citadel, and I Corps' MACV compound, on the south side of the Perfume River. The communists succeeded in isolating these two forces from each other by cutting their wire link.

Inadequate intelligence concerning the attack initially prompted Task Force X-Ray to dispatch a single rifle company, Company A, 1st Battalion, 1st Marines (1/1), to relieve the U.S. and ARVN forces under siege. Company A moved north to Hue from Phu Bai along Highway 1, linking up with four M48 tanks along the way. Because the Viet Cong were unsuccessful in their initial attempts to drop the An Cuu Bridge, Company A was able to cross over the Phu Cam Canal before they came under attack just short of the MACV complex. With Company A pinned down, Brigadier General LaHue attached Company G, 2d Battalion, 5th Marines (2/5), to Lt. Col. Marcus J. Gravel, the commander of 1/1, and dispatched him to Hue as well.

Upon linking up, the two companies continued their assault to reach the MACV compound, where they immediately took up positions around the headquarters and the navy's boat ramp on the river. Simultaneously they secured the base of the Nguyen Hoang Bridge, the Highway 1 crossing point over the Perfume River to the Citadel. Shortly thereafter, III MAF directed LaHue to order Company A, 1/1, and Company G, 2/5, to cross the river and link up with General Troung in the ARVN headquarters. To everyone on the ground, this order was a clear indication that III MAF was out of touch with the reality of the situation.[19] Nonetheless, Gravel sent Company G to secure the bridge. In a two-hour firefight, Golf Company succeeded in taking the bridge but was forced to retire back to the MACV compound about three hours later, when it became clear that they could not hold the bridge against an enemy counterattack.

On the second day of the battle, III MAF ordered Maj. Gen. John J. Tolson's 1st Cavalry Division to deploy the 2d Battalion, 12th Cavalry, to a landing zone along Highway 1, approximately ten kilometers northwest of Hue, in an effort to sever the NVA's LOC. The air cavalry fought in this area for several days but was unable to disrupt the enemy and isolate the city. Thus, the communist forces in Hue continued to receive reinforcements and resupply from the west. An additional five communist battalions eventually reinforced the nine that invaded Hue on the first day. There were also two sapper battalions, which brought the NVA strength in and around Hue to two divisions. The weather, too, began to favor the nontechnical enemy by hampering aerial support. Nevertheless, on the second day, Company F, 2/5, conducted a heliborne movement into the LZ adjacent to the MACV compound. Task Force X-Ray then issued yet another order to Gravel indicating the lack of situational awareness at the operational level. LaHue tasked him to secure the south side prison building. Because it was obvious to Gravel that the prisoners had already been liberated by the NVA, he successfully argued that the mission should be canceled. The following day, Company H, 2/5, joined the forces in the MACV compound as another unit "piecemealed" into the fight.

On the morning of the fourth day of fighting, Lt. Col. Ernest C. Cheatham, Jr., the commanding officer of 2/5, was at last ordered to move a convoy to Hue and assume command of the three companies he had fighting there under Lieutenant Colonel Gravel. The new commander of the 1st Marine Regiment, Col. Stanley S. Hughes, whom LaHue tasked to assume overall command of all U.S. Marine forces in Hue, accompanied the convoy. Racing through an ambush and into the MACV

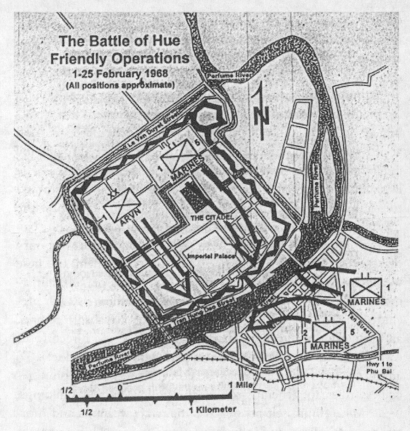

The Battle of Hue
Friendly Operations
1-25 February 1968
(All positions approximate)

U.S. attack axes[20]

compound, Hughes established his command post, took the reins from Gravel, and, still with no intelligence beyond that available in the MACV compound, issued an operations order to Cheatham and Gravel. Hughes ordered Cheatham to begin clearing the city's south side by advancing west from the compound generally along Le Loi Street and parallel to the Perfume River to where the Phu Cam Canal branched from the river. Hughes directed Gravel, with his single reinforced but casualty-ridden company, to move with 2/5, but along the Phu Cam, in order to keep Highway 1 open to the compound. The ARVN troops available to Hughes in the MACV compound would mop up snipers and pockets of resistance while caring for the civilian refugees in trace of the marines' advance.

Thus began the painstaking process of clearing Hue building by building through the prepared urban defenses of a determined enemy. Because every street constituted a prepared kill zone overwatched by snipers, the marines were forced to employ ingenious tactics and techniques to attain their objectives. The learning was by trial and error, and it was costly.[21] Accustomed to rural and jungle warfare against hit-and-run ambushes, the marines in Hue now faced both VC and NVA troops in an urban defense in depth.[22] Tanks were the only advantage in weaponry that the attacking marines had, and the movement of these weapons was greatly restricted by the NVA's use of B-40 antiarmor rockets. Restrictive U.S. rules of engagement (ROE) precluded the employment of aircraft munitions, naval surface fires, and artillery (despite the fact that the ARVN was directing its own Skyraider aircraft to attack targets within the Citadel). To advance, small infantry teams worked with tanks and 106mm recoilless rifles to generate routes through walls and buildings, while M42 40mm self-propelled antiaircraft weapons and mortars provided direct and indirect suppressive fires. Unfortunately, these tactics were unable to prevent high American casualty rates.

On several occasions during the street fighting, the marines assaulted buildings filled with noncombatants who were used as shields by the communist forces. United States tactical commanders implemented more restrictive, on-scene ROE accordingly; the NVA and the VC, on the other hand, did not. Both American and other international media representatives moved throughout the city along with attacking marine squads, consistently filming the actions of individual marines. By the fifth day of fighting, Maj. Ralph J. Salvati, 2/5's executive officer, acquired a number of E8 tear-gas launchers and distributed these to the fighting companies. The use of this nonlethal weapon helped the marines to force the NVA and VC out of buildings. In the open, the enemy could be engaged selectively without firing into buildings indiscriminately and risking civilian lives.

The marines methodically cleared the treasury, the university, the city hospital, the Joan of Arc School, and, on February 6, the rest of the provincial capital. Fighting by day and consolidating at night, Hughes was able to declare the south side of the city secure on February 10. The marines needed several more days, however, to completely sweep the area in and around the southern portion of the city of all communist forces. In so doing, more Americans became casualties. Also during these sweeps, the marines began uncovering the mass graves of South Vietnamese executed during the NVA's occupation.

Throughout the fighting, the civilian population remained essentially passive. According to TF X-Ray's after-action report, "There was little evidence of voluntary assistance to the VC/NVA. On the other hand, civilians volunteered no assistance to the Marines either."[23] Most of Hue's citizens had initially locked themselves in their homes, but now thousands began to stream into the MACV compound. Five thousand refugees gathered at the liberated Catholic Church, and another 17,000 accumulated at the university. When the mayor of Hue and the ARVN forces proved unable to adequately process and care for them alone, Da Nang dispatched a platoon from the 29th Civil Affairs Company to assume control of the humanitarian effort.

Because the Vietnamese refused to touch dead bodies, the Americans used enemy prisoners to bury the dead where they were found. Altogether, Hue had 22,000 displaced people to care for without adequate food, medical supplies, or sanitation facilities. To make matters worse, someone among the refugees or the ARVN promptly stole a significant portion of the emergency rations dispatched from Da Nang, beginning a black market enterprise even as the battle continued. Many refugees did not stop at the MACV compound but continued to flee the city south along Highway 1, further complicating movement along the main service route. Looting became commonplace. Although some marines were involved, the vast majority of looters were South Vietnamese, particularly the ARVN forces sweeping behind the marines. Lieutenant Colonel Gravel so feared that the media would accuse the marines of plunder that he warned American advisors to the ARVN that any ARVN soldier observed looting would be killed on sight. Although this statement did not completely solve the problem, it did succeed in greatly curtailing it.[24] Legitimacy remained a valid U.S. concern even in the midst of a conventional battle.

While the 2/5 and 1/1 were fighting for the south side, Brigadier General Troung consolidated his ARVN 1st Division to retake the Citadel. After the fourth day of his counteroffensive, the NVA proved too tough to dislodge and Troung requested American assistance. LaHue subsequently ordered Maj. Robert H. Thompson and his 1st Battalion, 5th Marines (1/5), to the Citadel. By late afternoon on February 11, Thompson positioned three of his line companies in the Citadel via a combination of heliborne and landing craft utility (LCU) transport lifts. The ARVN intelligence picture of what was going on within the Citadel was vague at best. Because the NVA held half of the northeast and most of the southeast walls, General Troung directed the marines to relieve his ARVN 1st Airborne Task Force along the 2,500–yard northeast wall and continue to clear that wall. Meanwhile, ARVN forces would focus on seizing the imperial palace and its adjacent southeast wall.

The marines stepped off on February 13, only to find the

NVA moving into the positions prematurely abandoned by the ARVN 1st Airborne Task Force. Just ten minutes later a meeting engagement began, and the NVA rendered A, 1/5, combat ineffective. With a full two weeks of preparation prior to the marines' arrival, the communists had hundreds of well-fortified and camouflaged, mutually supporting positions throughout the dense confines of the Citadel. As on the south side, NVA sniper fire proved exceptionally effective. Thompson's estimate of the situation caused Colonel Hughes to argue for, and successfully obtain, an easement of the restrictive ROE. Thompson then employed 5- and 6-inch naval guns, 8-inch and 155mm artillery, and fixed-wing zunni rockets along the wall, as well as riot control (CS) gas on structures inside the Citadel.

The fact that Gen. Creighton W. Abrams, the deputy theater commander, established a MACV forward command post at Phu Bai on the same day likely had much to do with the decision to ease the ROE. With intelligence on February 16 indicating that the communists were preparing to reinforce their troops in the Citadel, General Abrams hosted a meeting with Vice President Nguyen Cao Ky and Lieutenant General Lam, the I Corps commander. During this meeting, Ky concurred with the American assessment of an NVA buildup west of Hue, and stated his belief that the communists were willing to sacrifice thousands of their men to win a slight political gain. Ky then agreed that U.S. forces should be able to engage the enemy in pagodas, churches, and other religious buildings, and promised to accept responsibility for any destruction. The following day, Westmoreland met with both Abrams and Cushman and agreed to place two battalions of the 1st Brigade, 1st Cavalry Division, under TF X-Ray in order to block avenues of retreat to the south and southwest while the 2d Brigade, 1st Cavalry Division, pressed the NVA from the northwest.[25]

Following nine days of brutal fighting, 1/5 at last secured

the northeast wall of the Citadel on February 21. Yet, because
the ARVN had failed to make much progress against the southeast wall and the imperial palace, Thompson was forced to wheel
his battalion to the right and continue the fight. His battalion
largely exhausted, he turned to the recently arrived marines of
Company L, 3d Battalion, 5th Marines (3/5). As L, 3/5, continued the advance, four battalions of the 1st Cavalry Division
began a devastatingly effective combined-arms assault against the
NVA's supply installation established in the La Chu Woods just
west of the city. With their primary LOC severed and with little
hope of supporting their remaining forces inside the Citadel, the
NVA 6th Regiment at last gave the order to withdraw on the
twenty-third. On that same day, Thompson's marines rapidly secured the northeast wall and prepared to assault the final unse-
cured position, the imperial palace. In deference to the "host
nation," however, the elite ARVN Black Panther Company made
the final assault against very little resistance and replaced the VC
colors with those of the Republic of Vietnam.

On February 26, final mop-up operations began. Again, as
the marines and the ARVN moved through the Citadel in their
final sweep, they discovered several hundred civilian corpses, all
shot in the head. Apparently, in addition to executing those labeled as "Enemies of the People," the VC eliminated anyone
who could identify their infrastructure now that it had surfaced
as part of the Tet offensive. The communists took great care in
their attempts to bury and conceal the dead, and it took nearly a
full year after the battle for U.S. forces to gain an appreciation of
the true scale of the genocide. The South Vietnamese eventually
recovered 3,000 bodies in mass graves around the city; an additional 2,000 people were still unaccounted for.[26]

At midnight on February 27, the operation officially ended.
Lasting twenty-six days, the battle for Hue was the longest and
bloodiest of the Tet offensive. A total of three marine battal-

ions and eleven ARVN battalions were eventually committed to retaking the city. Ten thousand homes were damaged or destroyed. The battle created 116,000 homeless refugees and left 80 percent of the historic city in ruins. Americans lost 216 killed and 1,364 wounded in action; the ARVN lost 384 killed and 1,830 wounded. Some 5,800 civilians died, at least 2,800 of whom were killed by the VC, who sought out and exterminated those with pro-U.S. sentiments as well as those who could identify them and compromise their efforts. The United States estimated enemy casualties at 5,000, with 1,042 killed.[27]

The destruction of the culturally and spiritually significant city by military action was well publicized in the United States and had an important impact on public perceptions.[28] Clearly, Hue was a tactical victory as U.S. and ARVN forces regained control of the city. Because the Tet offensive was repelled and the North Vietnamese were soundly defeated militarily, it can also be argued that Hue was part of a larger operational success. It is just as clear, however, that the battle was a strategic failure. The effect of the Tet offensive on the American psyche was so dramatic that it caused the American public to lose faith in the Johnson administration. This led to erosion of public support for the war in Vietnam, the eventual withdrawal of all American forces from the country, and, ultimately, the defeat of South Vietnam.

Operational-Level Assessment

Command and Control

United States and ARVN command relationships remained disjointed and confused throughout the battle for Hue. Even after the initial surprise of the attack, General Westmoreland failed to coordinate with the South Vietnamese and establish a single operational-level commander in the area. The U.S. and ARVN units remained under separate chains for the duration of the fight. Lieutenant General Cushman was initially too absorbed by the situation in Khe Sanh to focus exclusively on the problem in Hue. With both the ARVN and MACV headquarters cut off and isolated, Cushman and LaHue lacked situational awareness of what was happening in the city, causing them to dispatch units to the city in a piecemeal fashion. The enemy took advantage of the slow U.S. response by consolidating its defenses and eventually dropping two key bridges to sever Highway 1. The lack of effective operational control in Hue resulted in haphazard and disjointed tactical actions. One officer involved in the fighting noted that "the lack of an overall commander resulted in no general battle plan and competition for supporting fires, air, and logistic support."[29]

The lack of situational awareness at the operational level also caused Westmoreland and Cushman to impose overly stringent ROE on the U.S. forces counterattacking in the city. The ARVN corps commander, General Lam, initially imposed strict ROE on the use of fire support in hopes of saving the historic city and preventing needless civilian casualties. Accordingly, U.S. forces initially agreed to prohibit the employment of artillery, naval gunfire, bombs, or napalm in the city. As a result, on several occasions marines were forced to allow the NVA to evacuate their wounded at night without engaging them with indirect neutralization fires. In one instance, a marine squad identified a group of NVA soldiers in a pagoda. Following the procedures, they requested a relaxation to the ROE to engage the soldiers in the structure. This request took two hours to route to the III MAF staff in Da Nang and back. By the time the marines were told that they could attack the pagoda (but only with direct-fire weapons), the NVA had successfully withdrawn from the building.[30]

Ironically, at the same time this was happening, the ARVN

forces under General Truong, located within the most culturally sensitive area of the city (the Citadel), were calling in their own air strikes. Only when General Abrams arrived did the operational picture become clear enough to initiate talks with the South Vietnamese and adjust the ROE appropriately. From that point, the U.S. ROE became increasingly liberal, and only the area immediately surrounding the imperial palace remained under tight restrictions.[31] When U.S. tactical commanders believed that noncombatants were threatened, they tightened the ROE accordingly. Hue is an example of where it may have been better to provide a clear operational commander's *intent for fires* rather than rigid ROE. It certainly does little good for one belligerent (the Americans) to be under one set of ROE while an ally (the ARVN) operates under different parameters. The primary purpose of ROE is to maintain the support, or at least the neutrality, of the noncombatant populace. In the case of Hue, this was not too difficult given the fact that the communists were an invading force engaging in genocide throughout the city.

Intelligence

Operational intelligence immediately before and during the Tet offensive was grossly lacking and resulted in the communists achieving near total surprise. United States intelligence correctly identified a large enemy buildup along both the demilitarized zone and the Laotian border. Unfortunately, it failed to correctly forecast the objective of these preparations. Flawed intelligence estimates caused operational planners to focus almost exclusively on Khe Sanh and the surrounding region as the communists' objective. The American operational intelligence failure caused a disoriented defensive posture, great initial confusion, and inadequate responses to Vietnamese actions.[32]

The primary sources of operational-level information were

the ARVN 1st Division and Thua Thien sector intelligence summaries and low-level agent reports.[33] American intelligence knew
that the NVA 4th and 6th Regiments were within a day's march
of Hue prior to Tet and preparing for an attack. Yet it completely
failed to identify the intent and magnitude of the communist offensive. It appears that no reliable human intelligence (HUMINT)
resources within Hue identified the several hundred VC who infiltrated the city two days prior to the attack in order to facilitate
the NVA invasion. Collection measures improved only after
Westmoreland, Cushman, and LaHue gained enough situational
awareness through "employment by trial and error" to focus on
Hue and bring superior American technology to bear. Only after
two weeks were appropriate collection assets put in place, and by
that time U.S. ground forces had already gained the initiative.
On February 16, American signals intelligence (SIGINT) intercepted an enemy radio transmission during which an officer reported the death of the communist force commander in Hue
and requested permission to withdraw. The officer was told to
remain in place and fight.[34]

Information dissemination was also a problem. On the night
of January 30, an army radio intercept field station at Phu Bai,
just south of Hue on Highway 1, intercepted NVA radio transmissions indicating an imminent attack on Hue. Rather than re-
laying the message immediately to Hue, the station followed the
bureaucratic procedure of sending it to Da Nang for posting and
analysis. As a result, MACV did not get the warning until well after the attack.[35] Despite the fact that American forces had long
been present in Hue, the commanders fighting in the city had to
scrounge city maps from a local gas station and the police headquarters to augment the few city maps they were able to obtain
from the MACV headquarters.[36]

Due to poor communications and information dissemination, it took far too long for the operational commanders to gain

appropriate situational awareness. On the second day of fighting, Brigadier General LaHue remained so confused that he assured a United Press International (UPI) reporter that the marines were in control of the city's south side. As author Keith William Nolan wrote, "The Marine command at Task Force X-Ray was separated from Hue by eight miles of road and by a wall of optimism, disbelief, and misinformation."[37] Intelligence was so bad that a full seven days after the An Cuu Bridge was dropped by communist sappers, TF X-Ray still unknowingly dispatched a convoy of 120 replacements to Hue without the means to repair the structure for crossing.[38]

By contrast, the communist intelligence effort was so effective that their two attacking regiments were given specific target lists with more than two hundred facilities, government officials, and other individuals. This list was so accurate that it included the names and location of agents at an American Central Intelligence Agency facility in Hue, which even officers at I Corps MACV headquarters knew nothing about.[39] The communists focused on both active and passive counterintelligence methods, impeding U.S. and ARVN communications by cutting their land lines and making a concerted effort to ensure that their troops had no documentation or unit markings that would indicate their force dispositions.[40] Nevertheless, in at least one respect the North Vietnamese HUMINT effort may not have been much superior to that of the Americans. Placing too much faith in their own propaganda, the communists appear to have been surprised when most of the citizens of Hue and the other cities and villages struck during the Tet offensive failed to view them as liberators and assist in their efforts against the ARVN and the marines.[41]

Maneuver

Hampered by poor intelligence and unable to fully ascertain the situation in Hue, Brigadier General LaHue elected to piecemeal infantry companies into the fight. This prevented a coordinated battalion-level attack until two days into the battle, and undoubtedly cost more lives than necessary. The delay in force deployment to Hue allowed the communists to solidify their defenses in preparation for the American counterattack. Because Hue was merely one of several simultaneous attacks conducted as part of the Tet offensive, III MAF did not have enough forces available to isolate Hue by sealing off the eight-mile perimeter around the city. Some authorities estimate that doing so would have required sixteen infantry battalions.[42] Nevertheless, the most effective operational maneuver during the course of the battle was the commitment of the 1st Cavalry Division to sever the NVA LOC into Hue. Short of completely isolating the city, this was likely the most effective maneuver that could have been performed at the operational level.

Poor tactical maneuver initially had operational consequences, because it produced excessive casualties. The marines of both 1/1 and 2/5 were ill trained for urban operations, both having been committed to Hue following extensive jungle fighting. The learning curve was very steep. What the marines lacked in formal urban training they made up for with "the imagination, aggressiveness, and esprit de corps of each combatant."[43] Although the marines were ill prepared for urban combat, it appears that the communist forces were also unprepared to exploit the advantages of defending urban terrain. In several instances, the VC/NVA initiated urban ambushes on the point element of American companies assaulting instead of waiting for the majority of the company to enter the kill zone. Both sides were accustomed to jungle fighting, and both learned as the battle progressed.

Moreover, although the Americans were unable to isolate Hue from the NVA, the reverse was also true. The NVA failed to seize their two most important initial objectives: the ARVN and the MACV headquarters. The communists also repeatedly failed to demolish the An Cuu Bridge over the Phu Cam to cut the LOC between Hue and Phu Bai until the night of February 4, five days into the fighting. By that time, five marine infantry companies, as well as additional ARVN forces, had successfully moved to reinforce the MACV compound. Similarly, the communists failed, despite repeated attempts, to capture any of the other bridges between those locations. Finally, they could not bring down the bridge across the Perfume River that separated the marines from the ARVN forces until the third day of fighting.[44] By failing to destroy the An Cuu Bridge and allowing the Americans to gain control of the navy boat ramp and helicopter landing zone near the MACV headquarters, the communist forces could not isolate the city. As a result, American forces were allowed to prosecute the battle for Hue from the "inside out" while being assured of reliable logistics resupply.

Fires

Beyond the limited fires to support the 1st Cavalry Division's effort to cut the NVA supply line in the La Chu Woods, operational fires in support of the counterattack on Hue were virtually nonexistent. Operational fires require sound intelligence to facilitate targeting; in the case of Hue, that intelligence was absent. The key learning point regarding operational fires from Hue was the necessity for the theater commander to make the appropriate weapons and munitions available to tactical commanders and to produce realistic ROE. By successfully negotiating an easement to the ROE, General Abrams later shaped the operational battle space so that tactical fires could be productive.

Airpower provides a case in point. Airpower played a relatively insignificant role because of the overcast skies and the highly restrictive ROE that were in effect during the majority of the battle.[45] When these ROE were eased, however, close air support proved effective in facilitating the infantry's advance in the Citadel. As described in TF X-Ray's after-action report, "On February 22, four flights of aircraft, loaded primarily with 250 pound Snakeye and 5,600 pound napalm bombs, laid down a devastating screen of destruction in the southeast sector of the Citadel City. Advancing directly behind the bombs, the ground units were able to secure the final portion of their objective with a minimum of casualties."[46]

Nonetheless, even after the easement of the ROE, the close confines of the city made the employment of tactical fires and combined arms especially challenging. Gaining accurate battle damage assessments from indirect-fire missions was difficult because the observer could rarely see the effects of the fires in the cluttered urban construction.[47] Real-time satellite and aerial imagery may help to alleviate this problem in the future, but only if the information can be relayed directly to the unit calling for the fires.

Riot control agents greatly assisted the counterattacking units. Lieutenant Colonel Chapman's battalion successfully employed CS gas to force NVA and VC soldiers from buildings without having to destroy Hue's infrastructure. This assisted immensely in limiting both collateral damage and noncombatant casualties. In future conflicts, the operational commander will likely be responsible for approving the use of such nonlethal weapons, and coordinating their use with the host nation or allied forces. Precautions and appropriate control measures should be established to ensure that these agents are productive. In Hue, during the confusion of the urban fight, 2/5 employed CS gas without first notifying an adjacent friendly unit, A 1/1, whose members did not have their protective masks.[48]

Hue clearly demonstrated the value of direct tank fire in mid- to high-scale urban combat. The M48s provided critical support to the infantry by opening "new" routes: knocking down walls and obstacles and blasting openings to enable troop movement and casualty evacuation under cover. By combining the M48 tanks with the Ontos antitank vehicles, the innovative marines dominated the close-range fighting along the confined streets of the Citadel. This technique was so effective that when tank ammunition ran out on February 17, the advance had to be halted.[49] When tank fires are to be employed at the tactical (in fact, the small-unit) level, it is critically important that the operational commander make armored assets available to his subordinate commanders in these circumstances. In studying armor employment during the battles of Hue and Khorramshahr, one officer found that "armor dominance in the urban setting translates to a four to sevenfold increase in the application of combat power in the close fight."[50]

In the long run, the nonlethal type were the most important operational fires that could and should have been employed during the Tet offensive. The information battle was the strategic battle that U.S. forces most needed to win, both within South Vietnam and at home. Cushman's pacification focus was consistent with this approach. Westmoreland's search-and-destroy philosophy was not. By focusing on superior firepower and an attrition-based operational strategy, while virtually ignoring the media, Westmoreland abandoned American public perception to communist propaganda efforts. As a result, despite the fact that the Tet offensive was an overwhelming U.S. tactical victory, it was a strategic defeat. Had Westmoreland made winning the information battle a central part of his campaign plan, things may have turned out differently.

Because of the rampant distrust that U.S. leaders held for the media, they potentially failed to capitalize on an opportunity to expose the American people to the NVA's callousness by publicizing the mass executions in Hue. This failure may be largely attributable to the fact that American forces did not have a good idea of the scale of the atrocities immediately following the operation.[51] At least one credible writer, however, believes that the communist genocide received little attention by the media because of the subsequent revelation of the My Lai massacre.[52]

Brigadier General LaHue made adequate psychological operations assets available to Colonel Hughes. Still, according to Hughes's after-action report, his "Psywar effort . . . had little apparent effect on the enemy force. The tenacious fighting and 'hold till death' attitude of the occupying NVA forces was not one that was receptive to psy ops, despite the deteriorating situation that worsened every day."[53] Notably, though, Hughes added, "Psy Ops directed towards the civilian population was successful and played an important role in the rapid response of the civilians to assist the GVN [Government of Vietnam] with information and rebuilding or clean up efforts."[54]

Logistics

Operational logistics throughout the battle for Hue was a resounding success, despite the fact that the NVA eventually succeeded in destroying the bridges along the main supply route (MSR, or Highway 1), thereby isolating the city from the ground. The marines surmounted this deficiency by using the landing zone and boat ramp immediately adjacent to the MACV compound. The boat ramp allowed the marines to use the Perfume

River effectively (which is accessible from the South China Sea) as an alternate line of supply and communication. Had the NVA succeeded in securing either or both the LZ and the boat ramp, the American logistics picture would likely have been much bleaker.

Although the American forces had immense difficulty in caring for the several thousand South Vietnamese refugees in Hue, they performed the combat service support function quite well. On only one day, February 17, were the marines of 1/5 forced to pause in their fighting in the Citadel due to a lack of both food and tank and 106mm recoilless rifle ammunition. An important operational logistics planning lesson is that both "wall busting" and nonlethal munitions must be made available to tactical units.

Logistics personnel skillfully employed mutually supporting air, land, and sea resupply means to keep the marines fighting. The 1st Marine Division G-4, Force Logistic Command, Force Logistic Support Group Alpha, and the Naval Support Activity headquarters, located in Da Nang, controlled this effort. Throughout the battle, more than a hundred ground convoys, many of which fought their way through ambushes, delivered critical ammunition to Hue. Both marine and army helicopters executed 270 medevac sorties to evacuate approximately a thousand casualties while bringing in 525 tons of supplies, despite the fact that they were flying into a hot landing zone. Sixty helicopters were hit over the city. Navy LCUs with Swift gunboat escorts brought in another 400 tons of supplies. As with the air and land routes, they, too, fought their way into and out of the navy ramp adjacent to the MACV compound. Three LCUs were literally blown to pieces.[55]

The fighting in Hue consumed an inordinate amount of ammunition, nearly ten times the normal combat rate experienced during the rural fighting.[56] Tanks alone fired 30 percent more ammunition than consumption rates specified for "heavy-intensity" combat in current planning manuals.[57] In addition to what the various marine units initially carried with them into the city, several tons of ammunition were sent in as resupply during the fight for Hue alone. This does not include the countless other units and engagements supported by Force Logistics Support Group Alpha throughout the entire Tet offensive. The logistical picture, however, was not perfect. A flawed combat replacement policy caused at least one group of replacements to be sent directly into Hue without any training in the theater. At least one marine died in Hue less than two weeks after completing recruit training.[58] These two weeks would have included stateside infantry training, a flight from California to Da Nang, and another flight into Hue itself.

With regard to the NVA logistics effort, at least until the second air cavalry operation, the communists' preparations were "sufficiently complete to insure adequate supplies of all types of ammunition and supply. . . . Prisoner interrogation indicated no shortages of ammunition during the battle, and indicated that resupply was constant and virtually automatic to front line units." The enemy developed regular and well-organized rear areas south and west of Hue in the nearby villages through which resupply was managed, and to which wounded personnel, prisoners of wars, persons freed from the Thua Thien Provincial Prison and numerous persons detained by the VC/NVA were taken.[59]

The enemy carried little food, apparently relying on the abundance of such provisions in the urban environment during a major holiday. Thus, with both sides assured of uninhibited supply throughout most of the battle, Hue turned into a logistics race, which the NVA simply could not win. The communists' inability to sever the American air, land, and sea LOCs likely cost them the battle.

Force Protection

Although American units implemented numerous force protection measures at the tactical level, those at the operational level were largely ignored. The best operational force protection measure taken was maneuvering to cut the NVA's LOC into Hue and thereby eliminate their ability to resupply their forces within the city. Making nonlethal weapons (in this case CS gas) available and successfully negotiating more liberal ROE with the host nation should also be viewed as operational force protection initiatives, because this groundwork made tactical force protection measures possible. Another significant force protection lesson is the danger in assigning forces inexperienced in urban fighting to battle in a city. Undoubtedly, numerous marines lost their lives as they learned the intricacies of urban combat through trial and error. In many cases, their jungle experience only made matters worse. The operational commander must ensure that tactical forces assigned to carry out missions in an urban environment are appropriately trained and equipped to handle such a mission.

Conclusion and Lessons Learned

Because the goal of the operational art is to translate strategic-level objectives into tactical actions that are conducive to attaining those objectives, this analysis has purposefully included significant detail on the tactical and strategic details of the battle for Hue. Additionally, Hue demonstrates the tendency for urban operations to cause the levels of war to blend. Thus, without strategic and tactical detail, it would be difficult to justify listing operational lessons learned from the battle that specifically pertain to urban conflict. This case study suggests that these lessons include the following:

- The principle of unity of command is of increased importance in urban areas. A single operational commander should be designated to lead the fight within large, significant cities. The commander must position himself, and structure his command and control assets, to maintain situational awareness in order to synchronize tactical elements spread throughout the urban infrastructure.

- The operational commander should coordinate realistic and consistent ROE with the host nation based on an awareness of the nature of the fight in the urban area. The ROE must balance maintaining the noncombatant populace's neutrality by preventing unnecessary casualties and infrastructure damage with giving friendly forces the ability to accomplish their mission without forfeiting their right to self-defense. In urban areas, where maintaining situational awareness at the operational level is exceptionally challenging, the commander should consider substituting a clear intent for fires in lieu of rigid ROE.

- Human intelligence is normally the most effective collection means in the urban environment. The operational commander should direct the development of his intelligence architecture accordingly. This requires recruiting and cultivating local informants throughout the theater of operations.

- The operational commander should maneuver to isolate his urban adversary from his base of support by locating and interdicting his lines of communication and supply. In some instances, this may preclude the necessity of committing tactical forces to an urban clearing operation altogether. Likewise, the commander should direct fires that target enemy LOCs into and within urban areas to further isolate the enemy from their base(s) of support.

- Where possible, the operational commander should commit only those tactical forces to the urban fight that are specifically trained, equipped, and organized for conducting operations in that environment. Individual combat replacements should likewise be properly trained and equipped. The operational commander should also ensure that his tactical units have weapons and equipment that are appropriate for urban combat. Hue indicates that nonlethal weapons (riot-control gas) and wall-breaching munitions are particularly important.

- Information operations can be among the most useful operational assets employed in the urban battle space. Engaging the media and ensuring that they are aware of U.S. objectives and efforts to prevent unnecessary noncombatant casualties and collateral damage are critical to shaping the environment for tactical success.

- Logistical planning must account for timely sustainment of widely dispersed and heavily engaged forces. Multiple, mutually supporting lines of supply by air, ground, and sea are useful in providing this sustainment. Operational logisticians must also recognize that materiel consumption rates during urban fights can be as much as ten times greater than those typically experienced in rural environments, and plan accordingly. Similarly, urban logistics planning must include provisions for refugee flow and care.

ENDNOTES

1.   Major Ron Christmas, USMC, *Hue City*, Monograph (Quantico, VA: U.S. Marine Corps Combat Development Command, Marine Corps University Archives, undated), 1.

2.   Jack Shulimson, et al., *U.S. Marines in Vietnam: The Defining Year, 1968* (Washington, DC: History and Museums Division, Headquarters, U.S. Marine Corps, 1997), 164.

3.   Christmas, 2.

4.   Map taken from The CIA World Factbook 1999 Homepage at www.odci.gov/cia/publications/factbook/vm/html#geo, January 29, 2000.

5.   Major Jonathan P. Hull, USMC, *Hue, The Mirror on the Pole View Around the Corner to Future Urban Combat*, MMS Thesis (Quantico, VA: U.S. Marine Corps Command and Staff College, April 16, 1997), 7.

6.   Keith William Nolan, *Battle for Hue, Tet 1968* (New York: Dell Publishing Company, Inc., 1983), 30–31. (Note: All of Mr. Nolan's extensive notes and interview material used in this volume are available at the Marine Corps Research Center, Quantico, VA.)

7.   The CAP was a unique approach to pacification, with the marines living alongside and sharing the suffering of the local populaces. The CAP was backed up by other marine units routinely conducting aggressive rural and jungle patrolling throughout the TAOR, where they were constantly the target of Viet Cong hit and run ambushes.

8.   Shumlimson, 170.

9.   Captain Jon E. Tellier, U.S. Army, "The Battle for Hue," in *Infantry* (July-August 1995), 21.

10.   Hull, 7–8.

11.   Tellier, 21–22.

12.   Shumlimson, 215.

13.   Ibid., 166.

14.   Nolan, 267.

15.   Hull, 8.

16.   Nolan, 22.

17.   Tellier, 24.

18.   At the height of the fighting, this strength would double.

19.   Nolan, 45.

20.   Tellier, 25.

21.   Christmas, 12–13.

22.   Brigadier General Michael P. Downs, USMC, from interview in

VHS film *Urban Warfare: Lessons From Hue City.* Produced by the Marine Corps University Foundation. 70 min. 1999.

23.   Combat Operations After Action Report (Operation HUE CITY), Commanding Officer, 1st Marines (-) (Rein), 1st Marine Division (Rein), 3480/3/TVB/twc dated March 20, 1968. Retained at Quantico, VA: U.S. Marine Corps Combat Development Command, Marine Corps University Archives, 8 (henceforth referred to as Operation Hue City After Action Report).

24.   Nolan, 130–34.

25.   Shumlinson, 205.

26.   Nolan, 267.

27.   Major Charles A. Preysler, U.S. Army, *MOUT Art: Operational Planning Considerations for MOUT,* Monograph (Fort Leavenworth, KS: School of Advanced Military Studies, U.S. Army Command and General Staff College, May 23, 1995), 15.

28.   Don Oberdorfer, *Tet* (New York: Doubleday & Company, 1971), 209.

29.   Shumlimson, 223.

30.   Nolan, 113–14.

31.   Preysler, 14.

32.   Hull, 8–9.

33.   Operation Hue City After Action Report, 7.

34.   Nolan, 203.

35.   Ibid., 20–21.

36.   Ibid., 77.

37.   Ibid., 54.

38.   Ibid., 145–47.

39.   Hull, 11.

40.   Operation Hue City After Action Report, 9.

41.   Ibid., 8.

42.   Nolan, 55.

43.   Christmas, 1.

44.   Nolan, 70. Interestingly, Nolan cites reports that indicate a strong possibility that the sappers who finally succeeded in taking down the Nguyen Hoang Bridge were Chinese communists.

45.   Preysler, 14.

46.   Operation Hue City After Action Report, 3.

47.   Ibid., 5.

48.   Russell W. Glenn, *"We Band of Brothers:" The Call for Joint Urban Operations Doctrine*, MDA 903–95–C-0059 (Santa Monica, CA: RAND, 1999), 46.

49.   Lieutenant Colonel R. W. Lamont, USMC, "A Tale of Two Cities–Hue and Khorramshahr," in *Armor* (May-June 1999), 25.

50.   Ibid., 26.

51.   Operation Hue City After Action Report, 8.

52.   Nolan, 267.

53.   Operation Hue City After Action Report, 82.

54.   Ibid., 82.

55.   Nolan, 208–9.

56.   Operation Hue City After Action Report, 75.

57.   Lamont, 25.

58.   Nolan, 221.

59.   Operation Hue City After Action Report, 7.

THIRTEEN

Da Nang–Hoi An

A Tank Skirmish in Quang Nam Province

by D. C. Fresch

For us the rice paddies and tree lines turned to asphalt and concrete . . .

> —D. C. Fresch (Editor's Note:
> The following is a firsthand account.)

The engagements chronicled in this story were undertaken by tanks from the 1st and 2d Platoon of Charlie Company, 1st Tank Battalion, 1st Marine Division. The 1st Tank Battalion arrived in the Republic of Vietnam in 1965 and was reinforced by elements of the 5th Tank Battalion in late 1968. The 1st Tank Battalion was scattered around the Da Nang "rocket belt" (a semicircular ring of hills and outposts some miles from the Da Nang airfield) and deployed in two- and four-tank units. Units in these positions were responsible for the suppression of 122mm and 140mm rockets that were fired by the Viet Cong into the airfield, sometimes on a nightly basis. The tanks used by the marines were M48A3 Patton tanks armed with a 90mm cannon. The newest modification was a cupola vision block ring.

The 2d Platoon operated in two- and four-tank sections: two tanks for bridge security on the Tu Cau road and at Nui Kim San on the main supply route (MSR) near the Marble Mountain and "Dodge City" area. While on sweeps we usually operated in a four-tank platoon and attached amtracs with the sweeping infantry element, and another four-tank platoon to act as a blocking force.

The 2d Platoon tanks were modified by their crews by taking the .50–caliber machine gun from the tank commander's (TC's) cupola and mounting it in the coaxial position with the main gun mount. Our .30–caliber coaxial guns were given over to the perimeter security bunkers with Charlie Company. We mounted M60 machine guns on a "skymount" attached to the TC's periscope. The guns were modified for reliable feeding from a rack to the left of the gun holding two 250–round boxes of 7.62 ammunition. The loader's hatches were fitted with any light machine guns available. Sometimes it would be the Chinese RPD that we felt was perhaps the best squad automatic weapon ever made. It was simple and light, had an attached folding bipod, and fed from a 100–round belt contained within an easily changed sheet metal drum. It also possessed an adjustable gas port, ensuring operation regardless of powder fouling.

The bustle racks on the back of the turret held a considerable amount of extra ammunition for both the M60 and the .50–caliber coax machine guns. Flares, smoke grenades, and assorted explosive and pyrotechnical devices were contained in 40mm ammo boxes attached to the bustle rack. We started the practice of collecting this stuff after a medevac was unable to come up with a green smoke for the medevac helo one day. If the grunts couldn't carry it, we would. Our personal weapons lay at the top of this pile; they consisted of everything from cutdown M14s to captured Chinese SKSs, AK-47s, and RPGs (rocket-propelled grenades). These field modifications and additional weapons were illegal as far as division was concerned. We always had a mad scramble to convert everything back to standard configuration on short notice of any inspection from higher headquarters.

To protect against enemy RPGs, we hung as much track block as we possibly could all around the turret from the infantry rails. We also strung steel cable in front of the driver's position in order to pack sandbags on the slope plate around him. The bustle racks were usually hung with 40mm ammo boxes fitted with hooks for our personal items and ponchos. This provided some predetonation protection to the rear of the turret.

Our TAOR (Tactical Area of Responsibility) spanned from the village of Nui Kim San, just south of Da Nang, to the city of Hoi An, some fifteen miles to the south on the coast, to an area called the Mud Flats, to the west. This area contained the infamous "Go Noi island" area, known as an in-country safe area for the NVA. Responsibilities included road reaction to mine incidents on the Tu Cau road and main supply route, night security at the Tu Cau and Nui Kim San bridges, security of the airstrip at the city of Hoi An with the 2d Blue Dragon Brigade of the Korean Marine Corps, and support of a small fire support/platoon patrol base in the Mud Flats with a company of Korean Marines and two amtracs. In addition, our tanks were "on call" as a reactionary force to support any unit within range that was in fear of getting overrun.

The sequence of moves and battles during this period came to be known as Operation Checkers. It led up to the infamous Tet offensive of January 30–31, 1968.

The Fight for Hoi An

The period of Tet 1968 was a strange week for the 2d Platoon, Charlie Company. The Khe Sanh combat base had its second battle of the year in the saddle of Hill 881 on January 20, 1968. An uneasy truce was declared by the Viet Cong for the Tet lunar holiday and was to run from January 27 through February 3. Rocket attacks against Da Nang, the Marble Mountain area, and Chu Lai put the truce to rest on the night of January 29–30.

The "Death Dealers" had been out with the infantry of the 2d Battalion, 3d Marines, cruising the tree lines for about three days looking for the enemy. We were all about to become heavily involved in what was probably the biggest running gun battle of the Vietnam war, the Tet lunar new year offensive.

Tet was the culmination of a long-planned offensive by Hanoi. The enemy had managed to attack almost every installation and city of any significance in South Vietnam. At the time, they believed that this would lead to a popular revolutionary uprising of the common people to overthrow and eject the Saigon government as well as the American allies. During the offensive the American press speculated that we had lost control of the war, despite the fact that virtually every battle was won by U.S. and South Vietnamese forces. Later in the war there were questions concerning the full commitment of Viet Cong forces as a means for the Hanoi government to avoid sharing power with the forces of the south. The Viet Cong were effectively eliminated from the battlefield during the aftermath of the offensive, and northern supply lines were drained to the extent that it would be two years until they were back at their previous effectiveness.

As gunner on an M48A3 tank, designated as C23, I often didn't leave the turret for three days at a time. Like the other crews, I ate and slept in the tank, urinating into the tank hull to be flushed out later. My tank commander, Sgt. Ralph MacDonald (Sargeant Mac), let me out every now and then to see the light of day for about five minutes.

Because tankers are cockier than most marines, we were having trouble coordinating with the infantry. Working as close to the tree lines as we did while evacuating wounded, it was essential that we have a team of infantry to suppress RPG attacks. It took a considerable number of complaints to get the support, and then it was quite a production to finally get our grunts to pull back when we needed to engage the main gun. Our second problem turned out to be the 2d Battalion, 3d Marines, commanding officer's inexperience at tank-infantry operations. As the sun was setting on about the third day of operations, after having found recent evidence of enemy activity in the area, he insisted on a night assault of the next tree line. Against our complaints and explanations of bad terrain, the assault went off, with our predicted result of two tanks severely bogged down in the mud and the other two engaged in removing them. It was a nasty job to recover a tank in the mud of a Vietnamese rice paddy.

The assault was called off and we spent an uneasy night in the open. Artillery dropped harassment and interdiction (H&I) fire around us, and gunships and fireflies overflew our position throughout the night. Very spooky. Considering we had yet to engage the enemy, someone higher up was taking great care to protect us. Did they know something we didn't?

It was the night of January 29–30. The next dawn would see all five provincial capitals attacked and the I Corps headquarters compound breached by VC and main force NVA. The communists had come out of their holes and hideouts to do battle.

With the arrival of morning, we hurriedly had our C rations and coffee and saddled up to hit the tree line from the night before. Monitoring the radios, we heard reports from the infantry of fighting holes and abandoned web gear. The enemy's positions had been hastily evacuated during the night.

Everyone cleared the tree line and stopped to regroup. Mac got out to confer with the infantry, and I climbed up to get a little daylight and man the TC's fire controls. Something did not feel right. I believe that everyone who has lived through combat has experienced this feeling at one time or another. I climbed down into the TC's seat and started to traverse the tree line by sweeping left to right across our front. The gun sights drifted across some horizontal banana trees and my alarms went off. "Bunker." Suddenly, I was looking down the tube of a 75mm Chinese recoilless rifle manned by six NVA ready to put a window in my tank's turret.

I squeezed off the main gun and got a click for my effort. I didn't know what the problem was, but I also didn't have time to deal with it. I climbed up on the tank, yelled to Mac what I had, opened up with the machine gun, and radioed the next tank down the line to put some 90mm cannon rounds where my fire was going. At that moment, all hell broke loose. About seven hundred NVA, the main effort of the NVA 2d Division, were moving out of the hills west of An Hoa to attack the Da Nang air base as part of the Tet offensive.

We were engaged most all day, working right up in the tree lines with canister rounds and beehives (90mm shells loaded with hundreds of small, arrowlike flechettes). When we needed more ammunition, we evacuated wounded, then returned to the fight.

As the battle wound down, the crew was talking on the intercom about how we could wrap this up and get back to the area for some rest and showers. I had been monitoring the radios and listening to the 1st Platoon mixing it up in Hoi An. From the transmissions I heard, it sounded as though they were in a very tough fight. Hoi An was about fifteen miles south of us on the Song Thu Bon River. An undetermined number of NVA had crossed the river from the south, out of the barrier island area, entered Hoi An, and not so politely requested that the ARVN soldiers leave town. There was a pitched battle, but the NVA won out, with most of the town in their hands. The small Military Assistance Command, Vietnam (MACV) compound in Hoi

An was surrounded, and the Americans there were fighting a desperate battle for survival. I had a friend with the fourteen-man marine security detachment at Hoi An. Our tanks based there took hits, most from RPGs, and several were knocked out of the fight.

We were low on ammo, and also running low on fuel from fighting for three days and being heavily engaged all morning. Just the same, we were instructed to head for Hoi An. We would be refueled and rearmed there. The trucks to resupply us were already on their way.

Leery of an ambush on the roads, we headed cross-country, flat out through the desert area above Hoi An, and arrived at the outskirts of the city without incident. Blitzing into the city proper, we crossed a bridge, which terrorized some locals, and soon passed a Shell gas station. We joked that we should pull in and fill up. We arrived at our rally point with the 1st Platoon to find that our fuel supply convoy had been ambushed on the road and blown up on Highway 538 west of the city. I since learned that a bulk fuel specialist was killed in the ambush attempting to get our fuel to us. I learned from another friend who was part of the convoy escort that the explosion was caused by a command-detonated mine.

We were facing a potentially disastrous situation. No fuel and no ammo is no way to enter a battle. Firefights were raging throughout the city as we linked up with elements of the 2d Blue Dragon Brigade of the Korean Marine Corps. We solved our re-supply problem by dragging out the hand pumps and hoses and siphoning fuel from the tanks that were out of service. We also stripped those tanks of their ammunition and distributed it among our four tanks.

Hoi An was a mess. There were firefights taking place all over, and four different military organizations were involved: the Korean Marines, the cut-off U.S. Army compound, the widely scattered ARVN, and us. In addition, the civilians were trying to get out of the middle of everything. Taking into consideration the damage to the 1st Platoon, it was decided that we would try to run two tanks north into the city from both the east and the west, then turn into the city. We'd just blow it away house by house by moving toward the MACV compound, supported by the Koreans. Language and communication problems quickly arose. This was the 2d Platoon's first time working with the Koreans and we were not communicating well. It was a moot point; everything would soon come apart.

The second of two tanks, we started up a narrow street to the west of the city. Closed in by buildings, we had limited visibility and maneuverability. We crept down the street, guns facing to the northeast, looking into every nook and cranny. The ROK troops were following us rather than supporting us as I watched our lead tank start its turn to the east.

WHAM! BLAM! The tank rocked to the left nearly on its side, and I saw smoke and flames shoot from both hatches. It slammed back to the street and just sat there and smoked. I couldn't believe what I had just seen through the limited vision of the gun sights. My world went into slow motion and all sound dropped away as I waited for movement from our lead tank and anticipated continued fire on ours. It seemed to take forever, but the crew, covered in soot, finally crawled out and sought cover at the side of the tank. They had taken two rapid-fire RPG hits in the space of a heartbeat. I would like to think that we always reacted quickly to circumstances, and perhaps we did; I suffered time compression throughout this incident. It seemed to take some time until several tankers with their .45 grease guns ran up to provide cover fire, allowing the crew to get back to us. We were effectively stopped in our advance. I remember thinking f—— this, just f—— this, I'm going home, good-bye! All I could see in my mind's eye was the next RPG coming

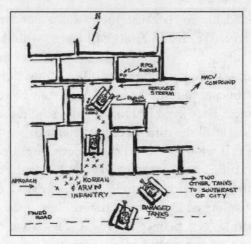

Position of engaged tanks

through my gun controls and turning me into paste. I actually pushed up from my seat to leave when I thought, where the hell am I gonna go? It's just as bad if not worse anywhere out there.

I really didn't want any of this, but I sat down and was determined to find that jerk with the rocket before he found us. I'm sure that other things were going on out there, but in the gunner's seat it was just the NVA and me. I traversed and traversed that street. I felt as though I burnt out both my eyes one at a time and soaked myself in nervous and real sweat while we idled in the street. I was trying to will those gun sights to show me something, anything.

The radios were squawking something about the NVA trying to withdraw as refugees, and we should try to separate the wheat from the chaff. A steady stream of civilians started to move out of the street that we had tried to turn into. An old man carrying a straw package appeared out of the alley and took cover under the front of the blown tank. Thinking that the package could conceal a rocket, I notified Mac, and was going nuts trying to get permission to fire. Permission was slow in coming, and understandably so, because there was a flood of evacuees leaving the area. We finally bounced some .50 under the tank and ran him off.

When our lead tank was hit, the ROKs left us, but the ARVN showed back up and fought like hell. These ARVN were fighting for their homes. They lived in Hoi An, and so did their families. I guess that made all the difference in the world.

Hearing that we were out in the street alone, I renewed my efforts to find the site from which the RPGs had been fired. I damned near went blind searching but finally noticed a slot at street level that looked like a storm drain. I keyed my combat vehicle crewman (CVC) helmet to tell Mac what we had, and in short order we ripped a load of .50 into the slot. Later exploration would reveal two dead North Vietnamese with an RPG in a belowground room. Unlike the fighting at Hue, we never got the opportunity to engage our main 90mm guns in the city. We were effectively blocked almost immediately by our damaged tank and were reduced to fighting a careful defensive machine-gun battle due to the flood of refugees fleeing the city.

We eventually worked our way into the city, but I couldn't tell you how. The rest of the day was a blur as we fought through the narrow streets. The next thing I remember was night falling as we had all of our tanks sitting outside the gates of the MACV compound. Some of the officers from the installation came out to bring us food and thank us for the rescue. They shared their tales of the last few days' madness. They were glad to have us there.

Everything about Hoi An seemed a bit otherworldly that night. We had never worked within a city before and were faced with an entirely new set of circumstances. As if to punctuate this feeling, a jeep with driver and a Vietnamese passenger roared out the gate and down the street. The vehicle ricocheted off the buildings on both sides of the street like a ball in a pinball machine, then flipped over. I just stood there and stared. The driver was drunk and taking one of the Vietnamese employees home. This was the capstone to this whole weird past week. They lay in the wreckage of the jeep moaning, and I was waiting for Rod Serling to step out of the wings and explain all of this. Strange days.

What We Learned

The challenges of using tanks were exacerbated by the harsh conditions of the urban environment. Tanks that were protected by infantry could act as effective close-in fire support. Tank main guns used against hardened targets yielded more precise results than could be achieved from artillery. Tank fire caused less collateral damage. Tanks that advanced with infantry protection also delivered a shock effect that intimidated defending dismounted troops.

Effective tank-infantry cooperation requires detailed coordination. Communication and command relationships must be established prior to an operation. Infantry and tank crewmen alike must be aware of each other's capabilities. All elements of the tank crew should be kept apprised of the tactical situation throughout the vicinity of their vehicle. The accompanying infantry must guard against snipers. The tanks must be regularly resupplied with fuel and ammo. We tried to move off the main roads to prevent creating easy targets for the enemy. Tanks could be used as armored resupply vehicles to meet the needs of the screening dismounts as required.

What We Did Wrong

I believe that plans for a helo air-transportable fuel bladder and air-delivered ammo resupply should have been rehearsed in the event that we exhausted these critical resources. The ambush of our resupply was always highly likely. Another option for resupply would have been to load supplies into armored personnel carriers for transport on a routine basis. In either case, resupply was a critical vulnerability, and good men died because of poor planning and lack of preparation.

Planning for a secondary insertion point into the heart of the city could allow tanks to get into the city and put steel on target if their primary route became blocked by disabled vehicles or debris. Often, destroyed vehicles become unexpected roadblocks. Plans for a city fight must include multiple directions of attack.

We often struggled with establishing communications between the tanks and the infantry. In a city fight, constant attention must be paid to every aspect of command and control. We did the best we could with what we had, and thankfully it worked out.

Other Conclusions

Tank drivers should remain situationally aware and stay ready to reverse out of ambush situations if necessary. The death by sniper or RPG of the tank commander can be catastrophic for a tank crew. If control of the tank is not immediately taken over by another crew member, and fought by the gunner or loader, panic can quickly lead to the loss of the entire crew and tank.

Gunners should keep apprised of the external situation for the same reasons. They must monitor the radios. The gunner, confined to the interior of the turret, requires a steady stream of information from his radios and fellow crewmen to remain aware of the tank's battle space. The gunner's ability to fight the tank should the TC become incapacitated rests on the gunner's situational awareness.

Loaders, at least in our situation, were best used as an extra set of eyes and a trigger finger on an auxiliary machine gun or even a rifle. City fighting is close work. Leaders should help spot and suppress antitank activity by a sector of observation agreed upon beforehand with the tank commander.

While operating with a security team at hand, tanks should have assigned overlapping sectors of fire and watch both high and low. Doing so will suppress fire from the rooftops to the sewers. The enemy will know his city; you probably won't, so pay attention. City fighting will always be house to house if not a window-by-window clearing operation. If you haven't cleared it or can't cover it with fire, don't move into it. Infantry finds and fixes the enemy positions. Tanks move forward and blow 'em away. The security team screens the tank.

The NVA showed us time and again how one or two determined kids armed with a cheap RPG could ambush a tank crew and effectively take out a half-million-dollar vehicle. The future will only bring more accurate weapons and even more fanatical opponents who are willing to trade their lives for the glory of taking out your tank and crew. They *will* be out there. Every move in a city is a move into an ambush. If you are not prepared to meet them, they will win!

Training is the only real answer to this endless dance of man and machine. Train until the tank-infantry team operates as one single deadly entity. The one cannot exist without the other in a successful city conflict.

FOURTEEN

Evolution of Urban Combat Doctrine

by Col. Mark J. Reardon

Written guidance, commonly known as doctrine, governs the actions of all armies on the battlefield. Doctrine addresses both enemy and friendly forces, from perspectives as varied as an individual soldier to that of a corps commander. Armies use doctrine to standardize how they train, equip, and maintain forces during peacetime and combat. Although actual combat can drive the development of doctrine, it is often derived solely from theory as untried weapons and tactics are introduced. The latter process characterized the initial development of U.S. Army urban combat doctrine. As late as the opening stages of World War II, American doctrine on fighting in cities was based almost exclusively on the experiences of other armies.

As war clouds darkened the horizon in 1939, it was readily apparent that American military theory had not kept pace with events taking place in Europe. The institutional knowledge necessary to fight a modern war, including in-depth discussion of urban combat, was often sorely lacking. Unlike European armies, American military leaders were not in a position to use their own recent experience to update outmoded doctrine. The U.S. Army, it seemed, had not found itself fighting in cities since the mid–nineteenth century.

Some of the first instances of urban combat involving American troops took place during the Mexican War of 1846–48. General Winfield Scott's army found itself drawn into battle as it approached the outskirts of Mexico City. An American column successfully penetrated the outer defenses of the Mexican capital when it captured the fortified convent at Churubusco on August 20, 1847. After a brief period of fruitless negotiation, U.S. troops surged forward once more to capture the gun foundry and old fort at Molino del Ray on September 8.

The following week, Scott's infantry captured the fortified hill of Chapultepec, a move that allowed them to advance to the San Cosme and Belen gates of Mexico City. Rather than continue the costly contest, the bulk of the Mexican troops under Gen. Santa Anna withdrew from the city the following night. At dawn, the remainder of the garrison surrendered just before the American bombardment began. Scott's victory at Mexico City came at a considerable cost; a total of 383 Americans were killed and 2,245 wounded.[1]

Scott's seizure of Mexico City does not represent the only instance of urban combat during the Mexican War. Indeed, toward the end of the conflict the Mexican army actively sought to enhance its own defensive capabilities by fighting in towns. On September 20, the battle of Monterey produced one of the few conflicts where U.S. losses exceeded those of their Mexican opponents. American troops storming the fortified city lost 120 killed and 368 wounded against 367 Mexican casualties.[2] It took the Americans three days of fierce fighting before they were able to surround the bulk of the defenders in the center of the city.

Rather than face the prospect of more street fighting, Gen. Zachary Taylor permitted the Mexican troops to depart unmolested. He also granted his opponents a provisional eight-week truce, albeit pending final approval by President James K. Polk. This was the first instance in which Mexican troops had been able to gain favorable terms from an American general. The war ended before further fighting took place. Urban combat had produced noticeably higher U.S. casualties than engagements conducted on open terrain, a trend that was apparently over-looked by the victors.

Less than twenty years later, U.S. armies clashed in a great civil war that took the lives of almost half a million combatants. Unlike the previous conflict in Mexico, urban combat proved the rare exception, not the rule, during the Civil War. The most famous instance took place when federal troops, tasked to seize a foothold across the Rappahannock River on December 12, 1862, encountered Brig. Gen. William Barksdale's Mississippi Brigade holding the town of Fredericksburg. The 20th Massachusetts Regiment lost ninety-seven men as it attacked Confederates defending Caroline Street.[3] Firing from basements, attics, and alleyways, Barksdale's men held out until late that afternoon before retreating to Marye's Heights.[4]

Although the trench warfare of World War I was remarkable for its absence of street fighting, the probability that we would engage the enemy in an urban environment was cause for concern at the start of World War II. When the United States entered that war, the only doctrine on urban combat possessed by the army was FM 100–5, *Field Service Regulations: Operations,* dated May 22, 1941. A separate manual on city fighting did not exist.

Based on observations of the Spanish Civil War and the early World War II campaigns in Western Europe, FM 100–5 stated that "bombardment aviation is of first importance in reducing a stubbornly defending city. Destruction is methodical and ordinarily progressive from front to rear." The manual also determined that "mechanized troops are of little value in combat within a defended town. Their use for such combat will probably result in excessive casualties, both in personnel and vehicles."[5] Much of the material on urban combat found in FM 100–5, however, proved to be misleading. Events would disclose that the

impact of aerial attack had been exaggerated, whereas the useful-
ness of tanks in city combat was significantly underestimated.

In the opening months of American involvement in World
War II, firsthand experience in urban warfare provided few opportunities to correct FM 100–5. In the Philippines, American
troops abandoned Manila without a fight. In North Africa, our
troops often found themselves fighting for the heights dominating the approaches to towns instead of the urban area
itself. Once U.S. troops invaded Italy, hard-fought urban
battles at Cassino, Rosignano, San Vittorio, and Benevento provided ample experience to support the publication of a new field
manual describing how operations in urban terrain were to be
conducted.

Faced with the prospect of continued fighting in Italy, as
well as the impending attack on the Atlantic Wall, the U.S. Army
published FM 31–50, *Attack on a Fortified Position and Combat
in Towns,* in January 1944. By combining both topics in a single
manual, FM 31–50 reflected the opinion of senior officers
who considered city fighting identical to "pillbox fighting." The
experiences of our allies also formed the foundation for the publication. Field Manual 31–50 was intended to provide U.S. commanders with a guide to training as well as the employment of
forces in combat.

Field Manual 31–50 stressed the fact that combat operations
in an urban environment should be conducted at a deliberate
pace. Preparatory fires would precede each assault, followed by a
methodical advance that continued until the attacker reached his
objective or halted to reorganize his forces at the end of the day.
Operating within a closely defined sector, regimental or battalion
commanders could expect to be assigned a limited objective,
such as a railroad station, telephone exchange, or gas and other
public utility buildings.[6] The manual also noted that "in no

other form of warfare except in dense jungle is observation so restricted. This condition makes centralized control difficult . . .
[M]ost of the fighting will resolve itself into small independent
actions and will place a premium on the initiative and aggressiveness of the small unit leader."[7] Clearly, the U.S. Army was convinced that the complex geography of urban areas would also
drive commanders to a decentralized approach when waging combat in cities.

Communications systems, a vital factor in exercising effective
command and control, would also be negatively impacted by
combat in built-up areas. According to FM 31–50, communications are "adversely affected by restriction in visibility, limitation
on physically traversable routes, and the effects of buildings, particularly those with steel frames, on the use of radios."[8] However,
the manual suggested that communications could be improved
by reducing the distance between units and their higher headquarters, as well as the existence of covered routes such as subways, basements, and sewers.

Not only would commanders have to operate among the
leading echelons due to limited observation and communications, but fire support assets would also have to displace well forward. Field Manual 31–50 explained that "due to the proximity
of forces in fighting within built up areas, much of the close-fire
support will be furnished by infantry cannon using direct fire,
and by elements of the antitank company. The bulk of the mortars and machineguns must be well forward."[9]

The impressive scale of mechanization within the U.S. Army
permitted the liberal allocation of tanks, tank destroyers, and
self-propelled guns to provide direct fire support to infantry
units. Significant numbers of artillery pieces were also allocated
to units attacking built-up areas. When a regiment of the 37th
Infantry Division assaulted the walled inner city of Manila, for

example, it was aided by 120 pieces of artillery.[10] During urban combat, the centralized control of fire support assets, which were usually positioned outside of the city, enabled commanders to switch fires rapidly from one target to the next. Although Americans often found themselves pitted against superior numbers during urban combat, they were never outgunned.

Field Manual 31–50 consistently reflected the aggressive nature of American doctrine. Although the manual discusses both attack and defense, it is heavily biased toward the former. Twenty-seven pages are devoted to offensive operations, whereas the discussion on urban defense is limited to sixteen pages, despite the fact that FM 31–50 freely acknowledged that "the characteristics of city, town, and village fighting favor the defense."[11] The manual also pointed out that urban areas offered opportunities to an attacker not found in other environments. The manual stated that cities and towns possessed a "third dimension not usually present in combat" that allowed an attacker to bypass an enemy force by going directly over or under him within the same building or city block.[12]

Accurately recognizing that the fight would begin outside of the city, FM 31–50 noted that offensive operations were preceded by the seizure of a lodgment designed to "eliminate fields of fire, reduce the effectiveness of hostile flat-trajectory fires, and limit enemy observation outside the built up area." When one or more infantry divisions assaulted a large city, this preliminary phase would be conducted at several points along the periphery of the urban area. By seizing the commanding terrain on the outskirts, U.S. forces would prevent their opponents from escaping by isolating the city. This move would also provide U.S. commanders with observation posts overlooking the periphery of the city or town while denying the enemy that key terrain.

Once the attacking troops entered the urban area, they

would systematically clear each building in their sector. Field Manual 31–50 stressed that this was necessary to reduce the possibility of leaving "hostile centers of resistance" behind friendly lines.[13] Streets, alleys, vacant lots, and open areas were avoided at all costs because they afforded the defender clear fields of fire. Troops were instructed to enter buildings by blowing a hole in the wall of an adjoining structure, or traveling along rooftops or sewers, or using the cover of smoke.

Field Manual 31–50 noted that civilians in large numbers would be encountered when fighting in cities. It indicated that civilians were normally driven out of the city by aerial bombing, whereas ground combat forced the population toward the center of the city. In liberated territory, American troops would receive the full cooperation of the civilian population. However, FM 31–50 cautioned commanders that both friendly and unfriendly civilian groups might exist in areas that had been occupied by the enemy for a lengthy period of time. Within Germany itself, FM 31–50 assumed "the population to be hostile and little in the way of cooperation may be expected. Spies and fifth columnists must be ceaselessly sought out and mercilessly dealt with."[14]

In liberated territory, the American army did not ignore civilian considerations during urban combat. In France, Holland, Luxembourg, and the Philippines, units often placed restrictions on the use of indirect and aerial fires in an attempt to limit civilian deaths and collateral damage. However, when losses increased to an unacceptable level, these restrictions were often relaxed or lifted.[15] Although frontline units rarely contemplated efforts to restore utilities and provide logistics support to civilians, there were instances of this type of support. For example, during the fighting in Manila, the 37th Infantry Division, fearing that flames from the north port area might spread to residential districts, used demolition charges to create a firebreak in the path of the inferno.[16]

By issuing FM 31–50, the U.S. Army made clear its belief that soldiers needed guidance to deal with the environment they would encounter when fighting in cities. Recognizing that most small-unit leaders lacked considerable experience in urban combat, FM 31–50 contained information on training techniques for individuals and units. The benefits that would be gained by educating leaders in urban combat tactics also did not go unnoticed. Field Manual 31–50 emphasized that "combat in built-up areas requires thorough individual and small-unit training and the exercise of the highest degree of initiative, skill, cunning, and courage on the part of the small unit leaders and individual soldiers."

Because every building in an urban area might conceivably require the formation of a combined-arms assault team, it was no wonder that FM 31–50 placed such a high premium on individual skill and initiative. There simply were not enough specialized units to go around. As a result, ordinary riflemen often found themselves saddled with tasks usually left to combat engineers. Rifle squads used satchel charges, crowbars, or axes to enter buildings through doors, walls, or rooftops. Infantry units were also organized into special detachments armed with smoke pots, hand grenades, flamethrowers, and rocket launchers.

In addition to the unique task organization required by urban combat, rifle squads and platoons divided themselves into covering and searching parties. The covering party would protect the searching party as it advanced toward the building under attack. The searching party, normally limited in size to ensure that the men did not get in one another's way, would clear the building in accordance with a prearranged plan. In some instances, an entire rifle company might employ these tactics to seize a large building such as a police station or city hall.

Field Manual 31–50 recommended that assault squads enter a building through the upper part of the structure. Access to the upper stories was to be gained by using ladders, grappling hooks, rain gutters, trellises, or the roof of an adjacent structure. Attacking soldiers would throw grenades down stairwells before descending to the lower floors. Holes could be chopped in the ceiling of lower floors to gain entry when using stairwells proved impossible. Once enemy troops were forced down to ground level, they would be more likely to retreat out of the building into the field of fire of the covering force rather than fight to the end if cornered on an upper floor.

Although FM 31–50 addressed tactics at individual soldier through battalion level, it focused primarily on the regimental combat team. Regiments normally attacked in a column of battalions across a narrow frontage of one to four city blocks. Factors such as strength of the defense and size, type, and construction of buildings, as well as density of structures within the area of operations, would impact on the designated frontage of an attacking regiment. Supporting weapons, to include tanks and tank destroyers, were pushed well forward to aid the assault troops. Antitank guns, as well as howitzers from the regimental cannon company, were employed to destroy strongpoints with direct fire. Chemical mortars would fire HE concentrations and smoke missions to blind enemy observation, cover attacks, and support deception.[17]

During the defense, an infantry regiment established its main line of resistance (MLR) either inside or outside the urban area but never along a clearly defined edge. The preferred method was to place the MLR inside the outskirts so as to command avenues leading into the city while also taking full advantage of observation, fields of fire, and opportunities for flanking fire against attacking forces. Artillery was also sited to support the defense by massing fires on likely avenues of approach. In the event that the enemy was successful in penetrating the town, the artillery would shift its fires against the penetrations and support counterattacks. Engineers were also attached to lay mines, maintain routes, and reinforce existing structures or construct new ones.

The War Department on June 15, 1944, published a new edition of FM 100–5, *Field Service Regulations.* Recognizing that airpower had proved less useful than artillery during urban operations, the newest edition of FM 100–5 dropped all reference to the employment of bombardment aviation to reduce a town. Whereas the 1941 edition had stated that troops attacking a town would be "strongly supported by artillery, combat aviation, and other supporting weapons," the 1944 manual noted that support would instead be provided by "artillery and other supporting weapons, and aided by combat aviation."[18]

Rather than downplay the utility of mechanized forces in an urban environment, the new FM 100–5 stated, "Strongly defended towns rarely present opportunities for tanks to exploit their mobility due to the restrictions of barricades, debris, streets, and short range antitank methods. However, opportunities will present themselves frequently where the support of tanks in such situations becomes desirable."[19] In addition, whereas the 1941 edition of FM 100–5 characterized towns as most suitable for a "defensive position, especially when mechanized attack is expected," the 1944 edition recognized that using an urban area as a defensive position would provide benefits in a wide range of situations as opposed to simply providing an antiarmor obstacle.

The 1944 edition explained that deliberately paced operations, limited objectives, and attack from unexpected directions were the hallmarks of urban operations. According to FM 100–5, urban areas strongly held by the enemy should not be attacked directly. The defenders would be fixed by a holding attack while the main body isolated the town by occupying the commanding terrain. When the immediate capture of a town was essential to the overall success of the operation, the main attack would be directed against the flank or rear of the town in order to "secure the advantages of enveloping attack." When frontal attack could not be avoided, U.S. commanders were instructed to secure the outskirts before reorganizing to continue their advance to the center of the city.

Field Manual 100–5 prophesized that combat actions within a city or town would be "necessarily decentralized to subordinate infantry leaders since lack of observation of the action precludes satisfactory centralized control."[20] This statement was borne out on the battlefield. The official army history, commenting on VII Corps operations at Cherbourg, noted that "the nature of the battle changed from a simultaneous effort to large-scale nibbling—a series of actions dictated by the local problems of each sector commander."[21] Similar situations were encountered during urban combat in Saint-Malo, Brest, Aachen, Aschaffenburg, Nuremberg, and Manila.

Even though FM 100–5 neatly complemented FM 31–50, it did offer several unique observations, including the fact that intensive reconnaissance was critical to success during combat in built-up areas. Field Manual 100–5 noted that "the larger the town and the longer it had been held by the enemy, the more thorough must be the preparation for attack."[22] The manual also stressed the vital importance of employing combined-arms forces when conducting combat in cities. As U.S. commanders quickly discovered, the use of well-coordinated tank-infantry teams would prove to be the vital factor in urban combat.

Although tanks provided infantry in cities with a decisive edge, armored divisions were not as suitable for urban combat as were infantry divisions augmented by separate general headquarters (GHQ) tank battalions. Despite the fact that tanks were a key player in urban combat, the employment of massed armor in cities violated approved armored force doctrine. Field Manual 71–100, *The Armored Division,* dated January 15, 1944, contained a number of caveats pertaining to the use of armored divisions in built-up areas.

In the opening sentences of the section on combat in cities, FM 71–100 stated, "Armored units avoid towns if practicable. While tanks can smash through flimsy houses, they cannot plough through rows of heavy houses and there is always the danger of falling into a basement. Tanks are, therefore, canalized in the streets where they can be stopped by barricades, concealed anti-tank guns, mines, and grenades thrown from roofs, second story windows, and basements."[23]

According to FM 71–100, armored divisions were capable of attacking villages, weakly held towns, and well-defended towns. Small villages could be reduced fairly quickly by an armored division's advance guard. A weakly held town could also be seized by armored units, provided the defenders were taken by surprise by tank columns rapidly entering the town from several directions. The use of an armored division to assault a well-defended town was strongly discouraged, a doctrinal tenet that was generally adhered to when fighting in Europe during 1944–45.

Despite its largely theoretical underpinnings at the onset of the war, U.S. doctrine on combat in cities proved remarkably successful in practice. This was evidenced by the fact that in many instances, U.S. troops were outnumbered by their opponents, yet they often inflicted greater casualties than they suffered themselves. In Manila, for example, 6,565 Americans were killed or wounded whereas 16,000 defending Japanese troops died. In Aschaffenburg, U.S. forces lost 320 killed and wounded whereas the German defenders suffered more than 4,800 killed, wounded, and captured. In Brest, the casualty ratio was 9,831 U.S. troops to 42,000 Germans, whereas at Saint-Malo the U.S. 83d Infantry Division inflicted 12,000 casualties while suffering "surprisingly light losses."[24] United States tactics had proved successful but suffered from several drawbacks, notably the length of time involved to execute operations, tremendous expenditures of ammunition, and significant collateral damage normally inflicted upon a city and its population.

Implementation of urban combat doctrine was also fairly consistent throughout the war, regardless of the theater of operations. In the Pacific, the 37th Infantry Division battling to recapture Manila in February 1945 adhered as closely to FM 31–50 as did the 45th Infantry Division fighting in Aschaffenburg and Nuremberg in March 1945. Despite the totally dissimilar environment and foe, it is difficult to distinguish between the tactics employed respectively by the 45th and 37th Infantry Divisions.

At the conclusion of World War II, the U.S. Army undertook steps to update its war-fighting doctrine using the lessons learned at such high cost in lives and materiel. Accordingly, a new version of FM 100–5 was published in August 1949. Although the majority of the section on combat in cities was repeated almost verbatim from the 1944 edition, the latest version of FM 100–5 did contain a significantly different approach when describing the employment of armor in urban combat.

When discussing the role of tanks in city fighting, FM 100–5 varied sharply from the 1944 edition of FM 71–100, *The Armored Division*. The new FM 100–5 noted that, "Small tank-infantry teams are particularly effective. Tanks are capable of breaking through light and medium construction. This, coupled with their ability to penetrate heavy walls with armor-piercing shells and to attack enemy personnel with high explosive shells and machinegun fire, makes them an effective combination with infantry for fighting inside towns."[25]

War broke out once again in June 1950 when the North Korean Peoples Army (NKPA) crossed the demilitarized zone that partitioned the Korean peninsula. Seoul was captured by the NKPA almost at the onset of the campaign. Less than three months later, the South Korean capital was liberated by elements of the 7th Infantry Division, 1st Marine Division, and South Korean units. The Americans and their Korean allies fought for six days before driving the NKPA from the city on September 29.

Although the North Koreans were routed with remarkably few American losses, the fierce fighting caused one marine to later remark, "Thank God we had tanks with us. Without them we'd still be fighting there."[26] Tank-infantry tactics developed during World War II once again proved their worth. Although the prodigious use of firepower did save lives, it left one American officer with the impression that Seoul's condition "was worse than Tokyo after the war. The first streets were obviously battle torn, but as they came to the center of town it was obvious that the retreating North Koreans had burned many of the buildings. Most of the windows in the Capitol building were smashed; its great copper dome was twisted and blackened."[27]

Motivated perhaps by the fighting that took place in Seoul, the existing FM 31–50 was revised in August 1952. Renamed *Combat in Fortified Areas and Towns*, the new manual underwent extensive changes before being reissued. For the first time, the definition of a built-up area as "any group of buildings designed for habitation or commercial purposes, such as villages, towns, cities, or factories" was included in army doctrine."[28] Field Manual 31–50 also recognized that combat in built-up areas did not always occur out of military necessity. The new manual explained that "the attacker attempts to bypass and isolate rather than attack a town that has been developed into a strongly defended position. The defender attempts to select towns for defense whose strategic or political importance will force the attacker to try to capture them in order to further his over-all plans."[29]

The 1952 edition acknowledged that the U.S. Army had considerable expertise in urban combat, but it did not attempt to eliminate discussion of individual and unit training. Although that section of the manual was significantly reduced, FM 31–50 did address the employment of individual weapons systems. However, the discussion of offensive and defensive operations at regimental level now formed the core of the manual.

Field Manual 31–50 noted that an infantry regiment assigned to a battle position in a city distributed its forces in three echelons: security force, holding force, and reserve force. Two battalions were normally assigned to defend the MLR while the third remained in reserve. Each infantry battalion was expected to defend a sector four to eight blocks in width. Built-up areas "suitable for the defense are located so that it forces the enemy to launch a direct attack or make a time consuming maneuver."[30] Likely avenues of enemy approach into the defended area were blocked by obstacles or covered by fire. Security elements on the forward edge of the town would warn of the enemy's approach, adjust supporting fires on the attacker, and deceive the enemy as to the location of the regimental MLR. If the defensive zone were penetrated, every effort would be made to contain the enemy until a counterattack could be launched to eject the attacker from his foothold.

When conducting offensive operations, a regiment would execute a three-phased attack on a built-up area. The first phase was designed to isolate the town or city by seizing terrain features that dominated the approaches. The second phase consisted of the seizure of a foothold on the outskirts of the city. The third phase featured the systematic house-by-house, block-by-block advance through the built-up area. The 1952 edition of FM 31–50 was quick to point out, however, that there was "no clear line of demarcation between the ending of the second phase and the beginning of the third. When each unit has secured its foothold, it immediately begins to displace its reserve and supporting weapons into the foothold area to support the third phase of the attack."[31]

The attack to seize the foothold in a built-up area was conducted similarly to an assault against a fortified area over normal terrain. Supporting weapons were used to neutralize the enemy and isolate the area from support and reinforcement from other parts of the built-up area. When troops were in assault position, supporting fires were lifted or shifted as required, and leading elements moved without delay to the first buildings to be seized. Once these buildings were cleared of enemy, supporting units and weapons displaced forward into the lodgment area.

The use of artillery in urban combat mirrored the three-phased approach to offensive maneuver. Constant artillery fire was laid on the approaches to the town and exits from the area to prevent reinforcement and to destroy withdrawing elements. During the first and second phase, artillery would fire concentrations on the built-up area and its approaches. Factors to consider when planning the weight and type of artillery included type of construction, whether or not producing rubble in the streets would provide the enemy with an advantage, restrictions on the movement of friendly tanks and supply vehicles caused by rubble, and the attitude of the population—friendly, neutral, or hostile.[32] The effectiveness of artillery support, however, was expected to decrease in the third phase due to lack of observation and the proximity of enemy forces to the attacking friendly troops.

The use of reconnaissance was stressed much more heavily in the 1952 manual than in previous editions. Gaining detailed information concerning the enemy, his defenses, and the terrain surrounding the built-up area was considered essential for the commander to make viable plans and decisions. As in all other types of operation, collection was based on the essential elements of information (EEI) established by the commander. Although air reconnaissance played a major part in collecting information, FM 31–50 emphasized that "as contact with the enemy becomes more imminent, ground reconnaissance agencies become more active . . . [B]oth air and ground reconnaissance collects exact and detailed information on the outposts and main defenses of the town or city."[33]

Increased confidence in the ability of commanders to effectively control their troops in a built-up area was reflected by extensive discussion of night operations. Field Manual 31–50 went so far as to state that "movement outside of buildings during daylight is greatly restricted; therefore, much of the fighting in towns will take place at night."[34] This section reflected lessons learned during the last six months of World War II, when Americans troops successfully used night infiltration tactics against German units defending villages and small towns.

Peace in Korea brought on a twelve-year lull in the further development of urban combat doctrine. Although several changes to the existing FM 31–50 were approved in the mid-1950s, a completely new manual retitled *Combat in Fortified and Built-Up Areas* was not published until March 1964. Reflecting the strategic challenges associated with the defense of Western Europe, the new edition of FM 31–50 noted that built-up areas may become battle areas "because their location controls routes of movement or because they contain valuable industrial or political installations."[35] The 1964 manual also contained a number of other significant revisions in U.S. urban doctrine.

For example, this version departed significantly from previous manuals by noting that the attacker could gain some significant advantages during urban combat. By seizing the initiative, an attacker could gain "the advantage of maneuver in isolating the town or city to be seized . . . [and] the attacker may be able to bypass strongly defended buildings by going under them, using cellars, sewers, subways, or other underground passages."[36] References to urban terrain providing clear advantage to the defender all but disappeared. In fact, the manual stated, "A built-up area that can be easily avoided has little defensive value."[37]

In the section on offensive operations, the 1964 edition clearly demonstrated that the U.S. Army was confident of its abilities to successfully conduct an attack against a built-up area. The manual repeated the three-phased technique discussed in earlier editions; however, much of the "mystique" of urban combat had vanished. Field Manual 31–50 noted that during the first two phases, an assault on a built-up area was to be treated in much the same manner as "other attacks of strong defensive positions." During the third phase, however, "the attack assumes more specialized characteristics."[38]

The chapter on offense in FM 31–50 proposed that commanders should take a much bolder approach to urban combat when circumstances warranted. For instance, when a built-up area was lightly defended, "it may be desirable for leading elements to push forward rapidly to seize critical areas. In such situations, supporting elements and reserves are given specific mopping up missions to clear sections of areas that have been bypassed or hastily cleared by leading elements."[39] The coordinated employment of multiple brigades during an attack on a large, built-up area was also mentioned for the first time. Previous editions had never ventured beyond the discussion of regimental-size formations.

President John Kennedy's interest in insurgent warfare and the newly created Special Forces also materialized within FM 31–50 in a section entitled "Counterguerilla Operations." The experiences of Algeria, Malaya, and Vietnam prompted FM 31–50 to unequivocally state that a guerrilla force in a built-up area "will not normally choose to fight . . . until it has reached the latter phases of its organizational development . . . [H]owever, clandestine elements in cities and towns often incite organized rioting, seize portions of urban areas, erect street barricades, and resist attempts to enter the area."[40]

Although U.S. commanders were urged to recapture areas seized by guerrillas forces as soon as possible, FM 31–50 cautioned against the use of indiscriminate force. The manual went on to explain that the sole objective of an urban guerrilla operation might be to provoke a violent reaction from counter-guerrilla forces that would gain sympathizers from the civil population and make the insurgents appear to be promoting a popular cause.

Discussion of nuclear and chemical weapons surfaced for the first time in the 1964 version of FM 31–50. During the conduct of the defense, the manual stated: "As the enemy comes under observation of security elements, he is subjected to long-range artillery fires . . . [N]uclear weapons may also be employed if suitable targets are located and developed . . . [U]pon withdrawal of the combat outpost (COP), Forward Edge of the Battle Area (FEBA) forces engage enemy targets as they appear, or fire against suspect or likely enemy assembly areas or other positions. Low-yield nuclear weapons (to include the Davy Crockett) may be fired against on-call targets."[41]

The offensive operations chapter, however, emphasized that it would not be desirable to use nuclear weapons in conjunction with a ground attack of a built-up area because of the casualties that would be inflicted on civilian populations, especially in friendly territory.

Emerging awareness of noncombatant issues, previously not a strong suit of urban doctrine, indicated that the U.S. Army realized it would have to deal with the populations of German cities, towns, and villages if the Cold War suddenly turned hot. The political considerations associated with such a conflict were touched upon when the manual noted that "the decision to evacuate civilians from a built-up area is normally made at the highest level of command." Field Manual 31–50 recognized the sovereignty of civilian government by noting that "friendly local authorities should be used to control the civilian population whenever possible . . . [W]hen local authorities were absent or ineffective, a Civil Affairs group composed of various teams would be assigned or attached to U.S. combat units to assist in the administration of a built-up area until fully effective civil government could be reestablished."[42]

The last substantive discussion of urban combat in FM 100–5 was found in the 1968 edition of that manual. Categorized as "Battle Under Special Conditions," FM 100–5 focused primarily on the impact that weapons of mass destruction would have on urban combat. It stated: "Built-up areas may be untenable because of their susceptibility to neutralization or destruction by conventional or nuclear munitions. These areas are also vulnerable to neutralization by biological or chemical munitions. Extensive subterranean systems may provide the defender with additional protection . . . [I]n employing NBC weapons the commander must consider their effect on the civilian population and make plans for control and evacuation." The manual went on to explain that "the advantages gained through the use of nuclear weapons must be weighed against the creation of obstacles to the assault force."[43]

Field Manual 31–50 underwent significant changes during this same period, resulting in the publication of an update in 1970. Lessons learned during the Tet offensive, particularly in the use of rotary wing aircraft in built-up areas, were included in this update. An airmobile assault on urban areas "usually will require modification of techniques which are otherwise normal for an airmobile operation in relatively unimproved or uninhabited areas . . . [A]irmobile operations at night in built-up areas require detailed and careful planning."[44] The update also discussed the use of rooftops as landing platforms, as well as the feasibility of rappelling techniques and troop ladders to unload troops and supplies from helicopters in built-up areas.

Contrary to popular images of battles in triple-canopy jungle, U.S. troops in Vietnam often found themselves fighting in villages and towns. Negative feedback resulting from the indiscriminate use of firepower against populated areas during the Tet offensive in 1968 resulted in the update forcefully iterating that "[t]actics which provide the most expedient military success may cause an adverse effect on the civilian population . . . [T]he time and effort in meticulous and coordinate planning can be well justified by the relatively inexpensive rehabilitation of friendly civilians from intact buildings . . . [T]ime and effort spent to conserve the life of noncombatants and nonmilitary personnel can be rewarded by the small effort subsequently required to reestablish a friendly populace as compared to the effort required to reestablish a hostile one."[45]

The U.S. Army renovated its urban doctrine once again when it published FM 90–10, *Military Operations in Urban Terrain (MOUT),* in 1979. Because the new manual dealt solely with urban combat versus fortified areas and city fighting, FM 90–10 represented a significant departure from previous doctrine. The new field manual did not differ greatly from its predecessor conceptually, but it did expand on a number of topics originally presented within FM 31–50. The inclusion of material, however, was somewhat offset by the disappearance of urban doctrine within FM 100–5, *Operations.* Readers of that manual would no longer be able to find mention of combat in cities following publication of the 1976 edition.

Field Manual 90–10 supported the concept of active defense introduced in the 1976 edition of FM 100–5. Active defense, simply put, consisted of trading time for space on a strategic scale while inflicting casualties on an attacker until he loses momentum and collapses. Military operations in urbanized terrain (MOUT), a new acronym in the U.S. Army's lexicon, was defined as "all military actions that are planned and conducted on a terrain complex where manmade construction impacts on the tactical options available to the commander."[46] The new MOUT manual also went on to explain that urban combat was unavoidable simply because towns and cities would always be a factor when set against the greatly expanded area of operations needed to conduct active defense.

Field Manual 90–10 also reflected the U.S. Army's renewed preoccupation with the Cold War after the "Decade of Vietnam." It classified urbanization using central European examples while glibly stating, "With minor modifications, it is applicable to other urban areas throughout the world."[47] Urban areas were divided into three classes: large cities, towns/small cities, and villages. Large cities, defined as having a population greater than 100,000 persons, formed the core of an urban complex consisting of the city, its suburban areas, and outlying towns. Towns/small cities, classified as having populations of 3,000 to 100,000, were normally located along major lines of communications and in river valleys. Villages were described as agriculturally oriented and distributed among cultivated areas. Field Manual 90–10 noted that there were "49 cities, 235 small cities/towns, and approximately 21,000 villages in the Federal Republic of Germany."[48]

Several familiar themes were included within FM 90–10. Deliberate attacks in an urban area remained divided into three phases: isolate, assault (to gain a foothold), and clearance. The manual stated that hasty attacks can be conducted when the enemy has not established strong defensive positions and attacking forces can exploit maneuver to overwhelm the defense. The manual explained that "an urban area is an obstacle to tactical maneuver and in that respect the hasty attack in MOUT is conducted somewhat differently than in open terrain."[49]

Field Manual 90–10 noted that urban sprawl added strength to the active defense by providing covered and concealed positions and restricting the attacker's mobility and observation. The manual stated that "the defender can prepare the ground in advance, build and reinforce obstacles, and select firing positions and observation posts, many of which require improvement only." The manual also explained that "every action of the attacker is made more difficult because he must feel his way through this complex of manmade and natural terrain features." Urban advantages were significant enough to create a combat multiplier effect that could be leveraged by U.S. commanders when they were tasked to retain key transportation centers, deny strategic/political objectives to the enemy, and control critical avenues of approach.[50]

Reflecting one of the more consistent beliefs in urban combat doctrine, FM 90–10 included extensive discussion of urban command and control (C2) difficulties. Among other things, city combat "placed a heavy strain on the command and control apparatus. Command of subordinate units and the control of fires is complicated by restrictive terrain, the proximity of opposing forces, reduced communications capabilities, and the numerous, small, isolated battles that may be fought."[51] The primary means of control measures were designation of battle areas, battle positions, and sectors, as well as phase lines, checkpoints, and restrictive fire control measures. The MOUT manual also recommended positioning commanders well forward and reducing distances between units to offset C2 problems found on the urban battlefield.

Field Manual 90–10 acknowledged that the decision to fight in an urban area, especially given the existence of the North Atlantic Treaty Organization (NATO), would be dictated primarily by political considerations. Coalition politics also demanded inclusion of paragraphs such as "in all circumstances, civilians are entitled to respect for their persons, their honor, their family rights, their religious convictions and practices, and their manners and customs. They shall at all times be humanely treated and shall be protected against all acts of violence or threats."[52] Written to support a doctrine founded on the conventional defense of Germany, FM 90–10 did not classify civilians as either friendly or hostile. As a matter of fact, FM 90–10 apparently assumed that U.S. forces would encounter only citizens of allied nations on the future urban battlefield.

Despite the conciliatory tone that the manual took when discussing civilians, domestic politics in Europe influenced the further refinement of MOUT doctrine. When left-wing German activists publicized excerpts from FM 90–10 that discussed the dynamics of fighting in cities, our allies began to argue that "the idea of fighting in cities is so abhorrent that it does not allow for closer scrutiny." Economic survival also figured prominently in the argument of NATO powers that emphasized that their "cities cannot be destroyed during a war, since they represent economic survival. The cities must be left alone, while the war is fought on the open countryside." The North Atlantic Treaty Organization itself came under scrutiny when the political opposition within several member countries claimed that it represented "a mutual pledge of intervention but not of self-sacrificial defense."[53] The resultant furor persuaded the U.S. Army to quickly lower the profile of its MOUT doctrine development.

Following the dissolution of the Soviet Union in 1991, the U.S. Army continued with development of MOUT doctrine in light of its expanded global commitment and the burgeoning nature of urban sprawl. Although FM 90–10 has not been updated in twenty years, doctrine writers at the Command and

General Staff College are currently working on a new version of that manual. At the conclusion of the Gulf War, the United States Army Infantry School began working on new doctrine. Field Manual 90–10–1, *An Infantryman's Guide to Combat in Built-Up Areas,* was published in 1993. Field Manual 90–10–1 was then supplemented by an extensive update published in 1995. The U.S. Army also issued TC 90–1, *Training for Military Operations on Urbanized Terrain,* in September 1993.

When the U.S. Army entered World War II, it possessed only a theoretical concept for fighting in cities. As American troops gained practical experience in North Africa, Sicily, and Italy, a separate manual on city combat was published. Few armies can lay claim to a similar ability to rapidly translate theory into practical battlefield expertise. In the 1980s, however, MOUT doctrinal development ended as a result of the political firestorm it created among our NATO allies. The physical, political, and economic characteristics of urban areas have evolved on a dramatic scale since then. Despite the solid foundation of experience gained by U.S. troops between 1944 and 1994, it still remains to be seen whether the U.S. Army can successfully combine those historical lessons with a new approach to urban combat that leverages twenty-first-century technology and tactics.

ENDNOTES

1. R. Ernest and Trevor N. Dupuy, *The Harper Encyclopedia of Military History—4th Edition* (New York: Harper Collins Publishers, 1993), 887.

2. Ibid., 883.

3. Fredericksburg and Spotsylvania National Military Park, U.S. Department of the Interior, *Fire in the Streets: A Civil War Walking Tour of Fredericksburg,* June 6, 1999 (Internet), p. 2; 4 pages (cited October 12, 1999), available from http://www.nps.gov/frsp/fire.htm.

4. Frank A. O'Reilly, *"Stonewall" Jackson at Fredericksburg: The Battle*

of Prospect Hill, December 13, 1862 (Lynchburg, VA: H. E. Howard, Inc., 1993), 16.

5.   U.S. War Department, War Department Field Manual 100–5, *Field Service Regulations: Operations* (Washington, DC: U.S. War Department, May 22, 1941), 210.

6.   U.S. War Department, War Department Field Manual 31–50, *Attack on a Fortified Position and Combat in Towns* (Washington, DC: U.S. War Department, January 31, 1944), 62.

7.   FM 31–50, 64.

8.   Ibid.

9.   Ibid., 65.

10.   Equivalent to a ten-battalion *groupement* of 105mm, 155mm, and 240mm howitzers and 8-inch guns. It also included a small number of tanks firing in the indirect mode as well as several 4.2-inch chemical mortars.

11.   FM 31–50, 61.

12.   Ibid., 63.

13.   Ibid., 83.

14.   Ibid., 46–47.

15.   Robert Ross Smith, *Triumph in the Philippines* (Washington, DC: Center of Military History, 1993), 264. American troops in Manila exercised great restraint in employing indirect artillery and aerial fires while clearing the northern suburbs and eastern portion of the city. When casualties began increasing dramatically as the troops moved south, the restrictions on artillery employment were lifted.

16.   Smith, *Triumph in the Philippines,* 255.

17.   FM 31–50, 73–75.

18.   FM 100–5, *Field Service Regulations: Operations* (Washington, DC: U.S. War Department, May 22, 1941), 210; FM 100–5, *Field Service Regulations: Operations* (Washington, DC: U.S. War Department, June 15, 1944), 248.

19.   FM 100–5, June 15, 1944, 248.

20.   Ibid., 247.

21.   Gordon A. Harrison, *Cross Channel Attack* (Washington, DC: U.S. Army Center of Military History, 1993), 643.

22.   FM 100–5, June 15, 1944, 247.

23.   U.S. War Department, War Department Field Manual FM 71–100, *The Armored Division* (Washington, DC: U.S. War Department, 1944), 78.

24. Martin Blumenson, *Breakout and Pursuit* (Washington, DC: U.S. Army Center of Military History, 1961); see p. 653 for information on casualties suffered at Brest. Losses at Saint-Malo are found in the same volume on pp. 401–4. Aschaffenburg figures are quoted from Maj. Quentin W. Schillaire's Military Masters of Arts and Sciences Paper, *The Battle of Aschaffenburg: An Example of Late World War II Urban Combat in Europe* (Fort Leavenworth, KS: U.S. Army Command and General Staff College, 1989), 137–38.

25. U.S. Department of the Army, Department of the Army Field Manual 100–5, *Field Service Regulations: Operations* (Washington, DC: Department of the Army, August 1949), 199.

26. Donald Knox, *The Korean War: An Oral History–Pusan to Chosin* (New York: Harcourt Brace Jovanovich Publishers, 1985), 293.

27. John Toland, *In Mortal Combat: Korea 1950–53* (New York: William Morrow and Company, 1991), 228.

28. U.S. Department of the Army, Department of the Army Field Manual 31–50, *Combat in Fortified Areas and Towns* (Washington, DC: Department of the Army, August 1952), 53.

29. Ibid.

30. Ibid., 60.

31. Ibid., 85.

32. Ibid., 78.

33. Ibid., 58.

34. Ibid., 54.

35. U.S. Department of the Army, Department of the Army Field Manual 31–50, *Combat in Fortified and Built Up Areas* (Washington, DC: Department of the Army, March 1964), 27.

36. Ibid., 32.

37. Ibid., 49.

38. Ibid., 32–33.

39. Ibid., 39.

40. Ibid., 46.

41. Ibid., 55.

42. Ibid., 30–31.

43. U.S. Department of the Army, FM 100–5, *Operations of Army Forces in the Field* (Washington, DC: Department of the Army, September 1968), 6–24.

44. Department of the Army, FM 31–50, Change 2, April 22, 1970, 3.

45.   Ibid.

46.   Department of the Army, FM 90–10, *Military Operations on Urbanized Terrain (MOUT)* (Washington, DC: Department of the Army, August 25, 1979), i.

47.   Ibid., 1–2.

48.   Ibid., 1–3.

49.   Ibid., 2–13.

50.   Ibid., 3–15, 3–16.

51.   Ibid., 3–19.

52.   Ibid., 5–7.

53.   U.S. Army Command and General Staff College, Lesson Plan A355, "Combined Arms Warfare on Urbanized Terrain" (Fort Leavenworth, KS: Department of the Army, U.S.ACGSC, August 1980), E-N111–1.

Lessons Learned from City Fights

1938–1968

by Col. John F. Antal and Maj. Bradley T. Gericke

The practical value of history is to throw the film of the past through the material projector of the present onto the screen of the future.
—B. H. Liddell Hart, *Thoughts on War,* 1944

Shaped by cultural, economic, and political factors, cities represent special conditions that place enormous strain upon military operations. Although warfare is ever changing, urban combat has remained relatively consistent. In the city fights covered in the chapters of this book, the advantages that accrued to the defender from the effective use of urban terrain were described. Defenders sought to shape conditions to their advantage to try to change the nature of the conflict and use the complex terrain of the urban environments to offset the attacking forces' advantages. *City Fights* establishes that urban areas are difficult to capture if defended by a determined foe.

If any trend can be discerned from the study of city fights in recorded history, it is that cities are often key to winning at the operational and strategic levels of war. At the same time, the distinction between the tactical, operational, and strategic levels of war is imprecise, frequently allowing tactical actions to directly influence operational and strategic objectives. The constricted confines of the urban battlefield compress the levels of war— tactical, operational, and strategic—and often blur the distinction and importance of each level.

Because of this compression, small-unit actions can directly affect the outcome of larger engagements and battles. Senior leaders must consequently anticipate the direction of fighting and make timely decisions to place units and resources in the correct locations to defeat the enemy and retain battlefield initiative in a city fight. In urban combat, the mundane matters tremendously, and the difference between victory and defeat is often narrow.

At the tactical level of war, urban combat also dramatically compresses time, distance, and combat power. The topography of a city restricts and compartmentalizes the military forces moving through the urban area. Mounted and dismounted movements are blocked by buildings and canalized along streets. In the human-made maze of an urban area, it is extremely difficult for military units to employ weapons, move and change direction, maneuver, employ combined arms, conduct logistical operations to sustain the fight, and command and control the forces conducting the battle. These factors, and many others, make fighting in cities a unique form of combat and one of the most deadly.

General Tactical Lessons Learned

Although every city fight is a unique situation, some general tactical trends did emerge. One of the simplest lessons learned is that combatants who were familiar with the urban battle space, either through careful reconnaissance and rehearsal or from having

grown up and lived in the city, were much more successful at optimizing the urban battlefield to their advantage. The defenders
of Stalingrad who knew the city were able to maneuver circles
around their German attackers. Likewise, the Polish defenders of
Warsaw were able to keep a bigger and better equipped German
army at bay for sixty-three days largely because of their expert
knowledge of the terrain.

Urban combat remained infantry intensive, and a well-
trained infantry was the centerpiece of any successful city fight.
Infantrymen used many techniques to improve survivability and
enhance maneuver. Tunneling or mouse-holing, where walls
were penetrated to create pathways between adjoining buildings,
was practiced widely by both attacker and defender and was an
extremely important tactic. Snipers were invaluable individuals
who ruled entire city blocks, freezing the maneuver of the opposing side when artfully employed. They frequently demonstrated that they could hold down large numbers of opposing
troops and hence became a favored tactic of the defender.

Man-portable antitank weapons came of age during the period of conflict covered in *City Fights* and became the weapon
of choice for infantrymen engaged in urban combat. From the
British-designed PIAT to the German-made panzerfaust, these
shoulder-launched antitank weapons became the hip-pocket artillery of the small, close-combat teams that ruled the city fight.
Such weapons also developed into today's lighter, more lethal
antitank weapons, as exhibited by the ubiquitous RPG used in
the streets of Hue, Vietnam.

Tanks were found to be essential to the successful defense or
offense of urban combat. Armor provided the protection and
firepower needed to move forward in a city and delivered concentrated, accurate, direct firepower. When tanks were protected
by infantry and employed as a critical part of the combined-arms
team, they helped to deliver tactical victory with fewer casualties.

During the battles of Manila and Aschaffenburg, the American use of armor, working in close cooperation with infantry, permitted the Americans to achieve victory with less than favorable odds and is a testament to the quality that combined arms brings to a battle. In the defense, armor became an integral part of the defense and often became the center of resistance, as we included in the chapters on the battles of Stalingrad, Budapest, and Berlin.

Antiaircraft weapons were found to be effective in city fighting because of their high rate and volume of fire. Weapons that provide concentrated, overwhelming firepower played a significant role in dislodging defenders in offensive urban combat. Such high-volume weapons as the American M16, a half-track equipped with quad .50–caliber machine guns, or the mobile 20mm flakpanzers could denude structures with their devastating firepower. Weapons such as the 20mm antiaircraft gun were effectively used in the defense by German forces in World War II, as related in the chapter on the battle of Aschaffenburg in 1945.

Although supporting close air support and artillery were important to most city fights described in this book, they were not decisive by themselves. Artillery and close air support are most effective against targets in the open and less effective against targets ensconced in concrete and steel-reinforced structures. Massive artillery and air bombardment failed to dislodge determined defenders. It took a combined-arms effort, particularly heavy in infantry, to capture or clear a city that was seriously prepared for defense. Nevertheless, artillery, particularly in the direct-fire mode, was often used to root out determined defenders. During the battle of Stalingrad, for instance, German commanders used artillery to flatten entire structures to defeat Soviet snipers. Artillery and air attacks at Hue in 1968 demolished buildings and created rubble that the defenders used to their advantage to inhibit maneuver in the city streets. Cratering city streets created significant obstacles to movement. In addition, in the battles described in this book, air superiority was essential to the attacker to maintain logistical support of the offensive effort in urban terrain but was not decisive in winning the battles. During the period covered in this book—before the development of precision air and artillery weapons—air and artillery fires alone could not capture a city or stop it from being taken.

Maneuver

Maneuver is the employment of forces, through movement combined with fire or fire potential, to achieve a position of advantage with respect to the enemy to accomplish a military mission. Maneuver is the means by which commanders concentrate combat power to achieve surprise, shock, momentum, and dominance. Napoleon said that an aptitude for war is aptitude for maneuver. The nature of urban terrain inhibits movement and drastically restricts maneuver. Advanced construction techniques practiced in recent decades have made multistory, high-rise buildings much more resilient. The reinforced concrete and high-strength steel utilized in these structures means that they would likely withstand initial attacks. The upper stories of such buildings can become virtually distinct battlefields within a single structure as forces become committed. It may be necessary to eliminate a foe from a building floor by floor to enable further movement in that structure's proximity.

Military operations in cities inhibit tactical maneuver because of the complexity of the urban battlefield. Road systems link urban areas, which in turn prompt further development of high-density building complexes. Rail corridors frequently parallel the road network, which, aligned with adjacent industrial construction, blocks traditional avenues of approach and restricts maneuver. Damage to structures provides cover and concealment, restricts fields of fire, makes foot traffic difficult, and hinders the employment of vehicles and heavy equipment.

During World War II, battles in major cities proved that many areas of a city could be prepared quickly for defense. Reinforced concrete and stone buildings were easily fortified and became bastions. Lesser structures that rapidly crumbled under the onslaught of armed attack became sources of rubble and provided material for the construction of obstacles. Both the intentional and unexpected demolition of buildings radically altered the battlefield. Soldiers found that landmarks, reference points, and roadways were often obliterated or made unrecognizable by heavy shelling.

In addition to fighting within buildings or in streets at ground level, subterranean systems were important as alternative routes. Subways, basements, utility lines, and sewers present opportunities for military forces to create safe mobility corridors for resupply and the movement of forces. In many cases ingenious methods were employed to minimize friendly casualties and gain freedom of maneuver. During the battle of Warsaw in 1944, the Germans employed an ingenious bomb, the Goliath—a small, remotely controlled tracked vehicle packed with five hundred kilograms of explosives—to blast through strong buildings defended by Polish forces and create freedom of movement for their units within the city.

Combined Arms

Close combat was required in offensive and defensive urban fights against an entrenched enemy in the battles described in this book. There were no "silver bullets" to take a city away from an enemy determined to keep it. The way cities have been captured since World War II—room by room, building by building, block by block—may continue into the future. The lesson that appears in the surveys of city fights from World War II and the Korean War is that there are no shortcuts to successful fights in urban centers. City fights remain harsh battlegrounds that place extraordinary demands on soldiers.

A decisive key to successful warfare, urban combat included, must be efficient combined-arms integration coupled with effective maneuver. In the examples in this book, city fighting quickly became a grinding ordeal. Most forces that engaged in close-quarter urban combat used overwhelming fire to get to a point of penetration in a strongpoint or building, make a penetration in a building, then painstakingly clear the building room by room. The combined-arms team of engineers, infantry, tanks, and artillery could get the force to and through the walls of the building, but to clear the building required infantry. This was a brutal form of warfare in which a potential ambush lurked behind every turn inside every structure.

A combined-arms organization sustains its lethality and effectiveness by combining with supporting arms. Taking advantage of the capabilities of different types of units creates a synergistic effect. Combining infantry, armor, engineers, fire support, and forward logistics multiplies combat power. It enhances force protection and thereby reduces casualties. But mutual support among combat units is difficult to achieve in a city fight. For the attacker, whose challenge is to bring his full power to bear within the confines of a narrow battle space, coordination in space and time strains command and control. Mutual support for the defender, who is often fixed to the protection of his defensive positions, is also difficult if the enemy does not enter the predesignated killing zones set up by the defender, as we saw in the battle of Troyes in 1944. It is clear that soldiers in a city fight must think in terms of multiple dimensions. They must consider how each of their units can contribute to one another in novel ways. The battle for a city must be fought in several directions simultaneously, from the tops of buildings to the sewers beneath the streets. The feat is difficult, but it can be done.

A major tactical lesson that should be learned from these urban battles is that operating as a combined-arms team is essential in a city fight. As Thomas Kelley explained in his chapter about the street-to-street fighting in Seoul, no single branch or type of unit can fight alone without facing extreme risk. Even when the enemy did not possess tanks or mines, the capabilities of armor and engineers provided friendly forces with significant advantages in firepower, mobility, countermobility, and survivability.

Alongside the importance of combined-arms organization as a principle is the vital lesson that combined-arms integration must be pushed to the lowest practical level. Successful combat in cities during the thirty-year period from 1938 to 1968 demonstrated that combined-arms integration within small tactical units—company, platoon, and squad—provided a tremendous advantage. In this kind of battle, the combatants learned that the spatial scale of tactical operations was drastically compressed and engagement ranges were short.

A major difference between fighting in cities and fighting in open terrain from 1938 to 1968 was the proportion and organization of combined-arms units. The necessity for a combined-arms approach persisted, but the ratio of required infantry, engineers, armor, and artillery varied with the situation. Armor and artillery were absolutely essential in city fights, as they were in all terrain conditions, but the demand for infantry and engineers was paramount and much greater in urban areas. More significantly, the forces that were most successful in urban combat executed combined-arms operations at the lowest level possible, and often as low as the company or platoon level. United States combined-arms tactics in the city fights during World War II and the Korean War, for instance, proved successful but suffered from several drawbacks, notably the length of time involved to execute operations, tremendous expenditures of ammunition, and significant collateral damage inflicted upon the city and its population. United States forces conducted combined-arms operations primarily at the battalion level, with some exceptions. Had the forces involved in these fights been better trained and equipped to use combined arms at the company, platoon, and squad level, the battles might have been won more quickly and with fewer casualties.

Examples of the successful employment of combined arms in the chapters of this book are plentiful, especially the challenges of assaulting or defending in the midst of a huge civil population. Peter Zwack, the author of the chapter on Budapest, aptly reported this trend when he said that heavy artillery, although effective, brought terrible incidental damage to structures and people. Mortars were more effective. Armor was useful primarily in a support role; both sides learned this costly lesson earlier in the war. Rarely were tanks engaged unsupported by infantry. Snipers ruled the streets during the daytime, which forced much of the action underground, inside and between buildings, and at night. In short, combined-arms tactics prevailed when they were synchronized.

Logistics

Logistical operations are critical to wage successful combat in cities. Fighting in cities consumes time, resources, and lives at a rapid pace. The well-known aphorism that amateurs study tactics and experts study logistics is true with regard to urban warfare. City fighting consumes tremendous amounts of ammunition. Casualty evacuation is also critical, and water resupply is essential. In several battles it was relatively easy to cut off water in a city.

Successful logistical planning for the urban fight required increased stores of ammunition, food, fuel, water, spare parts, and medical supplies. With the short engagement ranges that are the nature of the complex urban battlefield, targets were fleeting. Hence ammunition expenditure was high as units conducted reconnaissance by fire and attempted to suppress opposing forces. In addition, those who did not pay increased attention to threats to lines of communications, as the Germans failed to do at Stalingrad when they believed that they could supply the German Sixth Army from the air, paid dearly for their mistake.

At the tactical level, materials such as rope, grappling hooks, axes, explosives, and sandbags must be widely distributed or readily available to facilitate movement. Infantrymen can carry only so much equipment. Therefore, a system by which ammunition, grenades, and other expendable items can be replenished is essential. Soldiers fighting in cities need replacement weapons, batteries, signal devices, and a variety of other items. Resource demands heavily tax the logistical support system of any military force.

There is a toll on individual sustainment as well. The fleeting enemy, loud noise, and lack of refuge from hidden adversaries produce mental and physical strain to which leaders must attend by ensuring that soldiers receive adequate food, water, and sleep. In short, cities demand extraordinary commitment by forces fighting to seize them. But the fact that urban operations are brutally difficult and resource intensive must not obscure the fact that city fighting is never strictly a "military" affair.

Cities, of course, are built to serve the needs of the people. Military leaders must thus comprehend the human functions of cities, and consider how to use the various components of a city to their advantage. Some areas of the city provide potential resources for a military unit. Hospitals, medical clinics, schools, fuel storage areas, and transportation hubs should be identified and safeguarded if they are not under enemy control. Warehouses may contain needed construction equipment or supplies such as food or petroleum. Construction sites may have building materials. Stadiums and parks may serve as assembly areas, helicopter landing zones, or detainee holding facilities.

Command and Control

It is clear from our study of city fights in World War II and the Korean War that military leaders must plan, prepare, and execute to a high order of skill to meet the extreme conditions of city fighting. The city fights from 1938 to 1950 demonstrate that the victors based their planning, preparation, and execution on careful intelligence work, with special importance placed on the three-dimensional nature of the battlefield and with due consideration of the effects of battle on the local population.

To lead effectively, the leaders in these battles had to communicate. In a complex urban battle space, communications are the Achilles' heel of combined-arms integration. Urban operations place a premium on closely coordinated, combined-arms teams and carefully protected logistics. When communications break down, effective combined-arms execution is nearly impossible. In World War II and the Korean War, communications equipment was primitive by today's standards. Flares and flags were often the most reliable tools for visual communication. Such simple devices may be key in future city fights as well. Communication networks are often destroyed or suffer interference. To coordinate the actions of formations separated from line of sight and mutual support, couriers may supplement telephones and radio systems.

Communication is critical in warfare and even more so in the compressed time and space environment found in a city fight.

However, there are significant problems presented by cities. Wire lines are frequently cut and disrupted by the actions of the combatants. In addition, landlines were sometimes intercepted by wiretapping, and the maintenance and security of landline communications became a constant effort. Commercial and military telephone communication, however, was vital during the battles described in this book because radio communication was susceptible to interference, due to the nature of the urban battle space.

Most military FM radios require an unobstructed line of sight from transmitter to receiver. Radio signal degradation is a factor of building construction and the density of buildings. Electrical and trolley lines also adversely affected radio signals. Concrete and steel-reinforced buildings made radio communications problematic, because line-of-sight communications were often disrupted by dead spots. The British, in particular, lost control of the battle at Arnhem due to poor wireless communications. During the battle, the commander of the British 1st Airborne Division, Maj. Gen. Robert Urquhart, could not speak with higher headquarters for thirty-nine hours at Arnhem simply because he did not have the means to take the necessary communications equipment with him and use it effectively in urban terrain. The Germans, on the other hand, had similar problems but used the excellent Dutch telephone system to their advantage.

Successful urban combat operations from 1938 to 1950 required careful preparation and thorough rehearsal to master using combined-arms techniques in the close-quarters urban environment. Commanders must also carefully develop rules of engagement, adapting them to a variety of circumstances and ensuring that soldiers thoroughly understand, as was clearly illustrated by the holding of hostages by the Japanese during the battle of Manila.

At the tactical level, command and control was particularly

difficult. During these battles, as the urban terrain filled with debris, the resulting complex of broken and damaged vehicles and structures degraded the tactical leaders' ability to exert effective command and control. Soldiers and small units were often isolated, so they relied upon the preparation and initiative of junior leaders. Most of the decisions during these battles were in the hands of junior officers and noncommissioned officers. Individual initiative and small-unit aggressiveness paced the progress of armies. Commanders at higher echelons found it difficult to control the flow of the battle and maintain a clear mental picture of a dynamic situation. Of course the chaotic nature of urban combat was made more difficult by smoke and darkness. From the battle of Tai-erh-Chuang in 1938 to the fighting in Seoul during the Korean War of 1950 to the close-in fighting in Hue during the 1968 Tet offensive, the impact of effective small-unit leadership was decisive.

One solution to the challenge of communications in urban areas was to decentralize command and control to the lowest effective level and operate with minimal oversight and direction from higher headquarters. General Chuikov's small combined-arms teams, used so effectively in the defense of Stalingrad, and the U.S. Army's company-level tank-infantry-artillery cooperation at Aschaffenburg are cases in point. Units that were relatively self-contained and could execute the commander's intent minimized the challenge of communicating in urban areas.

Most importantly, effective command and control depends on the quality of the information concerning the enemy and terrain. The battles of World War II and Korea show that the force that develops information superiority has a tremendous advantage. In some cases, local civic officials may be key sources of information. Political and religious leaders can influence public opinion. Fire and police officials can assist with the preservation of order and identify hazardous material sites. Local governments may have access to translators or media expertise that can help a military force to communicate with the local population.

Conclusion

The world is in a period of massive urbanization. Today, more people than ever before live in major cities or megalopolises. In spite of this, few militaries are proficient at urban warfare, and few focus the majority of their training to fight in the urban complex. As in World War II, today's military thinking is to avoid urban fighting whenever possible. As this book relates, this was not possible in the bloody fighting that occurred in the cities of Europe, Asia, and the Middle East from 1938 to 1950. Likewise, fighting in urban areas during future conflicts will be an unavoidable reality.

The most significant conclusion is that there is no standard urban operation. Combat in cities is unique to the opponent, the city, the geography, the campaign, and the political considerations of the conflict. Urban operations are always complex and deadly. As the authors of *City Fights* have demonstrated, battles fought in Europe and Korea nearly sixty years ago remain portents of future war. The goal of the defender of a city is usually to use the complex urban terrain to negate the synergy of combined arms, bleed the attacker, gain time, and force his defeat. The attacker's goal, however, is to ensure that the city's complex topography does not have a decisive influence on the battle. Success usually came to the force that could utilize superior information, fires, and maneuver on the complex urban battlefield. To be successful in the difficult battle space of a city fight, commanders and units must be well trained, rehearsed, and ready.

Futurists frequently speak of the novel changes that await humankind in the coming years. Many contemporary military journals predict the benefits for soldiers through the technological enhancement of sensors, robots, and precision-guided weapons. Many of these military innovations will change how battles are conducted, but aerial attack, "information warfare," directed energy weapons, or nonlethal munitions do not provide dominant solutions to meet the challenges posed by urban warfare. In particular, as a recent U.S. Army and Marine Corps study concluded, *U.S. forces do not possess an overwhelming high technology advantage in urban combat as they do in virtually all other combat environments.* The historical fact remains that the calculus of fighting and winning in cities remains fundamentally unaltered. Absent a ready key to unlock the stasis, soldiers and military leaders must turn to the past for instruction.

Liddell Hart's admonition that we must study the past to glean value for the present is especially true for urban combat. The tales of combat related on these pages, of decisions made and destruction suffered, therefore serve to remind soldiers and interested civilians alike that the perils of urban warfare are genuine and ongoing. Defenders will use cities to negate the power of the attacker in future battles.

Because the world is largely urban in terms of population concentration, urban terrain will likely be the predominant battlefield of future wars. If geography is destiny, then fighting in cities makes close combat inevitable, and the experiences of urban combat of the soldiers who fought in World War II and Korea are likely to be repeated. To prevail on tomorrow's urban battlefield requires immediate attention to the records of the past. If *City Fights* has in a small way advanced that discussion, we must consider our brief foray into the past as a success.

City Fights Editors

Colonel John F. Antal III, an armor officer, has served predominately in tank and infantry units for the past twenty-three years. He is currently the G-3 (operations officer) for the U.S. Army's III Corps at Fort Hood, Texas. Until June 2002, Colonel Antal served as a special assistant to the chairman of the Joint Chiefs of Staff in Washington, D.C. Prior to that he commanded the 16th Cavalry Regiment at Fort Knox, Kentucky, and the 2d Battalion, 72d Armor, the "Dragon Force," an M1A1 tank battalion, stationed near the demilitarized zone in the Republic of Korea. Colonel Antal is a 1977 graduate of the United States Military Academy and has a master's degree in military arts and science from the Command and General Staff College at Fort Leavenworth, Kansas. Antal is recognized for his writings on tank warfare and combat operations in mountainous terrain. He has written four books: *Armor Attacks: The Tank Platoon* (1991), *Infantry Combat: The Rifle Platoon* (1995), *Combat Team: The Captain's War* (1998), and *Proud Legions: A Novel About America's Next War*. Since 1985 Antal has also published more than thirty-eight articles in professional journals.

    Major Bradley T. Gericke was commissioned in armor in 1988 from the United States Military Academy. He holds a Ph.D. from Vanderbilt University with an emphasis in early-modern European and British history. Major Gericke has published several college texts, numerous essays regarding military affairs, and is currently writing a book, *Spearhead: America's Third Armored Division in Peace and War, 1941–1992*. His assignments include service with tank battalions in the 3d Armored Division in Germany and Southwest Asia, the 2d Infantry Division in Korea, and as an assistant professor in the department of history at West Point. Major Gericke is currently assigned as a strategic planner and speechwriter within the Commanding General's Staff Group at U.S. Army Forces Command.

City Fights Authors

Colonel Kevin C. M. Benson recently commanded the U.S. 3d Battalion, 8th Cavalry, in the 1st Cavalry Division. He has served in armor and cavalry units in the United States and Europe. He served as the chief of war plans, U.S. Third Army; executive officer, 2d Cavalry Regiment; and chief of war plans, XVIII Airborne Corps. He also served as chief of staff, U.S. Forces Haiti. He is a graduate of the U.S. Army Command and General Staff College and the School of Advanced Military Studies.

Major Michael A. Boden is currently a student in the Army Command and General Staff College at Fort Leavenworth, Kansas. Prior to that, he was an assistant professor at the United States Military Academy, where he taught German and world history. He is a Ph.D. candidate at Vanderbilt University preparing a dissertation on "Friedrich Engels and the Art of War." An armor officer, he served during the Gulf War with the 1st (Tiger) Brigade, 2d Armored Division.

Major Norm Cooling is a marine infantry officer. A 1986 distinguished graduate of the U.S. Naval Academy, he has commanded both infantry and light armored reconnaissance platoons, as well as a light armored reconnaissance company in the 2d Marine Division. He participated in Operations Nimrod Dancer in Panama (the prelude to Just Cause) and Sharp Edge in Liberia. His nonoperational assignments have included a training command tour at the School of Infantry, two years as a Marine Corps liaison officer to the U.S. House of Representatives, and a year as a member of the 31st commandant of the Marine Corps Staff Group. Upon his graduation from the USMC Command and Staff College, he will report for joint duty with Special Operations Command, Europe.

Dennis C. Fresch was a corporal in the U.S. Marine Corps serving in 1967–68 as a gunner, then as a tank commander with the 2d and 3d Platoon, C Company, 1st Tank Battalion, 1st Marine Division FMF WESPAC. He has worked as a writer, art director, and electromechanical designer in the computer, medical, and aerospace fields. Fresch is currently an employee of the United States government.

Major Thomas A. Kelley was commissioned as an armor officer upon graduation from the United States Military Academy in 1986. Between 1986 and 1994 he served as a tank platoon leader, scout platoon leader, aide-de-camp, tank company commander, and assistant operations officer. Following graduate school at the John F. Kennedy School of Government at Harvard University, he returned to teach military science at the United States Military Academy before going on to attend the Command and General Staff College at Fort Leavenworth, Kansas.

Lieutenant Colonel G. A. Lofaro is a plans officer assigned to the U.S. Army's Forces Command headquarters. He formerly served as assistant professor of history at the United States Military Academy, where he taught military history. He is a 1981 graduate of West Point who was commissioned in the infantry. His assignments include tours with the 82d Airborne Division, the Ranger Training Brigade, and the 2d Infantry Division.

Lieutenant Colonel Peter R. Mansoor is an active-duty combat-arms officer in the United States Army. He is the author of *The GI Offensive in Europe: The Triumph of American Infantry Divisions, 1941–1945*, published by the University Press of Kansas in June 1999. He has served as an assistant professor of military history at the United States Military Academy at West Point. His degrees include a master's and doctorate in history from The Ohio State University. Lieutenant Colonel Mansoor is currently in command of the 1st Squadron, 10th Cavalry Regiment, 4th Infantry Division (Mechanized) at Fort Hood, Texas.

Colonel Mark J. Reardon was commissioned from Loyola College of Baltimore as an armor officer in 1979. He has since served in CONUS, Germany, Korea, and Saudi Arabia. He is a graduate of the airborne, air assault, and ranger schools, as well as the Armor Officer Advanced Course and USMC Command and Staff College. Major assignments include commander, B/2–72d Armor; commander, A/3–4th Cavalry; operations officer, 3–4th Cavalry; executive officer, 3–73d Armor (Airborne); and operations officer and deputy commander for Army Forces Central Command Saudi Arabia. Colonel Reardon is currently assigned to the Joint Staff in the Pentagon.

Benjamin Runkle is an International Security Fellow with the Belfer Center for Science and International Affairs and a Ph.D. candidate in the Department of Government at Harvard University. He has served as a fire support and fire direction officer with the 2d Infantry Division in Korea, and as a battery executive officer with the 82d Airborne. He has also worked for the Institute of Defense Analyses and the National Security Division of the Congressional Budget Office. His work has been published in the Harvard International Review and the Washington Times.

Major David M. Toczek is an infantry officer who currently serves as a plans officer for III Corps, Fort Hood, Texas. His previous assignments include instructor duty in the Department of History, United States Military Academy. After commissioning, he led an airborne rifle platoon and served as a company executive officer during Operation Provide Comfort in northern Iraq. He later served as a senior platoon trainer at the Infantry Officer Basic Course and commanded a Bradley company.

Second Lieutenant William M. Waddell, originally from Stillwater, New Jersey, is a 2001 graduate of the United States Military Academy at West Point. He received his degree in military history and was commissioned as an armor officer. He is currently serving as a Scout platoon leader in Eagle troop, 2/3 ACR.

Lieutenant Colonel Eric M. Walters is the assistant chief of staff, G-2 (intelligence), for the 3d Marine Aircraft Wing home stationed at Marine Corps Air Station Miramar, San Diego, California. A former director for Marine Corps Intelligence Training, he currently serves as a professor of intelligence, land warfare, and military history for American Military University. He is also an adjunct faculty member and seminar leader for the Marine Corps University's College of Continuing Education, teaching at the Amphibious Warfare School and Command and Staff College. Lieutenant Colonel Walters contributed to several commercial board wargames on the Stalingrad battle: Advanced Squad Leader Rules (The Avalon Hill Game Company, 1985; revised and republished by Multi-Man Publishing, 2001); Turning Point: Stalingrad (The Avalon Hill Game Company, 1989); and Streets of Stalingrad, 3d ed. (L2 Game Design, 2002).

Lieutenant Colonel Peter B. Zwack is both a U.S. Army military intelligence officer and a Russian foreign area officer. He is currently commanding the 524th Military Intelligence Battalion (CI/HUMINT) in South Korea. Prior assignments include service in the 2d, 3d, and 4th Infantry Divisions, the 66th MI Brigade, and the Defense Intelligence Agency. His last assignment was as a NATO policy staff officer in the JCS's J5 Directorate, where he was bestowed the Admiral William J. Crowe Jr. award as the Joint Staff's Action Officer of the Year for 1999. He has a master's degree in strategic intelligence from the Defense Intelligence College (DIA). His long interest in MOUT stems partially from the fact that his father was trapped in Budapest during the grim 1944–45 Soviet siege. He is currently writing a book about this siege.

Index